LINDLEY J. STILES
Professor of Education for Interdisciplinary Studies
Northwestern University
ADVISORY EDITOR TO DODD, MEAD & COMPANY

LEARNING TO TEACH IN
THE ELEMENTARY SCHOOL
INTRODUCTORY READINGS

EDITED BY

Hal D. Funk
*University of North Carolina
at Greensboro*

Robert T. Olberg
Northern Illinois University

LEARNING TO TEACH
IN THE
ELEMENTARY SCHOOL

INTRODUCTORY READINGS

Dodd, Mead & Company

NEW YORK   1971   TORONTO

ISBN 0-396-06314-4
Library of Congress catalog card number: 75-143290

Printed in the United States of America

PREFACE

The professional sequence of teacher education usually culminates with student teaching, which is without a doubt one of the most significant experiences in the preparation of prospective teachers. During this period students have the chance to put into practice the knowledge and theory they have acquired during their undergraduate study. Student teaching provides the opportunity for each student to develop and evaluate his competencies under the guidance of an experienced classroom teacher.

Much of the literature dealing with student teaching is concerned with the problems which challenge most students during this aspect of their professional education. Since 1940, considerable attention has been given to assessing the problems which cause anxiety for student teachers and several extensive studies have determined and categorized these areas of difficulty. The findings of these investigations indicate clearly that the most difficult problems encountered by student teachers are: (1) classroom control, (2) meeting individual differences, (3) planning and organizing learning activities, (4) presenting the lesson, and (5) motivating the students.

The editors of this book have used the research findings listed above as a guide in determining five of the chapters to be included in this volume. Although research has indicated that these difficulties cause the greatest anxiety for student teachers, there are other areas in which these prospective teachers have a genuine need for guidance and assistance. In acknowledgment of this fact two additional chapters have been added in an effort to include problems relating to the total student teaching experience. These chapters are: (1) evaluating and reporting pupil growth, and (2) assessing teaching behavior.

This book of readings is primarily designed for elementary student teachers. It could serve as a text or as a supplemental text in courses dealing with the student teaching experience. It could also provide a common background for student teachers engaged in seminar sessions. Since the articles chosen emphasize practical suggestions and solutions to the problems being discussed, these readings will be invaluable as a personal reference for each elementary student during his student teaching assignment. This book will also be a valuable reference tool for beginning teachers since they frequently experience the same anxieties as student teachers.

The editors have included a variety of articles within each of the chapters. Most of the articles have been written by recognized authorities in the field of education. Each chapter of the book has an introduction to help establish the relevance of that particular problem area to the total role of the student teacher and to give an overview of the selected articles.

The editors are indebted to the many authors and publishers who granted permission to use the material presented in this book.

HAL D. FUNK
ROBERT T. OLBERG

CONTENTS

Chapter 4. MOTIVATION

Chapter 5. INDIVIDUALIZING INSTRUCTION

Chapter 6. DEVELOPING PROPER PUPIL CONTROL AND DISCIPLINE

Chapter 7. EVALUATING AND REPORTING PUPIL PROGRESS

LEARNING TO TEACH IN THE ELEMENTARY SCHOOL
INTRODUCTORY READINGS

Chapter 1

ASSESSING TEACHING BEHAVIOR AND PROFESSIONAL GROWTH

INTRODUCTION

What is good teaching? What is a good teacher? These questions have been asked by many educators and much research has been conducted in an effort to provide acceptable answers. These research efforts have made significant contributions to the teaching profession and as a result we do have a better understanding of the teaching act and of what constitutes a good teacher. Although great strides have been made toward an acceptable definition of teaching and the delineation of the characteristics of a good teacher, the members of the teaching profession have not, at this time, reached a consensus on these issues.

During their pre-service education students often believe that there is a best way to teach and that certain personal and professional attributes guarantee teaching success. Research, as well as practical experience, indicates clearly that this is not true. Most educators agree that certain methods are more effective than others and that certain characteristics seem to be common to superior teachers, but that no specific set of methods and personal traits exists that would be best for every teacher.

Developing a philosophy of teaching by testing and constantly reassessing his beliefs is a major responsibility of every student teacher. It is important that each student teacher study the act of teaching and ascertain which methods and techniques are best suited to his personality and abilities. There are many alternative approaches to successful teaching, and the articles in this chapter discuss varied approaches and attempt to describe the effective classroom teacher.

The first article endeavors to analyze the teaching act. Louis Raths delineates twelve basic functions of teaching, and contends that these are the most essential functions, and that they are expected of all good teachers as they work with children in the classroom.

The uniqueness and individuality of good teaching is stressed in the next two articles. Arthur Combs explains his "perceptual view" of good teaching, based upon how teachers perceive themselves and their tasks. Laura Zirbes presents an explanation of "creative teaching" and discusses the challenges of creative teaching in the classroom.

Many reports have attempted to develop a teacher profile that would serve

1

as a blueprint for upgrading the performance of all classroom teachers. In his article, Don Hamachek maintains that effective teachers can be identified. He compares the personal and professional characteristics of good and poor teachers and points out the implications for teacher education.

During the last ten years many intern programs have become integral parts of teacher education. Martin Haberman explains the concept of a college intern, discusses a research study which attempted to describe the teaching behavior of interns, and includes a brief description of successful behaviors identified in the study.

Probably one of the oldest teaching methods is the lecture. William Hedges contends that teachers talk too much and that talking is not teaching. He maintains that learning is incomplete when the teacher does nothing more than talk and explains the shortcomings of the lecture method of teaching.

One of the greatest challenges facing the teaching profession today is the task of improving the educational program of our disadvantaged and culturally different children. Frank Riessman stresses the need to understand and respect these children and their families, and discusses methods, techniques, and teaching styles that may be effective in meeting the special needs of these children.

A vast amount of literature has been written about the effect of the classroom climate upon the pupils' attitudes and achievement. One of the outstanding researchers in this area is Ned Flanders. He reviews the research on verbal interaction and discusses how this interaction influences the classroom atmosphere, how interaction analysis can be used to study a teacher's behavior, and how this behavior affects the students.

Self-evaluation is an essential component of teaching. In his article, Kaoru Yamamoto proposes a scheme to systematize a teacher's attempt to evaluate the effectiveness of his own instruction and encourages teachers continuously to implement self-evaluation procedures so that evaluation may become an automatic habit in their teaching.

WHAT IS A GOOD TEACHER?

Louis Raths

When speaking about a *good teacher* we are probably thinking of many things—the teacher as a person, what he does in the classroom, how he interacts with other members of the faculty. We may also be thinking of him as a representative of the school in the community. We may be thinking of his background of experience and training. This article will concentrate on the most essential things which are expected of all good teachers as they work with children in the classroom.

What do we postulate as the functions of good teaching? This conception

From *Childhood Education,* May, 1964, 40:451–456. Reprinted by permission of Louis E. Raths and the Association for Childhood Education International, 3615 Wisconsin Avenue, N.W., Washington, D.C. Copyright © 1964 by the Association.

of good teaching will be greatly influenced by the culture to which we have been exposed and which we prize; good teaching depends upon one's philosophy of education and upon changing conceptions of what constitutes good teaching. No one pattern of good teaching exists. There are many different patterns—all of which are good.

Writings, conferences and researches of the past fifty years constitute a base for making some generalized proposals about the functions of teaching, proposals unbiased in that they do not imply goodness or badness of teaching. Judgment of the quality of teaching will follow the collection of data which bear upon these functions. Assuming the following twelve functions to be of great importance in almost every teaching day, we would then want to observe teaching with these twelve points in mind. Our discussions with teachers and those responsible for teacher education programs would revolve around these twelve points. Teachers themselves would be looking at their own work in terms of these same points.

It would be unfortunate if teachers were to be rated by some only in these terms. If these are the deepest areas of concern the data we collect should be used as a basis for improvement. Teachers themselves will probably want help in one or more of the functions. The points are proposed, not as a rating scale, but as a broad framework for teachers to discover more about themselves in relation to the functions of teaching.

1. Explaining, Informing, Showing How
2. Initiating, Directing, Administering
3. Unifying the Group
4. Giving Security
5. Clarifying Attitudes, Beliefs, Problems
6. Diagnosing Learning Problems
7. Making Curriculum Materials
8. Evaluating, Recording, Reporting
9. Enriching Community Activities
10. Organizing and Arranging Classroom
11. Participating in School Activities
12. Participating in Professional and Civic Life

EXPLAINING, INFORMING, SHOWING HOW

1. The good teacher is expected to be well informed in the areas in which he teaches. He is expected to be able to communicate information needed for background, enrichment and motivation, and on many occasions to *explain* relationships to children. The very word "explain" indicates that it isn't a fact to be explained; it is helping children to understand causal relationships; correlations; dependency relations; relationships of opposites, of larger and smaller, of heavier and lighter. In *showing how*, requirements vary for different age and grade levels. For instance, the teacher may be showing

children how to put on their boots and jackets or how to mix certain colors. He may be showing them how to handle the number system, how to analyze propaganda, how to draw maps, how to use a book and how to interview. In addition to clearness and comprehensiveness of the presentation, we expect some effort in getting the children ready for the demonstration. Most important of all, if the object is to show how, we expect the teacher to allow time in the curriculum for the children to practice until they have a certain grasp of the processes—enough so that they can do it at a level of quality which suits the purpose for the grade level at which it is being done. We expect all good teachers to do well at the task of informing, explaining and showing how.

INITIATING, DIRECTING, ADMINISTERING

2. One function of teaching is largely concerned with initiating, organizing, directing, and making many decisions. From the time he begins the day until he goes home at night the teacher faces decisions which might range from a thoughtful deliberation in making changes in a teaching schedule to a quick decision on sending an ailing child to the nurse's office, or what to do in the absence of a special teacher. His handling of the many unusual situations which turn up in the course of a week is indicative of his ability to reorganize and to direct.

It is becoming a much more common practice to include children in much of the planning of the school day. The teacher needs to initiate some of this work, to help get it organized and to direct it. In all these things he helps the children to see alternatives, to see additional resources and to anticipate consequences. Children look to the teacher for decision making in many situations. There are decisions to give more time on dramatics or science. There are decisions involving the use of consultants, meeting with parents, referring of some children for outside help. Observing teachers give some clue to their resourcefulness in organizing, managing and directing.

UNIFYING THE GROUP

3. At the beginning of each school year the teacher is confronted with a number of children. It is his hope and that of the children that as they live together they will become a unified group. When the children identify with each other and when the teacher's concerns overlap the children's, there is good reason to hope that a group spirit will emerge. When the teacher is fair and just to all he is making a contribution to classroom morale.

Discipline problems begin to be solved as children see that permissiveness is controlled by purposes. Children see that they may do those things which contribute to the agreed-upon purposes and that activities which conflict with those purposes are frowned upon or restricted. When there are some sub-groups, most children know what is going on in all of them. A rather wide variety of activities is going on, and children have a sense of participation. Having choices to make, they can frequently choose those in which they have some special skills or abilities to assert. Concentrated attention is relieved occasionally with games or with a dramatic presentation. There is a variety of teaching and learning procedures. Seating is not thought of as a permanent and fixed condition. The teacher is alert to the possibility of cliques and is doing many things to develop the idea of a group. An important task of the teacher is that of developing a group with a group spirit, an identification with common purposes and some common concerns.

GIVING SECURITY

4. Many children are in need of a warm, friendly atmosphere. The teacher with love and affection in abundance is creating a climate which makes it easier for these children to learn. Some children are greatly in need of praise and recognition, and one task of the teacher is to differentiate instruction so that all children may have a sense of achievement and accomplishment. Those children who feel a sense of loneliness, isolation and sometimes rejection need to be helped by teachers to feel that they belong, that they are wanted and needed. Some children are afraid of school, timid on playgrounds, fearful of many things in their lives. With them the teacher diminishes threats, warnings or unusually heavy penalties and provides support and assurance instead. The teacher tries to help those children plagued by feelings of guilt and shame by showing that all of us make mistakes and that we can profit by them; by indicating that we are all human and that at different times most of us have had these feelings. There are some children who have little respect for themselves and who feel that they are not worth very much. Here, the teacher asks them for their opinions and sees to it that they assume some responsibilities. Many children have dozens of questions about their relationships to the world and to their inner selves. To the teacher with insight these questions are not irrelevant. And there are some children who have a deep sense of economic insecurity, who wonder if they can count on next week or next month to be as secure as the present week. The classroom teacher brings to children a sense of security in the meeting of these needs. Whenever there are, in children, cases of aggressiveness, withdrawing, submission or psychosomatic disturbance, the teacher sees to it that the children's needs for special attention are met promptly.

There is pride in what the pupils are doing, and when they need protection the teacher protects them. In a classroom atmosphere which generates group cooperation rather than competition, children help each other. Because it is not altogether a teacher-dominated room—with all or nearly all questions coming from the teacher and every response going to him—children hold discussions with each other. It matters when a child is absent; it matters that birthdays are observed; it matters that returning to school after holidays is a time for reunion and rejoicing.

CLARIFYING ATTITUDES, BELIEFS, PROBLEMS

5. It is not unreasonable to assume that most of our children are utterly confused by the many social influences surrounding them. Looking at so many different ways of living on TV; listening to many things on radio; reading comics which again introduce new and unusual ideas; moving from one place to another every few years and meeting new people and new teachers; experiencing directly or vicariously the difficulties of a broken family; having few places to play and little opportunity to talk things over with parents who might both be working; living in the aftermath of cruel war and hearing much about possible new wars; being close to and sometimes a participant in racial problems; living under the ominous threat of unemployment; often seeing the glittering array of tempting goods in stores and realizing how little of it his own family has, the child of today must surely be very much confused. He hears nice things from the adults but sees and hears many things which contradict what they tell him.

To help clarify these matters, the teacher creates opportunities for children to state their attitudes, interests and problems; to talk about their purposes and aspirations; to speak their beliefs and convictions; to indicate what they think might and should be done; to reveal and to share some of the deeper feelings they have; and to tell about the activities in which they are engaging and those in which they would like to share. As deeper expressions of personality come out, the teacher limits questioning and tries to find out how much self-expression means to the children, whether they want help, whether they have thought of alternative action in solving their problems and consequences of actions. He raises questions with the children which only they can answer, for the questions concern the values which children hold. He gives the children opportunities to compare, observe, classify, interpret and puts them in a position to analyze, criticize and summarize. The teacher helps them to look for assumptions—those things which are taken for granted—and gives them opportunities to imagine and to create. There are problems to be solved and decisions of value to be made. In each specific instance a question or two is asked for the personal reaction of an individual or a small group and the responses accepted by the teacher. As this is carried on day by day and week by week, the assumption is made that some of the confusion surrounding children is being cleared up. Even more important is the idea that it is possible to clear it up and children are experiencing a teacher who believes that this is indeed possible. At the same time children are becoming accustomed to saying what they believe, stating what they think; they are becoming adapted to living in a world where people are not all alike, and they are beginning to prize the differences.

DIAGNOSING LEARNING PROBLEMS

6. In every classroom there are children who are not making the expected progress in their learning, growth and development. As the teacher lives

with these children, it is part of his task to have "hunches" and to suggest to himself possible courses of action. The teacher has to be alert to signs of ill health and sensitive to emotional problems of children. He has to be aware of limits of children's ability as well as of possible negative influences within the room, on the playground and at home. He has to feel his way around for evidence, lack of experience, and hence of maturity. The teacher faces behavior problems knowing that the behavior represents symptoms, that with the acting out of these symptoms children are asking for help. The naughty boy or girl is asking for help as much as the overshy and exclusively withdrawn. Apathy and flightiness, overconforming and overdissenting—all are taken as signs that the children want help in establishing direction. The impulsive child and the one who is always stuck, the one who seems to get little meaning out of the work and the one who wool-gathers, the one who is loudly assertive and the one who has little faith in his own ideas are asking for understanding. The prima donna, the rebel without a cause, the unpredictable student, the one who is unrevealing, the one who seeks the exclusive companionship of one other child, the cynic and the futilitarian all seem to be asking for a more important part in the power structure of the group. The teacher is alert to children who need special help in skills prized by the group. The teacher is grateful to the school with facilities for extra help for children who need more help than the teacher in the crowded school day can give. Surely one of the most important functions of a teacher is to make diagnoses which relate to learning and growth and suggestions which enable children to feel a sense of accomplishment and of identity with their peers.

MAKING CURRICULUM MATERIALS

7. All teachers recognize the inadequacy of the available books in meeting the needs of every child in the room. Every teacher is faced with the necessity of developing curriculum materials to supplement those provided by the local community. The teacher often hectographs or mimeographs materials which seem more appropriate for a particular group. He makes classroom tests; orders movies, slides and weekly newspapers; makes arrangements for visiting speakers; tries to get display materials of articles which are produced locally or at a great distance. The teacher asks a great many questions which do not appear in the books and makes suggestions for individual study. In a hundred ways he is modifying the curriculum for the needs of his particular group. Curriculum making is an important function of teaching. If a teacher has some practice in this area and some confidence in his ability to work with children in the development of new materials, he is more able to meet the learning needs of all children in the group.

EVALUATING, RECORDING, REPORTING

8. All teachers have the task of keeping records and making reports, of recording absences and tardiness. There is the oral report to individual chil-

dren, sometimes to the whole class about their progress. There are reports to parents, written and oral. Directed toward the plans to make life more productive and zestful for the child, there are reports to go to the administrator and on occasions to other teachers. Reports are necessary which indicate the planning of the schedule and the curriculum, such as a daily log or a projection into the future. In some instances there are anecdotal records to keep track of the behavior of a child, to see if he has decided to change certain of his behaviors. In spring some kind of reporting is usually asked which involves decisions about promotions, retardation and possible summer work. With respect to most of these things teachers come to their work well prepared, and what they do about this important task is largely dictated by local circumstances.

ENRICHING COMMUNITY ACTIVITIES

9. Most parents believe that a community is better when it has better schools, but the belief has little worth if the school itself is not concerned with the quality of community life. A classroom teacher who identifies himself with the community is sensitive to its problems and how they are solved, its growth and aspirations. The teacher is concerned about playgrounds, libraries, parks, museums, community health and transportation. As these things are discussed in school, the teacher is able to bring in appropriate illustrations from the community. Parents are frequent visitors and are thought of as colleagues with deep concerns about the education of their children. Community products are exhibited in the school.

There are field trips and visits to local institutions. The hobbies of mothers and fathers are sometimes shared with the children. Newcomers are oriented. Children who are leaving for another school get special attention and ways are sought to help them to a better start in a new location. In meetings with parents as much attention is paid to influential surroundings as to learning problems in the classroom. Harmonious relationships between school and community are a continuing, essential part of school life. When teachers have this concern, daily efforts are made to enrich the community—an important function of teaching.

ARRANGING AND ORGANIZING CLASSROOM

10. It is the task of every teacher with the help of pupils to make the classroom a beautiful, pleasant place in which to live. Appearance and arrangement can make a great impression on a visitor. Ideally, the room seems a wonderfully pleasant place in which to learn: lighting is appropriate; colors are pleasing; equipment and supplies are at hand. The room can be quickly reorganized for a variety of activities. In such a room children feel at home. A room organization which is flexible and adaptable to different purposes brings an additional sense of security to children, who like the

classroom better when they have shared in developing plans for its use. Many teachers initiate frequent change in the classroom during the year; for them a room is not fixed for all time in the first month of school. Children's exhibits are changed from time to time. Committees of children have different responsibilities for different tasks in arranging their classroom.

PARTICIPATING IN SCHOOL ACTIVITIES

11. In addition to all these classroom matters, there is the obligation of every teacher to participate in school activities, such as committee work, holiday programs to share in, lunchroom duty, bus duties, evening meetings. The teacher who believes that his tasks are fulfilled when he pays attention exclusively to his own classroom soon learns that there is the need to be concerned with the welfare of all children in all grades of the school. His participation in total school life is regarded as one of the important tasks of teaching.

PARTICIPATING IN PROFESSIONAL AND CIVIC LIFE

12. Every teacher is expected to enter wholly into professional life and to make his contribution to the improvement of the profession. He is expected to belong to professional societies, attend conferences, act in accord with professional ethics, keep up to date in the reading of literature, and make some attempt with his colleagues in the community to share new and pertinent research results. In addition, there is the usual expectation of his being a participating citizen in his community.

Those who discharge these responsibilities in an effective manner are making great contributions for good to a troubled world.

THE PERSONAL APPROACH TO GOOD TEACHING

Arthur W. Combs

To plan effective programs for teacher education we need the very best definition of good teaching we can acquire. That seems clear enough. How to arrive at such a definition, however, has proved to be a most difficult task. Despite millions of dollars and millions of man-hours poured into research on the problem over the past 50 years, the results have continued to be frustrating and disappointing—until recently. It now appears that our failure

Reprinted from *Educational Leadership* 21 (6):369–377, 399; March, 1964. Reprinted with permission of the Association for Supervision and Curriculum Development and Arthur W. Combs. Copyright © 1964 by the Association for Supervision and Curriculum Development.

to find useful definitions may be due to the inadequacies of the frame of reference from which we have attacked the problem.

THE TEACHER AS KNOWER

The earliest conception of the good teacher was that of the scholar. It was assumed that a person who knew could teach others. Of course it is true that a teacher has to know something but, even without research, it is apparent to anyone who looks that "knowing" is simply not enough. Most of us can recall out of our own experience the teacher who "knew his subject but could not put it across." In some places there can even be found good teachers whose depth of information in a particular field is woefully lacking! This is often a shocking discovery to some critics of education who still equate teaching with scholarship. One of my own studies on good teaching demonstrated that *both,* good teachers and bad ones, knew equally well what a good teaching situation *ought* to be like (Combs, 1961). Knowing is certainly important to teaching, but it is clear, good teaching involves much more.

THE "COMPETENCIES" APPROACH TO TEACHING

A second approach to defining good teaching has been in terms of teacher "competencies." The thinking goes something like this: If we know what the expert teachers do, or are like, then we can teach the beginners to be like that. This is a straightforward, uncomplicated approach to the problem and seems logically sound.

This idea has produced great quantities of research into the traits of good teachers and their methods. This has provided us with long lists of competencies supposedly characteristic of good teachers. In the beginning these lists were quite simple. Since, however, what people do is always related to the situations they are in, every situation calls for a different behavior and the more situations the researchers examine, the longer the lists of competencies have become.

The following, for example, is a list made by a conference of "Superior Teachers" in 1962:

Good teachers should:

Know their subject
Know much about related subjects
Be adaptable to new knowledge
Understand the process of becoming
Recognize individual differences
Be a good communicator
Develop an inquiring mind
Be available
Be committed
Be enthusiastic

Have a sense of humor
Have humility
Cherish his own individuality
Have convictions
Be sincere and honest
Act with integrity
Show tolerance and understanding
Be caring
Have compassion
Have courage
Have personal security
Be creative
Be versatile
Be willing to try
Be adaptable
Believe in God.

This is but a short list. There are much longer ones!

At first, attempts to discover the competencies of good teachers were highly specific. Hundreds of attempts were made to demonstrate that good teachers had this or that trait, used this or that method—all to no avail! Good teaching simply could not be defined in terms of any particular trait or method. In 1959, the American Association of School Administrators commissioned a team to review the research on the problem. Out of this the school administrators hoped to find some guidelines which might help them make the practical decisions about a high quality of teaching necessary in carrying on their jobs. Sadly, the team was forced to report that there is no specific trait or method sufficiently associated with good teaching to provide clear distinctions (Ellena, 1961).

Some investigators have thought better discriminations might be found in generic, rather than specific studies of the "teaching act." Accordingly, they have turned their attention to the *general* traits or methods used by the teacher. Approaching the problem in this way they have been able to find fairly stable distinctions in such general terms as, "good teachers are considerate," or "child centered," or "concerned about structure." The most significant of these is a study by Marie Hughes (1959) under a grant from the U.S. Office of Education, Cooperative Research Program. Dr. Hughes developed an exhaustive system for analyzing teacher behavior and applied this system to time sample observations of teachers in the classroom. She was able to demonstrate a number of general classes of behavior seemingly characteristic of good teachers. Among these were such categories as controlling, imposition, facilitating, content development, response, and positive or negative affectivity.

Similar attempts to analyze teacher behavior have been carried out by Flanders (1960), Smith (1961), Bowers (1961), Filson (1957), and Medley (1959). These attempts to examine the more global aspects of effective teaching have been somewhat more successful in discriminating between good and poor teaching than research directed at specific or detailed descriptions of behavior, or methods. But they still do not provide us with the definitive distinctions needed by the profession. Good teaching, it now seems clear, is not a direct function of general traits or methods.

SOME PRACTICAL DIFFICULTIES OF THE COMPETENCIES APPROACH

The attempt to develop a teacher education program based upon the competencies approach runs into some very knotty problems. In the first place, it is a fallacy to assume the methods of the experts either can, or should be, taught directly to the beginners. It is seldom we can determine what should be for the beginner by examining what the expert does well. I learned this some years ago when I was responsible for teaching failing university students more effective methods of study. At first glance it would seem logical to determine what should be taught to the failing students by determining the study habits of successful ones. Such an approach to curriculum construction, however, is disastrous!

Successful students study most whimsically. They operate without plan, go to the movies often, indulge in all sorts of extracurricular activities and generally behave in ways that would be suicidal for students teetering on the brink of failure. It simply does not follow that what is good for the expert is good for the novice too! Nor is it true, that the way to become expert is to do what the expert does.

Some of the methods used by the expert can only be used *because* he is expert. Many experienced teachers have learned to deal with most classroom disturbances by ignoring them. Yet beginners cannot ignore them! The expert is able to ignore matters precisely because he *is* expert. Some methods cannot even be comprehended without adequate prior experience. One must grow to achieve them. Asking the young teacher to use methods which do not fit him may only turn him loose in the blackboard jungle to fight for his life with inappropriate weapons.

The creation of long lists of competencies is likely to be deeply discouraging and disillusioning to the young teacher for another reason. Evaluations of "goodness" or "badness" become attached to methods, and students thereafter are expected to judge their own adequacies in these terms. The net effect is to set such impossible goals of excellence that no one can ever hope to reach them. This is a terribly depressing and discouraging prospect.

Discouraging and disillusioning as the competencies approach is for the young teacher, it has equally unhappy effects on the more experienced teachers. A vast complex of competencies, all of which are demanded as criteria for good teaching leaves the individual defenseless before criticism. No matter what he does well, it is never enough! There is always so much more that he might have done, or should have done, that he can rarely find pleasure or satisfaction in what he actually has done. Add to this the fact that many of the competencies demanded do not fit his particular personality, and so could probably never be achieved anyhow, and the defeat of the individual becomes almost inevitable. In time, the feeling of inadequacy produced by continual failure to meet impossible goals undermines professional pride and is likely to produce a guilt-ridden teacher suffering from a secret feeling of being "too little and too late." It should not be surprising if, after years of this kind of experience, the will to try shrivels and dies on the vine.

To use particular competencies as a measure of good teaching, irrespective of personalities, situations or purposes, leads us to the ridiculous conclusion that some of the very people who taught us most, were poor teachers. When I hear young teachers-in-training remark, "Oh, he is a lousy teacher but you sure learn a lot!" I am forced to conclude that the determination of the goodness of teaching on the basis of competencies is highly questionable.

The methods people use are highly personal. These methods cannot be judged apart from the personality they express. No one, after all, looks well, feels well, or behaves well, in another person's clothing. Methods, like the clothes we wear, must fit the people we are. Good teaching is a highly personal matter.

THE PERSONAL CHARACTER OF GOOD TEACHING

Is there a better approach? I think there is. As we have seen, the research on good teaching is unable to isolate any common trait or practice of good teachers. Yet these unanimous results, themselves, represent a most important commonality. They demonstrate the uniqueness and individuality of good teachers! The very failure of research to define common factors is, itself, a demonstration that a good teacher is primarily a personality. If good teachers are unique individuals we could predict from the start that the attempt to find *common uniqueness* would be unfruitful!

A good teacher is first and foremost a person. He has competence, to be sure, but not a *common* set of competencies like anyone else. Like the students he teaches, he is infinitely unique and becoming more so all the time. The fact of his personness is the most important and determining thing about him. The personal character of good teaching can be documented by almost any of us from our own experience. If one thinks back to his own school days he will probably discover that the good teachers he had in his own lifetime did not all behave alike or, even, with great similarity. Rather, each stands out as a person, an individual, some for one reason, some for another.

Apparently, there can be no such thing as a "good" or "bad" method of teaching. The terms "good" and "bad" can be applied to results, outcomes, purposes or ends. The methods we use to achieve these ends, however, only derive their value from the goals and purposes for which they are used. The good teacher is not one who behaves in a "given" way. He is an artist, skillful in producing a desirable result. The *result* may be considered "good" or "bad," but not the method.

THE "SELF AS INSTRUMENT" CONCEPT

This shift in our thinking from a mechanistic to a personal view of teaching is by no means confined to our profession alone. In fact, most other professions dealing with human problems have preceded us in this direction. The effective professional worker, in medicine, social work, clinical psychology, guidance or nursing is no longer seen as a technician applying methods in more or less mechanical fashion the way he has been taught. We now understand him as an intelligent human being using himself, his knowledge and the resources at hand to solve the problems for which he is responsible. He is a person who has learned to use himself as an effective instrument (Combs, 1961).

If we adapt this "self as instrument" concept of the professional worker to teaching, it means that teachers colleges must concern themselves with *persons* rather than competencies. It means the individualization of instruction we have sought for the public schools must be applied to the teachers colleges as well. It calls for the production of creative individuals, capable of shifting and changing to meet the demands and opportunities afforded in daily tasks. Such a teacher will not behave in a set way. His behavior will change from moment to moment, from day to day, rapidly adjusting to the needs of his students, the situations he is in, the purposes he seeks to fulfill and the methods and materials he has at hand.

The good teacher is no carbon copy but stands out as a unique and effective personality, sometimes for one reason, sometimes for another, but always for something intensely and personally his own. He has found ways of using himself, his talents and his environment in a fashion that aids both his students and himself to achieve satisfaction—their own and society's too. Artists sometimes refer to "the discovery of one's personal idiom" and the expression seems very apt applied to teaching as well. We may define the effective teacher *as a unique human being who has learned to use his self effectively and efficiently for carrying out his own and society's purposes.*

The production of this kind of person is not a question of teaching him what to do. Modern perceptual psychology tells us that a person's behavior is the direct result of his perceptions, how things seem to him at the moment of his behaving. To change an individual's behavior, it is necessary to help him see himself and his world differently. It is here that teacher education must direct its effort. The modern giant computer is able to provide "best answers" to vast quantities of data depending upon the formulas built into the machine. In a similar fashion, the effectiveness of the teacher is dependent upon the internal "formulas" which select and control his behavior as he is confronted with changing situations. These human formulas are the perceptions he holds of himself, his purposes and the world in which he must live and operate.

Whether an individual can behave effectively and efficiently in a given situation, according to the perceptual psychologists, will depend upon how he is perceiving at the time. To change his behavior, furthermore, it will be necessary to produce a change in his perceptions of himself and his world. This means for teacher education, we need first to know how good teachers perceive. Knowing that, we may then be able to help teachers perceive themselves and their tasks in those ways.

A PERCEPTUAL VIEW OF GOOD TEACHING

What kinds of beliefs, understandings, values and concepts make up the perceptual organization of good teachers?

This way of looking at teacher education is so new that we do not yet have the precise research we need to guide us. This need not deter us, however, for there is evidence enough at least to start us thinking on new tracks, designing new techniques and planning for the research we need. To this point we have the following sources of information to draw upon for defining the probable dimensions of good teaching in perceptual terms:

1. Perceptual psychological theory, especially that having to do with the nature of the self and fully functioning behavior

2. Research on the perceptions of good practioners in other helping professions (Combs and Soper, 1963)

3. The research already existing in our profession

4. The experiences accumulated by thousands of teachers engaged in day to day "action research" in the classroom.

Drawing upon these four sources it would appear that a good teacher is characterized by typical perceptual organizations in six general areas:

A. His knowledge of his subject

B. His frame of reference for approaching his problems

C. His perceptions of others

D. His perceptions of self

E. His perceptions of the purpose and process of learning

F. His perceptions of appropriate methods.

Under each of these major headings a series of hypotheses can be drawn concerning the teacher's characteristic perceptual organization in that area. The following is a list developed at the University of Florida by the author and his colleagues over the past five years. These were originally drawn up to serve as suggestions for future research. The list is presented here both as an amplification of the "self as instrument" concept and as possible propositions for further research by others who may be interested in the problem. The list is by no means a complete one but it serves as a point of departure for consideration of the self as instrument approach. It is presented as a promising series of leads which may excite other researchers, as it has my colleagues and me, to explore these matters further. Some of the following hypotheses (marked by *) we have already corroborated in research on good and poor counselors (Combs, 1963). Others (marked by †) are currently being explored in several researches on the perceptual organization of good teachers. Each hypothesis is stated as the two ends of a continuum with the perceptions presumed characteristic of the good teacher at the left and those of the poor teacher at the right. Those hypotheses already studied or currently under investigation include more extensive definitions. Several items, not yet subjected to research test, do not have definitions included.

HYPOTHESES REGARDING THE PERCEPTUAL
ORGANIZATION OF EFFECTIVE TEACHERS

A. *A Good Teacher Has Rich Perceptions About His Subject:* The good teacher will need to be well informed about the subject matter he is responsible for teaching. That is to say, he must have a rich and extensive field of perceptions about his subject upon which he can call as required. The good teacher is not stupid. This aspect of good teaching provides us with nothing new. It is the aspect of the teaching function we have known best and developed most fully in the past.

B. *The Good Teacher's Frame of Reference:* The good teacher is always keenly aware of how things seem from the point of view of those with whom he works. His frame of reference for approaching problems and people is humanistic rather than mechanistic. He is deeply sensitive to the private worlds of his students and colleagues and accepts their feelings, attitudes, beliefs and understandings as legitimate and important data in human interaction.

Hypothesis 1 * †—Internal-External frame of reference: The teacher's general frame of reference can be described as internal rather than external; that is to say, he seems sensitive to and concerned with how things look to others with whom he interacts and uses this as a basis for his own behavior.

Hypothesis 2 * †—People-Things orientation: Central to the thinking of the teacher is a concern with people and their reactions rather than with things and events.

Hypothesis 3 * †—Meanings-Facts orientation: The teacher is more concerned with the perceptual experience of people than with the objective events. He is sensitive to how things seem to people rather than being exclusively concerned with concrete events.

Hypothesis 4 * †—Immediate-Historical causation: The teacher seeks the causes of people's behavior in their current thinking, feeling, beliefs and understandings rather than in objective descriptions of the forces exerted upon them now or in the past.

Hypothesis 5—Hopeful-Despairing.

C. *Perceptions About What People Are Like and How They Behave:* Teaching is a human relationship. To behave effectively good teachers must possess the most accurate understandings about people and their behavior available in our generation. Each of us can only behave in terms of what we believe is so. What a teacher believes, therefore, about the nature of his students will have a most important effect on how he behaves toward them. Let us take a simple example to illustrate this point.

If a teacher believes his students have the capacity to learn, he will behave quite differently from the teacher who has serious doubts about the capacities of his charges. The teacher who believes his students *can,* begins his task with hope and assurance that both he and his students may be successful. He can place confidence and trust in his students and be certain that, if he is successful in facilitating and encouraging the learning process, they can, they *will* learn.

The teacher, on the other hand, who does not believe his students are capable approaches his task with two strikes against him. He is licked before he starts. If you do not believe that children *can,* then it is certainly not safe to trust them. False beliefs about the nature of people can only result in the selection of inappropriate ways of dealing with them. A prime function of the teachers college must be to assist its students to clear and accurate understandings of the nature of people and their behavior.

Hypothesis 6 * †—Able-Unable: The teacher perceives others as having the capacities to deal with their problems. He believes that they can find adequate solutions to events as opposed to doubting the capacity of people to handle themselves and their lives.

Hypothesis 7 * †—Friendly-Unfriendly: The teacher sees others as being friendly and enhancing. He does not regard them as threatening to himself but rather sees them as essentially well intentioned rather than evil intentioned.

Hypothesis 8 * †—Worthy-Unworthy: The teacher tends to see other people as being of worth rather than unworthy. He sees them as possessing a dignity and integrity which must be respected and maintained rather than seeing people as unimportant, whose integrity may be violated or treated as of little account.

Hypothesis 9 †—Internally-Externally motivated: The teacher sees people and their behavior as essentially developing from within rather than as a product of external events to be molded, directed; sees people as creative, dynamic rather than passive or inert.

Hypothesis 10 * †—Dependable-Undependable: The teacher sees people as essentially trustworthy and dependable in the sense of behaving in a lawful way. He regards their behavior as understandable rather than capricious, unpredictable or negative.

Hypothesis 11 †—Helpful-Hindering: The teacher sees people as being potentially fulfilling and enhancing to self rather than impeding or threatening. He regards people as important sources of satisfaction rather than sources of frustration and suspicion.

Hypothesis 12—Unthreatening-Threatening.

Hypothesis 13—Respectable-Of no account.

D. *The Teacher's Perception of Self:* Perceptual psychology indicates that the behavior of the individual at any moment is a function of how he sees his situation and himself. In recent years we have come to understand the crucial importance of the self concept in affecting every aspect of a person's life. It makes a vast difference what people believe about themselves.

The behavior of a teacher, like that of everyone else, is a function of his concepts of self. Teachers who believe they are able will try. Teachers who do not think they are able will avoid responsibilities. Teachers who feel they are liked by their students will behave quite differently from those who feel they are unliked. Teachers who feel they are acceptable to the administration can behave quite differently from those who have serious doubts about their acceptability. Teachers who feel their profession has dignity and integrity can themselves behave with dignity and integrity. Teachers who have grave doubts about the importance and value of their profession may behave apologetically or overly aggressively with their students and with their colleagues. It is apparent that, if the self concept is a fundamental in producing the behavior of an individual as has been suggested by modern psychology, then teacher education programs must give it a vital place in the production of new teachers.

Hypothesis 14 * †—Identified with-Apart from: The teacher tends to see himself as a part of all mankind; he sees himself as identified with people rather than as withdrawn, removed, apart or alienated from others.

Hypothesis 15 * †—Adequate-Inadequate: The teacher generally sees himself as enough; as having what is needed to deal with his problems. He does not see himself as lacking and as unable to cope with problems.

Hypothesis 16 * †—Trustworthy-Untrustworthy: The teacher has trust in his own organism. He sees himself as essentially dependable, reliable, as having the potentiality for coping with events as opposed to seeing self in a tentative fashion with doubts about the potentiality and reliability of the organism.

Hypothesis 17 * †—Worthy-Unworthy: The teacher sees himself as a person of consequence, dignity, integrity and worthy of respect; as opposed to being a person of little consequence who can be overlooked, discounted, whose dignity and integrity do not matter.

Hypothesis 18 * †—Wanted-Unwanted: The teacher sees himself as essentially likeable, attractive (in personal, not physical appearance sense), wanted, and in general capable of bringing forth a warm response from those people important to him; as opposed to feeling ignored, unwanted, or rejected by others.

Hypothesis 19—Accepted-Not accepted

Hypothesis 20—Certain, sure-Doubting

Hypothesis 21—Feels aware-Unaware.

E. *The Purpose and Process of Learning:* Behavior always has direction. Whatever we do is always determined by the purposes we have in mind at the time of our behaving or misbehaving. What teachers perceive to be their own and society's purposes makes a great deal of difference in their behavior. The teacher who believes schools exist only for the able and that "it is a waste of time to fool with the poorer students," behaves quite differently from the teacher who perceives society's purpose as that of helping *all* children become the best they can. Similarly, what the teacher believes about how students learn will markedly affect his behavior. One teacher, believing children must be molded, teaches loyalty to country by carefully censoring what students read and hear about democracy and communism. Another teacher, believing children learn best when confronted with all kinds of evidence, takes a different tack in teaching his class. The clarity and accuracy of perceptions about the purposes and processes of learning will have profound effects on the behavior of teachers.

How the teacher sees the task of teaching, in the immediate sense, as it applies to moment to moment operations in the classroom, or in the broadest sense, of society's needs and purposes, will determine the way he behaves on the job. The teachers college must help him find these understandings and make them a part of his very being. Only the best and most accurate perceptions will suffice.

Hypothesis 22 * †—Freeing-Controlling: The teacher perceives the purpose of the helping task as one of freeing, assisting, releasing, facilitating rather than a matter of controlling, manipulating, coercing, blocking, inhibiting.

Hypothesis 23 * †—Larger-Smaller perceptions: The teacher tends to view events in a broad rather than narrow perspective. He is concerned with larger connotations of events, with larger, more extensive implications than the immediate and specific. He is not exclusively concerned with details but can perceive beyond the immediate to future and larger meanings.

Hypothesis 24 * †—Self revealing-Self concealing: The teacher sees his appropriate role as self revealing rather than self concealing; that is, he appears to be willing to disclose himself. He can treat his feelings and shortcomings as important and significant rather than hiding them or covering them up. He seems willing to be himself.

Hypothesis 25 †—Self involved-Self withheld: The teacher sees his appropriate role as one of commitment to the helping process, a willingness to enter into interaction, as opposed to being inert or remaining aloof or remote from interaction.

Hypothesis 26 †—Furthering process-Achieving goals: The teacher sees his appropriate role as one of encouraging and facilitating the process of search and discovery, as opposed to promoting, or working for a personal goal or preconceived solution.

Hypothesis 27—Helping-Dominating

Hypothesis 28—Understanding-Condemning

Hypothesis 29—Accepting-Rejecting

Hypothesis 30—Valuing integrity-Violating integrity

Hypothesis 31—Positive-Negative

Hypothesis 32—Open-Closed to experience

Hypothesis 33—Tolerant of ambiguity-Intolerant.

F. *Perception of Appropriate Methods:* The methods teachers use must fit the kinds of people they are. An effective teacher must have an armamentarium of methods upon which he may call as these are needed to carry out his teaching duties. These may vary widely from teacher to teacher and even from moment to moment. Whatever their nature they must fit the situations and purposes of the teacher and be appropriate for the students with whom they are used.

The teacher education program must help each student find the methods best suited to him, to his purposes, his task and the peculiar populations and problems with which he must deal on the job. This is not so much a matter of *teaching* methods as one of helping students *discover* methods.

While methods must always be highly personal, certain perceptions about appropriate methods may be characteristic of good teaching. Among the hypotheses we hope to explore in this area are the following:

Hypothesis 34—Helping methods seen as superior to manipulating methods

Hypothesis 35—Cooperation superior to competition

Hypothesis 36—Acceptance superior to appeasing

Hypothesis 37—Acceptance superior to rejecting (attacking)

Hypothesis 38—Permissiveness superior to authoritarianism

Hypothesis 39—Open communication superior to closed communication

Hypothesis 40—"Giving" methods superior to withholding.

REFERENCES

N. D. Bowers and R. S. Soar. *Studies in Human Relations in the Teaching Learning Process V*. Final Report, Cooperative Research Project No. 469, 1961.

A. W. Combs. "A Perceptual View of the Nature of 'Helpers,' in Personality Theory and Counseling Practice." Papers of First Annual Conference on Personality Theory and Counseling Practice. Gainesville, Florida: University of Florida, 1961, pp. 53–58.

A. W. Combs and D. W. Soper. "The Perceptual Organization of Effective Counselors." *Journal of Counseling Psychology* 10:222–26; 1963.

W. J. Ellena, M. Stevenson and H. V. Webb. *Who's a Good Teacher?* Washington, D.C.: American Association of School Administrators, NEA, 1961.

T. N. Filson. "Factors Influencing the Level of Dependence in the Classroom." Unpublished Ph.D. Thesis. Minneapolis: University of Minnesota, 1957.

N. A. Flanders, *Teacher Influence, Pupil Attitudes and Achievement: Studies in Interaction Analysis*. Final Report, Cooperative Research Project No. 397, U.S. Office of Education, 1960.

Marie M. Hughes. *Development of the Means for Assessing the Quality of Teaching in Elementary Schools*. Report of Research, Cooperative Research Program, U.S. Office of Education Project No. 353, 1959.

Donald M. Medley and Harold E. Mitzel. "A Technique for Measuring Classroom Behavior." *Journal of Educational Psychology* 49:86–92; 1958.

B. Othanel Smith. "A Concept of Teaching." *Language and Concepts in Education*. Chicago: Rand McNally & Company, 1961.

WHAT CREATIVE TEACHING MEANS

Laura Zirbes

It would not be a creative approach to begin an article on creative teaching with a definition. Meanings can be developed creatively, formatively, from

"What Creative Teaching Means," by Laura Zirbes. From *Childhood Education*, December 1967, Vol. 44, No. 4. Reprinted by permission of the Association for Childhood Education International, 3615 Wisconsin Avenue, N.W., Washington, D.C.

contexts, from illustrative examples, from discriminative comparison, from shared experiences, and from a combination of some of these with other "makings." Meanings can also be enriched, reconstructed, and expanded by reworking them. These are, in fact, ways in which creative teaching proceeds, sometimes coming out with tentative formulations that are purposely left open for further development or test or extension and for use.

Bread can be defined, but even the clear grasp of Webster's definition cannot match the meanings which creative teaching built into it for a second grade.

At lunch one day a child said, "The bread my mother bakes is not like this." That started comparisons and discussions that led to a decision to visit a farm where wheat was growing and almost ready for the reaper. Two bundles of stalks were brought back. Pictures of sheaves of wheat were put on the bulletin board with a poem, and the poet's reference to the waving fields of growing grain led to a discussion of other grains used in making flour and bread. The machinery used for harvesting and threshing wheat today was compared with old-fashioned methods. Brueghel's picture, "The Harvesters," was compared with views of modern farm implements, a threshing machine and a modern combine at work in a great wheat field in Kansas. Of course there was a great deal of discussion, and in the course of it questions arose which led to a visit to a mill. Here children watched the process and got as dusty as the proverbial miller. Afterward one of them said:

> "We watched the great sieves sifting;
> They look like huge drums dancing."

They threshed the wheat they had brought from the farm and tried in vain to grind it and get it as fine as the flour they had brought from the mill, but they found that it made good muffins. Muffins brought the talk around to other things made of flour, and to different grains and different kinds of bread, and to bread in other lands. Finally, after visiting a big bakery where hundreds of loaves were baked and wrapped for delivery, one of the mothers helped the children make bread, and they relived the whole sequence of experiences in creative rhythms while waiting for their bread to bake. Then they bowed their heads after the bread was passed before eating, and said:
"For this bread we give thanks."

Creative Teaching—What does it mean? It means the development of opportunities for such life-related learnings, for such understandings. It means guidance which catches a child's question about some phase of his experience and makes something of it—something significant in his further development and in the development of his associates.

Creative teaching took the words *colonial* and *heritage,* which came up in a broadcast, and made them mean more than any history text could convey.

The children in an intermediate grade took a walk with their teacher. They found colonial doorways, colonial windows, colonial architecture in two churches and several homes. They went into two homes by invitation later, and found colonial heirlooms—furniture, silver, and pewter. They found that they were themselves, in fact, heirs, and that these things were all part of that colonial heritage, as was the Declaration of Independence, the town meeting, the lore and literature of pre-Revolutionary days, the heroism and statesmanship of the settlers and the founding fathers.

Creative teaching makes something fine out of learning situations, whatever they are, and in so doing, develops the creative potentialities of learners.

Out of a sudden flood, creative teaching made an occasion for inquiry into what water does and how man has learned to use it and control it, to cross it on bridges, fly over it in planes, or tunnel under it. Something of man's resourcefulness challenged the creative potentialities of those children because creative teaching was resourceful enough to make a situational adjustment by a timely use of what had befallen a community.

Where teaching is not creative, such vital leads would be missed, and the creative potentialities of children would miss the challenge to fulfillment!

Teachers need the challenge to the fulfillment of *their* creative potentialities, too! Every teacher can catch the challenge and do things to foster creativity; to cultivate active curiosity, initiative, openmindedness, resourcefulness, and originality in children. Personalities are in the making in childhood, and the qualities which creative teaching encourages are developed as children respond to guidance which awakens their aspirations and involves their wholehearted endeavor. Striving to develop these qualities in children is a creative experience which transforms the tasks and routines of teaching into creative opportunities in human development. This does not sanction an escape from teaching responsibilities, but proposes a higher level of intelligent concern about them, and a formative forward adjustment in approaches and procedures to a fuller concern for creative values. It calls for an abandonment of reliance on stereotyped ways of conceiving teaching-learning situations.

The teacher who guided her children toward a more flexible functional approach in spelling saw spelling as something very different from a list of words a day, to be assigned, studied, pronounced, marked, and reviewed or forgotten. She saw it as an integral part of all written expression, and as a matter contingent on the cumulative outcomes of clear perception—auditory and visual— and of diagnostic guidance in which misspellings and causal factors in misspelling were systematically considered. Her children kept two files, one for the alphabetized list of words which they used in their writing, each clearly marked as mastered or as still in need of mastery because new or because of error or uncertainty, the other for an expanded list. In this one children entered words they thought they might like to use in their writing, words derived from words they had mastered and words for which they had looked up synonyms or syllabication or other information in dictionaries. They offered to proofread each other's papers, and worked in teams on their expanded lists. It was therefore not surprising to find that this creative teaching had raised the standard of spelling performance far above the usual expectations in that group. Furthermore, the level of writing and the attitudes toward written work were involved in creative ways.

There are challenges to creative teaching in other phases of school experience.

A teacher whose children developed a collection of implements used in measuring made the approach to denominate numbers a creative adventure in which meanings were enriched and arithmetic took on social significance.

There is no field of learning or curricular concern in which creative teaching cannot raise the level of attention, insight, achievement, and aspiration.

Assuming that what has gone before in this article serves to challenge many readers to a more creative approach in their own teaching, the following suggestions for self-directed inservice growth are given.

An unsolved problem or a matter in which you cannot fall back on habits or skills acquired by training or long experience is a challenge to exploratory learning in which you try out two or more ways of proceeding, seeking to "learn by doing."

By discovering one or more points in one's practice which are examples of stereotyped, habit-bound teaching performance, anyone can project at least one alternative on the way to less rigid, more flexible teaching, and less dependence on routines which get in the way of creative forward adjustments.

By getting rid of the accumulated stock of devices on which one has come to depend in a more or less mechanical way, one can open one's mind to the creative possibilities of a more resourceful use of recurrent phases of one's teaching, instead of succumbing to the temptation to go stale.

By involving children in the cooperative planning and projection of certain phases of school living and learning, one can gradually outgrow the tendency to get them to adjust and conform to a pre-planned, teacher-directed regimen in which their initiative and creative potentialities are not valued or developed.

One must sometimes give one's self the advantage of a new situation, a change of work, new leadership, or new associations to throw off the inhibitions and fixities that block one's creative aspirations, and lull one into stultifying complacency or fill one with anxious resistance to new ideas.

One can actually face up to what creative teaching means, and proceed on one's own initiative or with one's professional associates to project aspirations to creativity into action. Leadership can do much to provide impetus to such efforts and to develop the conditions in which creative potentialities are challenged and realized. This process of facing up to *what creative teaching means* implies a willingness to *act* on the meanings—an involvement in the kinds of formative forward adjustment that contribute to creativity and to creative teaching—an evaluative concern in the whole process and its impacts on personalities and human relations, aspirations, and outcomes.

If, for example, creativity is discouraged when spontaneity is inhibited, and conformity is valued above initiative and originality, it becomes clear that *creative teaching* means a departure from regimented routines such as following directions for drawing, using patterns, stencils to be "colored in," or models to be imitated. It also means provision for spontaneity of movement and expression, as contrasted with imposed restraints that hold expression and voluntary action in check in compliance with repressive demands that stifle creative impulses.

If creativity is developed by freedom to explore and experiment with new ideas, new materials, or resources, then *creative teaching means* fuller provision for such opportunities.

If creative forward adjustments are safeguards against habit-bound rigidity —that complicates human advance—*creative teaching means* an acceptance of the social challenge of forward adjustments in education, and that calls for guidance in adaptive, insightful living and learning, particularly in *childhood education.*

"In interpersonal relations it (creativity) is the ability to invent or improvise new roles or alternative lines of action in problematic situations, and to involve such behavior in others. Among other things, it seems to involve curiosity, self-confidence, something of the venturesome and risk-taking tendencies of the explorer, a flexible mind with the kind of freedom which permits the orientation of spontaneous play."

CHARACTERISTICS OF GOOD TEACHERS AND IMPLICATIONS FOR TEACHER EDUCATION

Don Hamachek

It is, I think, a sad commentary about our educational system that it keeps announcing both publicly and privately that "good" and "poor" teachers cannot be distinguished one from the other. Probably no issue in education has been so voluminously researched as has teacher effectiveness and considerations which enhance or restrict this effectiveness. Nonetheless, we still read that we cannot tell the good guys from the bad guys. For example, Biddle and Ellena [2] in their book, *Contemporary Research on Teacher Effectiveness,* begin by stating that "the problem of teacher effectiveness is so complex that no one today knows what *The Competent Teacher* is." I think we *do* know what the competent—or effective, or good, or whatever you care to call him— teacher is, and in the remainder of this paper I will be as specific as possible in citing *why* I think we know along with implications for our teacher-education programs.

Reprinted from *Phi Delta Kappan* 50:341–345 (February, 1969), by permission of author and publisher.

WHAT THE RESEARCH SAYS

By and large, most research efforts aimed at investigating teacher effectiveness have attempted to probe one or more of the following dimensions of teacher personality and behavior: 1) personal characteristics, 2) instructional procedures and interaction styles, 3) perceptions of self, 4) perceptions of others. Because of space limits this is by no means an exhaustive review of the research related to the problem, but it is, I think, representative of the kind and variety of research findings linked to questions of teacher effectiveness.

Personal Characteristics of Good Versus Poor Teachers. We would probably agree that it is quite possible to have two teachers of equal intelligence, training, and grasp of subject matter who nevertheless differ considerably in the results they achieve with students. Part of the difference can be accounted for by the effect of a teacher's personality on the learners. What kinds of personality do students respond to?

Hart[7] conducted a study based upon the opinions of 3,725 high school seniors concerning best-liked and least-liked teachers and found a total of 43 different reasons for "liking Teacher A best" and 30 different reasons for "liking Teacher Z least." Not surprisingly, over 51 percent of the students said that they liked best those teachers who were "helpful in school work, who explained lessons and assignments clearly, and who used examples in teaching." Also, better than 40 percent responded favorably to teachers with a "sense of humor." Those teachers assessed most negatively were "unable to explain clearly, were partial to brighter students, and had superior, aloof, overbearing attitudes." In addition, over 50 percent of the respondents mentioned behaviors such as "too cross, crabby, grouchy, and sarcastic" as reasons for disliking many teachers. Interestingly enough, mastery of subject matter, which is vital but badly overemphasized by specialists, ranked sixteenth on both lists. Somehow students seem willing to take more or less for granted that a teacher "knows" his material. What seems to make a difference is the teacher's personal style in *communicating* what he knows. Studies by Witty[14] and Bousfield[3] tend to support these conclusions at both the high school *and* college level.

Having desirable personal qualities is one thing, but what are the results of rigorous tests of whether the teacher's having them makes any difference in the performance of students?

Cogan[4] found that warm, considerate teachers got an unusual amount of original poetry and art from their high school students. Reed[10] found that teachers higher in a capacity for warmth favorably affected their pupils' interests in science. Using scores from achievement tests as their criterion measure, Heil, Powell, and Fiefer[8] compared various teacher-pupil personality combinations and found that the well-integrated (healthy, well-rounded, flexible) teachers were most effective with *all* types of students. Spaulding[12] found that the self-concepts of elementary school children were apt to be higher and more positive in classrooms in which the teacher was "socially integrative" and "learner supportive."

In essence, I think the evidence is quite clear when it comes to sorting out good or effective from bad or ineffective teachers on the basis of personal characteristics. Effective teachers appear to be those who are, shall we say, "human" in the fullest sense of the word. They have a sense of humor, are fair, empathetic, more democratic than autocratic, and apparently are more able to relate easily and naturally to students on either a one-to-one or group basis. Their classrooms seem to reflect miniature enterprise operations in the sense that they are more open, spontaneous, and adaptable to change. Ineffective teachers apparently lack a sense of humor, grow impatient easily, use cutting, ego-reducing comments in class, are less well-integrated, are inclined to be somewhat authoritarian, and are generally less sensitive to the needs of their students. Indeed, research related to authoritarianism suggests that the bureaucratic conduct and rigid overtones of the ineffective teacher's classroom are desperate measures to support the weak pillars of his own personality structure.

Instructional Procedures and Interaction Styles of Good Versus Poor Teachers. If there really are polar extremes such as "good" or "poor" teachers, then we can reasonably assume that these teachers differ not only in personal characteristics but in the way they conduct themselves in the classroom.

Flanders [6] found that classrooms in which achievement and attitudes were superior were likely to be conducted by teachers who did not blindly pursue a single behavioral-instructional path to the exclusion of other possibilities. In other words, the more successful teachers were better able to range along a continuum of interaction styles which varied from fairly active, dominative support on the one hand to a more reflective, discriminating support on the other. Interestingly, those teachers who were *not* successful were the very ones who were inclined to use the same interaction styles in a more or less rigid fashion.

Barr [1] discovered that not only did poor teachers make more assignments than good teachers but, almost without exception, they made some sort of textbook assignment as part of their unyielding daily procedure. The majority of good teachers used more outside books and problem-project assignments. When the text was assigned they were more likely to supplement it with topics, questions, or other references.

Research findings related to interaction styles variously called "learner-centered" or "teacher-centered" point to similar conclusions. In general, it appears that the amount of cognitive gain is largely unaffected by the autocratic or democratic tendencies of the instructor. However, when affective gains are considered, the results are somewhat different. For example, Stern [13] reviewed 34 studies comparing nondirective with directive instruction and concluded:

Regardless of whether the investigator was concerned with attitudes toward the cultural out group, toward other participants in the class, or toward the self, the results generally have indicated that nondirective instruction facilitates a shift in a more favorable, acceptant direction.

When it comes to classroom behavior, interaction patterns, and teaching styles, good or effective teachers seem to reflect more of the following behaviors:

1. Willingness to be flexible, to be direct or indirect as the situation demands
2. Ability to perceive the world from the student's point of view
3. Ability to "personalize" their teaching
4. Willingness to experiment, to try out new things
5. Skill in asking questions (as opposed to seeing self as a kind of answering service)
6. Knowledge of subject matter and related areas
7. Provision of well-established examination procedures
8. Provision of definite study helps
9. Reflection of an appreciative attitude (evidenced by nods, comments, smiles, etc.)
10. Use of conversational manner in teaching—informal, easy style

Self-Perceptions of Good Versus Poor Teachers. We probably do not have to go any further than our own personal life experiences to know that the way we see, regard, and feel about ourselves has an enormous impact on both our private and public lives. How about good and poor teachers? How do they see themselves?

Ryans [11] found that there are, indeed, differences between the self-related reports of teachers with high emotional stability and those with low emotional stability. For example, the more emotionally stable teachers 1) more frequently named self-confidence and cheerfulness as dominant traits in themselves, 2) said they liked active contact with other people, 3) expressed interests in hobbies and handicrafts, 4) reported their childhoods to be happy experiences.

On the other hand, teachers with lower emotional maturity scores 1) had unhappy memories of childhood, 2) seemed *not* to prefer contact with others, 3) were more directive and authoritarian, 4) expressed less self-confidence.

We can be even more specific. Combs,[5] in his book *The Professional Education of Teachers,* cites several studies which reached similar conclusions about the way good teachers typically see themselves, as follows:

1. Good teachers see themselves as identified with people rather than withdrawn, removed, apart from, or alienated from others.

2. Good teachers feel basically adequate rather than inadequate. They do not see themselves as generally unable to cope with problems.

3. Good teachers feel trustworthy rather than untrustworthy. They see themselves as reliable, dependable individuals with the potential for coping with events as they happen.

4. Good teachers see themselves as wanted rather than unwanted. They see themselves as likable and attractive (in a personal, not a physical sense) as opposed to feeling ignored and rejected.

5. Good teachers see themselves as worthy rather than unworthy. They see themselves as people of consequence, dignity, and integrity as opposed to feeling they matter little, can be overlooked and discounted.

In the broadest sense of the word, good teachers are more likely to see themselves as good people. Their self-perceptions are, for the most part, positive, tinged with an air of optimism and colored with tones of healthy self-acceptance. I dare say that self-perceptions of good teachers are not unlike the self-perceptions of any basically healthy person, whether he be a good bricklayer, a good manager, a good doctor, a good lawyer, a good experimental psychologist, or you name it. Clinical evidence has told us time and again that *any* person is more apt to be happier, more productive, and more effective when he is able to see himself as fundamentally and basically "enough."

Perceptions of Others by Good Versus Poor Teachers. Research is showing us that not only do good and poor teachers view themselves differently, there are also some characteristic differences in the way they perceive others. For example, Ryans [11] reported several studies which have produced findings that are in agreement when it comes to sorting out the differences between how good and poor teachers view others. He found, among other things, that outstandingly "good" teachers rated significantly higher than notably "poor" teachers in at least five different ways with respect to how they viewed others. The good teachers had 1) more favorable opinions of students, 2) more favorable opinions of democratic classroom behavior, 3) more favorable opinions of administrators and colleagues, 4) a greater expressed liking for personal contacts with other people, 5) more favorable estimates of other people generally. That is, they expressed belief that very few students are difficult behavior problems, that very few people are influenced in their opinions and attitudes toward others by feelings of jealousy, and that most teachers are willing to assume their full share of extra duties outside of school.

Interestingly, the characteristics that distinguished the "lowly assessed" teacher group suggested that the relatively "ineffective" teacher is self-centered, anxious, and restricted. One is left with the distinct impression that poor or ineffective teachers have more than the usual number of paranoid defenses.

It comes as no surprise that how we perceive others is highly dependent on how we perceive ourselves. If a potential teacher (or anyone else for that matter) likes himself, trusts himself, and has confidence in himself, he is likely to see others in somewhat this same light. Research is beginning to tell us what common sense has always told us; namely, people grow, flourish, and develop much more easily when in relationship with someone who projects an inherent trust and belief in their capacity to become what they have the potential to become.

It seems to me that we can sketch at least five interrelated generalizations from what research is telling us about how good teachers differ from poor teachers when it comes to how they perceive others.

1. They seem to have generally more positive views of others—students, colleagues, and administrators.

2. They do not seem to be as prone to view others as critical, attacking people with ulterior motives; rather they are seen as potentially friendly and worthy in their own right.

3. They have a more favorable view of democratic classroom procedures.

4. They seem to have the ability and capacity to see things as they seem to others—i.e., the ability to see things from the other person's point of view.

5. They do not seem to see students as persons "you do things to" but rather as individuals capable of doing for themselves once they feel trusted, respected, and valued.

WHO, THEN, IS A GOOD TEACHER?

1. A good teacher is a good person. Simple and true. A good teacher rather likes life, is reasonably at peace with himself, has a sense of humor, and enjoys other people. If I interpret the research correctly, what it says is that there is no one best better-than-all-others type of teacher. Nonetheless there are clearly distinguishable "good" and "poor" teachers. Among other things, a good teacher is good because he does not seem to be dominated by a narcissistic self which demands a spotlight, or a neurotic need for power and authority, or a host of anxieties and tremblings which reduce him from the master of his class to its mechanic.

2. The good teacher is flexible. By far the single most repeated adjective used to describe good teachers is "flexibility." Either implicitly or explicitly (most often the latter), this characteristic emerges time and again over all others when good teaching is discussed in the research. In other words, the good teacher does not seem to be overwhelmed by a single point of view or approach to the point of intellectual myopia. A good teacher knows that he cannot be just one sort of person and use just one kind of approach if he intends to meet the multiple needs of his students. Good teachers are, in a sense, "total" teachers. That is, they seem able to be what they have to be to meet the demands of the moment. They seem able to move with the shifting tides of their own needs, the student's, and do what has to be done to handle the situation. A total teacher can be firm when necessary (say "no" and mean it) or permissive (say "why not try it your way?" and mean that, too) when appropriate. It depends on many things, and good teachers seem to know the difference.

THE NEED FOR "TOTAL" TEACHERS

There probably is not an educational psychology course taught which does not, in some way, deal with the highly complex area of individual differences.

Even the most unsophisticated undergraduate is aware that people differ in readiness and capacity to handle academic learning. For the most part, our educational technology (audio-visual aids, programmed texts, teaching machines, etc.) is making significant advances designed to assist teachers in coping with intellectual differences among students. We have been making strides in the direction of offering flexible programs and curricula, but we are somewhat remiss when it comes to preparing flexible, "total" teachers. Just as there are intellectual differences among students, there are also personality and self-concept differences which can have just as much impact on achievement. If this is true, then perhaps we need to do more about preparing teachers who are sensitive to the nature of these differences and who are able to take them into account as they plan for their classes.

The point here is that what is important for one student is not important to another. This is one reason why cookbook formulas for good teachers are of so little value and why teaching is inevitably something of an art. The choice of instructional methods makes a big difference for certain kinds of pupils, and a search for the "best" way to teach can succeed only when learners' intellectual *and* personality differences are taken into account. Available evidence does not support the belief that successful teaching is possible only through the use of some specific methodology. A reasonable inference from existing data is that methods which provide for adaptation to individual differences, encourage student initiative, and stimulate individual and group participation are superior to methods which do not. In order for things of this sort to happen, perhaps what we need first of all are flexible, "total" teachers who are capable of planning around people as they are around ideas.

IMPLICATIONS FOR TEACHER EDUCATION

Research is teaching us many things about the differences between good and poor teachers, and I see at least four related implications for teacher education programs.

1. If it is true that good teachers are good because they view teaching as primarily a human process involving human relationships and human meanings, then this may imply that we should spend at least as much time exposing and sensitizing teacher candidates to the subtle complexities of personality structure as we do to introducing them to the structure of knowledge itself. Does this mean personality development, group dynamics, basic counseling processes, sensitivity training, and techniques such as life-space interviewing and encounter grouping?

2. If it is true that good teachers have a positive view of themselves and others, then this may suggest that we provide more opportunities for teacher candidates to acquire more positive self-other perceptions. Self-concept research tells us that how one feels about himself is learned. If it is learned, it is teachable. Too often, those of us in teacher education are dominated by a concern for long-term goals, while the student is fundamentally motivated by

short-term goals. Forecasting what a student will need to know six months or two years from now, we operate on the assumption that he, too, perceives such goals as meaningful. It seems logical enough, but unfortunately it doesn't work out too well in practice. Hence much of what we may do with our teacher candidates is non-self-related—that is, to the student it doesn't seem connected with his own life, time, and needs. Rather than talk about group processes in the abstract, why can't we first assist students to a deeper understanding of their own roles in groups in which they already participate? Rather than simply theorize and cite research evidence related to individual differences, why not also encourage students to analyze the individual differences which exist in *this* class at *this* time and then allow them to express and discuss what these differences mean at a more personal level? If one values the self-concept idea at all, then there are literally endless ways to encourage more positive self-other perceptions through teaching strategies aimed at personalizing what goes on in a classroom. Indeed, Jersild [9] has demonstrated that when "teachers face themselves," they feel more adequate as individuals and function more effectively as teachers.

3. If it is true that good teachers are well-informed, then it is clear that we must neither negate nor relax our efforts to provide them with as rich an intellectual background as is possible. Teachers are usually knowledgeable people, and knowledge inculcation is the aspect of preparation with which teacher education has traditionally been most successful. Nonetheless, teachers rarely fail because of lack of knowledge. They fail more often because they are unable to communicate what they know so that it makes a difference to their students. Which brings us to our final implication for teacher-education programs.

4. If it is true that good teachers are able to communicate what they know in a manner that makes sense to their students, then we must assist our teacher candidates both through example and appropriate experiences to the most effective ways of doing this. Communication is not just a process of presenting information. It is also a function of discovery and the development of personal meanings. I wonder what would happen to our expectations of the teacher's role if we viewed him less as dispenser, answerer, coercer, and provoker and more as stimulator, questioner, challenger, and puzzler. With the former, the emphasis is on "giving to," while with the latter the focus is on "guiding to." In developing ability to hold and keep attention, not to mention techniques of encouraging people to adopt the reflective, thoughtful mood, I wonder what the departments of speech, theater, and drama on our college and university campuses could teach us? We expose our students to theories of learning and personality; perhaps what we need to do now is develop some "theories of presentation" with the help of those who know this field best.

This paper has attempted to point out that even though there is no single best or worst kind of teacher, there are clearly distinguishable characteristics associated with "good" and "bad" teachers. There is no one *best* kind of teaching because there is no *one kind* of student. Nonetheless, there seems to be enough evidence to suggest that whether the criteria for good teaching is on the basis of student and/or peer evaluations or in terms of student achievement gains, there are characteristics between both which consistently overlap. That is, the good teacher is able to influence both student feeling and achievement in positive ways.

Research is teaching us many things about the differences between good and bad teachers and there are many ways we can put these research findings into our teacher-education programs.

Good teachers do exist and can be identified. Perhaps the next most fruitful vineyard for research is in the classrooms of good teachers so we can determine, by whatever tools we have, just what makes them good in the first place.

NOTES

1. A. S. Barr, *Characteristic Differences in the Teaching Performance of Good and Poor Teachers of the Social Studies.* Bloomington, Ill.: The Public School Publishing Co., 1929.
2. B. J. Biddle and W. J. Ellena, *Contemporary Research on Teacher Effectiveness.* New York: Holt, Rinehart, and Winston, 1964, p. 2.
3. W. A. Bousfield, "Student's Rating on Qualities Considered Desirable in College Professors," *School and Society,* February 24, 1940, pp. 253–56.
4. M. L. Cogan, "The Behavior of Teachers and the Productive Behavior of Their Pupils," *Journal of Experimental Education,* December, 1958, pp. 89–124.
5. A. W. Combs, *The Professional Education of Teachers.* Boston: Allyn and Bacon, 1965, pp. 70–71.
6. N. A. Flanders, *Teacher Influence, Pupil Attitudes and Achievement: Studies in Interaction Analysis.* University of Minnesota, U.S. Office of Education Cooperative Research Project No. 397, 1960.
7. W. F. Hart, *Teachers and Teaching.* New York: Macmillan, 1934, pp. 131–32.
8. L. M. Heil, M. Powell, and I. Feifer, *Characteristics of Teacher Behavior Related to the Achievement of Children in Several Elementary Grades.* Washington, D.C.: Office of Education, Cooperative Research Branch, 1960.
9. A. T. Jersild, *When Teachers Face Themselves.* New York: Bureau of Publications, Teachers College, Columbia University, 1955.
10. H. B. Reed, "Implications for Science Education of a Teacher Competence Research," *Science Education,* December, 1962, pp. 473–86.
11. D. G. Ryans, "Prediction of Teacher Effectiveness," *Encyclopedia of Educational Research,* 3rd Edition. New York: Macmillan, 1960, pp. 1,486–90.
12. R. Spaulding, "Achievement, Creativity, and Self-Concept Correlates of Teacher-Pupil Transactions in Elementary Schools." University of Illinois, U.S. Office of Education Cooperative Research Project No. 1352, 1963.
13. G. C. Stern, "Measuring Non-Cognitive Variables in Research on Teaching," in *Handbook of Research on Teaching,* N. L. Gage (ed.). Chicago: Rand McNally, 1963, p. 427.
14. P. Witty, "An Analysis of the Personality Traits of the Effective Teacher," *Journal of Educational Research,* May, 1947, pp. 662–71.

THE TEACHING BEHAVIOR
OF SUCCESSFUL INTERNS

Martin Haberman

Since intern teachers have minimal professional preparation before assuming instructional responsibilities, the controversy over the intern approach usually focuses on a single issue: Do intern teachers act on the basis of educational principles or do they focus on the expedient techniques which will enable them to survive? In essence, this question is asking whether teachers should be prepared as independent, professional decision-makers or as skilled craftsmen. Unfortunately, the experiences of successful interns indicate that they act on some principles and ignore others, and that they grasp at and utilize ineffective as well as effective techniques. In place of the either-or question of whether interns act on principle or expediency, it would be more fruitful to take an intensive look at the nature of the principles and methods interns actually do employ. The discussion which follows will describe the kinds of behaviors which seem to characterize a particular group of successful intern teachers in order to determine implications of these behaviors for the development of teacher education programs.

Since 1895, over one hundred colleges and universities have offered some form of teacher education program which included intern teaching.[1] Although the term "intern" has been used in a variety of ways, five characteristics are generally used to define the concept. An intern is a college graduate who, as an undergraduate, specializes in some field other than education, begins the study of education on an advanced level, bears major responsibility for the instruction of children and youth as part of his preparation, is paid by the school district, and is supervised by college and public school personnel.[2,3]

Critics of the intern approach point out that the intent of some programs is merely to make financial arrangements which will serve as recruiting devices; that since interns begin their professional preparation as graduate students, these experiences are lumped on, rather than integrated with, students' liberal and general education; that the telescoped period of preparation does not allow sufficient time for the interns to be changed in important ways; that inexperienced interns may seriously harm the children and youth placed under their aegis; and that intern programs must of necessity focus on the techniques which will help inexperienced beginners to survive rather than the fundamental knowledge which is basic to the development of professional practitioners.[4]

Reprinted from *Journal of Teacher Education* 16:215–220 (June, 1965), by permission of author and publisher.

Proponents of the intern approach point to the high academic and personal standards usually required for admission, the elimination of inappropriate or repetitive professional courses, the increased cooperation of public schools and universities in the preparation of teachers, the new knowledge gained from the experimental designs of many intern programs, and the high degree to which theory and practice can be interrelated in a period of internship.[5, 6]

Critics and proponents alike would agree that intern programs have served a useful exploratory function. Practices which should be disseminated to all teacher education programs, and others which might best be discontinued, have been identified and tested. For example, a variety of new supervisory arrangements between public schools and universities have proved helpful in bridging the gap between preservice preparation and the first year of regular teaching. At the same time, the notion that interns may successfully begin without a minimal degree of course work and direct experiences with youngsters has been dispelled.[7]

In an effort to determine the actual behaviors in which interns engage, a colleague and I spent fifty-six full school days observing twenty-eight beginning interns over a two-year period. These interns had experienced one summer session which included part-time student teaching, a course in general methods, and a course in child development. They were then given full responsibility (under supervision) for classes of children in grades one to six. Almost all of these classes were in schools serving the urban disadvantaged.

As it became evident that some interns were doing better than others, we tried to specify what was different between the performance of successful and less successful interns. Several factors were used to determine the "success" of interns; these included the reading gain scores of pupils, the interns' indirect-direct ratio on a Flanders Interaction Analysis, and the subjective judgment of the two observers. Although all three of these criteria tended to identify the same interns as successful, it was the third criterion (the judgment of the classroom observers) which was weighted most heavily. We considered a successful situation to be one in which interns and pupils seemed active, enthusiastic, and interested; and where we perceived the classroom to be a pleasant place to work.

Clearly, then, some of the distinctions between successful and unsuccessful interns are the unprovable perceptions of two observers; these distinctions might also be viewed as the calculated hunches of experienced supervisors familiar with the particular schools and interns, and as such, fruitful hypotheses for future study. In an effort to focus on the nature of the principles and gimmicks employed by beginning interns, there will be a brief description of the characteristics and behaviors which do and *do not* seem to discriminate between successful and unsuccessful interns.

Factors which do not discriminate between the successful and unsuccessful interns in our program include: (1) academic achievement as a graduate student, (2) communication skills, and (3) positive attitudes toward children, as measured on written instruments or in personal conferences.

Academic achievement. There has been a clearly scattered pattern in trying to relate on-the-job success with students' records as graduate students. The "A" student whose pupils learn little and who is most directive and rigid in his teaching and the "C" student on probation in the graduate school who successfully elicits learning behaviors from his pupils are common occurrences in our program. Since we deal with adults who have, in some cases, been away from college for a long time, it may be they are potentially good graduate students who have suffered a loss of study skills. Actually, however, we find the same inability to relate graduate grades with teaching performance among our younger interns who are essentially in a fifth year of preparation.

Positive attitudes toward pupils. We have found that there is no relationship between scores on tests such as the MTAI and interns designated as successful. The same range and frequency of scores will characterize unsuccessful as successful interns. We have also found little relationship between verbally expressed attitudes toward children and what is actually done with children. Some of our most vitriolic interns engage in warm behaviors while some of our softest-spoken are harsh and rejecting in practice; and in neither case can the pattern of written and verbal attitudes be identified as characteristic of successful or unsuccessful interns.

Communication skills. We have had interns from low-income and deprived southern areas who have done very well in practice but who are below the level of reading, writing, and speech characteristic of other graduate students. Once again, however, there does not seem to be a pattern.

On the basis of our experience we do not believe that it is possible to predict the success or failure of an individual intern on the basis of the above characteristics. Neither do we believe it is possible to use these factors to predict the success of groups of interns.

Moving from these background characteristics to actual teaching behaviors we discovered little in the behavior of successful or unsuccessful interns that would indicate they were implementing the educational principles of planning cooperatively, utilizing pupils' background experiences, helping pupils see purpose in their work, or attempting to interest and motivate the youngsters.

Cooperative planning. Few interns ever behaved as if the school curriculum were not completely preestablished. Although involvement of pupils in goal setting is a frequently cited principle of education, there was little indication that interns were aware of it. Successful interns were as directive as others in deciding what should be done, how, by whom, for how long, and with which materials.

Utilizing pupils' backgrounds. There was little evidence that interns knew much about their pupils and less that they attempted to utilize this information in their teaching. Both successful and less successful interns possessed much inaccurate information. Interns' knowledge of their youngsters and the use of such knowledge in the classroom were not related to their rating of success.

Helping pupils see purpose. In few classrooms was there any attempt consistently to help children understand why they did what they did. The usual mode was one of establishing organization and schedules so that teacher and pupils moved through a series of activities. Unsuccessful interns could not be distinguished from others on the basis of their efforts to help children see purpose in activities. Most children in all the classrooms seemed to accept the premise that they were supposed to do what was expected of them by the teacher.

Motivating youngsters. As in the case of the above three principles, there was little evidence that interns consciously planned activities for the express purpose of interesting the pupils in particular subject matter. Neither, in this regard, did there seem to be a difference between what successful interns did in comparison with others. This is not to say that the pupils of interns designated as successful were not motivated but that pupils seemed to become interested in response to teacher behaviors which were not specifically intended as motivational procedures.

There are, however, five behavioral patterns which do seem to distinguish successful interns—a behavioral demonstration of a belief in the youngsters' potentialities, an ability to organize a classroom situation, a real enthusiasm for some subject matter, an ability to set appropriate standards, and a willingness to listen.

Belief in the youngsters. Belief in and respect for the abilities of youngsters mean that the intern manifests behaviors which indicate he does not believe he can know the limits of his pupils' potentialities. Through verbal patterns, body gestures, facial expressions, written communication, and a combination of all of these, successful interns demonstrate clearly that they believe in the youngsters. Their behavior indicates not only that they think pupils can learn, but further, that they have no real way of estimating the potential insights of which the youngsters are capable. Rather than sentimental, maudlin, or condescending behaviors, the intern's work is characterized by an obvious respect for the youngsters as people and by a clear assumption that nothing is beyond them—provided the teacher knows the appropriate teaching procedures. Essentially, the interns who do not manifest this behavior place the blame for learning failures on the pupils, while interns who do believe in the youngsters are willing to assume professional responsibility for what their pupils learn. Their first reaction in evaluating a lesson is not a search for what is wrong with the youngsters but for what might be lacking in their own teaching skills and approach. Statements such as, "This is good work for these kinds of youngsters" or "This is all you can expect of these kids," imply that the teacher thinks he can know the maximum which can be expected of the pupils, and are examples of an essentially deprecating teacher attitude. Successful interns, although praising and reinforcing pupil achievement, exhibit behaviors which demonstrate that they expect the pupils to move to new levels and much beyond.

Enthusiasm for some subject matter. Some scholars limit definitions of subject matter to the study of the traditional fields of human inquiry and describe the passion which envelops the student of literature, music, biology, etc. Some professional educators focus on the youngsters rather than on the fields of knowledge and describe the enthusiasm which develops when a teacher deals with content that has meaning to pupils in terms of their own backgrounds of life experiences. Neither of these approaches adequately accounts for the enthusiasm of successful intern teachers.

Utilizing a wide range of subject matter, successful interns demonstrate that their pupils can become interested in many topics and problems which are clearly beyond their fields of experience. One intern, for example, gives his disadvantaged sixth graders oral instructions in Japanese. He also uses old Caruso records as a basic part of his music program. In these and other cases, it is evident that the enthusiasm of the intern for some discipline, topic, problem, or area of interest can be contagious. The critical elements do not seem to be inherent in the subjects themselves, in the manner in which the content is organized, or in the basic ideas which characterize the material. The critical element seems to be the teacher's innumerable and pervasive behavioral demonstrations that *he* values the material, that *he* thinks it is important, that *he* regards it as useful.

The same phenomenon of intern's interest seems to be true for the teaching of processes. In cases where interns value selected media of creative expression, procedures of brainstorming, and selected patterns of classroom learning, the pupils adapt to the processes favored by the intern.

This suggestion is, of course, contrary to one of the most common generalizations cited as a principle of learning; that is, pupils learn in terms of their previous experience. Our observation would lead us to hypothesize that the tendency of pupils to learn what is of great interest to the teacher is more powerful than the influence of their previous experiences.

Ability to organize. The classrooms of successful interns are rooms in which individuals are able to predict the behavior of others: pupils know what they are about and what their peers and the teacher are doing. But more important, pupils seem to know the written and the unwritten rules guiding these behaviors. The ease which seems to characterize the successful situations may also be due in part to the fact that teacher and pupils share common understandings regarding materials and their use. The result of these mutual understandings is that the participants in these classroom interactions have the power to predict their own actions and, to a great degree, the responses of others.

These conditions are the result of behaviors by interns who are capable of administrative action. These interns do not confuse the eliciting acts of instruction with the directive behaviors required to organize a classroom. Even the most indirective acts of instruction require that the teacher set time limits, determine the pupils to be involved and the materials to be used. The interns who organize successfully do so by directing, telling, explaining, gathering materials, and making a host of administrative decisions regarding schedules, materials, and pupils' responsibilities.

Successful interns seem able to make the management decisions which establish them as the organizational head of the classroom and to use this authority to organize efficiently. The personal styles of interns who demonstrate these organizational skills vary. There is no single pattern discernible in what they do, say, or write. There is a similarity, however, in the responses of the youngsters, and the dimension which seems critical is the intern's ability to demonstrate the organizational behaviors which become the ground rules by which the class operates.

Ability to set appropriate standards. Some ineffective interns expect too little of their pupils and rationalize about what might reasonably be expected of "these kinds of kids." Others, on the pretext that the curriculum must be covered, set rigid goals which are beyond even their most able pupils. Interns who are successful, however, are able to set standards which reflect pupils' needs without pandering to them. As a result, pupils of successful interns learn more.

A second dimension of this standard-setting is that successful interns frequently have more than a single expectation: there are different expectancies for various youngsters. Teacher behaviors which lock a class together (e.g., giving the total class the same assignment to be completed in the same period of time; using the same reading material with the total class; explaining, giving information, and discussing with the whole group) are not so common as teacher behaviors which open up youngsters to realize divergent standards (e.g., working with individuals and subgroups within a classroom, giving multilevel assignments, setting a variety of time limits and assignment lengths, allowing pupils to make choices).

The essence of these behaviors is that the teacher's acts encourage pupils to believe that if they try they can succeed. It is unnatural enthusiastically to enter a race in which there is no hope of winning.

It is not uncharacteristic of some interns to regard the youngsters who "act out" as their major problems. Successful interns, however, more frequently cite the quiet, unobtrusive youngster who is difficult to involve as among their most important problems. This is because, in their attempt to set realizable goals, successful interns come to understand the challenge being posed by the overly quiet, withdrawn youngster. When an effective teacher interests reluctant youngsters who then take hold and complete tasks, the classroom observer who appreciates this dynamic of teaching is witness to an esthetic experience. Because they accomplish tasks which they themselves value and because they are capable of evaluating their own success, pupils in these classrooms seek little external reinforcement.

The willingness to listen. There are three aspects to the professional behavior of listening; these require that the teacher (1) be attentive, (2) remember, and (3) utilize pupils' talk. Being attentive means giving the youngster real attention—not allowing him to address a teacher distracted by other tasks or engaged in other responsibilities. It is necessary for the teacher to remember pupils' ideas in order to help them relate what they are saying to what they may have said before and for using what the pupil says at a later date with the whole class.

The skill and art of teaching are embodied in this ability to use public ideas. By questioning, by reflecting back to the pupil for reconsideration, and by combining and extending his thoughts, the successful intern engages in the basic acts of teaching. All of these critical behaviors are derived from the interns' initial willingness and ability to listen. The elementary truth is that less successful interns tend to regard their pupils' talk as some form of interference, while successful interns tend to regard the eliciting of pupil talk as a major objective of their lessons.

The question of whether beginning interns act on principle or expediency is unimportant. A more fruitful question is to determine the behaviors which successful interns employ and conceptualize the sources and causes of these actions. On the basis of our observations, successful interns act on principle *and* in terms of the immediate needs of the situation. The principles involved, however, are not the usual ones couched in terms of the educational psychologist focused on learning. Perhaps the reason we did not observe successful interns using pupils' backgrounds of experiences and engaging in motivational activities is that these are not principles of teaching at all but rather attempts to extrapolate from principles of learning to the work of the teacher. Unfortunately, a principle of learning does not tell a teacher what to do. In what specific behaviors does a teacher engage to help a student see purpose, feel motivated, etc.?

The five kinds of behavior described as characteristic of successful interns are behaviors of teachers, not learners. They can be rationalized on the basis of several psychological learning theories. They can also be explained by theories in the fields of sociology, anthropology, and even political science.

Rather than begin with the logical assumption that psychological explanations of learning can also provide the principles for guiding teacher behavior, we have attempted to describe the teaching behavior characteristic of successful interns. Our observations lead us to raise the following questions regarding preservice teacher education:

What are the means for affecting preservice students' belief in the potentialities of pupils?

What are the means for developing preservice students' willingness to listen and use pupils' ideas?

What are the means for fostering preservice students' enthusiasm to share various areas of subject matter with their youngsters?

What are the means for helping preservice students develop the self-confidence and skill to organize a classroom?

What are the means for teaching preservice students to individualize standards of achievement?

In the final instance, it is the demonstrated teacher behaviors which should be the goals of the program of preparation. In the absence of such demonstration, the debate about the bases of teacher actions has a hollow ring. Considering the actions of successful intern teachers as objectives may cause us to reexamine the justification of the elements of preservice preparation now considered basic.

NOTES

1. Shaplin, J. T., and Powell, A. G. "Comparison of Internship Programs." *Journal of Teacher Education* 15:175–83; June 1964.
2. Michaelis, J. V. "Teacher Education—Student Teaching and Internship." *The Encyclopedia of Educational Research*. Third edition. (Edited by W. S. Monroe.) New York: The Macmillan Co., 1960. p. 1474.
3. Haberman, M. "Intern Concept in Teacher Education." *Wisconsin Journal of Education* 96:12–13; January 1964.
4. Hermanowicz, H. J. "The Professional Education of Teachers." *Concern for the Individual in Student Teaching*. Forty-Second Yearbook. Cedar Falls, Iowa: Association for Student Teaching, 1963. pp. 59–125.
5. Whitelaw, J. B. "Teacher Preparation: Five Targets for the Next 10 Years." *School Life* 46:11–13. January–February 1964.
6. Whitelaw, J. B. "The Most Important Breakthrough in the History of Teacher Education: The Teaching Internship." An address to the Annual Conference of Idaho School Administrators and Trustees at Sun Valley, Idaho, August 14, 1964. (Mimeographed)
7. Halliwell, J. W. "A Review of the Research Concerning the Teaching Effectiveness of Elementary School Teachers Prepared in Intensive Teacher Training Programs and in Regular Undergraduate Programs." *Journal of Teacher Education* 15:184–92; June 1964.

IS TALKING TEACHING?

William D. Hedges

Most teaching, from first grade through graduate school, can be described in a single sentence: "Teaching is talking." This cannot, however, be followed with its logical corollary: "Learning is listening." If it could, our problems with the methodology of effective teaching would be largely solved.

In support of my assertion that teacher talk dominates our classrooms, I merely ask you to walk by 20 classrooms in any school and count the number of times you hear the teacher talking. If you make your survey in a junior or senior high school or a college, the chances are that you will hear the teacher talking in at least 15 of the 20 classrooms; if in an elementary school, the teacher will probably be talking in about ten of the classes. My

Reprinted from *The Clearing House* 41:334–337 (February, 1967), by permission of author and publisher.

own most recent tally, secured during a trip down the hall of a local senior high school, was as follows: in 16 classrooms, teachers were talking; in two, students were talking; in one, the class was taking an examination; and in one, the class was engaged in silent study. Should you wish more reliable evidence, you are referred to the work of Ned Flanders,[1] who has conducted extensive studies of what actually takes place in classrooms, and to the *Handbook of Research on Teaching,*[2] which contains copious references to related studies.

All of this teacher talk has many purposes. The teachers may be explaining a concept, asking a question, modifying and clarifying a student's statement, responding to a question, giving a lecture, administering a test, reading a story, reciting a poem, preparing students to view a film, making an assignment, dictating spelling, typing, or language practice, describing a science demonstration, admonishing a student for mischievous behavior, taking the roll, reading the daily bulletin, or telling a joke. One researcher, Withal,[3] devised seven categories into which all forms of teacher verbalization seem to fit: *learner-supportive,* as in commending the student; *acceptant and clarifying,* as in letting the student know he is understood; *problem-structuring,* as in asking leading questions or giving clues; *neutral,* as in reading an announcement; *directive,* as in describing procedures to be followed; *reproving,* as in admonishing students to cease certain types of activity; and *teacher self-supporting,* as in the teacher's defending an action or point of view.

There is nothing inherently wrong with talking as a method of teaching. There are times when talking is the most efficient, most effective method a teacher can use. Thus, a teacher often needs to talk in order to question students, to challenge them, to probe their thinking. And there are times when a lecture is the best way to present a series of related ideas in an organized fashion.

There are other times, however, when talking is the least efficient, least effective method a teacher can use. When the teacher is doing most of the talking, the classroom is teacher centered, teacher directed, teacher dominated. The teacher, in short, is doing the explaining, setting the goals, and performing the evaluation. The teacher is at the center of the stage and hence is often doing most of the learning. He is doing most of the learning because he is the one who is the most involved in the whole process. Learning theory tells us that we learn most effectively when we are involved, when we participate actively in discussing and using ideas. This is precisely what the teacher is doing when he is talking. He is highly motivated, he reads, he ruminates, he writes lesson plans, he discusses, he waves his arms, he writes on the board. He is internalizing the concepts because most of his senses are involved, in varying degree. This accounts for the old cliché about learning something by teaching it. This is essentially true, but unfortunately the teacher does not always perceive the implications for student learning. He does not recognize that for the very reasons *he* is learning while *he* is teaching, the students may be learning precious little. *They are not necessarily involved.*

I have often thought how wonderful it would be if teachers were forced to teach one entire week of each year with their mouths taped shut. A drastic measure, perhaps—but I believe it would be an effective way of forcing them to devise and use other methods of teaching. These other methods, once used, might become a part of their repertoire of teaching practices.

Professors in schools of education spend too much of their time lecturing—telling future teachers how to teach. In the process they violate much of what they are saying. They confuse listening with learning, and when accused, rationalize by citing the maturity of the students and the need to "cover" a great amount of material in a limited time. Is it strange that teachers so "trained" are prone to follow suit?

If one is to become an effective teacher, he must teach. And during the processes of teaching, he must be led to examine his behavior—to think and talk and write about the ways he and the students interact. He must be guided to analyze the students' reactions, as expressed through their behavior, and to consider the implications for his teaching. He must be involved. He cannot be passive if he is to be an effective learner. There must be participation.

But when it comes to teaching "subjects," these techniques are often neglected! The principle of pupil involvement is ignored. It is ignored by the education professor and, not surprisingly, it is subsequently ignored by his student teacher when he marches forth to do battle in the classroom. This principle is most often ignored in subject classes because it is much harder to get mental than physical involvement. The music, art, and typing teachers and the coach have a somewhat easier time of it because the obvious necessity for physical involvement more naturally facilitates mental interaction.

Observe a history class, for example. What do you see? The teacher is a talking machine. He is describing a battle; he is pointing at a map and explaining an aspect of the terrain; he is asking a question (and, more often than not, interrupting to answer it)—he is talking.

Learning is incomplete when the teacher does nothing more than talk. It is incomplete even when there is almost perfect reception—even when the student hears and understands almost exactly what the teacher is trying to communicate. I said, "almost perfect reception" because we know that what is in the teacher's mind *cannot be conveyed in that form* directly to the students' minds. There is distortion. There is misunderstanding. There are differing interpretations of the same words. Each student, in a sense, views the world through a pair of glasses which are tinted in a different way from everyone else's. These glasses, and the way they distort what the teacher says and does, are shaped by the needs, the interests, the attitudes, the experiences, the expectations which the students bring with them to the classroom.

Innumerable examples of this phenomenon can be cited by any experienced teacher. He recognizes that there are times when some of the students just don't hear what he means for them to hear. Primary teachers are especially alert to this problem. But somehow many teachers in the upper grades lack an awareness of the inadequacy of just words. And then they think the problem is with the students rather than with themselves. They think the students are stupid or apathetic, or unable to follow directions, or just plain lazy.

The loquacious teacher somehow feels he can actually short circuit the learning process. Exhilarated and enthusiastic about his subject, he sincerely believes that in a few minutes of talking he can communicate a concept, an idea, an attitude, an emotion that required years for him to acquire and perhaps (if the truth be known) only came to him with a flash the night before *as he was involved* in planning the lesson. I was one of the worst offenders.

Zooming into class each morning I would plunge enthusiastically into some mathematics or physics concept—and meet blank, uncomprehending stares. Backing off, I would give another example, use another analogy, and then another and another and another. Still the blank stares. Mouth dry, throat sore, exhausted, I would desperately make an assignment, somehow hoping the students would "get it." My assignment would emphasize that they must follow the directions very, very carefully.

Every experienced teacher knows what I mean when I describe this blind, blank, virtually impregnable wall of student resistance, student apathy, student reliance on the teacher to make sure they understand—this "you make me understand because that's your job" attitude. At the end of such a day we depart emotionally and physically exhausted and sometimes even a trifle bitter and cynical. Contrast this, however, with those days when, for some perhaps unaccountable reason, the lecturing *was* appropriate, when the kids *did* learn. On such days we depart tired, but still exhilarated (and happy).

I'll never forget what a supervisor said to me years ago. It was during my first year of teaching and he had come to supervise my geometry class. He observed the pyrotechnics—the neat drawings, the splendid verbal illustrations with just the right enunciation, all the gyrations of the well prepared teacher trying to snow the supervisor. After the session, as we sat in the room, I asked him, "How did I do?"

There was a rather lengthy pause. "Well," he finally said, "it was a splendid example of the geometry *you* know, but I don't think the students learned a great deal. Some did, perhaps, but not many."

"What do you mean?" I stammered.

"Good teaching implies that the students learn," he said. "You have the makings of a good teacher, but you'll never be effective until you realize that teaching involves more than just skillful presentations, more than skillful lectures, if you please. The students were there in the classroom, but how do I know (and how do you know) that they were really involved? And even if they were involved, even if they did follow you, that doesn't mean they can solve any of the problems themselves."

Frankly, what he said to me that day just did not make sense at the time. I heard the words, but they did not mean anything to me. I secretly dismissed his "lecture" with an angry, almost contemptuous shrug and the thought that he just didn't understand. Here is precisely the phenomenon about which I have been speaking. *Momentarily I was the student and the words spoken by the supervisor did not convey the insight about teaching intended by the supervisor.*

It was only as I continued to experience that wall of resistance, that deadly air of apathy, that firm resolve of the students that the responsibility for learning should rest on *my* shoulders and not on theirs, and the glaring evidence of the test scores, that I seriously began to entertain doubts about the validity of talking as my major teaching method. And it was not until the following summer when, in some desperation, I enrolled in several professional education courses, that the supervisor's words began to take on meaning. For me, desperately motivated to improve, searching for insights into the behavior of youngsters, the lectures of those professional educators fell as welcome rain on a parched lawn. Notice that I said lectures. But notice that for me, at that time, with my desperate need to know, my interest in finding out, based on experience in the classroom, those lectures were meaningful. Is the typical talking teacher this fortunate each day?

Even more significant is the measurable drop in student attention over time. The best orator is seldom able to hold the complete attention of most of his audience for more than 35 or 40 minutes. How, then, can the average teacher expect to hold attention for 55 minutes? And how can he expect to hold the attention of students in his class when those same students have just sat through one, two, three, or even four other such classes?

What are the alternatives to teaching by talking? There are many, but they cannot be cited as items on a grocery list. They are found in methods books on teaching. They are found in the sociology of groups. Bits and pieces of clues are to be found in the writings of men such as Dewey, Piaget, Neill, Noar, and Combs. But above all, the alternatives are found as the teacher applies the laws of learning to himself. Just listening to lectures won't provide the answers. Nor will just reading books, or observing other teachers in action, or viewing films, or asking questions, or trying out ideas in the classroom by themselves accomplish the goal. But all these techniques, tried and evaluated by a person strongly motivated to become a good teacher, will result in learning—just as in an analogous way they will succeed with students who are allowed to become involved. Teaching is not just talking. Learning is not just listening.

NOTES

1. Ned A. Flanders, *Interaction Analysis in the Classroom*. University of Minnesota, College of Education, 1960.
2. N. L. Gage (Ed.), *Handbook of Research on Teaching*. Chicago: Rand McNally and Company, 1963.
3. J. Withal, "Development of a Technique for the Measurement of Socio-Emotional Climate in Classrooms," *Journal of Experimental Education*, Vol. 17, 1949, p. 349.

TEACHERS OF THE POOR:
A FIVE-POINT PLAN[1]

Frank Riessman

INTRODUCTION

There are numerous paths to improved education of the educationally deprived, culturally different child: the curriculum, parent involvement, school administration. The teacher and his approach stand at a central point; more-over, in the present hopeful atmosphere, the teacher is more open to change than ever before. However, it would be naïve to suppose that teacher change can occur independently of other relevant variables, particularly administra-tion.[2] Presented below is a fivefold plan for the training of both preservice and in-service teachers of urban disadvantaged children:

1. Building teacher respect for disadvantaged children and their families. This involves attitude change and a proposed method of producing it.

2. Supplying teacher experiences with the disadvantaged.

3. Some general do's and don't's in teaching the urban poor.

4. A teaching technology appropriate for low-income youngsters.

5. The development of a variety of teacher styles through integrating other parts of the plan with the idiosyncratic potential of each teacher. This con-cerns the *art of teaching* and how it can be developed and organized.

1. ATTITUDE CHANGE THROUGH INTEREST

Many people stress the importance of respecting disadvantaged children as the key to their education, but the secret of respect for someone is to know his positives, his strengths. Unfortunately, too many who talk of respecting these children really see nothing to respect. Hence, it is crucial for teachers to know such positives in the culture, behavior, and style of the disadvantaged as the cooperativeness and mutual aid that mark the extended family; the avoidance of the strain accompanying competitiveness and individualism; the equalitarianism, informality, and humor; the freedom from self-blame and parental overprotection; the children's enjoyment of each other's company and lessened sibling rivalry; the security and traditional out-look found in an extended family; the enjoyment of music, games, sports, and cards; the ability to express anger; the freedom from being word bound; and finally, the physical style involved in learning.

These positives must be spelled out in detail lest they become vague, romantic, sentimental, and demagogic. We need clear vision regarding the

Reprinted from *Journal of Teacher Education* 18:326–336 (Fall, 1967), by per-mission of the author, Frank Riessman, and publisher.

positives in people who cope with a difficult environment, who can express their anger toward the school, and who are disturbed at being discriminated against. The point is that you cannot have respect in a general way. To have genuine respect, you must know the culture and its positives, you must appreciate how these people cope with their environment, and how in coping with it, they have built their culture.

However, it is not enough to build respect and knowledge; teacher attitudes must also be changed. This is not so difficult as may be imagined; the most important element is to *interest* the teacher in disadvantaged people and their culture. Generally, school personnel have not been especially interested in the make-up of the disadvantaged; the poor, for the most part, are seen as an undifferentiated, drab mass. Surprisingly, providing teachers with sociological analyses of disadvantaged groups, though valuable, is not sufficient to develop deep interest and excitement. Oscar Lewis's literary anthropology is more useful, but it is still not enough; the time has come for teacher preparation to include the novels, films, art, dance, and music of low-income groups, particularly Negro and Spanish. Discussions around books such as *The Cool World* [3] and the movie made from it are more helpful and stimulating than any anthropological text.

Contrasts and issues can be stimulated by books and movies about the disadvantaged elsewhere, such as the British *The Sporting Life* and *Saturday Night and Sunday Morning*.[4] Such films and literature offer prospective teachers a different perspective and a closer feeling for these cultures. Valuable, too, is the study of Negro history and Negro contributions in science, art, and engineering.[5] Discussion of "hip" language may help overcome the stereotype of the nonverbal, inarticulate poor! A look through *Hiptionary* [6] is especially valuable in creating a feeling for the language of certain disadvantaged groups; it reveals their wonderful ability to verbalize and destroys the absurd illusion that they lack verbal ability. They have a highly imaginative language, though they are limited in its formal structure, and the school should certainly work on this need. The first area in the proposed program, then, is to build teacher respect for these people by developing interest and excitement in their psychology and culture.

2. PREPARED EXPOSURE

The second area considers appropriate laboratory experiences for teachers. Several programs are emerging in this area: one is the Hunter College preservice program described in *The Culturally Deprived Child;* [7] another is the Mobilization for Youth in-service program in New York City. Such programs stress visiting the homes and neighborhoods of the poor. Many people think that this *exposure* will prove positive in and of itself; actually, simple exposure may only reinforce existing stereotypes. Teachers, like everyone else, see selectively what they want and expect to see; consequently, what is needed is a carefully directed, prepared exposure showing *what* to look at and *how* to look at the culture. Instead of merely a broken home, they see an extended female-based family which may be highly organized, although in ways very different from the traditional nuclear family. They learn to see how functions are delegated and organized, how child rearing is handled, how cooking is assigned, how members of the family care for the house, how some go to work, and how responsibility is divided.

Teachers can learn not to confuse the normal with the pathological. The normal female-based family is not pathological, although pathology may occur in some families. The difference may be clarified by a look at the middle-class family. In some middle-class strata, child rearing includes parental over-protection and overindulgence. This is the norm, just as less intensive loving is normative in lower socioeconomic groups. But neither pattern by itself is abnormal, even though pathologies in both classes may well be related to the norm, reflecting it in an extreme form or expressing the constitutional reactions of particular children. What teachers need is an emphasis on the under-standing of the basic culture (the norm) rather than on pathology. They should not focus on the environment as such (the crowdedness, the lack of privacy, the lack of economic security) but upon how these people struggle with their environment, how they have thereby forged a culture, and how this culture can be utilized in the school. It is clear, then, that we cannot simply call for tours and home visits. Teachers must be carefully prepared to look beyond the environment and the surface behavior in comprehending the meaning of the life and behavior of the poor.

3. SOME GENERAL DO'S AND DON'TS

The third area briefly considers some do's and don'ts in teaching edu-cationally deprived children. Consistency, structure, and order are funda-mental. *Informality and authority are not seen as contradictions, and the poor like both.* Extrinsic rewards and punishments are understood, but brutality is strongly rejected. The teacher should be straightforward, direct, and should clearly define what is to be done. *Values related to order, tardiness, or aggression should be strictly oriented toward their usefulness in learning.* (We can't conduct a class if children fight, come late, walk around, etc. This does not mean that fighting is "bad.")

Goldberg states:

The successful teacher meets the disadvantaged child on equal terms, as person to person, individual to individual. But while he *accepts, he doesn't condone.* He sets clearly defined limits for his pupils and will brook few transgressions. He is aware that, unlike middle-class children, they rarely respond to exhortations in-tended to control behavior through invoking feelings of guilt and shame. He, therefore, sets the rules, fixes the boundaries, establishes the routines with a minimum of discussion. Here he is impersonal, undeviating, strict, but never punitive. Within these boundaries, the successful teacher is business-like and or-derly, knowing that he is there to do a job. But he is also warm and outgoing, adapting his behavior to the individual pupils in his class. He shows his respect and liking for his pupils and makes known his belief in their latent abilities.[8]

Different stages of the teaching process should also be considered. There are two crucial stages: first, achieving contact; and second, developing educational power. In the contact stage, comes the special "breaking through" to the child, winning his attention, etc.; although this problem is sometimes exaggerated, it is nevertheless a definite issue in preparing teachers who must develop effective techniques. Unfortunately, a good many teachers who succeed at the contact stage (maintaining orderly, attentive classes) are unable to move on to the next stage and develop educational power. They have done well to achieve the contact stage, but to stop short of the next and most crucial stage is indeed unfortunate.[9]

4. APPROPRIATE TEACHING TECHNOLOGY

Listed below are a number of approaches that may have special value for low-income children:

1. The "organics" approach of Sylvia Ashton-Warner[10] should be especially valuable in utilizing the interests and strengths of the youngsters and should guard against their being "acted upon." (The latter is the current trend in many programs designed for the disadvantaged, who are supposedly deficit-ridden.)

2. The Montessori System, which envisions a 35 to 1 ratio of children to teacher, may provide valuable leads. The stress on sensory materials and on order in this approach should be particularly congenial to low-income children.[11] (Dr. Ronald Kregler, a neuropsychiatrist at the University of California, Los Angeles, is experimenting with a Montessori nursery program for disadvantaged children.)

3. Various game techniques may be valuable: In the Manner of the Adverb, Robbins Auditory Set Game, etc.[12]

4. Senesch's techniques for teaching economics to first- and second-graders seem promising.[13]

5. *Scope,* the new magazine published by Scholastic Magazines, is particularly attuned to teaching the disadvantaged.

The Special Significance of Role Playing.[14] Role-playing techniques have long been popular with blue-collar workers in labor unions and industry. Experiences at Mobilization for Youth and various community organizations also indicate an exceptionally positive response to role-play technology by low-income people. Although more systematic research is needed regarding these observations, it would appear that this technology is very congenial to the low-income person's style—physical (action-oriented, doing rather than talking); down to earth, concrete, problem-directed; externally oriented rather than introspective; group-centered; gamelike rather than test-oriented, easy, informal in tempo.

Miller and others,[15] on the basis of investigations, concluded that an outstanding characteristic of the low-income person's style is an emphasis on the physical, especially the motoric (the large muscles involved in voluntary action). They prefer to do rather than to talk. It is not simply that the poor *are* physical: that their labor is characterized by working with things, that their child rearing typically utilizes physical punishment, that their religious expressions more often include physical manifestations of emotion such as handclapping, that when they become mentally ill they appear more likely to develop motoric symptoms such as conversion hysteria and catatonia (disorders involving malfunctions of the voluntary muscles), that they are strongly interested in sports, that they are especially responsive to extraverbal forms of communication such as gestures; [16] the significant factor from the point of view of style is that low-income people tend to *work out mental problems best when they can do things physically*. This is their *habit* or style of work, and it appears when they work on academic problems, personal problems, or whatever.

Role playing appears admirably suited to this physical, action-centered, motoric style that requires a wholistic doing or acting out of situations, a mode of problem solving that low-income males, and young males in particular, find attractive. They frequently have a strong dislike for talk, especially talk that is isolated from experience; they want action and prefer talk that is related to action. They also like vivid (e.g., hip slang), down-to-earth, situationally rooted talk; and this, too, is more likely to emerge in the role-play format. Role playing is much more lively, physical, and active than the typical interview.

There are numerous other dimensions of role playing which are congruent with various aspects of the low-income person's style: Low-income groups typically do not like the traditional test format, and this limits diagnostic work with them. The requirements of their style seem to be better met by gamelike atmospheres and situational measures, both of which are found more readily in role-play technology.[17] They are generally less introspective, less introverted, and less concerned with self. They respond more to the external, to the outside, to action. They are more likely to see the causes of their problems in external forces; they project more and tend to externalize their guilt.[18] Kohn notes that their child-rearing patterns center on conformity to external prescriptions in contrast to the self-direction focus of the middle class.[19] He relates this, in part, to the fact that working-class occupations require that one follow explicit rules set down by an authority; middle-class positions are more subject to self-direction.[20]

Although the style of the poor probably includes a strong emphasis on informality, humor, and warmth, the disadvantaged also like a content that is structured, definite, and specific. It is often assumed that role playing is highly unstructured, open, and free. In part, this is true, particularly in the early phase of setting the problem and mood; but in the middle and later phases (especially the role-*training* stage), where the effort is made to teach very specific behaviors, role playing can be highly structured, reviewing in minute detail the various operations to be learned (such as how to run a meeting, organize a conference, talk to a housing manager). Educationally disadvantaged people appear to prefer a mood or feeling tone that is informal and easy but a *content* that is more structured and task-centered. Role playing may suit both needs.

A Route to Verbalization. In role-playing sessions we have had occasion to observe that the verbal performance of deprived children is markedly improved in the discussion period following the session. When talking about some action they have seen, deprived children are apparently able to verbalize much more fully. Typically, they do not verbalize well in response to words alone. They express themselves more readily when reacting to things they can see and do. Words as stimuli are not sufficient for them as a rule. Ask a juvenile delinquent who comes from a disadvantaged background what he doesn't like about school or the teacher and you will get an abbreviated, inarticulate reply. But have a group of these youngsters act out a school scene in which someone plays the teacher, and you will discover a stream of verbal consciousness that is almost impossible to shut off.[21]

Role playing can have various beneficial results in the teaching of academic material in the school. Considerable excitement is added to a lecture when the instructor illustrates a point this way; for example, if an inquiring student should wonder what Abraham Lincoln would think of our present civil rights policy, let Lincoln and Johnson stage a debate enacted by two students! The impossibilities of time and space are eliminated, and the civics lesson will be well remembered.

The Use of Hip Language—A description of the use of hip language (combined with role playing) in teaching disadvantaged children in the Madison Area Project in Syracuse was given in the *Syracuse Herald-Journal* of November 11, 1963.[22]

A teacher had complained to Gerald Weinstein, curriculum coordinator of the Madison Area Project, that her students "practically fell asleep" while she was reading poems from a standard anthology. He responded by distributing to the class copies of "Motto," a poem by the Negro author Langston Hughes:

> I play it cool and dig all jive.
> That's the reason I stay alive.
> My motto, as I live and learn,
> Is: Dig and be Dug in Return.

After the students had read the poem, there was a long silence, followed by exclamations, such as, "Hey this is tough"; "Hey, Mr. Weinstein, this cat is pretty cool"; "It's written in our talk." However, when asked the meaning of "playing it cool," the students had difficulty in verbalizing the idea, but a boy volunteered to act it out, with Mr. Weinstein taking the part of the teacher.

During the discussion of the phrase "dig all jive," Weinstein was able to impress upon the class that, in addition to understanding their own jive, their chances of "staying alive" would be infinitely increased if they also understood the school jive.

The enthusiasm of the students for "Motto" led them into more of Hughes' poetry. Later they moved into other kinds of literature, written in more conventional language. But the students were not the only ones to learn from that exciting class. Weinstein learned too: he learned the advantage of being familiar with the language of the children you are teaching and establishing a rapport with them. If a teacher doesn't "start where the child is," Weinstein says, he only reinforces the failures and frustration that have become the normal pattern for disadvantaged students.

Exposure to the best cultural works produces no magical results, and the phony literature that often characterizes school readers, especially in the lower grades, is even less effective. Exposure must begin "where the child is" and proceed to other varieties of art forms. The method applies to all kinds of students, Weinstein says; for the student who has read Shakespeare but has not read Langston Hughes, for example, is also disadvantaged.

It should be clear that we are *not* suggesting that teachers employ hip language in normal conversation with underprivileged youngsters. It is not intended as a device for attempting to be friendly with the child through imitating his culture; this would indeed be patronizing and dangerous. Rather the use of hip materials in a formal lesson plan can become an excellent avenue to the style and interests of the disadvantaged and contribute to the development of their verbalization.

Recently in tutoring a disadvantaged high school student in English, I employed a hiptionary in a completely systematic and formal fashion. The first and rather immediate result was that the student learned a great many new English word definitions for the hip words with which she had been familiar:

Hip Word [23]	Definition
"bug"	to disturb, bother, annoy
"cop out"	to avoid conflict by running away, not considered admirable or honorably accepted
"cool it"	to be quiet, peaceful, tranquil
"far out"	not comprehendible
"weak"	inadequate, inappropriate

Words such as "tranquil," "inappropriate," etc., were unknown to this youngster, but through use of the hip word game, she quickly became familiar with them and derived great pleasure from a new-found use of various "big" words. I then used the hiptionary to clarify the meaning and significance of the metaphor (e.g., the hip phrases for bisexual are "AC-DC," "switch hitter," and "swings from both sides of the fence"). Similarly, many other linguistic concepts can be introduced by utilizing hip language in this word game.

In addition to teaching technology, there is great need for curriculum materials that appear to promise success with disadvantaged youngsters. Both the Bank Street College of Education, through its proposed Educational

Resources Center, and Mobilization for Youth have been developing such curriculum laboratories, which should be closely related to the teacher institutes and should contain not only materials but also reports (and films) [24] of positive experiments in the teaching of the disadvantaged, functional illiterates, etc.[25]

5. EFFECTIVE TEACHER STYLES

There is some tendency to develop a hypothetical model of the ideal teacher. We tend to assume that effective teachers must be healthy and well adjusted. I seriously question this idea. I am not suggesting, of course, that we look for sick people and make them teachers; what I am suggesting is that we think about the development of individual teacher styles, and some of these may have significant nonhealthy components. There appear to be many styles that function well with low-income youngsters; teachers succeed in different ways. In visits to schools in low-income areas in over thirty-five cities, I have always found at least one teacher in a school who, it was agreed by everyone (children, parents, colleagues, and administrators), was an effective teacher, but the personality of each of these teachers, the manner of approach, and point of view were vastly different.[26]

For example, there is the fussy, compulsive type, whom I find it difficult to query, who teaches things over and over, is very concerned that I understand him, and treats me like a child. But, actually, in the classroom the behavior that annoys me can be quite effective. This kind of person might well be called a "sublimated compulsive"; he directs his compulsivity into the functional order and structure which disadvantaged children like.

Another type of teacher is the "boomer." He shouts out in a loud, strong voice: "You're going to learn. I'm here to teach you, and there is no nonsense in this classroom." He lays the ground rules early, and the kids know immediately that there is a point beyond which they cannot go. They may not like him, but they learn. Some psychologists and educators might call this person hostile; yet he has learned to use this quality effectively in the classroom.

Another kind of teacher might be called the maverick. Everybody loves him but the boss. He upsets everything because he's always raising difficult questions and presenting ideas that disturb. This teacher is convinced that ideas are meant to stir people up, and consequently he develops a close link with his young and eager students. He is as surprised and curious as they at each turn of mind, each new discovery, and it is this fresh quality that comes through to them.

Then there is the coach. He is informal, earthy, and may be an athlete, but in any case, he is physically expressive in conducting his dialogue with the world. Many low-income youngsters like this. Coming from homes characterized by activity and motion, they connect with this quality quickly and naturally.

In sharp contrast is the quiet one. This teacher accomplishes much the same goal by sincerity, calmness, and definitiveness. His essential dignity pervades the situation and commands both respect and attention.

We also have the entertainer, colorful, melodramatic, and most importantly, not afraid to have fun with the children. He may make mistakes through his sheer flair for the comic, but he is free enough to laugh with the children at his own blunders. His inventiveness may furrow his supervisor's brow, as when he has children make western hats from a paper-reading assignment about cowboys. But they learn more about cowboys than if a traditional method had been applied. This teacher actively involves the children—their opinions count, and they know it.

A striking example of another teacher style is the secular. This fellow is relaxed and informal with the kids, may have lunch with them, or use their bathroom. You would be amazed at how many children do not *really* believe that teachers eat and sleep and go to the bathroom like other people! This fellow is comfortable talking turkey with the kids.

There are many other styles, but I will cite just one more—the secular intellectual. He is not academic, but he is interested in knowledge and its transmission to youngsters. He is really interested in the substance and not just the academic correctness of the material. He doesn't like classical music because he is supposed to but because he likes all types of music; and it so happens that he also likes blues, jazz, and popular music. He really has *broader* horizons. One such person I met was especially interested in hip language, which he was learning from the youngsters—a normally unwise action against which I would warn most people. However, this teacher, because of his deep interest in all language, could show a genuine interest in hip language without being false or condescending.

Teacher preparation should include learning about these types of teachers, with films and observation of them in action, but above all, with an opportunity for student teachers to play each type. Each student should develop his repertoire by trying out the roles in permissive, unthreatening situations in his own group; he should play the classroom and the different problems that arise. Out of this role play, he develops his own repertoire. No matter what is talked about in general, he must formulate these things in his own individual way for his own specific personality. He needs more than practice teaching for this, since the actual classroom cannot allow full experimentation. He needs a practice situation—experimental and permissive—in which he can actually try out various techniques and approaches, experiment with different styles, see which ones fit, blend them to his personality, and develop his own strengths.

ORGANIZATION OF THE TEACHER INSTITUTES

Without detailing the methods whereby teachers would receive the training proposed in the five-point plan, a number of general principles can be outlined:

Where possible, teachers themselves (master teachers, consulting teachers) should do the teaching or group leading. It may be necessary first to hold master institutes where teachers who would later train other teachers would be exposed to the five-point program. At a later point, these master teachers would be supervised as they translated the program for their local schools. The master institute could call on all kinds of specialists, including sociologists, psychologists, Montessori specialists, role-playing leaders, etc. The institutes could be introduced as special courses in preservice training (in regular sessions or summer sessions) as well as for in-service programs.

Training that is provided close to the operations in which it will be utilized will be most effective.[27] Teachers, for example, should be worked with around their specific school and classroom problems and the trainers should visit the classrooms, observe the teachers closely, and discuss problems and suggestions with them in considerable detail. The ideas embodied in the five-point plan would thus be selectively applied in relation to on-the-job problems experienced by the teacher trainees. An interesting variant of this approach is to be found in the Bank Street College proposal for an Educational Resources Center which will be devoted to "development, collection and dissemination of new instructional materials, new teaching methods, and curriculum innovations specifically designed to raise the achievement of the educationally handicapped minority group child."

Teachers and their pupils selected for demonstration will actually move into the Center for a designated period—say three weeks—where they will receive special instruction from master teachers and other specialists. When the class returns to its home school following the instruction period at the Center, the teacher will continue to use methods and skills acquired at the ERC and will also consult frequently with specialists from the Center who will visit the school. Eventually it is hoped that each school will boast a number of teachers who, with their classes, have had instructional periods at the Center.[28]

A group or team approach should be a central feature in the training, with a strong emphasis on building esprit de corps in the groups. The group experience would be examined and utilized for the development of concepts, understanding of group process, etc. (T (training)-group approach).

Full participation of the trainees should be intensively solicited with regard to encouraging them to formulate their needs, the way they see their problems, and their suggestions for meeting these problems. Hence, small teacher meetings should be organized to discuss (and role play) ways of meeting classroom difficulties, teaching techniques, and approaches. In this context, the trainers would offer for discussion techniques that have evolved elsewhere.

In order to have the training become a part of the neuromuscular make-up of the trainees, a variety of techniques should be instituted: supervisory conferences, role-playing films, demonstrations, quizzes, intensive brief reading, small group discussions, lectures, debates, and the writing of a paper. This methodology is based on two principles: (a) People learn through a variety of styles—some learn best from doing (e.g., role playing), others from lectures, still others from films, etc. (b) In order to internalize material taught over a relatively short period of time, it is necessary to provide as much active practice and involvement as possible, along with corrective feedback from the supervisory staff; hence the emphasis on role playing and supervisor's sessions. In addition, having the learner teach the material to other trainees appears to be an excellent device for the development of deep learning.

There is constant criticism today of education in the United States—the school system, the curriculum, the teachers, and the administration. There are constant attacks by authors such as Paul Goodman, Edgar Friedenberg, and others upon the conformity of the system and the lack of any real learning. There is also constant, powerful criticism of the middle class in our country by authors like Erich Fromm and Paul Goodman, who see the middle class as conformists who have lost their spontaneity and inner convictions. Yet, although this criticism is very widespread, it is rarely applied to the teaching of disadvantaged children, who, apparently, are to adapt to the oft-criticized school and be made into middle-class people by its culture. When we talk about disadvantaged children, we seem suddenly to acquire an idealized picture of the school and the middle-class life for which these children are to be prepared, even though many of us might agree with the David Riesmans, Paul Goodmans, and Erich Fromms that a great deal must be done to change both the middle class and the school. Disadvantaged children have much to contribute to this needed change; their culture, their style, and their positives can aid greatly in the remaking of our middle-class society.[29]

NOTES

1. Prepared for presentation to the Syracuse University Conference on Urban Education and Cultural Deprivation, July 15–16, 1964.
2. It is striking that significant teacher improvement in morale and performance appears to have taken place in the Banneker District in St. Louis where Assistant Superintendent Samuel Shepard has introduced marked administrative modifications vis-à-vis the teaching staff.
3. Miller, Warren. *The Cool World.* Boston, Mass.: Little, 1959.
4. Sillitoe, Alan. *Saturday Night and Sunday Morning.* New York: Knopf, 1959.
5. See *Negro Heritage,* published monthly in Chicago.
6. Horne, Elliot. *The Hiptionary: A Hipster's View of the World Scene.* New York: Simon & Schuster, 1963.
7. Riessman, Frank. *The Culturally Deprived Child.* New York: Harper, 1962. pp. 118–19.
8. Goldberg, Miriam. "Adapting Teacher Style to Pupil Differences." A paper delivered at Teachers College Conference on Disadvantaged Children, July 1963. p. 9.
9. For a fuller discussion of these stages, see Riessman, *op. cit.,* pp. 94–95.
10. Ashton-Warner, Sylvia. *The Teacher.* New York: Simon & Schuster, 1963.
11. See Mayer, Martin. "Schools, Slums, and Montessori." *Commentary* 37: 33–39; June 1964.
12. Riessman, *op. cit.,* pp. 84–85.
13. Senesch, Lawrence. "The Organic Curriculum: A New Experiment in Economic Education." Reprint Series No. 22. Lafayette, Indiana: Purdue University, School of Industrial Management.
14. The following discussion of role playing is taken from Riessman, Frank, and Goldfarb, Jean. "Role Playing and the Poor." *Group Psychotherapy,* Vol. 17, No. 1, 1964.

15. Miller, D. R., and others. *Inner Conflict and Defense.* New York: Holt, 1960. p. 24.
16. For a discussion of many of these items see Miller and others, *op. cit.*
17. Becker, Jerome, and others. "Situational Testing of Social Psychological Variables in Personality." *Mental Health of the Poor: New Treatment Approaches for Low-Income People.* (Edited by Frank Riessman and others.) New York: The Free Press, 1964.
18. Miller and others, *op. cit.*, p. 396.
19. Kohn, Melvin L. "Social Class and Parent-Child Relationships: An Interpretation." *American Journal of Sociology* 68: 471–80; January 1963.
20. *Ibid.*
21. Riessman, *op. cit.*, p. 77.
22. Kanasola, Robert. "Students Dig Jive When It's Played Cool." *Syracuse Herald-Journal,* November 11, 1963.
23. The words in this list were taken from a hiptionary entitled "The Other Language" developed by Anthony Romeo at Mobilization for Youth, January 1962.
24. The Lincoln Filene Center of Tufts University and McGraw-Hill Publishing Company are jointly preparing three films related to the teaching of disadvantaged children.
25. An illustration would be the Bank Street experiment conducted in the summer of 1963 where disadvantaged youngsters showed marked academic and emotional improvement as a result of a special one-month program. Shepard's project in the Banneker District of St. Louis is another illustration. Shepard's program is especially noteworthy because he has demonstrated that disadvantaged youngsters at the elementary and junior high school levels can be quickly improved to grade level. Much more comprehensive efforts than Shepard's might very well produce even more startling results. It is time to put an end to the tendency toward educational surrender on all but preschool disadvantaged children.
26. The discussion of teacher types that follows is based on a joint unpublished paper with Arlene Hannah entitled "Teachers of the Poor," 1964.
27. This proposal, called site training, as well as a number of other proposals in this section were developed for the Rutgers University Training Center, a grant for which has been requested from the President's Committee on Juvenile Delinquency.
28. *Bank Street Reporting,* Vol. 1, No. 1, 1964.
29. For an excellent discussion of the Negro contributions to our age, see Killens, John Oliver. "Explanation of the 'Black Psyche.' " *New York Times* Magazine Section; June 7, 1964. p. 37.

TEACHER INFLUENCE, PUPIL ATTITUDES, AND ACHIEVEMENT

Ned A. Flanders

TEACHER INFLUENCE AND TALKING

COMMUNICATION AND TEACHER INFLUENCE

Step inside a classroom and what do you hear? The chances are better than 60 per cent you will hear someone talking if you are in an elementary or secondary school classroom.

Reprinted from Cooperative Research Monograph No. 12, Office of Education, U.S. Department of Health, Education, and Welfare. (Washington, D.C., Government Printing Office) 1965, pages 1–23, 111–121.

If someone is talking, the chances are that it will be the teacher more than 70 per cent of the time. Yes, the teacher talks more than all the students combined. He manages class activities by giving directions. He expresses his ideas by lecturing. He stimulates student participation by asking questions. He clarifies student ideas by applying them to the solution of a problem. He praises and encourages students from time to time. On rare occasions he may clarify or diagnose the feelings and attitudes expressed by students or inferred from their behavior. He may also criticize the behavior of a student or class. All are types of teacher statements that can be heard in a classroom.

Most of the functions associated with teaching are implemented by verbal communication. Of course, nonverbal communication does exist and is not unimportant. The nod of the head to encourage student participation, the finger to the lips to warn against talking, the smile, and the frown, these all communicate to students. But nonverbal communication occurs less frequently than verbal communication and the two are usually highly correlated. The frown is most often associated with statements that express disapproval, the smile with statements of approval.

The first step toward systematic classroom management is made when a teacher understands how to control his verbal communication so that he can use his influence as a social force. Unfortunately, this kind of knowledge and the corresponding skill don't always go together. As one teacher put it, "I know what I'm doing and I am usually aware of most mistakes that I make, but I don't know what to do about it."

The research reported in this monograph concerns the verbal statements of teachers as they occur in the spontaneous interaction of the classroom. We will explain what has been called a system of classroom interaction analysis, our method of recording and analyzing teacher statements. A theory of teacher influence or, more modestly, some hypotheses of teacher influence will be developed and tested. The data were obtained from research carried out in the Minneapolis and St. Paul public schools before March 1957 and after March 1958. Additional data came from research in Wellington, New Zealand, carried out under a Fulbright Research Scholarship during 1957.

Our basic purpose is greater understanding of the teacher's role, the control he provides while teaching, and the patterns of influence he uses in classroom management.

There are at least two theoretical models that are currently being used to understand interaction analysis data collected in a classroom. One model makes use of the logical steps of problem-solving and draws heavily from what we know about inductive and deductive reasoning, scientific method, procedures for defining terms, level of abstraction, and principles from the field of semantics. This approach is being used in the research of B. Othaniel Smith (14) at the University of Illinois.

The second model, the one we use, is based less on the intellectual skills mentioned above and more on a set of social skills used by teachers to control and manage class activities. This model is based on a psychology of superior-subordinate relationships, adapted to fit classroom conditions. An earlier development can be found in the 59th Yearbook, National Society for the Study of Educational Research (9).

The differences between these two models can be illustrated by the teacher's orientation to classroom behavior. Suppose a teacher becomes aware of intellectual confusion in the remarks of a student because the student uses the same word as if it had two quite different meanings. The teacher's knowledge and skill in defining words and his understanding of level of abstraction will help in diagnosing the intellectual aspects of the problem in terms of the first model. Just how he chooses to provide this information—by lecturing, by asking a series of questions so that the student can "discover" the difficulty, or by directing the student in some semantic exercise—is the kind of choice on which the second model is based. Here the teacher is concerned with his own behavior and how he can best use his authority to enhance student learning.

Neither model is "right" or "wrong," and an understanding of both models is likely to improve teaching. Each model is a frame of reference for organizing ideas about behavior; such an organization guides research. Research within either frame of reference is difficult and tedious; to work in both simultaneously would require more resources than were available at Minnesota when the research reported in this monograph was planned and conducted.

To summarize, this monograph is concerned with analyzing the spontaneous verbal communication of the teacher. A system of interaction analysis is used for this purpose. The procedure involves the classification of statements every 3 seconds and the tabulation of data in special matrices for later analysis. Measures of academic achievement and student attitudes are correlated with the verbal patterns observed in the classroom. Most of the conclusions refer to the role of the teacher in classroom management.

EARLY RESEARCH ON CLASSROOM CLIMATE

Most research programs have antecedents in the work of other researchers. The research reported in this monograph is no exception. We are indebted to a number of individuals whose work has contributed to our thinking.

The term "classroom climate" refers to generalized attitudes toward the teacher and the class that the pupils share in common despite individual differences. The development of these attitudes is an outgrowth of classroom social interaction. As a result of participating in classroom activities, pupils soon develop common attitudes about how they like their class, the kind of person the teacher is, and how he will act in certain typical situations. These common attitudes color all aspects of classroom behavior, creating a social atmosphere, or climate, that appears to be fairly stable, once established.

Thus, the word "climate" [1] is merely a shorthand reference to those qualities that consistently predominate in most teacher-pupil contacts and in contacts among the pupils in the presence or absence of the teacher.

The earliest systematic studies of spontaneous pupil and teacher behavior that relate directly to classroom climate are those of H. H. Anderson and his colleagues, Helen and Joseph Brewer and Mary Frances Reed (2, 3, 4, and 5 in the bibliography at the end of this monograph); these studies are based on the observation of "dominative" and "integrative" contacts. It is essential to understand the qualitative differences between an integrative and a dominative social contact, because most of the research on classroom climate makes similar behavioral distinctions.

A preliminary study showed that it was possible to devise reliable measures of behavior of young children. Behavior was recorded as "contacts" divided into two groups of categories. If a child snatched a toy, struck a playmate, or commanded him, or if he attempted to force him in some way, such contacts were included under the term "domination." By such behavior he ignored the rights of the companion; he tended to reduce the free interplay of differences and to lead toward resistance or conformity in responding or adapting to another.

Other contacts were recorded which tended to increase the interplay of differences. Offering a companion a choice or soliciting an expression of his desires were gestures of flexibility and adaptation. These tended in the direction of discovering common purposes among differences. Such contacts were grouped under the term "socially integrative behavior." (5, p. 12)

The findings of Anderson are based on the study of preschool, primary school, and elementary school classrooms involving five different teachers and extending over several years. The imaginative research of Anderson and his colleagues has produced a series of internally consistent and significant findings: First, the dominative and integrative contacts of the teacher set a pattern of behavior that spreads throughout the classroom; the behavior of the teacher, more than of any other individual, sets the climate of the class. The rule is that a climate of domination incites further domination, and one of integration stimulates further integration. It is the teacher's tendency that spreads among pupils and is continued even when the teacher is no longer in the room. Furthermore, the pattern a teacher develops in one year is likely to persist in his classroom the following year with different pupils. Second, when a teacher has a higher proportion of integrative contacts, pupils show more spontaneity and initiative, more voluntary social contributions, and more acts of problem-solving. Third, when a teacher has a higher proportion of dominative contacts, the pupils are more easily distracted from school-

---

[1] Climate is assessed either by analyzing teacher-pupil interaction and inferring underlying attitudes from the interaction, or by the use of a pupil-attitude inventory and predicting the quality of classroom interaction from the results. Its precise meaning, as commonly used, is seldom clear—just as its synonyms, "morale," "rapport," and "emotional tone," are also ambiguous. To have any meaning at all, the word is always qualified by an adjective, and it is in the choice of adjectives that researchers become reformers and too often lose their objectivity.

work, and show greater compliance to, as well as rejection of, teacher domination.

A year or so after Anderson started his work, Lippitt and White (12), working with Kurt Lewin, carried out laboratory experiments to analyze the effects of adult leaders' influence on boys' groups. The laboratory approach used had certain advantages in studying the effects of the adult leader's behavior. First, the contrasting patterns of leader behavior were purified and made more consistent as a result of training and role-playing. Second, differences in the underlying personality and appearance of the adult leaders were minimized through role rotation. Third, the effect of the pattern of leader behavior was intensified, compared with the effect in an ordinary classroom, since there were only 5 boys to a group. Roughly speaking, the pattern Lippitt and White named "authoritarian leadership" consisted of dominative contacts; "democratic leadership" consisted of an integrative pattern; and "laissez-faire" consisted of irregular and infrequent integrative contacts with an element of indifference to the total group that is seldom found in a classroom and was not present in the Anderson *et al.* studies.

Most of the conclusions of the Lippitt and White study and others confirm or extend the general conclusions of Anderson *et al.,* with some semantic modification but very little change, if any, in behavioral meaning. From the point of view of classroom teaching, one interesting extension was the conceptualization of "dependence on the leader" by Lippitt and White. This is a state of affairs in which group members are unable to proceed without directions from the leader. Anderson *et al.* used the category "conforming to teacher domination" and thus noted similar events, but in the more concentrated social climates of the laboratory experiments, it was clearly seen that extensive compliance occurs when there is a generalized condition of dependence.

These two mutually supportive and independent studies aroused considerable interest in the notion of social climate. Additional research revealed minor variations of the central theme already established. Withall (15) showed that a simple classification of the teacher's verbal statements into 7 categories produced an index of teacher behavior almost identical to the integrative-dominative (I/D) ratio of Anderson *et al.* Flanders (8) created laboratory situations in which contrasting patterns of teacher behavior were exposed to one pupil at a time. A sustained dominative pattern was consistently disliked by pupils: it reduced their ability to recall the material studied, and it produced disruptive anxiety, as indicated by galvanic skin response and changes in the heartbeat rates. The reverse trends were noted as pupil reactions to integrative contacts. Perkins (13), using Withall's technique, studied groups of teachers organized to discuss the topic of child growth and development. He found that greater learning about child growth and development occurred when group discussion was free to focus on that topic; groups with an integrative type of leader were able to do this more frequently than were groups led by a dominative type of leader.

In a large cross-sectional study that did not use observations of spontaneous teacher behavior, Cogan (6) administered to 987 eighth-grade students in 33 classrooms a single paper-and-pencil instrument that contained three scales: (*a*) a scale assessing student perceptions of the teacher; (*b*) a scale on which students reported how often they did required schoolwork; and (*c*) a scale on which students reported how often they did extra, nonrequired schoolwork. Cogan's first scale assessed traits which he developed in terms of Murray's list of major personality needs. There were two patterns in this scale. The items of one pattern were grouped as "dominative," "aggressive," and "rejectant." The second pattern was "integrative," "affiliative," and "nurturant"; these correspond to Anderson's dominative and integrative patterns. Cogan found that students reported doing more assigned and extra schoolwork when they perceived the teacher's behavior as falling into the integrative pattern rather than the dominative pattern.

All together, these research projects support the definition given earlier of classroom climate. The two teacher behavior patterns that create the contrasting classroom climates are shown below:

The Integrative Pattern

a. Accepts, clarifies, and supports the ideas and feelings of pupils.
b. Praises and encourages.
c. Asks questions to stimulate pupil participation in decision-making.
d. Asks questions to orient pupils to schoolwork.

The Dominative Pattern

a. Expresses or lectures about own ideas or knowledge.
b. Gives directions or orders.
c. Criticizes or deprecates pupil behavior with intent to change it.
d. Justifies own position or authority.

CONCEPTS FOR UNDERSTANDING CLASSROOM INTERACTION

One contribution of research on classroom climate has been the identification of different kinds of verbal statements that the teacher uses. This information has been used in the development of our system of interaction analysis.

A less consistent contribution of this early research concerns the words used to designate patterns of teacher behavior. In fact, there is quite a choice: Anderson (2)—"dominative" and "integrative"; Lippitt and White—"authoritarian," "democratic," and "laissez-faire" (12); Withall (15), Flanders (8), Perkins (13)—"teacher-centered" and "student-centered"; and Cogan (6)—"preclusive" and "inclusive." All these come from a short stroll in the conceptual garden of psychology; an overnight hike could extend the list indefinitely. Faced with such a choice, we might first pause to discuss the concepts used in this type of research.

Concepts used to describe teacher influence refer to a series of acts occurring during some time period. When a particular series occurs again and again, it becomes familiar to an observer and he can identify it. We call such a series a "pattern" of influence.

It is interesting to distinguish between an influence pattern and the concept of "role," as it is commonly used in the literature of social psychology. The difference is in the degree of behavioral specificity that is implied. For example, it may be said that a teacher plays in the classroom a "democratic" or "authoritarian" role. These concepts not only connote value judgments, but they are so abstract that they fail to denote very much about the behavior of the teacher. If someone tries to create either role, his choice of influence patterns depends primarily on his personal and often unique understanding of the concept. Such a choice involves too many alternatives; specificity is lacking.

The only path through these difficulties is to increase understanding by insisting that the concepts used have explicit behavioral meaning. In the rest of this section, certain concepts that refer to the teacher's behavior, the student's reactions, and the nature of the learning goals will be presented. In each instance, a description of behavior in a social setting will be given first. Next, concepts will be used to abstract the behavior events, and in the process, a theoretical definition of the concept will become clear. Finally, the procedures used in this study to measure or quantify the concept will be briefly stated.

The reader may wish to evaluate the development of these concepts by applying the following criteria. First, what are the concepts that are given theoretical meaning by analysis of the behavior that commonly occurs in a classroom? Second, are the procedures used for quantifying behavior that is associated with a concept (a) practical: that is, can they be used in a classroom; (b) representative: that is, do they adequately sample all behavior that could logically be associated with the concept; and (c) reliable: that is, can the error factor be determined and is it low, compared with the differences studied? Third, can the concepts be organized into hypotheses or principles (cause and effect statements) to predict behavior or the consequences of behavior?

Concepts for Describing Teacher Influence. Teacher influence exists as a series of acts along a time line. It is most often expressed as verbal communication. In this study we assume that verbal communication constitutes an adequate sample of the teacher's total influence pattern. A single act of a teacher occupies a segment of time. Before this act a particular state of affairs exists; after the act is completed, a different state of affairs exists. Some acts are more potent than others and have greater consequences. Furthermore, a long series of similar acts may have more extensive effects than just an isolated few.

A researcher is free to choose concepts that will be used to describe the state of affairs before and after an act, and concepts that will be used to describe the act itself.

Suppose a teacher says, "Please close the door," to a student. The chances are that the student will close the door. Before this act of influence, the student was engaged in some activity, such as thinking or reading. But since he was expected to comply with the teacher's command, he interrupted his train of thought to get up and close the door.

Actually, this sequence of behavior is as complex as we wish to make it. We could theorize about the social expectations that exist when a teacher makes what adults call a reasonable demand of a student. Much could be said, if we had the facts, about how past contacts with other authority figures have helped to form this particular student's reactions to a command. It might be that the student resented this intrusion and chose to push the door so that it slammed, rather than gently closing it. A lesser degree of resentment could be expressed by an audible sigh followed by slow movements.

Because of all the concepts that could be used to describe behavior, there is a choice here along a continuum. The genotypic concepts that describe inner motives or feelings are at one end, and the phenotypic concepts that describe more superficial aspects of behavior are at the other end. The choice should fit the purpose. A psychiatrist would prefer certain concepts for his purposes that would probably be too genotypic for the majority of interpretations that a teacher needs to make.

Our choice in this instance leads to the following explanation. The teacher exerted *direct influence,* which restricted the *freedom of action* of the student, making him momentarily more *dependent* on the teacher. From this illustration we hope the reader will understand that an act of direct influence restricts freedom of action, usually by focusing on a problem and, in this case, it made the student more dependent on teacher influence for a short period of time.

By the way, you the reader may have felt uneasy when you thought of a teacher's restricting the freedom of action of a student. These are terms that often elicit value judgments. However, it seems sensible to assert that a student's freedom of action is restricted when he is told to shut the door. Nevertheless, it is difficult to make an objective description of such events.

Now, suppose the same door is closed, but with a completely different script. The teacher asks, "Does anyone feel a draft in here?" Johnny says, "Yes, it's cold. I think it's coming from this open door." The teacher says, "Well, since it seems cold, please close the door." So Johnny gets up and closes the door.

The second example includes the same command and ultimately leads to the same compliance, yet most of us would agree that the state of affairs would be different at the termination of the episode. Consider, too, differences after a series of such episodes extending over hours, days, weeks, or the school year.

Again we face a choice in conceptualizing the behavior. Our choice is as follows: The command, "Close the door," was modified first by a question, "Does anyone feel a draft in here?"; second, by a student response, "Yes, it's cold. I think it's coming from this open door," the latter phrase being a student-initiated idea; and third, by the teacher's acknowledging the student's idea, "Well, since it seems cold. . . ." Taken all together, the teacher's acts of influence are more indirect than direct. While the student's freedom of action was restricted, his perception of this restriction was probably modified in the second example because he was solving a problem that he had helped to identify, rather than merely complying with the command of an authority figure. In fact, the teacher's behavior encouraged the student's initiative and, in this sense, his freedom of action was expanded. Later on, after more examples are given, we hope it will become clear that an act of indirect influence expands freedom of action and usually makes a student less dependent on the teacher. He often has greater orientation to a problem, because he helped to identify it.

Most teachers who hear these ideas expressed immediately conclude that indirect influence is superior to direct influence. We believe that the basis of this value judgment lies less in the ideas just expressed than in the social pressures that affect teachers' self-concepts. Most teachers apparently want to believe that they are "indirect teachers," even before they hear how these concepts are defined or are told about any research findings. If being an indirect teacher means consistently using indirect influence, we can state categorically that no such teacher exists, because no teacher employs a pure pattern of influence. All teachers establish some kind of balance based on a combination of direct and indirect influence.

At this point, further objection often arises. It seems obvious that any "intelligent teacher" would prefer to have his students "problem-oriented," as illustrated in the second episode, rather than "authority-oriented," as illustrated in the first episode. (The quotation marks are used here to empha-size how quickly abstract value judgments enter the discussion.) Our experi-ence would suggest that, in the long run, most teachers want the students in their classes to react to the demands of problem-solving rather than to their own authority. Yet does it necessarily follow that indirect influence is superior to direct influence? Is the student in the first illustration any less "problem-oriented" than the student in the second?

Our system of interaction analysis provides an explicit procedure for quantifying direct and indirect influence that is closely related to the teacher behaviors identified by research on classroom climate. Direct influence con-sists of those verbal statements of the teacher that restrict freedom of action, by focusing attention on a problem, interjecting teacher authority, or both. These statements include lecturing, giving directions, criticizing, and justifying his own use of authority. Indirect influence consists of those verbal statements of the teacher that expand a student's freedom of action by encouraging his verbal participation and initiative. These include asking questions, accepting and clarifying the ideas or feelings of students, and praising or encouraging students' responses.

Concepts for Describing Student Dependence. One way to start describing student reactions to teacher influence is to postulate that dependence is always present in some degree in any teacher-pupil relationship. The maturity and power advantages of a teacher, reinforced by social expectations, are such that the student anticipates teacher direction and supervision. The student is more often ready to comply with teacher influence than not, and when he does not comply, his anxiety increases because the teacher can control an effective system of rewards and punishments.

One way to describe the process of instruction is to say that the teacher strives to change the response pattern of a student from mere compliance to independent action, determined by the student's own analysis of the problems confronting him. A student who recognizes no learning problem is much more dependent on the teacher in deciding what is or is not acceptable behavior, and will solicit direction. On the other hand, a student hard at work on a problem responds to the requirements for its solution; these requirements form a set of criteria with which to evaluate his own behavior as well as that of the teacher.

The first complication of this over-simplification is that students differ in their ability to give up dependence on the teacher by shifting orientation to the problem-solving requirements. Some students can hardly separate the problem-solving requirements from teacher approval, and continually seek teacher support at nearly all stages of their activities. We call such students *dependent-prone*. Even the most skillful teachers find it difficult to stimulate self-directed problem-solving among highly dependent-prone students. Dependence-proneness is a personality trait that is established early in childhood, and the extent to which it can be modified by school experiences is unknown.

We must distinguish here between *compliance* and *dependence*. When a teacher directs, demands, or forces, compliance is not voluntary. But when a student imagines or expects that the teacher wants a job done in a particular fashion and voluntarily does what he imagines the teacher wants, his reaction is an act of dependence.

By way of illustration, let us apply the concepts of dependence-proneness, compliance, and dependent behavior to the episode of the boy closing the door. Most students, whether they are dependent-prone or not, will comply when told or asked to do something by the teacher. Most students, for example, will get up and close the door. This is an act of compliance. Suppose, however, that we could turn this episode into a little experiment in which closing the door gradually becomes more and more of an imposition. Suppose that we could move the door farther and farther away, put flights of stairs in the way as physical barriers, and, in general, make the task increasingly cumbersome and difficult. Even when the task became most difficult, a highly dependent-prone student would probably get up and close the door, but a student with low dependency-proneness might be stimulated to think of an alternative, such as "Let's close the window. That will stop the circulation of cold air." The dependent-prone student has a lower threshold or resistance to compliance than the independent-prone.

Illustrating acts of dependence within the context of this episode becomes a bit absurd, since the episode involves only a simple act of common courtesy. But suppose that the student, with no sign from the teacher, simply volunteers to close the door, and that we can prove he wasn't doing it for his own comfort. Such an action is not compliance, but an act of dependence. A more typical dependent act in the classroom consists of soliciting approval and permission. For example, a student does an arithmetic problem and then asks the teacher: "Is this the way you wanted it done?"

Over a long period of time, continuous compliance will increase the incidence of dependent behavior. Students begin to anticipate teacher demands and respond dependently. Being ordered to act in a certain way and being subjected to standards of behavior imposed by an authority figure will, in the long run, set these expectations. The more dependent-prone respond with compliance and acts of dependence. The more independent-prone will comply when forced, and, depending on other factors, may engage in subtle and not so subtle acts of aggressive counter-dependence, or rebelliousness.

Compliance, then, consists of doing what one is told to do by an authority figure. This type of behavior is best quantified by the analysis of spontaneous behavior, for example, by analyzing a tape recording or developing a system of observation.

Dependent behavior consists of voluntarily bowing to expected teacher influence or to imagined restraints associated with the teacher's authority. The problems of measurement are difficult, since acts of dependence must be separated from acts of compliance on the basis of difference in intent.

We might note here that conformity to group standards, real or imagined, often has a self-initiated and thus voluntary aspect to it. In this sense, acts of conformity and acts of dependence both differ from compliance because of the absence of a teacher directive and the presence of the pupil's intent to please. The imagined directive or group force-field that creates conformity and dependence can be just as potent and seem just as real for the pupil as those creating compliance.

Dependence-proneness is a personality trait representing the tendency of a student to engage in dependent acts. Dependence-proneness is a concept necessary to explain why some children respond dependently, and others do not, when exposed to identical social stimuli. Dependent behavior may be caused by a number of psychological forces, one of which is dependence-proneness.

In past laboratory experiments dependent behavior has been successfully measured by observing teacher-pupil contacts and noting, in particular, requests for help and solicitations of approval. Filson (7) used a paper-and-pencil questionnaire on which students indicated their need for approval and help, or their lack of it, during a teacher-directed learning task. We have been particularly unsuccessful in developing procedures for measuring dependent behavior in the classroom under field conditions.

In this study, dependence-proneness is measured by an attitude inventory consisting of 45 items. The reliability and validity of this scale have been cited by Flanders, Amidon, and Anderson (10) for seventh-grade and eighth-grade boys and girls.

Concepts for Describing Learning Goals. Learning goals are usually described in terms of curriculum organization and content. In all classroom activities the learning of certain skills, understandings, or facts is central to a plan for which the teacher has ultimate responsibility.

However, certain dimensions of learning goals, particularly the goal perceptions of the students and the teacher, can be conceptualized and measured without specifying the curriculum content involved. For example, the following dimensions of students' goal perceptions seem independent of content. First, there is a dimension of motivation; how attractive and interesting are these goals? Second, there is a dimension of realism; are the resources of time, ability, and energy adequate to reach a goal? Third, there is a dimension of clarity; how well do students understand the steps necessary to reach a goal and how clearly is the end product visualized?

The last-named dimension, goal clarity, received special emphasis in this monograph because variation of this variable is crucial to our hypotheses about teacher influence. In the analysis of results, we will distinguish between situations in which goals are presumed to be clear and those in which goals are presumed to be less clear.

The first two dimensions, motivation and realism, are ignored in our studies, even though they are important, because the consequences of their variation are more self-evident. Lewin (11) and many others have discussed goals with high positive valence which create strong motivation and result in greater progress in learning. The consequences of sufficient or insufficient time, ability, and energy are self-evident. The assumption that motivation and realism are approximately equal among the groups being compared later in this monograph seems to us quite reasonable. Certainly the students all had an equal opportunity for work, they often had more than enough energy, and individual differences were distributed within each class in a manner that did not seriously affect our results.

We assume that the dimension of goal clarity can be described by conceiving of a continuum that extends from *clear goals* at one end to *ambiguous goals* at the opposite end. We define having *clear goals* as a condition in which a student knows what steps are necessary to reach the goal and has a clear picture of the end product. Having *ambiguous goals* is defined as a condition in which a student is not sure of the steps necessary to reach the goal and has an uncertain picture of the end product. The perceptions of the students, not the teacher, are essential to any measure of the clarity or ambiguity of goals.

As goals become clear, a student at work on a problem can use his understanding of the problem-solving requirements to guide his own behavior or to evaluate teacher influence. In either case, he is less dependent on teacher influence. It seems reasonable to suppose that a student will benefit most from problem-solving experiences when he works at the lowest level of dependence on the teacher that both he and the teacher can tolerate that permits necessary coordination and maintenance of classroom learning activities. A certain amount of dependence is desirable and will always be present in the classroom, but the teacher can and should control the general level of dependence by appropriate use of teacher influence.

The level of dependence at some moment in the classroom is a function of the student's dependence-proneness, the restraints set by the teacher's pattern of influence, and the student's perception of the learning goal. In a specific situation, we assume the dependence-proneness of the student is "given," that is, fixed by the personality trait. The restraints set by the teacher are a function of his use of direct and indirect influence and the perception of this influence held by the student from past experience. When goals are ambiguous, the student is more likely to respond to teacher influence in a dependent fashion. When goals are clear he can evaluate teacher influence by analyzing the intent of the teacher in terms of the problem-solving requirements.

It takes time to establish a learning goal, to identify the steps of problem-solving, and to begin work activities. During this period of time, clear goals gradually emerge from ambiguous goals. Because the student expects to comply with the teacher's authority, an expectation founded on past experience with authority figures, he responds initially in a dependent manner or at least with compliance. The natural tendency of a teacher, when faced with a situation in which goals are ambiguous, is to establish clarity by using a pattern of influence that is primarily direct. Direct influence, under these circumstances, leads to higher levels of dependence that can interfere with self-directed problem-solving. In effect the student must take into consideration both the demands of the teacher and the demands of the problem. A dependent-prone student remains oriented to the demands of the teacher, even when goals become clear. Dependence, once established under these conditions, is difficult to reduce.

The case of closing the door can again serve as an illustration. When the teacher said, "Please close the door," the student's orientation to action was in terms of compliance. In one sense, problem-solving was not possible for him unless he chose to make an issue out of complying. Repeated over and over again, such compliance increases dependence. In the second example of closing the door, the action taken was a solution to the problem of eliminating a cold draft. The teacher's indirect approach permitted the student to participate in the identification of the problem; when such an approach is used, students are more likely to suggest an alternative solution, such as closing a window. Dependence-proneness is thus held constant rather than being intensified. The point here is that the teacher's choice of direct or indirect influence while goals are still ambiguous is crucial to the control of dependence.

When the activity under consideration is an important part of the curriculum and not a routine closing of a door, the consequences of alternative teacher influence patterns are much more significant. Our observation of teachers in many classrooms gives us the conviction that teachers are more likely to exert direct influence while goals are ambiguous or when progress is halted and diagnosis needed. Add to this the tendency of students to comply and to become dependent, and a good deal of the dependent behavior that occurs in the classroom is explained.

Amidon (1) has successfully measured the goal perceptions of students during laboratory experiments involving eighth-grade students learning geometry. He manipulated the initial conditions by presenting information on tape recordings: one to create goal ambiguity and the other, goal clarity. At different points during the learning activities, a paper-and-pencil scale was used to assess the students' perceptions of next steps and end products.

In the field studies to be reported in this monograph, conditions of greater goal ambiguity are presumed to exist during the initial two days of the 2-week units of study and during those periods in which the teacher introduces new material. During the middle and terminal phases of the 2-week unit of study, excluding the introduction of new material, greater goal clarity is presumed to exist.

Concepts for Describing Teacher Flexibility and Homogeneous Classroom Activities. Anyone who has observed many hours in a classroom soon notices that classroom interaction occurs in a sequence of activity periods. First, there may be a routine 3 to 5 minutes for settling down to work. Next, perhaps, homework is corrected and handed in. Next, a student or group may give a report. This may be followed by a 15-minute discussion, and so on. We have found it advantageous to tabulate interaction analysis data separately for these periods.

The main reason for separating data from different activities is that we can then discover whether a teacher shifts his balance of direct and indirect influence in various activity periods. Is a teacher more indirect when new material is being introduced? Is he more indirect when helping diagnose difficulties? Is he more direct when supervising seatwork? What about evaluating homework or test results?

Identifying activity periods is almost a second system of categorization that is superimposed on the system for classifying verbal statements. In junior-high academic classrooms, we use 5 activity categories: introducing new material; evaluating homework, tests, or learning products; other class discussion; supervising seatwork or group activities; and routine clean-up, passing of materials, or settling down to work. In general, a change from one activity to another is indicated by the statements made, a change of class formation, or a change in the communication pattern.

Tabulating data separately for homogeneous activities permits us to define teacher flexibility and measure it. Teacher flexibility is a measure of the change a teacher makes in his verbal influence from one activity period to another. We measure this by noting the ratio of indirect influence (I) to direct influence (D) in one activity period and comparing it with the corresponding ratio in other activity periods. If we wish to avoid a measure which is a ratio of a ratio, that is, an I/D ratio as a per cent divided by a per cent, we can compare changes in the per cent of indirect influence across different activities, and then make the same comparison for direct influence. Unfortunately, this does not eliminate the statistical problems. Distributions of I/D ratios, comparative per cents of indirect statements, and raw tallies all form a "J"-shaped curve.

HYPOTHESES OF TEACHER INFLUENCE FOR THIS STUDY

In the preceding section, a series of concepts necessary to understand teacher influence were described and defined. Included among these concepts were direct and indirect teacher influence, freedom of action of the student, dependent and independent behavior, the personality trait of dependence-proneness, clear and ambiguous goals, and teacher flexibility. These concepts are tools for thinking about teacher behavior.

In the long run, the purpose of testing hypotheses about teacher influence is to establish principles of teacher behavior that can guide a teacher who wishes to control his own behavior as part of his plan for classroom management. Each principle, if it is to be useful, must be a cause-and-effect statement. Accordingly, this report will express principles in statements that adhere to the following general pattern: if such and such is true, then action "X" will produce result "Y."

This study is concerned with the following hypotheses, which will be stated in terms of the concepts described in the preceding section:

Hypothesis One: Indirect teacher influence increases learning when a student's perception of the goal is confused and ambiguous.

Hypothesis Two: Direct teacher influence increases learning when a student's perception of the goal is clear and acceptable.

Hypothesis Three: Direct teacher influence decreases learning when a student's perception of the goal is ambiguous.

In these three hypotheses, the concept *learning* refers to the development of skills and understandings that can be measured by pre- and post-tests of achievement. In this project, tests were administered before and after a 2-week unit of study, so that an operational definition of learning consists of final achievement, adjusted for initial ability.

By way of brief review, the dynamic explanation of these hypotheses rests on the following reasoning: First, indirect influence increases learning when goals are ambiguous because less disabling dependence develops. During the initial stages of learning, goals are ambiguous. Indirect influence increases student freedom of action, allowing the student the opportunity to question goals and the procedures for reaching them. The net effect of this participation in clarifying goals is less compliance to authority per se and more attention to problem-solving requirements, or at least a more balanced orientation for those students who have high dependence-proneness.

Second, direct influence increases learning when goals are clear because the criteria for accepting or rejecting teacher influence as well as various alternative actions can be recognized in terms of the problem-solving requirements. The student is presumably oriented toward the problem; direct teacher influence is likely to be oriented toward the problem and be helpful; and the net effect is more efficient action toward problem solution. Dependence on the teacher remains steady or is decreased as a result of successful progress toward the goal.

Third, direct influence decreases learning when goals are ambiguous because it increases dependence sharply. The primary response of the student is compliance with teacher authority when goals are unclear. This, in turn, develops dependence. Unless the student understands the goal that the teacher has in mind, he has no other acceptable alternative, given our present cultural expectations. The high dependence that quickly develops means that the student is oriented more toward pleasing the teacher than toward meeting the problem-solving requirements.

These hypotheses are generalized predictions across a range of individual differences. The interaction between a teacher and a particular student in a specific situation is modified by unique personality characteristics and situational factors.

RESEARCH TOOLS FOR ANALYZING CLASSROOM INTERACTION

The studies of classroom interaction reported in this monograph made use of the following research tools: first, an observation procedure called classroom interaction analysis; second, several student-attitude inventories assessing student perceptions of the teacher and the schoolwork; third, a dependence-proneness test used for scaling this attribute among students; and fourth, achievement tests used to measure learning achievement. Each of these will be described in turn.

CLASSROOM INTERACTION ANALYSIS

The spontaneous behavior of a teacher is so complex and variable that an accurate description of it is most difficult to obtain. Even trained observers struggle with the same biases that distort the testimony of witnesses at the scene of an accident. Too often an observer's preconceptions of what he thinks should happen allow him to perceive certain behaviors but prevent him from perceiving others. Interaction analysis is an observation procedure designed to minimize these difficulties, to permit a systematic record of spontaneous acts, and to scrutinize the process of instruction by taking into account each small bit of interaction.

Classroom interaction analysis is particularly concerned with the influence pattern of the teacher. This might be considered a bias, but it is a bias of purpose and interest. Our purpose is to record a series of acts in terms of predetermined concepts. The concepts in this case refer to the teacher's control of the students' freedom of action. Our interest is to distinguish those acts of the teacher that increase students' freedom of action from those acts that decrease students' freedom of action, and to keep a record of both. The system of categories is used by the observer to separate those acts which result in compliance from those acts which invite more creative and voluntary participation; at the same time, it prevents him from being diverted by the subject matter which is irrelevant to this study.

Interaction analysis is concerned primarily with verbal behavior because it can be observed with higher reliability than most nonverbal behavior. The assumption is made that the verbal behavior of the teacher is an adequate sample of his total behavior; that is, his verbal statements are consistent with his nonverbal gestures, in fact, his total behavior. This assumption seems reasonable in terms of our experience.

The Procedure. The observer sits in the classroom in the best position to hear and see the participants. At the end of each 3-second period, he decides which of a prescribed set of numbered categories best represents the communication events just completed. He writes this category number down while simultaneously assessing communication in the next period. He continues at a rate of about 20 to 25 observations per minute, keeping his tempo as steady as possible. His notes are merely a sequence of numbers written in a column, top to bottom, so that the original sequence of events is preserved. Occasionally, marginal notes are used to explain the class formation or any unusual circumstances. When there is a major change in class formation, the communication pattern, or the subject under discussion, the observer draws a double line and indicates the time. As soon as he has completed the total observation, he retires to a nearby room and writes up a general description of each separate activity period. This includes the nature of the activities, the class formation, and the position of the teacher. The observer also notes any additional facts that seem pertinent to an adequate interpretation and recall of the total observation period.

The Categories. There are 10 categories in the system. Seven are assigned to teacher talk and two to student talk. The 10th category covers pauses, short periods of silence, and talk that is confusing or noisy. The category system is outlined in Table 1.

Of the seven categories assigned to teacher talk, categories 1 through 4 represent indirect influence, and categories 5, 6, and 7, direct influence.

Indirect influence encourages participation by the student and increases his freedom of action. To ask a question (category 4) is an invitation to participate and express ideas, opinions, or facts. It is true that a question can be so phrased as to leave very little freedom of action, but at least the student can refuse to answer, a reaction which reflects more freedom than does passive listening. The more general a teacher's question, the greater the opportunity for the student to assert his own ideas.

When the teacher accepts, clarifies, or uses constructively the ideas and opinions of students (category 3), they are encouraged to participate further.

TABLE 1. CATEGORIES FOR INTERACTION ANALYSIS, 1959

Teacher Talk	*Indirect Influence*	1.* ACCEPTS FEELING: accepts and clarifies the tone of feeling of the students in an unthreatening manner. Feelings may be positive or negative. Predicting or recalling feelings are included. 2.* PRAISES OR ENCOURAGES: praises or encourages student action or behavior. Jokes that release tension, but not at the expense of another individual, nodding head or saying "um hm?" or "go on" are included. 3.* ACCEPTS OR USES IDEAS OF STUDENT: clarifying, building, or developing ideas suggested by a student. As teacher brings more of his own ideas into play, shift to category 5. 4.* ASKS QUESTIONS: asking a question about content or procedure with the intent that a student answer.
	Direct Influence	5.* LECTURING: giving facts or opinions about content or procedure; expressing his own ideas, asking rhetorical questions. 6.* GIVING DIRECTIONS: directions, commands, or orders which students are expected to comply with. 7.* CRITICIZING OR JUSTIFYING AUTHORITY: statements intended to change student behavior from unacceptable to acceptable pattern; bawling someone out; stating why the teacher is doing what he is doing; extreme self-reference.
Student Talk		8.* STUDENT TALK—RESPONSE: talk by students in response to teacher. Teacher initiates the contact or solicits student statement. 9.* STUDENT TALK—INITIATION: talk initiated by students. If "calling on" student is only to indicate who may talk next, observer must decide whether student wanted to talk.
Silence		10.* SILENCE OR CONFUSION: pauses, short periods of silence and periods of confusion in which communication cannot be understood by the observer.

* There is NO scale implied by these numbers. Each number is classificatory, designating a particular kind of communication event. To write these numbers down during observation is merely to identify and enumerate communication events, not to judge them.

Often teachers act as if they do not hear what a student says; to acknowledge and make use of an idea is a powerful form of recognition. To praise or encourage student participation directly (category 2) is to solicit even more participation by giving a reward. The ability to use the feeling tone of a student constructively, to react to feeling and clarify it (category 1), is a rare skill. Teachers with this ability can often mobilize positive feelings in motivation and successfully control negative feelings that might otherwise get out of hand.

All the actions falling into categories 1 through 4 tend to increase and reward student participation, and to give students the opportunity to become more influential. The net effect is greater freedom of action for the students.

Direct influence increases the active control of the teacher and often stimulates compliance. The lecture (category 5) focuses the attention of the students on ideas chosen by the teacher. To give directions or commands (category 6) is to direct the activities of the class with the intent of obtaining compliance. Category 7 refers to criticizing student behavior or justifying the teacher's use of authority. These actions concentrate authority in the hands of the teacher. Direct influence tends to increase teacher participation and to establish restraints on student behavior. The ensuing restriction of freedom may occur in the form of compliance to the teacher or of adjustment to the requirements of problem-solving activities. The net effect is less freedom of action for the students.

The division of student talk into categories 8 and 9 provides an automatic check on freedom of student action within the system of categories. Ordinarily, but not always, a pattern of direct teacher influence is associated with less student talk, which generally consists of responses to the teacher (category 8). A pattern of indirect influence is ordinarily associated with more student talk, which is often initiated by the students (category 9). The use of only two categories to record all kinds of student talk neglects a great deal of information, but the major purpose of these categories is the analysis of teacher influence. The greatest information will accrue from observation if category 9 is used sparingly and only on those occasions when the communication is truly student-initiated.

For example, the act of a student in answering a specific question asked by a teacher obviously falls into category 8. Even the act of giving an oral report may be placed in this category when the student is restricted to a specific outline and is probably responding to the teacher's directions.

Category 9 should be used by the observer only to indicate the student's spontaneous expression of his own ideas. General questions are often a clue that a student may be initiating his own ideas. When a teacher calls on a student who voluntarily raised his hand to speak and asks, "Have you anything to add, Robert?" the chances are that the use of category 9 is correct.

The purpose of category 10 is to record short pauses, silences, and periods of confusion as they occur during classroom interaction. It is not intended to record periods of silence or confusion lasting for more than 2 minutes. The continuous use of this category to designate long periods of silence serves no useful purpose.

The system of categories is designed for situations in which the teachers and the students are actively discussing schoolwork. It is an inappropriate tool when the verbal communication is discontinuous, separated by fairly long periods of silence, or when one person is engaged in prolonged lecturing or in reading aloud to the class. In situations in which two-way communication does not exist and is not likely to exist, the observer should stop and make a note of the exact time at which spontaneous interaction lapsed and the reasons for the interruption. The observer must remain alert to the resumption of spontaneous interaction.

Marking Activity Periods. Teacher influence is a pattern that is constantly changing over time. The most effective teachers, in fact, have a large repertoire of behaviors, and systematic observation shows that they can present many different influence patterns.

The identification of activity periods is one way that flexibility can be studied. In effect, a second system of categories is superimposed on the 10 interaction categories; this second system is likely to be different in each research study. For example, it may be sufficient in a study of high school mathematics classes to indicate periods of (*a*) settling down to work, (*b*) introducing new material, (*c*) teacher-directed discussion or work on material that is not new, (*d*) supervision and direction of individual seatwork, and (*e*) periods of evaluation, in which homework and test results are discussed.

In an elementary classroom, it would be reasonable to keep interaction data collected during show-and-tell separate from reading instruction, and these in turn from arithmetic, music, games, penmanship, etc.

If interaction analysis is to be used to discover whether a teacher's pattern of influence in planning work with students is different, for example, from his influence pattern while supervising work already planned, then even finer discriminations would be necessary to identify the boundaries of the required time periods.

One way to develop sensitivity to these different activity periods is to train the observer to draw a double line whenever there is a change in the class formation, the communication pattern, the subject matter to be learned, or in the presumed purpose of instruction. After the classroom visit is completed, the observer can use his double lines and marginal notes to recreate a brief chronology of the classroom activities. Interaction data gathered by this procedure can be grouped in a variety of ways for special comparisons.

No matter whether one is discussing a set of categories for interaction analysis or a set of categories for classifying activity periods, there are two requirements that must be satisfied in order to make generalizations about total class interaction. First, the system should be designed to include all possible events, that is, the categories should be totally inclusive. Second, a single event must be recorded in one, and only one, category so that the categories will be mutually exclusive.

Any system of observation that fails to meet the first requirement is selective, and under it the data are not representative of all the events that occurred. Failure to meet the second requirement produces an inconsistent enumeration of events; the comparison of category frequencies then becomes meaningless or at least biased in some unknown way.

CONCLUSIONS AND IMPLICATIONS OF THE PROJECT

METATHEORY

Theorizing about theory is not a common pastime, especially in the field of education, but some questions should be raised about the theoretical hypotheses around which this project is organized. What kind of theorizing will be of most help in creating a theory of instruction? Can the present hypotheses contribute to a theory of instruction? These two questions will occupy our attention for a page or two before we go on to discuss the conclusions and implications of the project.

To theorize about the behavior of a classroom teacher, one must draw from the fields of learning theory, motivation, personality, group dynamics, sociometry, and practically everything else, and direction signs are not well-posted.

Educators are not yet ready to start the ambitious task of developing a theory of instruction that takes into account all behavior that occurs in a classroom. In one bold step of oversimplification, we postulated that a theory of instruction must at least concern itself with the teacher's acts of influence and the reactions of the students, using the goals of learning as a reference for interpretation. There must be concepts that describe teacher influence, concepts that describe student reactions, and concepts that describe learning goals. In the analysis of behavior, the order is reversed. Given particular learning goals, students' perceptions of these goals are developed through classroom interaction. The work that follows also involves interaction. The analysis of student and teacher interaction is carried out in terms of the learning goals. We found that classroom behavior makes the most sense when viewed within this frame of reference.

In order to contribute to a theory of instruction, a hypothesis must propose dynamic cause-and-effect relationships among learning goals, teacher behavior, and student behavior. If the hypothesis is verified empirically, it can become a principle of instruction that a teacher can then use to predict the consequences of his own behavior under certain conditions. To illustrate, one of our hypotheses is that direct influence when goals are ambiguous produces high dependence on the teacher and less learning. Direct influence is a concept describing teacher behavior; it is operationally defined as the enumeration of a series of verbal statements occurring in sequence and theoretically defined as those acts which restrict alternative actions of the student. Goals are conceptualized along a continuum from ambiguous to clear, and are operationally defined in terms of the student's perceptions. Acts of dependence and learning are aspects of the student's behavior. Each can be assessed and given operational meaning by either paper-and-pencil tests or observation.

The ultimate value of this kind of engineering research will be tested by pragmatic criteria. As this chapter is being written, arrangements have been completed for an inservice training program in a nearby school district. The project will attempt to answer the question, if teachers learn our theories about the consequences of indirect and direct influence, will this help them control their behavior and become more effective teachers? The results of the present project will become part of the content of this inservice training.

SOME ASSUMPTIONS INHERENT IN OUR APPROACH

Certain assumptions are necessary in our analysis of teacher influence. First, acts of influence are expressed primarily through verbal statements. Nonverbal acts of influence do occur, but are not recorded by interaction analysis. The reasonableness of this assumption rests on the assertion that the quality of the nonverbal acts is similar to the verbal acts; to assess verbal influence therefore is to adequately sample all influence.

Second, how much teachers talk and what they say determine to a large extent the reactions of the students. This is another way of saying that the teacher is an influential authority figure. Given the teacher's position of authority, his greater maturity, and the common expectations of students, we find this assumption reasonable.

Third, an assumption necessary to the application of these research results in any program designed to increase teacher effectiveness is that teachers can control their verbal participation in the classroom. We believe that the average teacher can control his behavior and use it as a psychological force in classroom management. He can be indirect if he chooses, or direct, according to his assessment of the situation. What we hope to provide are principles which he can use in making the choice.

These assumptions focus our attention on the verbal participation of teachers and students. We are in the business of evaluating classroom communication in terms of the teacher's control. Our procedures tend to emphasize control processes and to ignore subject matter, or content. The latter is important, but so is the former, and we prefer to work on one thing at a time at our present stage of development.

MAJOR CONCLUSIONS OF THE 1955–57 STUDIES

The purpose of the early studies was to develop research tools and to use these tools to study relationships between teacher statements and average classroom scores on a pupil attitude inventory. These early studies were conducted in eighth-grade combined English/social studies in Minnesota and Standard Four elementary classrooms in New Zealand. A sample of Minnesota elementary classrooms provided additional interaction analysis data.

These early studies establish clear and significant relationships among teacher statements, pupil attitudes toward the teacher, and the classroom learning activities. Furthermore, the same relationships were shown to exist in more formal and less formal classroom situations in two countries some 8,000 miles apart.

It was shown that when a class scored higher on scales of teacher attractiveness, motivation for schoolwork, fair rewards and punishments, independence, and lack of disabling anxiety, its teacher showed more acceptance of, interest in, and constructive use of the student ideas expressed in classroom discussion. In New Zealand, the teachers of higher-scoring classes also gave fewer directions and made fewer criticisms. The incidence of corporal punishment was also much lower in high-scoring New Zealand class-rooms. In the lower-scoring classrooms, the opposite trends occurred. The findings of these early studies were consistent with the research carried out almost 20 years before the present studies by H. H. Anderson and his colleagues.

If one accepts the assumptions and theoretical formulations presented in the first part of this monograph, one sees that these studies demonstrate a cause-and-effect relationship between teacher influence, as expressed by the verbal statements of teachers, and pupil attitudes, as measured by our paper-and-pencil instruments. At the different age levels that exist at primary, elementary, junior high, and senior high grade levels, across different combinations of pupil personality and individual differences, with different types of teaching styles, and even in two countries which differ in the formality of teacher-pupil relationships, students react similarly to the same differences in teacher influence.

These early studies did not include any measure of subject matter achieve-ment. Such measures were purposely delayed until the larger field study could be conducted with the necessary experimental controls.

THE MAJOR CONCLUSIONS REGARDING ACHIEVEMENT

In this project we have isolated situations in which students learned more, and have compared these with situations in which students learned less. Our method of isolation was not to administer a test of achievement first and then study the differences in teacher behavior. Instead, we made theoretical pre-dictions of the following sort.

First, we assessed acts of teacher influence as they occurred spontaneously in the classroom. By using the technique of interaction analysis, we were able to isolate teachers who had an above-average pattern of indirect influence. We found that they were far more flexible than those teachers who exerted below-average indirect influence. That is, they could be just as direct as the latter teachers in certain situations, but they could be far more indirect in other situations. The net effect was a higher average of indirect influence.

Second, we predicted certain patterns would occur among the more flexible teachers: (1) they would be most indirect while goals were being clarified and new content material was being introduced; (2) they would be most direct after goals had been clarified, while work was in progress.

Finally, we predicted that the students of those teachers who were less flexible would learn less, as measured by our achievement tests. It was on this basis that we isolated classes of higher achievement and classes of lower achievement.

When we initially contacted teachers to solicit their participation in the project, we expected certain types of students to learn more while working with direct teachers and other types of students to learn more while working with indirect teachers. We were wrong. All types of students learned more while working with the more flexible teachers. We also thought that classes in the field of mathematics might learn more while working with a direct teacher and that classes in the field of social studies would learn more while working with an indirect teacher. Again we were wrong. It is true that teachers of mathematics use time and methods differently than do teachers of social studies, but students of the more flexible teachers scored higher on the achievement tests in both content areas.

We are not yet prepared to discard the notion that particular types of students work more effectively toward learning goals with particular types of teachers even though our field studies failed to support it. In a series of experiments with geometry classes, we found significant differences indicating that dependent-prone students learned more than independent-prone students while working with a more indirect teacher. Perhaps subsequent experiments will reveal what types of students learn the most while working with direct teachers. Furthermore, there are a number of improvements that can be made in our methods of classifying students into types, and these should be tried out before discarding expectations which at first glance seemed quite reasonable.

With our present data, a factor-analysis can be made of student attitudes toward direct and indirect teachers. An item analysis of the factors in the M.S.A.I. test, made separately for our five types of students, may reveal that different attitudes do develop from contacts with different types of teachers, even though these attitudes did not affect achievement in this study.

SOME IMPLICATIONS OF THE RESEARCH

Implications for Classroom Teachers. To those of us on the staff, the most interesting implication of the project concerns the timing of direct and indirect influence. We find this most interesting because our theoretical predictions are contrary to accepted teaching practice. Nearly all teachers agree that immediate action should be taken in any situation in which the learning goals are ambiguous and students do not know what to do. "Students who are unable to go on with their work are wasting time," the reasoning goes, "Something should be done!" So far we are all in agreement.

Should the initial contacts made by a teacher in such a situation be direct or indirect? Our theory suggests an indirect approach; most teachers use a direct approach. Teachers can find many justifications for their direct approach. Often they think that to tell the students what to do is only to remind them of something they already know. Sometimes teachers are quite sure that the students are lazy or are pretending confusion. A direct approach seems more efficient at the moment, and a teacher is a busy person. These and many other reasons are often mentioned by teachers as a justification for the following pattern: (*a*) the teacher decides students are confused; (*b*) the teacher makes his best guess on the cause of this confusion; and (*c*) the teacher, acting on his own diagnosis, proceeds to give information, direction, and, in some cases, criticism in order to reestablish patterns of work.

The two most common situations in which a teacher faces this choice are those in which new material is being introduced, such as a new topic, a new procedure, or a new method of problem-solving, and those in which a group already at work runs into difficulty—when Johnny won't cooperate, information cannot be found, the answer doesn't check with an independent proof, materials are missing, and so forth.

It is obvious to any person with teaching experience that no valid generalizations can be made on how the teacher should handle these and similar situations. That is, it is obvious that there are some situations in which a teacher should be primarily direct and others in which he should be primarily indirect. However, we can make a statistical generalization which will hold for 100 such situations. In this study, the teachers of students who learned less employed a pattern of direct influence more often in such a situation. Our theory predicts higher achievement and less dependence when goals are clarified by an indirect approach.

An indirect approach stimulates verbal participation by students and discloses to the teacher students' perceptions of the situation. Such an approach not only provides the teacher with more information about students' understanding of a particular problem, but also often encourages students to develop more responsibility for diagnosing their difficulties and for suggesting a plan of action.

A direct approach increases student compliance to teacher opinion and direction. It conditions students to seek the teacher's help and to check with the teacher more often to be sure they are on the right track.

A second implication for classroom teachers is that the major differences in the use of influence between the teachers whose students learned the most and those whose students learned the least are illustrated by the use of actions classified under categories 1, 2, and 3. The direct teachers lack those social skills of communication that are involved in accepting, clarifying, and making use of the ideas and feelings of students. The indirect teachers have these skills, even though they are not in use most of the time. Although these skills are used sparingly, they are employed when needed.

Associated with this increased social skill is less need for directions and criticism. The most direct teachers give twice as many directions as the most indirect, and express eight times as much criticism. These figures are consistent with what has been said about dependence. Lack of clarifying and using student ideas places the teacher in a position of giving more directions; in short, he must work harder to keep his students working successfully. When dependence is higher, progress by students depends much more on continuous teacher supervision.

There are interesting comparisons to be made between what we have found in this project and some of the more common criticisms of the public schools that have attained national prominence during the last several years. Some critics of the public schools have advocated that teachers "get tough," tell students what to do, and demand high standards. Our data show that higher standards can be achieved not by telling students what to do in some sort of misguided "get tough" policy, but by asking questions and then using student ideas, perceptions, and reactions to build toward greater student self-direction, responsibility, and understanding. If "getting tough" means helping students face the consequences of their own ideas and opinions, as contrasted against living with the consequences of the teacher's ideas and opinions, then indirect teachers are much tougher.

The third implication for classroom teachers that we would like to mention is that variability in teacher influence, or flexibility, is associated with teachers whose students learned the most. One consequence of this finding is that our better teachers were less alike and our poorer teachers were more alike. It suggests that creative teaching is an expression of a particular teacher's personality, working with a particular group of students, in a particular subject.

We should emphasize again that our six most indirect social studies teachers fell clearly into two types. Three lectured much more and placed greater emphasis on content material, but all six shared the common characteristic of a higher I/D ratio. The more content-oriented teachers worked with student ideas less, but when they did, their pattern was essentially indirect. The other three teachers worked in a very different style that included 31.6 per cent student talk, the highest average in the entire study. The average student achievement of this latter group was a nonsignificant one-half point higher, indicating that achievement was high for two rather different styles of teaching. It also indicates that a variation from 20 per cent student talk in the content-oriented style to 31.6 per cent student talk in the other three classrooms is not associated with a significant difference in achievement.

The differences between the direct and indirect teachers may be interpreted in terms of the different roles the teacher is able to play in the classroom. The direct teachers could not shift their style of interaction as much as the indirect teachers. Because the direct teachers had fewer ways of working with students, they could provide only a limited number of roles. On the other hand, the indirect teachers were able to adopt many different roles, and they shifted from one to another in a manner consistent with the theories that have already been stated.

Implications for Preservice and Inservice Education. There is no substitute for knowledge of what is being taught. Two of the mathematics teachers were not adequately trained. One of these two classes showed an average mean gain in achievement that was last in rank order and *one-sixteenth* of the mean gain of the highest-ranking class. The other class was ninth in rank order. The teacher of this latter class used more social skill in guiding classroom communication. His attitude was, "I'm no math teacher, but we'll have to make the best of it and learn this material together." While his class exceeded the achievement of one or two other classes whose teachers had more extensive training in mathematics, the achievement could not match that of those classes whose teachers were both socially skillful and well-qualified.

The two cases just described illustrate a general implication of this project for the training of teachers. Teachers who are qualified in a content area should be exposed to some type of human relations training that will help them attain the following objectives: first, the ability to use the social skills of accepting, clarifying, and using the ideas of students in planning work and diagnosing difficulties; second, knowledge of those acts of influence that restrict student reactions and those that expand student reactions; and third, understanding of a theory of instruction that he can use to control his own behavior as he guides classroom communication.

It is reasonable to suppose that these objectives cannot be reached without supervised practice. The person supervising this practice should be able to provide the practice-teacher with information about his own behavior. One way to do this is to use the technique of interaction analysis. The procedure is likely to involve threat for the practice-teacher and will require a skillful, indirect approach on the part of the supervisor.

One possible procedure would permit practice-teachers to try out different patterns of influence. Suppose that on one occasion the practice-teacher tried introducing material with a highly direct pattern and that on another occasion he tried with an indirect pattern. A qualified observer could collect interaction analysis data, tabulate the two matrices, and discuss the resulting communication patterns with the practice-teacher. This could be done if all practice-teachers were trained to become reliable observers so that they could alternate between the roles of observer and teacher in teams of two.

Implications for Merit Pay. In the present decade, the issue of merit pay for gifted teachers will probably receive more and more attention. Already many school districts are experimenting with different systems. Since this study deals with teacher effectiveness, inferences about the merit pay issue are inescapable.

Two warnings should be issued to anyone who reads this project report and then makes inferences about merit pay. The first warning is that it is easier to identify poor teaching than good teaching. This study found that teachers were quite similar whose students learned the least and had the poorest attitudes toward the teacher and class activities. The teachers who presented the opposite picture were more flexible. By refining the research techniques of this project, reliable distinctions between high- and low-scoring classrooms could be made concerning the amount of students' talk, teachers' use of their time, and the distinction between the 8 and 9 categories of student talk (i.e., student response versus student initiation). The possibility of making such distinctions looks promising, but much more preliminary work will be necessary.

The second warning is that the correlations between various measures derived from interaction analysis, student attitude inventories, and tests of achievement are still so low that evaluation of an individual teacher is subject to considerable error, even though the general trends of the research are statistically significant. So much for the warnings.

The major aim of all systems of merit pay is to reward competence in such a way that all teachers who can improve their teaching skills will do so.

A secondary objective, which is to give higher pay for more difficult jobs, must await a more dramatic modification of school organization leading to specialized teaching functions.

Our staff, after making such a close analysis of teacher-pupil contacts, has developed a number of basic beliefs about some of the issues of merit pay. First, programs for the improvement of instruction should be designed and controlled by teachers as part of their professional responsibility. Teacher control, rather than administrative control, is necessary because changing one's methods of teaching is very personal, often involves emotional adjustments, cannot be coerced by administrative fiat, and therefore must be a voluntary, self-directed process.

Second, no system of teacher evaluation will be accepted by teachers until it has been tested and found satisfactory by the teachers whose professional welfare will be affected. Teachers must have confidence in the valuative methods, criteria, and control before they will cooperate.

Third, a system of inservice training that teachers think is successful in helping improve their own ability to teach can become, with care, a stepping-stone to a satisfactory system of rewarding the exceptionally competent. In our opinion, this means that merit pay would normally follow a 4- to 6-year active, voluntary inservice training program that, in the opinion of the majority of teachers, has been successful. As teachers experience success in improving their teaching and develop confidence in the criteria used to identify improvement, they will be closer to accepting a system that provides monetary reward for those who make the best progress.

It is our opinion that whenever systems of merit pay are forced from "the top down," the program will fail to meet its major objectives. Administrators and school boards following this path will meet with failure. In the same breath, it can be predicted that teachers who resist schedule policies that have served well in the past will be confronted with increasing criticism from the public and from school board members. Sooner or later the minimum teachers' salary will stop improving in relation to the general economy, and it will then be in the best interests of the profession to raise the ceiling of teacher income for those who are most qualified and most effective.

It follows from the foregoing assertions that the development of objective criteria and procedures to evaluate teacher effectiveness is a professional responsibility. The most rugged test of any procedure is an objective research program that not only provides evidence of the highest quality attainable, but also employs procedures that nearly all teachers can understand and use in a self-improvement program.

The Implications of Interaction Analysis. The system of interaction analysis used in this study is content-free. It is concerned primarily with the social skills of classroom management, as expressed through verbal communication. It is costly and cumbersome, and it requires some form of automation in collecting, tabulating, and analyzing the raw data. It is not yet a finished research tool.

Nevertheless, our staff has experienced minor triumphs that we will never forget. We have, for instance, played the following game with considerable success: A single observer collects interaction analysis data, tabulates a matrix, and presents the matrix at a staff meeting. The only information supplied to the staff is the presumed objective of the lesson, the grade level of the class, and the sex of the teacher. The observer who collected the data remains silent as the rest of the staff reconstruct the social interaction. Conclusions about the tempo or speed of interaction, the relative domination of the teacher, whether he asks long or short questions, how much he lectures, and many other aspects of interaction are listed. After the group has finished crawling out on the end of a limb, the observer corrects any misconceptions that may have developed. The number of correct speculations is usually very high, well over 80 per cent. Occasionally a single misconception colors other guesses until a picture develops that is quite incorrect, but these latter outcomes are remarkably infrequent.

Much of the inferential power of this system of interaction analysis comes from tabulating the data as sequence pairs in a 10×10 matrix. This is a time-consuming process. It can be and should be done mechanically by electronic computers. Once the high cost of tedious tabulation is under control, the problem of training reliable observers and maintaining their reliability will still remain.

We have reason to be optimistic about the value of interaction analysis. Its potential as a research tool, however, for a wide application to problems in education remains to be explored.

REFERENCES

1. Amidon, E. and N. A. Flanders, "The Effects of Direct and Indirect Teacher Influence on Dependent-Prone Students Learning Geometry," *Journal of Educational Psychology,* LII, No. 6 (December 1961), 286–91.
2. Anderson, H. H., "The Measurement of Domination and of Socially Integrative Behavior in Teacher's Contact with Children," *Child Development,* X, No. 2 (June 1939), 73–89.
3. —— and H. M. Brewer, "Studies of Teachers' Classroom Personalities, I: Dominative and Socially Integrative Behavior of Kindergarten Teachers," *Applied Psychology Monographs,* No. 6, 1945.
4. —— and J. E. Brewer, "Studies of Teachers' Classroom Personalities, II: Effects of Teacher's Dominative and Integrative Contacts on Children's Classroom Behavior," *Applied Psychology Monographs,* No. 8, 1946.
5. —— and M. F. Reed, "Studies of Teachers' Classroom Personalities, III: Follow-Up Studies of the Effects of Dominative and Integrative Contacts on Children's Behavior," *Applied Psychology Monographs of the American Psychological Association,* Stanford, Calif.: Stanford University Press, No. 11, December 1946.
6. Cogan, M. L., "Theory and Design of a Study of Teacher-Pupil Interaction," *The Harvard Educational Review,* XXVI, No. 4 (Fall 1956), 315–42.
7. Filson, T. N., "Factors Influencing the Level of Dependence in the Classroom." Unpublished Ph.D. Thesis, University of Minnesota, 1957.
8. Flanders, N. A., "Personal-Social Anxiety as a Factor in Experimental Learning Situations," *Journal of Educational Research,* XLV (October 1951), 100–110.
9. ——, "Diagnosing and Utilizing Social Structures in Classroom Learning," 59th Yearbook of the National Society for the Study of Educational Research, *Part II, The Dynamics of Instructional Groups.* Chicago: University of Chicago Press, 1960. Chap. IX, pp. 187–217.

10. —— and J. P. Anderson and E. J. Amidon, "Measuring Dependence Proneness in the Classroom," *Educational and Psychological Measurement,* XXI, No. 3 (Autumn 1961), 575–87.
11. Lewin, K., *A Dynamic Theory of Personality.* New York: McGraw-Hill Book Company, 1935. Chap. IV, pp. 114–70.
12. Lippitt, R. and R. K. White, "The 'Social Climate' of Children's Groups," in R. G. Barker, J. S. Kounin, and H. F. Wright, eds., *Child Behavior and Development.* New York: McGraw-Hill Book Company, 1943, pp. 458–508.
13. Perkins, H. V., "Climate Influences Group Learning," *Journal of Educational Research,* XLV (October 1951), 115–19.
14. Smith, B. O., "A Concept of Teaching," *Teachers College Record,* LXI, No. 5 (February 1960), 229–41.
15. Withall, J., "The Development of a Technique for the Measurement of Social-Emotional Climate in Classroom," *Journal of Experimental Education,* XVII (March 1949), 347–61.

EVALUATION IN TEACHING

Kaoru Yamamoto

We, as active teachers, have wondered about many matters in teaching and raised numerous questions about education and our role in it. Most of these queries have been private in nature, while some remained even subconscious. For the purposes of the present discussion, however, let us make the basic questions explicit.

TEACHING AND ITS QUESTIONS

All our questions point to one central inquiry: "What is teaching?" The latter can be answered in myriad ways, but I submit here (see Table 1) a convenient scheme to systematize most of these questions and answers. The questions are classified by interrogative pronouns and further divided into normative (prescriptive) and descriptive forms.

For example, one of the fundamental questions takes the form, "Why should we teach?" This asks for the rationale of teaching, probably in terms of cultural values, goals, intentions, and motives, and the answer is expressed as an *ought,* or normative, statement (e.g., "we ought to teach our children to convert them from animals to humans"). Our concept of the nature of the universe and of *Homo sapiens* determines the specific form of the answer to this question.[1]

A variant of the above question is, "Why are we teaching?" This version asks for a description of our present, working rationale, and the answer must therefore clarify the immediate and real reasons for teaching, instead of some ideals. We may insist, in response to the normative form of the question, that our aim is to induce insight and innovation in our students because

Reprinted from *Texas Journal of Secondary Education* 21:4–11 (Spring, 1968), by permission of author and publisher.

TABLE 1. TEACHING—SCHEMATIZATION OF QUESTIONS

QUESTION		
Prescriptive	*Descriptive*	AREA OF CONCERN
Why should we be teaching?	Why are we teaching?	Values, goals, intentions, and motives
Who should be teaching?	Who are teaching?	Teacher qualification (recruitment, selection, and preparation)
Whom should we be teaching?	Whom are we teaching?	Student characteristics (recruitment, selection, and distribution)
When should we be teaching?	When are we teaching?	Readiness and logistics (physical, cognitive, and social development, timing, duration and continuity)
What should we be teaching?	What are we teaching?	Curriculum (types and quantity of material, structure, and sequence)
How should we be teaching?	How are we teaching?	Instruction and demonstration (methods, media, climate, and control)
Where should we be teaching?	Where are we teaching?	Ecology and logistics (locale, physical facilities, and geocultural administration)

they are destined to grow up in an unknowable world; but in fact, the actual goal of our teaching may be mere conservation and perpetuation of the past. The two answers, therefore, may or may not agree with each other.

Similarly, when the question, "Whom should we teach?," is raised, we may answer that we should teach every child, regardless of his race, color, sex, creed, social status, and aptitude. If, however, the question is in the descriptive form, "Whom are we teaching?," our answer will be radically different from the above, due to a wide gap between our dream and practice.[2]

Now, my thesis is that we are engaged in "evaluation" whenever we compare our answer to the normative question with that to the descriptive question. In other words, we are evaluating our current activities against what we know or believe we should be doing. Accordingly, if we are conscientious, we will be continuously involved in evaluation which, quite often, we express as feelings of dissatisfaction, insecurity, and anxiety.

In this sense, we cannot escape evaluating various aspects of education, including ourselves as teachers. It is nothing mysterious or threatening. Whether such action is carried out consciously or unconsciously, publicly or privately, constructively or destructively, and systematically or randomly— that is, however, another matter. In any case, evaluation is here to stay as an essential component of teaching activities.

PROCESS OF EVALUATION

We said that evaluation is fundamentally the comparison between our answer to the normative question and that to the descriptive question. Thus, no matter what specific aspects of teaching we are concerned with, evaluation follows the basic pattern shown in Table 2.

Let us take an example of the curriculum question, "What should we teach?" The general goal here may be to teach students the use of American language, while a more specific goal could be to teach certain children of the poor [3] how to understand a formal version of this language used by teachers, other children, and textbook writers.[4]

We next answer the descriptive question, "What are we teaching?," by an examination of the current status of curriculum. To arrive at a diagnosis of

TABLE 2. AN EVALUATIVE LOOP

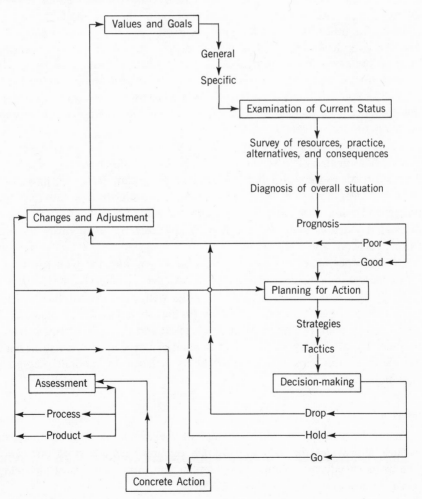

the situation, we survey our resources (what different curricula are available to be taught?), practice (what is actually being taught?), alternatives (what other choices are possible in curriculum material, structure, and sequence?), and consequences (what are the possible results of the current practice and of the alternatives?). On the basis of such diagnosis, we derive a prognosis for the original goal, forecasting the probability of reaching it.

Specifically, we may find that no attention has been paid to the possibility of communication difficulty between students of the poor who use a particular vernacular and teachers who use another.[5] No teaching material has been prepared in such informal dialects and a wholesale shifting to the informal language may entail confusion on the part of both teachers and students. It may be advisable for the teacher to find out the kind and extent of such communication gaps on both sides, that is, what he does not understand in children and what they do not understand in him.[6] If the gap is too large, the prognosis for the original intention to teach students to understand teachers' formal vernacular would be poor and, hence, would demand either reformulation of the values and goals or re-examination of the current status, or both.

If, on the other hand, the prognosis is good, we start planning for action, first the overall strategy and next the specific tactics. A gradual transition may be preferred to an outright showdown, while a frank and open comparison of the different languages may be a successful tactic (we call them "police"—you call them "fuzz," etc.).[7] We must use our imagination in making up plans since there is no safe and sure way which is applicable to every teaching situation.

When a plan is ready, we must make a final decision before plunging into action. A re-analysis of the plan and of the overall situation may reveal that we have to drop the particular blueprint at this point. If so, we have to go back to several earlier points and re-loop. Administrative, interpersonal, financial, health, and various other reasons may make it impracticable to execute the action plan. It may have to be held up temporarily, pending further revisions and elaboration.

On the other hand, the decision may be a "go" and the plan can be put into concrete action. Then, both the process and product (results) must be carefully observed and assessed. If things go well, keep the action up; if not, changes and adjustment are necessary to the operation, or its plan, or its goals. In this manner, the entire loop is closed and the self-corrective feature becomes clear. This is why we say evaluation is a crucial component in teaching. Without this closed loop, teaching is reduced to random, haphazard activities.

IN A LOOP

As we have seen, the closed nature of the evaluative loop is important because it provides the only way we can get any feedback from our action. The word, "feedback," should be a familiar one to us, since most physiological functions, mediated by the central nervous system, work on this principle. For example, it is important for a person to be able to hear what he is saying in order for him to adjust his speech continuously to the temporal and situational requirements. For another example, try to remember the feelings of powerlessness and panic you experienced if you have ever had to drive on solid ice at night; in that situation, a minimum of information is fed back through your tactile or visual sense organs, and you realize how much you normally use that feedback to guide you in making corrections.

Not only humans but other animals also depend on information feedback to guide their behavior. It is well known that bats and porpoises, among others, emit high-frequency signals and navigate by judging the feedback, the sounds reflected by other objects standing in their way. Needless to say, this is exactly the mechanism used in our sonars, radars, and guided missile systems. Without such feedback, neither these animals nor many scientific apparatuses would operate successfully.

Another familar word is "reward" or "reinforcement" in learning. Something is reinforcing precisely because it gives the learner some information concerning his performance, namely, whether he is operating on a right level or plane, whether he is moving in the proper direction, and whether he is traveling at a satisfactory speed. Even though many of us disliked certain aspects of the grade system when we were students, we depended heavily on our teachers' grading to steer our course, and we used to complain bitterly when no information was made available because we could not know what was expected of us and how we were doing. Under the circumstances, our efforts were something like blasting a shotgun in the dark.

So, students need some information from teachers to set up their own goals, to examine their current status, to map out a plan for action, to assess their actual moves, and to make necessary changes and revisions. It is certainly one of our duties to provide whatever feedback is relevant to students' progress and development.

But let us keep in mind that the closed evaluative loop is indispensable, first and foremost, to teachers themselves in their teaching activities. It is not primarily for the sake of students that we ask the normative and descriptive questions. We evaluate teaching, not out of any immediately altruistic motives, but because we will be unable to function as teachers without it. If we think we can teach without engaging at the same time in evaluation, we are deceiving ourselves and we will soon be lost and useless.

It was earlier mentioned that many evaluative efforts are executed informally and even subconsciously. In fact, if evaluation becomes an automatic habit in teaching, and if we can forget about it just as we ordinarily do the presence and role of our autonomic or involuntary nervous system, this will be wonderful. Unfortunately, we tend to forget about evaluation long *before* we have established it as a habit. We must therefore make some conscious efforts to build such activities where there have been few and to recognize the loop clearly where its existence has, till now, been only implied.

By now it has grown apparent that the familiar appraisal activity of test administration and score-reporting is but a fraction of the entire evaluative function performed by teachers. More fundamental questions have to be asked first and any such part operations should be interpreted in the total context of an evaluative loop. The specific methods of assessment to be used are obviously determined by the full sequence and not by whims and fads.

For example, when we answer the normative question on instruction, "How should we teach?," our response may be phrased in terms of some rules (logical, evidential, or social), of certain criteria, or of personal preferences and desires.[8] In each case, a different loop will be planned and executed, and different assessment techniques will be employed. If, therefore, we decide that we should teach according to the rules of deductive logic or discovery method, our assessment will be different from one made in terms of the distribution of time among various subactivities (such as lecture, discussion, prompting, disciplining, etc.). Likewise, if our normative definition is made in reference to the proportion of students surpassing national norms of a standardized achievement-test battery, the techniques used will be quite dissimilar to those adopted when the definition is couched in terms of personal feelings.

Actually, most of these forms of answers are intermixed and, hence, evaluation is seldom complete with a single loop. Both quantitative and qualitative approaches are adopted and judgments are made on both (so-called) objective and subjective bases. Teacher and peer nominations, students' writings and oral reports, observation, anecdotal records, interview results, and projective techniques are as useful as standardized and non-standardized tests, inventories, course examinations, and grades. A close working relationship with other teachers and parents, as well as with specialists, including remedial teachers, doctors, school nurses, social workers, school counselors, and school psychologists, is obviously desirable. Here, it can easily be seen that public and communicable evaluative efforts are necessary to facilitate each other's work for the ultimate benefit of our students.[9]

By all means, therefore, let us ask the basic questions on teaching and continue to ask them time and again to keep the evaluative loop working well. What, in your mind, is teaching?

NOTES

1. See, for example:

Gordon C. Lee. *Education and Democratic Ideals.* New York: Harcourt, Brace & World, 1965.

Israel Scheffler. "Philosophical Models of Teaching," *Harvard Educational Review* 35: 131–143; Spring 1965.

Kaoru Yamamoto. "The Rewards and Results of Teaching," *Education* 87: 67–72; October 1966.

2. See, for example:

Gunnar Myrdal. *An American Dilemma.* New York: Harper & Brothers, 1944.

Harry Passow, Ed. *Education in Depressed Areas.* New York: Teachers College Press, Teachers College, Columbia University, 1963.

W. Lloyd Warner. *American Life: Dream and Reality* (rev. ed.). Chicago: University of Chicago Press, 1962.

3. This presumes our treatment of another set of questions, namely, "Whom should we teach?" and, "Whom are we teaching?" It seems that we usually do well to think of more than one aspect of teaching.

4. We may further wish to define what is meant by such concepts as "to understand," or "a formal version." The more specific our goals and intentions are, the easier it is to plan for an action, to carry it out, and to assess the results. Often, however, too specific efforts are rendered ineffective because of the absence of consideration of broader factors.

5. Incidentally, this kind of information comes from activities labeled "research." Research can take many forms but here, in contrast with evaluation, we can ask various questions singly and in their own right. Thus, we ask, "Who should teach?" or, "Who do you think should teach?," without coupling it with another question, "Who are teaching?" For this reason, it is sometimes said that evaluation needs criteria (the normative question), while research does not. Naturally, we can conduct research on evaluation or do research on research operations themselves.

6. As for the specific form such a gap takes, see, for example:

Basil Bernstein. "Language and Social Class," *British Journal of Sociology* 11: 271–276; September 1960.

Martin Deutsch. "The Role of Social Class in Language Development and Cognition," *American Journal of Orthopsychiatry* 35: 78–88; January 1965.

Frank Riessman and Frank Alberts. "Digging 'The Man's' Language," *Saturday Review* 49: 80–81 & 98; September 17, 1966.

Estelle Cherry Peisach. "Children's Comprehension of Teacher and Peer Speech," *Child Development* 36: 467–480; June 1965.

7. Here again we see the close relationships among different sets of questions. The matter of what-to-teach is actually intermeshed with that of how-to-teach and also with the question of whom-to-teach.

8. The readers may be interested in consulting such references as the following for further discussion of this point:

Milton Meux. "The Evaluating Operation in the Classroom," In Arno A. Bellack, Ed. *Theory and Research in Teaching.* New York: Bureau of Publications, Teachers College, Columbia University, 1963. Pp. 11–24.

Hilda Taba. *Curriculum Development.* New York: Harcourt, Brace & World, 1962.

Fred T. Wilhelms, Ed. *Evaluation as Feedback and Guide.* (1967 ASCD Yearbook) Washington: Association for Supervision and Curriculum Development, 1967.

9. Meaningful integration of all the information is a skill to be developed through practice. See, for example:

Robert L. Brackenbury. *Getting Down to Cases.* New York: G. P. Putnam's Sons, 1959.

James L. Hymes, Jr. *Behavior and Misbehavior.* Englewood Cliffs, N.J.: Prentice-Hall, 1955.

Bel Kaufman. *Up the Down Staircase.* New York: Avon Books, 1966. (N-130)

Sybil Marshall. *An Experiment in Education.* New York: Cambridge University Press, 1963.

Pauline Sears and Vivian Sherman. *In Pursuit of Self-Esteem.* Belmont, Calif.: Wadsworth Publishing, 1964.

Robert W. White. *Lives in Progress.* (2nd ed.) New York: Holt, Rinehart & Winston, 1966.

Chapter 2
PLANNING AND ORGANIZING LEARNING ACTIVITIES

INTRODUCTION

Although there is frequent disagreement regarding the form which planning should take, most teachers agree that good teaching is the result of careful planning. This planning includes specific daily lesson plans, long-range instructional plans, plans for organizing groups of children, and plans to help each child achieve his individual goals.

Student teachers often are astonished when they begin to realize how much time and effort are required to plan effectively for full-time teaching. They begin to understand that what children learn depends upon the quality of the children's experiences, a quality determined greatly by the kind of planning done by the classroom teacher.

Student teachers learn that no single approach to instructional planning will work for all teachers. Such factors as the teacher's mastery of subject matter, degree of confidence, and experience with children will dictate not only the type of plans used but the intensity of planning necessary for success in the classroom. Increased skill in instructional planning is one of the most important goals of the student teaching experience.

The readings included in this chapter have been selected to define, delineate, and clarify what planning is, and to offer suggestions on how to plan effectively. The three articles dealing with lesson plans contain numerous proposals for the classroom teacher. Robert Olberg and Hal Funk answer the question, "Why plan for teaching?" Kenneth and Helene Hoover attempt to clarify some basic relationships between unit planning and lesson planning and, as example, include a lesson plan which is consistent with unit teaching. John Etten deals specifically with lesson plans for the inner city, and evaluates four basic teaching methods in terms of practicality for use in the inner city.

Most teachers probably would agree that dividing material into logical teaching units is a good idea. Three readings in this section pertain to unit teaching. Raymond Muessig's article will be helpful to those student teachers who have been exposed to textbook teaching only. Walter McPhie offers suggestions for planning and executing a teaching unit. Jerrold Kemp stresses the necessity for stating specific behavioral objectives in planning and organizing the content for a teaching unit. These behavioral objectives serve as the basis for selecting learning activities, deciding on the most appropriate media to be used, and evaluating the learning experience.

Edward Ponder's article makes a plea for teachers to plan with each individual child by helping him in setting learning goals within his reach. JoAnn Strickland suggests that since parents play an important part in educating their children, it would be wise to have joint parent-teacher planning in considering beneficial experiences for each child. Bruce McLaren emphasizes the belief that since learning will result in changed behavior, the teacher should plan with behavioral objectives in mind. He suggests four steps which a teacher should follow in preparing behavioral objectives.

Kopple Freidman examines the need for curriculum guides and calls for an intelligent use of these resource materials by the teacher.

PLANNING FOR TEACHING

Robert J. Olberg and Hal D. Funk

Travelers who plan trips and teachers who plan lessons are confronted with many similar tasks. For example, both need to include long range goals and more immediate objectives. The plans of travelers and teachers should include methods for achieving the objectives, and supplies for facilitating the efficient utilization of their methods. Teachers and travelers also should assess their experiences in light of their goals to determine if they received full value for the time, effort, and money invested during their endeavors.

Careful planning gives purpose and direction to any venture. For travelers as well as teachers the success of the endeavor is related closely to the adequacy of the plans prior to its beginning.

OBJECTIVES

In planning a trip most travelers have a destination or objective in mind as well as points of interest which they do not want to miss as they are traveling. In education these destinations often are referred to as teaching objectives, goals, or aims. Regardless of the names attached to these teaching destinations, the fact remains that no teacher should begin instructing a group of children without specific objectives. These objectives indicate what learnings the teacher expects the children to derive from his instruction.

Objectives may be in the form of knowledge, concepts, behaviors, skills, attitudes, appreciations, or any combination of the above. All activities included in the lesson should be related directly or indirectly to the objectives of that instructional endeavor.

This article was written especially for this book.

METHODS

It is a rare traveler who has a destination in mind but gives no thought to the method he will use to reach his destination. Likewise, in teaching it would be foolish to have an objective in mind and give no thought to the methods which will be used to accomplish this objective.

Just as two travelers might choose different means to achieve the same traveling goal, so two teachers also might choose different techniques to achieve the same teaching objective. It also is probable that in different situations the same teacher may use entirely different methods to reach the same objective.

Techniques such as lecture, class discussion, group work, individual instruction, and field trips are employed frequently by teachers. The techniques an instructor chooses should depend on the objectives of the lesson, the teacher's abilities, the group of children to be taught, and any other variables which might affect the desired objectives.

MATERIALS

A traveler's plans would be incomplete if he gave no attention to the supplies needed for the journey. Similarly, a teacher should give careful attention to the materials he will need in teaching a lesson. Materials such as films, filmstrips, paints, pencils, paper, textbooks, supplementary books, maps, pictures, and countless other materials are usually at the teacher's disposal. The teacher must decide which of these tools or media are the most suitable for a specific lesson. He also must make the necessary arrangements to have these materials available when the lesson is to be taught.

ASSESSMENT

After travelers have completed their journeys, they evaluate the actual outcomes of their trips in light of their original objectives. On the basis of the evaluation they frequently begin planning for their next trip.

Teachers also must assess any instructional endeavor on the basis of their objectives for that lesson, the methods they chose to achieve those objectives, and the appropriateness of the materials used during their instruction. Future lessons are planned on the basis of this appraisal.

Techniques such as standardized- and teacher-made tests, classroom discussions, pupil evaluations, sociometric tests, and observation by the teacher all have been found to be valuable in assessing the effectiveness of a lesson. The technique of evaluation is frequently dependent upon the objective of the lesson.

Frequently when people travel they discover points of interest which they had not anticipated. To take advantage of these new interests it becomes necessary to make slight changes in the daily travel plans. It does not usually mean a complete change of the previously planned itinerary. These additional points of interest frequently enhance the original objectives of the trip.

In like manner, a student or an entire class which "takes side trips" in a study has not destroyed the general plan of the teacher. The educational benefits of the lesson probably have been increased by this deviation for the purpose of studying a topic of particular interest to the group. Instructional plans must be flexible enough to permit the class to pursue related activities that will contribute to worthwhile educational objectives.

LESSON PLANNING: KEY TO EFFECTIVE TEACHING

Kenneth H. and Helene M. Hoover

Planning, like map making, enables one to predict the future course of events. In essence, a plan is a blueprint—a plan of action. Although even the best laid plans sometimes go awry, they are necessary for effective living.

In like manner, teachers must plan classroom experiences. While few would deny the necessity of planning, there is considerable controversy with respect to its scope and nature. Indeed, methods specialists themselves differ about the essential scope of planning (5). Some feel that unit planning renders lesson planning almost unnecessary (3). Others would emphasize lesson over unit planning.

The purpose of this paper is to clarify certain basic relationships between unit and lesson planning and to illustrate one type of lesson plan which seems to be consistent with the unit approach to teaching.

BOTH UNIT AND LESSON PLANS NEEDED

Since the appearance of the Morrison unit some three or four decades ago, the importance of unit planning has been generally accepted (6). Although there is still some controversy over the nature of unit planning, most authorities seem to prefer the "basic theme or concept" approach (2), (4). This approach is seen as an effective means of giving unity or structure to learning (1). When units are built around basic themes or concepts, they provide a basis for the formulation of related *problems* (7). At this point the student may become actively involved in pursuing the solution of a problem appropriate to his motives, interests, and abilities.

In the foregoing paragraph we advanced from general to specific activities of teaching. In like manner, the effective teacher must move from unit to lesson planning. *The lesson plan is an expanded portion of a unit plan.* It represents a more or less detailed analysis of a particular *activity* suggested in the unit plan. To illustrate: Let us suppose that in a world history class

Reprinted from *The Clearing House*, 42:41–44 (September, 1967), by permission of authors and publisher.

we have developed a unit around the central theme, "Population Pressures." (Let us assume our text materials focus upon problems of Asia.) As one related topic the class (or the teacher) might suggest an exploration of our relationships with Communist China. Formulated as a problem of policy appropriate for class exploration and analysis, a problem could be stated as follows: *What steps should the United States take to improve diplomatic relationships with Communist China?* (5:112–13) Let us assume that the teacher decides to handle this particular problem by means of a class discussion.

Thus far, in our illustration, the unit plan has sufficed. From this point forward, however, the teacher must expand each selected activity into more detailed lesson plans. The mere title of a class discussion is simply not a sufficient basis for conducting one! Careful planning, including "pump-priming" questions, is essential. Instead of a *daily* lesson plan (a different plan for each class period), as was common prior to the development of the teaching unit, the same plan may carry one through for two, three, or more class periods. In the problem illustrated, it is likely that two or three class periods would be necessary for a thorough analysis. Likewise, a panel discussion and its follow-through discussion usually requires at least two class periods. There are times when the nature of an activity may render a *formal* lesson plan unnecessary. One may not need a special plan when the day's schedule calls for oral reports, studying reference materials, or engaging in collateral reading activities.

The particular nature of a lesson plan will be determined by the type of activity involved. Each class activity usually necessitates a different plan as well as a different type of plan. The nature of the activity also will influence its length. There are additional factors, however, that affect the length of a plan. These will include the particular teacher involved (some more experienced teachers need less detailed plans than beginning teachers), the general nature of the course, and the administrative policies of the school.

AN ILLUSTRATED LESSON PLAN

Although it is quite true that each teacher must personally evolve his own particular approach to lesson planning, there are certain basic essentials that should be included in most plans. Two common deficiencies are often apparent: (1) Inadequately stated goals and (2) the omission of certain basic class activity steps. (The latter is frequently apparent in class discussion experiences.) We hope that the following lesson plan will clarify the issue.

WORLD HISTORY (8)

Unit: Population Pressures
Method: Class Discussion
Problem: What steps should the United States take to improve diplomatic relationships with Communist China?

Goals: After this lesson the student should have furthered his understanding of the influence of population pressures upon our diplomatic relations with Communist China, as evidenced by:

1. His contributions and questions posed during the discussion.
2. His ability to draw conclusions during a follow-through discussion of the problem.

Lesson Approach: Yesterday we saw a movie which summarized the foreign relations of Communist China up to 1949. What were some of the major reasons for the tension that existed?

What is hate? How is it propagated? What purposes does it serve? What fundamental bases of hate were implied?

What techniques are being employed in Communist China today which suggest a similar campaign is being waged against the United States?

Why do "hungry nations" sometimes fall prey to Communism? What are our best defenses against their propaganda?

What historical conditions have implanted the seeds of distrust among the Chinese?

What bases for distrust exist in Southeast Asian nations? (Vietnam, for example.)

Lesson Development:

I. *Analysis of the Problem*

1. What other things happening in Communist China and America suggest to you that we need better relations?
2. What are some of the causes which led to the present tension?
3. Why is it crucial that we establish better relations?
4. What might be some effects if we do not establish better relations?
5. Do you feel that China's aggressive attitude is likely to persist? Why or why not?
6. How does the problem relate to population pressures? Do other Asiatic nations have similar problems? If so, how are they solving them?
7. What have the Chinese done in the past to alleviate food shortages? How effective have these techniques been?
8. What conditions are similar (and different) in the world today?

II. *Establishment of the Hypotheses*

Now in view of our discussion, WHAT STEPS SHOULD THE UNITED STATES TAKE TO IMPROVE DIPLOMATIC RELATIONSHIPS WITH COMMUNIST CHINA?

Possible solutions (suggestive only):

1. Recognize China in the United Nations.
2. De-escalate the air war in North Vietnam.
3. Withdraw support of Nationalist China in the United Nations.

4. Get out of Southeast Asia.

5. Embark upon a regional assistance and development program.

What might be some advantages and disadvantages of each of these solutions?

Summary: We have discussed one of the hottest problems facing the United States today. We know that the solutions we have developed can not be realized by the direct action of this class. But we do know that indirectly, through intelligent conversation with our parents who are voters, we can help choose those governmental officials who feel much the same as we do. We are also preparing ourselves to be intelligent citizens and policy makers of the future.

Let us restate some major ideas or concepts which seem to have emerged as a consequence of this discussion. (Suggestive only.)

1. The present conflict is indirectly related to inadequate food supplies and overpopulation pressures.

2. Decisions relative to one aspect of the problem will influence many other areas.

3. Asiatic mistrust of foreigners has a historical basis.

CONCLUSION

The foregoing plan contains the basic essentials of any fundamental lesson plan: goals, motivation (lesson approach), major activities (lesson development), and summary. In addition, it contains essentials of a problem-solving class discussion. The first portion of the lesson development, analysis of the problem, deals with definition of terms, cause and effect relationships, and so on. It is in this phase of the lesson that the basic historical facts will be introduced and evaluated—in terms of the problem being discussed. Normally some two thirds or three fourths of the discussion time will focus upon this phase of the experience. The latter part of the lesson development, called establishment of the hypotheses, focuses directly upon the problem. It is designed to lead the student from the facts of the situation to a plan of action for solving the problem.

Teachers who neglect formal planning all too often omit the hypothesis phase of class discussion. This is particularly unfortunate since, without this phase of the discussion, such an experience is of minimal value. The major class purpose is not reached.

The questions posed in the plan serve as guidelines only. They are asked only if and when they are needed. They also serve to guide the teacher as he moves from one phase of discussion to another. An experienced teacher, of course, will tend to have fewer questions in his plan than will an inexperienced teacher. It is imperative, nevertheless, that all teachers pose at least a few such questions for each of the discussion phases described.

Many teachers apparently fail to realize that each major class activity demands a different type of lesson plan, structured *within* the framework of the basic essentials described. Thus the lesson development phase of a problem handled with the sociodramatic technique will differ markedly from that of a review lesson, and so on (9).

Finally, we remind the reader that the foregoing lesson illustration is merely one of many approaches to planning. There is evidence, however, that in too many cases such a generalization has been used as a "straw man" to avoid adequate planning. Unit and lesson planning take time—sometimes more time than the beginning teacher has available. Nevertheless, it pays high dividends in increased learning for boys and girls. In essence, planning is a *dress rehearsal* for the real thing. It forces a teacher to think through his task in advance of the experience.

REFERENCES

1. Bruner, Jerome S., *The Process of Education* (Cambridge, Mass.: Harvard University Press), 1960.
2. Chase, John B. and James L. Howard, "Changing Concepts of Unit Teaching," *High School Journal,* Vol. 47, No. 4 (February 1964), pp. 180–187.
3. Grambs, Jean D. and others, *Modern Methods in Secondary Schools,* Rev. Ed. (N.Y.: Holt, Rinehart and Winston, Inc.), 1958.
4. Hennis, R. Sterling, Jr., "A Broad Unit Approach to Literature," *High School Journal,* Vol. 45, No. 5 (February 1962), pp. 201–207.
5. Hoover, Kenneth H., *Learning and Teaching in the Secondary School* (Boston: Allyn and Bacon, Inc.), 1964.
6. Morrison, Henry C., *The Practice of Teaching in the Secondary School* (Chicago: University of Chicago Press), 1931.
7. For an excellent treatment of this process, the reader is referred to John B. Chase and James L. Howard, "Changing Concepts of Unit Teaching," *High School Journal,* Vol. 47, No. 4 (February 1964), pp. 180–187.
8. This plan is adapted from one submitted to the writer by Mr. Dennis Gibbons, a college student.
9. Other lesson illustrations can be found in a methods book prepared by the writer, *Learning and Teaching in the Secondary School* (Boston: Allyn & Bacon, Inc.), 1964.

LESSON PLANNING FOR THE INNER CITY

John F. Etten

Although inexperienced in teaching, a graduate from a teacher training institution may have had considerable practice in writing lesson plans. His student teaching experience may have been in a middle-class neighborhood and if so, his lesson plans have been directed toward teaching middle class students. Picture his frustration when he faces an assignment to a school in the inner city! His lesson plans may be a work of art. The students he is to

Reprinted from *Education,* 87:347–353 (February, 1967), by permission of author and publisher, The Bobbs-Merrill Company, Inc.

teach, however, do not work into the theoretical plans. On the first day, he is discouraged, disappointed, and unhappy in his new surroundings. He may blame himself for his failure to keep order in the class or he may blame the college professors who prepared him for his teaching career.

This failure is not a criticism of the beginning teacher or of the teacher training institution from which he graduated. Rather, it is hoped that by analyzing the following steps toward realistic methods of lesson planning, the beginning teacher will come to realize that with a succinct appraisal of the problem, he will be able to create successful plans for inner-city classrooms of the megalopolis.

However, before the beginning teacher can write a lesson plan, he must ask himself two questions:

1. What do children in the inner-city schools need to make learning meaningful and successful?

2. Where does the teacher in the inner city start in the planning of a rewarding learning experience?

In the first place, the teacher decides which teaching approaches he is going to use. Many factors are involved in selecting the best methods of teaching in the inner city. Let us examine four methods and evaluate each one as to the practicality of its use in the inner city. As the new teacher gains experience, he will modify and adapt these and other methods as each individual class requires.

THE LECTURE

The lecture has very little value to beginning teachers in the inner city because they generally do not have the acceptance of the class on the topic under discussion. In other words, if a beginning teacher lectures about the way an astronaut prepares for a flight in space, the class will probably dissociate the young teacher with the actual success of the astronaut in this accomplishment. If, however, the beginning teacher is able to bring a tape recording of the astronaut's voice or a film of the astronaut going through his briefing activities before flight, then the realism of the situation arouses interest and the attention of the group is held by the real-life materials.

Often the inner-city teacher will call upon successful men and women of the community who have been products of the local community area to visit the school and speak or demonstrate on topics of concern to the students. The reality of seeing a successful citizen as "one of their own" offers a big lift to pupils and a lecture by someone with whom they can identify is often accepted very easily. It has even been worthwhile to have a person who "went wrong" return to school to show the error of his ways and caution pupils *not* to follow in his footsteps.

The traditional lecture method will probably be less successful for beginning teachers in the inner city than anywhere else in the megalopolis and is best used sparingly.

THE RECITATION

The recitation method or the "assign-study-recite-test" method has been a standard method of planning for many years and with few exceptions, is utilized by most teachers today. Briefly, it consists of a teacher giving the assignment to the class, followed by a period of study. The study time may be during the scheduled class period or it may be a homework study plan. Following the study period, the pupils discuss the assignment with the teacher and the teacher asks questions of the pupils. Lastly, the test phase of this method covers the review of the assignment and concepts are evaluated.

This type of planning obviously leans heavily on the textbook as the focal point of the lesson. Facts, rules, phrases, and definitions are of utmost importance and drilling subject matter into the students seems to be the desired end.

The inner-city classroom is not the place for the assign-study-recite-test method because, in order to be successful, pupils need interests and purposes that fit in with the subject being taught. Because it does not capture the attention of the pupils, it fails as a vehicle for learning. If, however, children can adapt themselves to the method and if it is used within limitations, it can be a useful *tool* for the beginning teacher.

"SEATWORK"

All beginning teachers are going to find that planning for multiple activities at the same time is one of the most difficult tasks of teaching. The teacher must be able to have two or more groups of students working on different activities if he is to keep the class interested, and make some provision for the individual differences in achievement identified in the pupils.

One successful way in which this group work can be initiated is by incorporating, at spaced intervals, meaningful "seatwork."

Seatwork is class work that is pursued by students at their desks. The seatwork focuses attention on related learnings to the teaching unit underway and is realistically correlated with the objectives of the unit. Seatwork is not "busy work," for there is no place for "busy work" in the classroom. When students mark time by writing a sentence twenty-five times so that the teacher can devote time in the lesson plan for an oral activity with another group, the children writing the assignment are wasting valuable class time which could be spent on profitable, educationally enriching experiences.

Examples of successful seatwork have been programed worksheets, teacher improvised, which reinforce prior learning or lead to new learnings which can be understood by pupils on an independent basis. Seatwork of this type does have a vital role in the lesson plan and it is especially well-suited for inner-city children. It can accomplish at least the following purposes:

1. Aid in providing for individual differences.
2. Aid in the establishment of good classroom management (discipline).

3. Aid in freeing the teacher from directed observation of the total class in order to go from desk to desk, helping individuals with their work.

4. Aid in offering a new type of approach to the learner as a vehicle of instruction, thus creating an added interest in the development of the unit under study.

Seatwork, properly prepared, augments the daily plan and is one of the most vital tools beginning teachers can utilize in planning lessons for their classes in the inner city.

THE PUPIL EXPERIENCES METHOD

It has been said that drawing upon pupil experiences for the study of a desired subject is fragmentary and piecemeal. The teacher allows the class to play leapfrog with discussions and contributions to the subject being discussed. The free association of experiences and the scattered facts and concepts brought forth seem to leave children without a central thought at the close of each period. There seem to be no goals and the lesson plan seems disjointed and lacking purpose.

Nevertheless, the beginning teacher in the inner city may wish to employ this method to a degree, because by permitting peripheral contributions from pupils on the subject to be discussed, children are allowed to express themselves. This pupil expression is vital to the inner-city teacher. For the beginning teacher, the motivation created by this method acts as a powerful stimulant for an inattentive class. The inattentive student responds when given an opportunity to express his personal thoughts. The child makes a personal identification with the subject, and the teacher has passed the biggest hurdle of teaching—proper motivation.

Caution should be exercised in the work that follows this free association of responses, because the child may think that accumulation of facts or concepts without the organization of a complete plan or understanding is acceptable.

After sufficient interest has been established, the teacher should move directly into the pre-planned lesson formulated for the day.

Once the choice of method and approach are established in the pre-planning stage, the teacher is ready to construct the actual lesson plan. Teachers who have had little experience in teaching will find it desirable to plan their work so that every lesson will occupy a logical place in a well-conceived teaching unit.

To accomplish this, two plans will have to be made: the long-range unit plan and the daily lesson plan. The unit plan considers the concepts to be learned over a period of from two to four weeks and is formulated in advance of the daily plans. All lesson plans should be detailed enough to show the activities and instructional materials to be used, and at the same time attention must be focused on the outcomes one hopes to achieve. The more specific the plan is, the more efficient it will be.

VARYING THE LESSON PLAN

Let us look at a lesson plan outline and see what a teacher might do with it to facilitate instruction on three different levels to accommodate the slow learner, the average learner, and the more rapid learner. Let us divide the plan into four broad topics:

1. Daily Objectives
2. Subject Matter Materials
3. Work Period Activities
4. Evaluation.

1. The *objectives* are specific goals or tasks to be accomplished each day. These objectives are achievable in terms of the children being taught. The student backgrounds, abilities, strengths, and weaknesses are all reflected in the pre-planning estimates of the teacher. The child who is a remedial reader will fulfill specific objectives tailored for his special needs. The average and advanced learners will have objectives which may be the same in kind, but different in degree.

For example, "Developing an understanding of the usefulness of simple weather instruments," might be a specific daily objective in teaching a unit on *Atmosphere Around Us*. Once this objective has been realized, the students should understand the importance of weather instruments, e.g., anemometer, barometer, wind gauge, rain gauge, hygrometer, thermometer. The slow learner should be able to grasp the names of instruments and tell what they do in simple terms. The average and advanced learners should be able to read, write, and discuss the applications of these instruments on weather forecasting and develop insights into phenomena using scientific instrumentation for navigational purposes, predictability, and advanced applications of weather instruments of meteorology.

Since class periods in the elementary school are usually single period sessions of 30 to 45 minutes duration, the teacher must exercise good judgment in selecting daily objectives that are attainable within the restrictions of the time schedule which has been established.

The main consideration with daily objectives in lesson planning is to remember that *all* the children must be capable of realizing the objectives set forth if they have exerted normal efforts.

2. The second topic in the outline is *subject matter materials*. Here the teacher lists the materials of instruction that will be the vehicle through which the daily objectives are borne. They are the textbooks, the maps, globes, visuals, mockups, filmstrips, pamphlets, etc., that provide the information and assistance to accomplish the objectives of the day.

In the inner city, the subject matter materials must be plentiful and scaled in interest and ability level on a programed basis to attract the child who might have little background in subject matter. Each teacher should act as a clearing house of information and select appropriate instructional materials from as many sources as possible to provide the class with a variety of learning aids.

3. The third area of the lesson plan outline is the *work period activities* section. This segment of the lesson plan is important because it contains an analysis of the teaching activities planned by the teacher to realize effectively the stated objectives. Here again, the beginning teacher must provide for individual differences in learning by differentiating assignments and procedures to accommodate *all* the children. Take for example, the slow learner in arithmetic who finds success with simple computations, adding and subtracting coins and currency in our money system. The average learner has work period activities designed to provide him opportunity to add numbers in the base five or multiplying by base two.

4. The fourth and last topic in the lesson plan outline is the *evaluation* section. Here, the teacher determines whether or not he has accomplished the daily objectives and through use of available instruments of measure determines his degree of success.

For example, he may decide to employ a review, short outline or quiz to assess the accomplishments of the daily plan. He may decide to place the students in a practical exercise and observe their reactions in terms of the concepts developed in that particular lesson. A teacher who has attempted to describe the process by which plants make their food may elect to have students come forward to the science demonstration table and describe what happens when chlorophyll, carbon dioxide, and water associate in the presence of sunlight. If the students demonstrate that this association is a chemical change called "photosynthesis" and that it is the process by which plants make their food, then the teacher can give the students and himself an "A."

In summary, an example of a lesson plan done by a beginning teacher in the inner city follows. It has proved effective for the neophyte who used it and it hopefully incorporates the basic tenets of the exposition given in the preceding pages.

DAILY LESSON PLAN OUTLINE
Science—Fourth Grade
Subject: Inclined Planes

I. Daily Objective
   To demonstrate how an inclined plane helps us to do work
II. Concepts to be covered:
   A. Definition (on board): An inclined plane is a sloping or slanting flat surface.
   B. Less energy is needed to pull a weight up an inclined plane than to lift it straight up, but the load must be moved a greater distance up the incline.
   C. The longer the inclined plane, the easier it is to lift a load.
   D. More force is required to lift an object up a short, steep incline than is required to lift the same object up a long gradual incline.

III. Subject Matter Materials
   A. Text: D.C. Heath Science Series
   B. Pictures of inclined planes in use have been collected by the teacher. Pupils will be asked to start a collection for the Bulletin Board Committee.
   C. Wooden board
   D. Several books
   E. Object to be used as weight (large wooden block)
   F. Cardboard
   G. Rubber bands
   H. String
   I. Paper clips
   J. Quarters or metal weights (drapery weights may be used)
   K. Commercial scale
IV. Work Period Activities
   A. Teacher makes an inclined plane in the classroom, using a smooth board several feet long and a stack of books.
   B. Teacher and students (in groups of four) construct spring scales by using a piece of cardboard, rubber band, string, paper clips and quarters. Tape the quarters in equal groups, hang from the scale and make a mark as each group is added.
   C. Use the scale to weigh the object as it hangs freely.
   D. Weigh the object as it is being pulled up the inclined plane. Note the difference, that less force is required to lift up an incline than straight up.
   E. Let children use commercial scale to weigh other objects.
      1. How do people and materials get aboard a ship or an airplane?
      2. How are heavy packages loaded into a truck?
      3. Have you ever walked up a board, maybe when a sidewalk is being repaired?
      4. Is a stairway an inclined plane?
      5. Is a step ladder an inclined plane?
      6. Is the ramp to an expressway an inclined plane?
V. Evaluation
   A. Teacher:
      1. Was I able to hold the attention of most of the children?
      2. Were my materials organized well in advance?
      3. Did I assign at least one mature child to each group of four?
      4. Did the students enjoy the lesson? Was their response enthusiastic?
   B. Student:
      1. Did the children participate actively?
      2. Was each group able to construct a spring scale?
      3. Were the students able to collect pictures of inclined planes?
      4. Were they able to make generalizations from the material covered in class?
VI. Additional Resources
   A. Films:
      Simple Machines: Inclined Planes, Coronet Instructional Films (to be used to introduce this lesson, or on the following day to reinforce the material)

B. Filmstrips
   Simple Machines (Encyclopaedia Britannica)
   Simple Machines, Jam Handy Organization
   Simple Machines Make Work Easier, McGraw-Hill Publishing Co., Inc.

BRIDGING THE GAP BETWEEN TEXTBOOK TEACHING AND UNIT TEACHING

Raymond H. Muessig

One of the perennial problems in the history of mankind is the difference which has often existed between the ideal and the real, the gap between theory and practice, or the dichotomy between what is said and what is done. The stereotypic view of a politician includes in it the assumption that the campaign promises made before election and the activities engaged in after the person has taken over the duties of the office may be widely separated or even unrelated. Kneeling before his beloved, the young suitor promises the object of his affection the moon, the stars, castles, furs, and jewels. Imagine the young lady's disillusionment a few years after their marriage when she is still cooking over a leaky gas stove, waiting for more hot water so she can finish washing the dishes, and doing the family laundry by hand in a set tub in the basement! In a more serious vein, the "Sunday Christian" may be a long way from the Sermon on the Mount when he composes an advertisement for a forthcoming "bargain" sale in a department store.

Countless articles in professional education journals have discussed the cultural lag which exists between rather widely accepted educational theories and actual practices in classrooms. Perhaps there is no more profound or troublesome breach than the one that exists between the theory of unit teaching so widely espoused in the social studies and other content areas and the highly structured, constricting, uncreative use of textbooks which one may observe in so many social studies classrooms. Almost four decades have elapsed since Professor Henry C. Morrison championed an early unit plan which was one of the forerunners of today's unit method, yet many teachers still fall short of mastery of this procedure—let alone more advanced practices like the problems approach.

Simply deploring this condition does little good. Exhorting teachers to throw down their textbook crutches and run to the unit seems to have had a negligible impact. Giving in to the dead weight and long-standing tradition of the single textbook is a solution which might appeal to a substantial num-

Reprinted from *The Social Studies,* 54:43–47 (February, 1963), by permission of author and publisher.

ber of teachers, but this is the coward's way out and would mean denying our students the best of which our profession is capable.

Just as the skillful teacher "begins where the students are" in their developmental levels and their academic mastery, it is only reasonable to assume that the teacher has to walk before he can run, master some basic methods before attempting more complex ones, and move from the approaches where he feels secure to those where he feels less secure.

The approach which I am going to outline very briefly is not a panacea. It must be considered as tentative, subject to error, open to revision and improvement. As a matter of fact it is proposed as a *temporary* measure to aid teachers in getting a feeling for unit teaching. Once this feeling has been grasped, I hope that this idea will be discarded and new operational levels sought. I worked out this procedure initially to help a group of experienced teachers, used to single textbook teaching, move into unit work. They reported that the idea "worked." Whether this suggestion is good, right, new, or old, it is at least "pragmatic."

The only task which remains before I attempt an explanation of this system for bridging the gap between textbook teaching and unit teaching is a definition of terms. What do I mean by "textbook" and "unit" teaching as I perceive them? I hope that I am not creating two "straw men" just for the sake of contrast, but I see a rather significant difference in these two methods and in their underlying philosophies.

Textbook-centered teaching has a medieval heritage. The teacher who could secure a book or commit the contents of a manuscript to memory was "in business." The text was a source of authority, often unquestioned and unchallenged. The more faithfully the learner could return its contents to his teacher, the more approbation he earned. This approach, therefore, has been with us a long time. To many it seems to have the same kind of familiarity as a well-worn smoking jacket. There are many allies in the textbook-centered camp including husky bruisers like Status Quo, Custom, Mental Discipline, and Apathy. The facts contained in the single source have some kind of magical intrinsic value—worthy in and of themselves. The assign-study-recite-test procedure is generally followed. The teacher generally originates, directs, and passes judgment upon all learning activity. Only those evaluation techniques which attempt to assess the degree to which the names, dates, places, and events have been "learned" are employed. Motivation is provided by the teacher by way of grades and other extrinsic rewards. The teacher's main aim in life seems to be "covering the text." More and more facts accumulate as research continues over the years and as man's stay on earth is extended; textbooks get larger; and it gets harder and harder for the teacher to reach first Page 523, then Page 678, and later Page 751 by the end of the year. A teacher's life is further complicated by parents who can conceive of no other approach and who believe in "fundamental" learning void of "fads and frills," by administrators who insist that various kinds of standardized tests be given to all groups as a means of comparing teachers or schools, by students who either cannot read the text or are bored by it, and by the fact that his courses seem to be more dull and drab each year they are repeated.

This is not to say that the use of a textbook is wrong. That assumption would be absurd. The textbook can be one of the finest resources available to a class and a teacher. Textbooks are often written by persons who are well qualified both as scholars and teachers. Texts may be well documented and illustrated and may even be graded in an endeavor to meet some of the reading problems. They may even contain suggestions for meaningful activities which can enhance learning. The problem is, however, that too many teachers rely exclusively upon the text and never move out to other green pastures like additional books containing related but varied material and written at different reading levels, pamphlets and booklets, newspapers and magazines, films and filmstrips, recordings, field trips, resource persons, community studies, independent research, *ad infinitum*.

Unit teaching in a more simplified form is not always a radical departure from the most enlightened textbook teaching, nor is it any kind of a final answer; but it does attempt to correct many of the shortcomings of narrowly conceived textbook-centered methodology. Unit teaching at its best can be a thing of beauty, however, and has some unique properties which distinguish it from its more mundane cousin, the textbook approach. Unit teaching attempts to integrate, combine, coordinate, or articulate understandings, skills, attitudes, and appreciations around large significant topics. It seeks wholeness rather than fragmentation, clusters of ideas and data rather than isolated particles, more of a montage than a series of single snapshots taken one by one. The unit approach does not avoid facts, but it does try to build facts into concepts and generalizations which may have more meaning, may be transferable in more situations, and may be more lasting. This method recognizes that any single source of information, however good it may be, imposes unnecessary limitations upon the class and the teacher. Pupil-teacher planning in the drafting of objectives, search for materials, selection of methods of study, and development of evaluative processes is more common. Actual interests, needs, aspirations, and problems of students are tapped and kept in mind, and greater student involvement and identification with objectives of learning tends to upstage intrinsic rather than extrinsic motivation. The unit may deal with material similar in content to that which the textbook approach gives its allegiance, but there is no pressure to cover any given text. Unit teaching encourages creative, independent, critical thought rather than memorization for its own sake. It relies on a variety of evaluation techniques in addition to the typical standardized and teacher-made tests. We could go on, but the basic thing, it seems to me, is that the unit teacher is after more *meaning* in what goes on in a classroom.

I believe that one of the reasons the unit approach has not found its way into more social studies classes is that the distance from basic textbook teaching to full-blown unit teaching is too great to travel all at once. I propose that the teacher already used to the text begin there. The first step is to make the most of the textbook, to get more meaning out of it, to emphasize relatedness. Later, a few added resources may be brought in and some activities with a "unit flavor" blended in. Still later, a simple unit could be worked out with the students, and so on until a complete unit approach is attempted in the spring.

This article begins with and stops at the first stage of this process—using the text as a more unified teaching tool. The steps for the procedure are outlined below:

1. Let us assume for the sake of this illustration that it is a few weeks before the start of the school year. Taking the basic textbook for the course, the teacher might begin by writing the chapter titles on separate 3 x 5 cards. It is sometimes useful to jot down a few of the sub-topics under the chapter title just to have a reminder of some of the basic things included in the chapter. The cards should be separated into several stacks by priority. Some chapters which the teacher considers to be of primary importance will fall into the "essential" pile; others of secondary importance will fall into the "helpful" stack; and still others which may have doubtful value for a particular class would go into a "possible," "hold," or "delete" group. (Realizing that many textbooks try to be all things to all people, the teacher is already beginning a discrimination process by seeking significant aspects of the course for his point of focus.)

2. Next, the teacher works out a rough approximation of the number of teaching weeks in the school year. His purpose for doing this is not to see how much material—regardless of its importance—he can cram into the course but to work out *areas of emphasis* or "unit" topics. Now he roughly divides the total number of weeks into blocks of approximately five weeks. Later, as actual "units" emerge they may vary from three to six weeks in length depending on the teacher's objectives, the interest of the class, and other factors. In a typical school year, there would be from six to eight of these textbook units. Glancing quickly at the 3 x 5 cards in the "helpful" stack and thumbing more carefully through those in the "essential" pile, the teacher tries to list from six to eight over-all problems, topics, or content areas around which the units can be constructed.

3. The remainder of the 3 x 5 cards in the top priority group, probably most of the cards of secondary importance, and perhaps even a few of the cards in the third questionable pile may now be separated under the basic unit copies. This unit distribution may or may not follow the organization of the textbook. The important thing is whether the over-all topics make sense to the teacher and the students. The order of the unit topics can be arranged chronologically, logically, psychologically, or developmentally according to the teacher's perception of the nature of the class and the content discipline. The first unit might be so placed because it is fundamental or foundational in its content, interest arousing, more concrete or understandable, or for some other reason.

4. Now the teacher is ready to build the first of the units. He takes the 3 x 5 cards in the group assigned to the initial topic and notes the chapters they represent. (Each unit would include from about three to six chapters in the typical social studies text.) It is at this point that a rather tedious, but rewarding, process begins. The teacher carefully reads only those chapters which will be used for the first unit. On fresh, additional 3 x 5 cards he writes down the *crucial, basic* facts contained in each chapter, using one card for each factual statement. Just "any old facts" will not do! These must be facts with lasting importance, facts which will lead to significant understandings, attitudes, and appreciations. Altogether, though it is not possible to assign a magic number, the teacher might have from one hundred to two hundred essential facts.

5. The "fact" cards are now separated into three basic piles, "understandings," "attitudes," and "appreciations." The "understandings" pile will probably be the largest by far.

6. The cards in the "understandings" pile are again subdivided. The teacher tries to find groups of facts which support a given concept. A concept is a class of related information, a "basket" which holds a cluster of facts and gives them real meaning. A given unit might contain from ten to twenty concepts each of which would be supported by from five to ten basic facts which "add up to something." One last refinement is necessary, however, to complete the treatment of "understandings." This is the formulation of from one generalization up to five generalizations. A generalization is the interrelationship of two or more concepts and should emerge quite naturally when the teacher analyzes the concepts already developed. One of the most important goals in social studies education is the ability to generalize, to fit particulars into a configuration, to draw inferences from data, or to perceive applications. The generalization, therefore, is the cognitive capstone of the unit. It is the vein of gold which is the product of all of the digging which the students and the teacher do throughout the unit.

7. A single unit may lead to only one or two important attitudes and appreciations. The "attitude" pile may contain only two or three concept cards and the group of fact cards which buttress the concepts, and a similar situation usually exists with the "appreciation" pile. Attitudes and appreciations are mixtures of both facts and feelings, cognitive and emotive elements. They carry the values, predispositions, and aesthetic elements of the unit.

8. The teacher is now at the "blueprint" stage of building a textbook-oriented unit. He takes a large piece of butcher paper and divides it into three columns. At the top and center of each of the three columns he prints "Content," "Activities," and "Evaluation" from left to right, respectively.

9. In the "Content" column the teacher prints a complete structural outline of the material he has gathered on the 3 x 5 cards. A Roman numeral is assigned to each generalization, attitude, and appreciation. Capital letters are

given to supporting concepts which go under each generalization, attitude, and appreciation. Arabic numbers are assigned to the facts which undergird their respective concepts. Now the teacher can "see" what he is after, where he is going, what he wants to build. This view can be quite satisfying, for it gives a textbook teacher a sense of purpose which he may have missed before.

10. In the "Activities" column the teacher prints *over-all activities* which will serve the purposes and content of the unit like reading from the text, group discussion, etc. and *specific activities* like student panels, individual student papers, etc. which match up on a one-to-one basis with particular generalizations, attitudes, and appreciations or individual concepts which support them. Later, these more traditional activities may be augmented with procedures typical of a full-blown unit approach. The teacher could begin this expansion process on the second unit by having students write for free and inexpensive materials, by ordering several films, by forming a few research committees, by securing a resource person, etc.

11. In the "Evaluation" column the teacher would again list both general and specific procedures for assessing student growth on the unit as a whole and on given generalizations, attitudes, appreciations, or underlying concepts. During the first trial "unit" the teacher might be contented with just teacher-made essay tests, multiple choice tests, etc. In later units, the teacher may include inventories, check lists, observation, open-ended procedures, etc.

12. The final step in the process is for the teacher to ditto copies of the "unit" for all of the students. A cover with a "catchy" title and a clever illustration can help a great deal to interest the students. The teacher should write a one paragraph over-view of the nature of the unit to secure student involvement. A group of basic unit objectives might be listed. This time they will be the teacher's, but later they will come out of class discussion. Also included would be a copy of the teacher's outline of content, activities, and evaluation so the students have a "preview of coming attractions." The first dittoed unit might contain daily assignments with some options for differences in students' interests and capacities. Students will read selectively from the text and use it as a genuine resource. Additional enrichment activities could be suggested too. Culminating, or wrap-up activities might be planned by the students themselves after they have a feeling for this approach. This would also initiate some pupil-teacher planning. Finally, if the teacher has caught the spirit by now, the unit might have a brief bibliography for the students so they could start getting in the habit of consulting other sources.

This has been an attempt to suggest a procedure by which teachers in secondary social studies could bridge the gap between textbook-centered teaching and unit teaching. The "bridge" suggested probably bears a closer resemblance to a log dropped across a creek than a sleek, steel suspension bridge, but it is a beginning. The rest of the construction task is up to the dedicated teacher who wants to do more for the wonderful, unique, challenging young people who walk through his door.

THE TEACHING UNIT:
WHAT MAKES IT TICK?

Walter E. McPhie

Anyone who has completed a teacher preparation program at some university or teachers college has heard the word *unit*—and heard it often. It may be a teaching technique or method to some, a part of curriculum structure to others, or a combination of both to still others, but one thing is clear: the word itself is no stranger in the teaching profession.

Most of the literature on units in teaching is supportive. It is a rare methods text for either secondary or elementary school teachers that does not promote, either openly or by implication, teaching with units. It is championed as the *modern* way of teaching, the most effective method of curriculum arrangement.

Occasionally in the professional literature a questioning voice is heard which suggests that another look at the basic assumptions about unit teaching is needed. Criticism, however, is more often heard from practitioners in the field, new and experienced teachers who honestly and sincerely prefer to teach on a day-to-day basis. To some of the critics, developing units of study is "busy work," a nonsensical submission to the whimsical desires of people in ivory towers who are too far removed from reality. To others, unit teaching is still a hazy concept; these people are not really sure what a teaching unit is. In their eyes the literature seems to be contradictory, professors of education do not appear to be in full accord on the matter, and discussions with colleagues shed little additional light. For this group of teachers, unit teaching is not clearly enough defined to be seriously considered as an alternative to already established daily routine.

What is a "unit"? Perhaps the easiest way to define a unit of teaching is to draw back and look at the word in other contexts. For example, a busy mother, while shopping in a local department store, sees a skirt-blouse combination on sale which would just fit her daughter. She really likes the skirt but does not care for the blouse.

"How much would it cost if I just bought the skirt?" she inquires.

"I'm sorry," replies the clerk, "but we must sell this set as a *unit*."

Some people who become a little panic-stricken at the thought of being forced into using teaching units would not give a second thought to the explanation given by the clerk. They would immediately understand that for some reason the composite parts of the skirt-blouse set belong together as a whole entity and that to use them otherwise would be disadvantageous.

Reprinted from *The Clearing House*, 38:70–73 (October, 1963), by permission of author and publisher.

Other examples of the word *unit* could be given which would demonstrate the general use of the term (automobile mechanics speak of the various units in the complex make-up of their machines; refrigerator and radio repairmen often refer to units in their work; and so on). Certain common elements emerge from these examples, which should help to clarify the meaning of the term *unit* as it applies to teaching. First, there is a single mass or entity characteristic which is often composed of minor parts. Second, there appears to be some logical reason for the kind and/or size of the mass or entity and this reason most often is based on function or purpose. Therefore, a unit of teaching would be a single mass or quantity of subject matter (concepts, skills, symbols, and so forth) which for some logical reason appears to belong together or to form some reasonable single entity. Units of teaching involving *The American Revolutionary Period, Punctuation,* or *The Back-Stroke in Swimming* serve as good examples. In each case smaller bits and pieces of information are grouped together into a larger, meaningful mass of subject matter which can be identified easily as an entity and which can be referred to logically as a *unit.* Such a process is no more complex or confusing than seeing a skirt and blouse kept together for a given reason.

Why teach with units? Having established that the word *unit* is neither awesome nor difficult to understand in teaching or any other context, there still remains the task of demonstrating the advisability of using such an approach. Once again, it may prove helpful if activities in life other than teaching are examined first.

For example, consider the businessman who must drive from Salt Lake City to attend a conference in San Francisco. If asked where he is going he will respond unhesitatingly, "San Francisco." This response indicates an awareness of the *ultimate* goal—just as a teacher if asked what he is teaching might respond, "United States history," "home economics," or "algebra." If it were possible, however, for the questioner to look secretly inside the businessman's mind and just as secretly accompany him on his trip, he would discover that he does not *actually* drive from Salt Lake City to San Francisco but that he drives from Salt Lake City to *Grantsville, from Grantsville to Wendover, from Wendover to Wells, from Wells to Elko, from Elko to Carlin,* and so on *until he reaches his ultimate goal,* San Francisco. The 800-mile trip is too distant, too remote, and too time-consuming to represent a realistic, workable goal. Therefore, the traveler breaks the trip into smaller, identifiable goals which are more satisfying because progress is more easily seen and because achievement is in the immediate foreseeable future. It is significant to note, however, that he does not carry the breakdown of the ultimate goal to the extreme. For example, he does not attempt to drive from tar-strip to tar-strip on the highway, from telephone pole to telephone pole, or from mile to mile as indicated on his speedometer. Such short, unchallenging goals would be too small, too insignificant, and too unrelated to the ultimate goal for the traveler to find them useful.

Once home from his trip, the businessman notes that he has a backlog of unfinished tasks. As he starts to take care of the unattended chores, he once again demonstrates the natural tendency to approach major tasks in terms of *units*.

While mowing his lawn he finds himself cutting a swath across the middle of a particularly large section, dividing it into two or three smaller areas rather than working his way tediously toward the center of the apparently never-ending larger section. He does not, however, pluck the grass blade by blade, nor does he cut his lawn in square foot or square yard sections.

While other examples are plentiful, the foregoing clearly illustrate several obvious facts: (1) when man is faced with a large task, he naturally—almost automatically—divides the task into smaller segments which are more easily handled and are psychologically more motivating; (2) the smaller segments are not just selected at random, but represent logical, meaningful portions of the larger goal; (3) if the smaller segments of the large task become too small, they lose appeal, challenge, and identity with the larger task.

Teaching with the unit approach offers no exceptions to the generalizations given above. In teaching, the larger goal is represented by the basic knowledge which the students should acquire from a given course. Since this task of teaching is so large, it is unmanageable and too distant to be challenging. Therefore, the teacher divides the basic understandings of the course into smaller segments. These smaller segments (or units) are chosen on the basis of their logical cohesiveness and their ability to stand alone as subject matter entities. Teaching on a day-to-day basis rather than from within the framework of a unit is the equivalent of breaking the large goal into areas that are too small to be challenging and that are not easily related to the larger task.

How is a unit planned? Once a person has convinced himself that the unit approach to teaching is not mysterious and that it is the natural way to attack any large task, he is ready to start with actual unit planning. This will involve four basic steps: (1) selection of objectives, (2) determination of teaching procedures, (3) identification of teaching materials, and (4) justification of the three previous steps.

The teacher's first step, within the confines of the unit chosen, is to *select* the basic understandings (concepts), skills, or new vocabulary which need to be developed. This suggests that the teacher will analyze the subject matter contained within the unit very carefully and will decide on certain things to be emphasized, learned, and remembered. Some authorities disagree with such a suggestion; they maintain that such an authoritarian approach kills the incentive and initiative of the students. Such opposition is based on a misunderstanding of the proposal. The suggestion that the teacher should select the fundamental objectives to be achieved in advance *does not* imply a lack of flexibility. It simply suggests that it is necessary for the teacher to be prepared to give focus and direction in his teaching. It allows for deviation from the advance plan, *but offers something from which to deviate*.

The second consideration for the teacher is the procedures necessary to achieve the objectives. Most literature on unit planning speaks of multitudinous lists of activities which could conceivably fit within the framework of a given unit, but it seems advisable to seek out methods, techniques, and procedures which apply *specifically* to the individual objectives. Whether the teacher includes many or just a few procedures for teaching each objective depends upon whether the teacher wants the unit to be a resource unit or a unit plan from which to teach directly. In either case, however, there should be a specific relationship between the stated objective and the procedures proposed. Then nothing is left to chance; each objective has its corresponding procedures which have been planned to insure that the desired learning takes place. Again, this does not suggest rigidity. Rather, it insists on basic preparation with the clear understanding that the teacher has the right and obligation to deviate and make adjustments whenever the current situation demands.

Identifying materials which will aid in the achievement of the objectives is in reality part of the responsibility in determining procedures. It is given separate space here since many teachers feel that it is important to list the materials in a special place on the unit plan where the list can be quickly checked prior to commencing a lesson. This helps to prevent an often-heard statement: "I had meant to bring such-and-such today to demonstrate this point, but I seem to have forgotten." The advisability of using materials such as films, slides, realia, charts, graphs, pictures, the chalkboard, and other audio-visual aids is generally conceded by most teachers. The most important thing to be remembered is that these materials are only *means*—not ends.

The fourth task in unit planning is one which rightfully encompasses the other three. What is the justification for the objectives selected? For the procedures chosen? For the materials to be used? The teacher should ask: "Am I attempting to teach this basic concept because I have thought it over carefully and believe it is important for the students to understand *in the light of some purpose*—or am I attempting to teach something simply because it is today and I taught something yesterday which seemed to precede this? Am I going to show this film because it will really help to clarify a justifiable concept or skill—or is it because film-showing takes up most of the period and requires relatively little of me?" Unit planning which is scrutinized with such introspection cannot help but yield superior results.

In summary, the unit approach to teaching is a simple, natural one. It has been demonstrated that man uses this approach in nearly every large task. Unit planning involves the segmenting of large teaching goals into smaller, cohesive, and meaningful entities of subject matter. It also involves the selection of basic objectives within the smaller segments (units) which are important for the students to learn and retain. Once the latter has been done, it is then necessary for the teacher to determine the proper procedures to be employed in achieving the objectives, to identify appropriate materials to be used in the learning process, and to justify the objectives, procedures, and materials. With all of this clearly in mind, and with a determination to teach well, teachers should be able to look forward to the security and satisfaction which comes from knowing what needs to be done and how to do it.

TEACHING THE ONE AND THE MANY—AT THE SAME TIME

Jerrold E. Kemp

Dissatisfaction with present methods and levels of accomplishment is often the seed that leads to effort for change in an educational program. In this instance, recognized limitations in the adopted textbook and special characteristics of students were the factors that started the search for a new approach.

The biology textbook used at our school, from the B.S.C.S. program, *Molecules to Man,* incorporates the laboratory approach, the inquiry method, and the newest discoveries of science. All this is bound together with an excellent series of conceptual themes. What it lacks is individuality in terms of the needs of our students.

As teachers, we tend to imitate our texts. We throw a great quantity of material at our students and expect the best to learn the most, and so on down the line. This approach can only lead to frustration and problems—for both students and teacher. Also, special techniques, like the inquiry method, are fine, but they are basically for high achievers only.

When we look at our classes we see individuals, not stereotyped human forms. Our students are predominantly culturally and economically deprived. They vary greatly in reading abilities. The classes, including a few high achievers, produce an extremely heterogeneous grouping.

These students need variety; they need individually structured materials that will interest and challenge them on their own levels, and opportunities to learn through experiences that they can satisfactorily complete. The wide range of abilities dictates the need for a wide range of learning experiences and these can only be met with a variety of instructional media.

PLANNING THE NEW APPROACH

In developing a new approach with an emphasis on individualized activity, it immediately became apparent that two things had to be done before we could select and design specific learning activities. First, there was consideration of objectives and content. Second, we had to become acquainted with the various media that would be available and gain some understanding of the potentials, advantages, and limitations of each type.

We started with vaguely stated purposes, but as we organized the content for a unit the purposes became clearer and gradually we were able to state specific behavioral objectives for students. We've read that this is a slow,

Reprinted from *Educational Screen and Audiovisual Guide,* 46: 26,27,32 (November, 1967), by permission of author and publisher.

painful process, but not until you actually do it do you realize how difficult it is! The final statement of the objectives for a specific topic now sounds simple and straight-forward (see box #1).

As we listed and organized the content of a unit we realized that the textbook did not include some points we felt were important. Other items in the book were over-emphasized, in terms of our objectives and student needs. Therefore, it was necessary to balance the single text with other references, periodicals, and our own experiences.

As the content became organized all facts and details were listed on cards. The cards were displayed. This became a kind of "storyboard" for examination. We could see the relationship among elements, whether there was a smooth flow of ideas and content, and the loop-holes that had to be filled or places that needed re-arranging.

It was then a short step to select specific activities to carry the content in terms of the objectives.

SELECTING LEARNING ACTIVITIES

Using the storyboard we developed student activities. The outcome was the *student study guide* (see box #2). This is the direction sheet for the activities that will allow each student to satisfy the objectives set down at the beginning. Notice the variety of media and activities to be used—8mm film clips, worksheets, picture folio, readings, laboratory, pre-test, post-test, and discussion.

What this represents is a concise package. The package places a boundary around each student goal. He knows what must be done and approximately how long it will take. He also knows that he will not be able to pass the post-test unless he completes the package successfully.

Some teachers may feel that creative thinking and open-ended learning are lost with this method. We do not feel so. Such experiences must occur at the right time. If you wish to use this kind of activity you may do so during a discussion period or at the end of the package. However, the student must satisfy the given objectives first, before he is confronted with new ideas.

As we developed the package we always kept in mind the variety of activities and media to be used, how many kinds of activities were repeated, and the order in which they appeared. We felt that the greater the variety the better would be the student response (see Sequential Flow Pattern in box #3).

LOCATING AND PREPARING MEDIA

On the basis of the specified activities, we either located or prepared materials. This was even more demanding than the previous planning steps.

Our school A/V coordinator helped us with catalogs, equipment, and materials. We located one commercial 8mm single concept film for use, prepared another one as a test, found magazine pictures and mounted them for

Box #1

OBJECTIVES

At the Completion of This Unit Each Student Should Be Able to:

1. Define the following: Innate   reflex

2. If given examples of behavior, identify which are innate and which are not innate.

3. Label the parts of a reflex arc. (On a diagram or model, trace the path of the nerve impulse as it completes a reflex arc.)

4. Explain the difference between innate reflex action and other behavioral actions (in discussion or on paper).

Box #2

STUDY GUIDE—Innate Animal Behavior

____1. View film clip #40. At the same time answer questions found on Worksheet #40.

____2. Read pages 70–73 in ANIMAL BEHAVIOR; Life Nature Library.

____3. Read any two (2) of the following:
A. Pages 106–07; *Fishes;* Life Nature Library

B. Pages 162–167; *Insects;* Life Nature Library

C. Pages 2–7; *Courtship in Animals;* B.S.C.S. Pamphlet series

____4. Read picture portfolio on Innate Animal Behavior and answer questions.

____5. Do Lab #65—Reflex action. Collect data, answer questions and write an interpretation.

____6. Read section 25-8 in *Molecules to Man:* Houghton Mifflin.

____7. View film clip #41.

____8. Sign up and attend Discussion Group on Innate Animal Behavior.

____9. Take Post-test on Package #2.

Box #3

Sequential Flow Pattern of Media Uses

1. Pretest	6. Laboratory
2. Film	7. Textbook
3. Worksheet	8. Film
4. Nature Book	9. Discussion
5. Still Pictures	10. Post-test

---

students to handle, developed the specific worksheets, selected reading assignments, planned for laboratory activity, and so forth.

There is a definite challenge in deciding what picture or what words can best describe content, interest students, and stimulate correct responses. You must use some ingenuity in this selection and development, and also get reactions and suggestions from other people as often as possible as you are too close to the work to see things objectively.

EVALUATION

As materials were prepared we evaluated them in terms of the content and how well they served the specific objectives. The best way to do this was by trying out materials with a few students. If students are unable to satisfy an objective we improved or altered the activities which guided that particular objective. This is the same procedure used in more formalized programmed learning.

Results so far have been very good. In addition to definite growth in content knowledge, there are apparent attitude changes in students. Because they work at their own rate, students seem to be more interested and self-sufficient. The responsibility for learning the material has been given directly to them. If a student fails to complete the work necessary to satisfy an objective he cannot expect to rank high on the post-test. He knows this because he can see the direct relationship between his efforts and his test grade.

Finally, we should recognize the value of the multi-media approach to adjust for differences in student ability. The poor reader can obtain information from a film clip or from a tape-slide series much better than by reading or listening to a verbal lecture. With more concrete experiential background reading levels improve. By altering the paths on the Study Guide we hope to better provide for different abilities in learning. The poor reading student takes more time but covers the basic material. The good student covers the basic material rapidly and is then able to take on extra activities.

This approach takes time, cooperation among people with various skills, and many frustrations. But it looks like the effort is worth it.

DIAGNOSTIC TEACHING

Edward G. Ponder

Perhaps we should begin to discuss diagnostic teaching by saying what it is not. We are not talking here about the general concept of the term *diagnostic* which centers primarily on the problems of children with learning disorders.

Reprinted from *The Instructor,* 78:21,52 (December, 1968), by permission of author and publisher.

Nor is it a special device for very bright or more mature children. It is not limited to any particular segment of the student population. Rather, diagnostic teaching focuses on ordering learning goals so that any learner can set out to reach the goal which suits his current need. It accomplishes this by setting up necessary sequences and then breaking them down into manageable steps.

A recent editorial in the *Wall Street Journal* accused educators of confusing the public by using a professional jargon which it termed Educanto. But I find that no one is more wary of jargon than the experienced teacher. You are probably asking whether diagnostic teaching isn't just a new name for what you've been trying to do in your classroom all along. If it isn't, you are probably wondering how to take on extra tasks of setting up sequences and partitioning learnings within them, when you are already bombarded by limitless tasks and emotional demands.

What I hope to do here is to sell you on the idea that diagnostic teaching is indeed worth the effort—that it is what you professional teachers have been striving for: a way to focus on each learner's learning level.

Diagnostic teaching calls on the teacher to analyze and assess the level at which each child is functioning. Then the teacher enters into a partnership with the child, helping him set realistic goals for his learning. The next step is critical, calling for genuine professional skill—the learning goals must be translated into behavioral terms so that sequential learning continua for accomplishing them can be established. These provide the means by which the child and the teacher can constantly assess the degree to which the child is accomplishing his goals. In this way, diagnostic teaching provides for individualization of student learning.

Traditional instruments of diagnosis presently cast long shadows over your planbooks. Teachers are relying on such measures as the IQ, standardized achievement and readiness test scores, and profiles from psychological tests. These tests certainly have their uses, but when you and Melinda face each other in the critical interactions of the learning process, you wonder: How can this child with an IQ of 130 be so slow to learn fractions?

When you diagnose, you analyze the child's skills to find his problem. Then, through *programmed teaching,* you concentrate specifically on his particular difficulties, using a program tailored to his learning behavior. Rather than relying primarily on traditional yardsticks, you begin to depend on critical interactions between you and the *one* child who is involved.

Based on the precepts of programmed instruction, diagnostic teaching has these features:

1. Class time and space are planned so that you work with children individually during the day.

2. Skills become more important than "information."

3. Before you face any child, you have available many sequences of small, appropriate steps leading to the acquisition of the skill involved.

4. You and the child examine the continuum of small, appropriate steps required to go from incapacity to capacity in a specific skill. Together you

decide where he must begin, and as he proceeds he has access to the skill-building process and its goals.

5. You keep close track of the child's progress and record many observations. Like the writer of a programmed-instruction manual, you give additional practice where it is needed, or you allow a child to skip steps if it is appropriate *for him*.

6. You are concerned with motivation, for achieved goals build the child's confidence or ego. Unlike a person writing a programmed-instruction manual, you are on the scene in the flesh; you can be warm and responsive.

7. Your goals are defined in terms of behavior that can be measured or in some way assessed. As the child proceeds from one manageable step to the next, you are able to measure what you have taught in terms of his achievements.

8. The teaching-learning experience is nonpunitive. The child is both learner and observer of himself as learner, with at least partial control over the process. He sees his own weaknesses and strengths almost impersonally, knowing that only one step on the stairway to a skill is at stake—not his class status.

9. The learner competes with his "yesterday self" rather than with others in the class—except in the general competition to grow towards "becoming."

Let's think together about a familiar example. We all agree that we want to teach the concept of democracy, but it is too global and complex an idea to be taught as such. The general concept must be broken down into a group of concepts whose mastery can be measured. Each concept must be further divided into learning continua. Some of these would be voting (you might lead the child from understanding eligibility to exercising the franchise); petitioning the government (from recognizing a problem connected with government responsibilities, to wording the complaint, to collecting the signatures, to submitting the petition, to reacting to the response); and obedience to law rather than to a ruler's whim (from differentiating between rules [laws] and whims, to making and unmaking rules [laws], to breaking or respecting laws).

Within these working parts of the concept of democracy there is still much that is abstract, but each of the parts can "work" because both the learning goals and the steps to each goal are measurable in behavioral terms. As the diagnostic teacher, you break down each working part of the global concept of democracy into a sequence of learning steps which both you and the learner can recognize as logical and progressive.

Or take the simpler example of teaching color to a preschooler. You find that he cannot name the colors. You have to diagnose further to see if he can place his finger on a particular color when he hears it named. Or you need to go further back in a presumed sequence to see if he can match and sort colors.

Diagnostic teaching is not easy. However, it is more exciting and more attuned to the learner. It moves us as teachers beyond the attitude, "I take the child where he is." For we as teachers often say we value the individual learner, and yet we penalize him if he is not at grade level or not within the approved context of someone else's curriculum mold. As a system of live interaction in the classroom between teacher and child, diagnostic (programmed) teaching is a technology whose time has come. Let's give it a try!

WHO GOES TO SCHOOL?
IS THE CHILD REALLY THERE?

JoAnn H. Strickland

The child at school is a person possessing a special combination of learned behaviors. Such behaviors may sometimes reflect the feelings of one or both parents, the rejection of a sibling, the experience of being lost, or frightened of the dark, the fear of making a mistake and being punished. Who goes to school cannot be determined by studying the normal population of children and concluding to generalities. The classroom teacher—the educator who sees the child each day—is the logical investigator of children's differences.

The statement, "each child is different," as a basis for challenging the teacher to individualize instruction, may have been posed too frequently in educational literature and lecture. Perhaps this statement needs clarification stemming from the following logical set of sequences: "Why does each child differ?" "How can differences be detected?" and "What teaching-learning designs promote individualization?" The simple recognition that children differ is meaningless unless answers to such questions are adopted as both the theoretical and technical framework for governing the development of the child's curriculum.

Some major considerations of this article are important determinants of children's differences—determinants that are both inside and outside the classroom but are not generally evaluated as basic to the learning process. Additional attention is given to recommendations in program and observation models which may facilitate the detection and treatment of the individual's uniqueness.

PARENTAL INFLUENCES

To answer the first question, "Why does each child differ?" speculation herein is limited to the prime influences of the parent-child and teacher-child interactions. The child learns a unique set of behaviors and responses as he interacts with his environment, which is composed of a unique set of things, events, and others.

The most significant others in any child's life are his parents. The person he is and will become is primarily determined by the parent-child interaction. In fact, the child's degree of social-emotional adjustment and intellectual development may be, in a large measure, a result of such parent behaviors as acceptance-rejection, consistency-inconsistency, permissiveness-dominance. These factors seem to have a prevailing influence on the child as he grows older.

Hurley [1] found that third-grade children who rate low in intelligence have parents who exhibit a high degree of rejecting behavior. From a study of the attitudes of 400 college students, Itkin [2] reported a significant positive correlation between the subjects' attitudes of acceptance-rejection toward parents and their parents' attitudes of acceptance-rejection toward children. It can be assumed then that one major and continuing educational effect on the child is the parental effect. The process of acquiring uniqueness may include stabilizing misinformation and being underdeveloped, as well as learning acceptable behaviors.

The classroom teacher must accept the child rearing process as a major educative process and, therefore, design with parents programs which will benefit children. Such programs should supply the parent with information, suggest appropriate adult-child interactions, and provide situations through which the parent can develop problem-solving skills that will better equip him to function in the parent-child relationship.

When launching a program that includes parents, the school must recognize that parents differ as to needs, concerns, and problems. The values, expectations, and social skills of various socioeconomic and ethnic groups are often dissimilar. Diversity among parents, as individuals and groups, necessitates the utilization of many approaches to parent involvement. Provisions may be made for the following approaches: individual parent-teacher contact via home visitation and/or school visitation by the parent; child study groups and interest groups at the school or, more conveniently, at a neighborhood facility or home; observation of children engaged in learning activities; participation in school activities or as teacher assistants, parent curriculum improvement committees, and others. All parents should not be expected to engage in *all* activities of a program, and especially in all activities at the same time.

The behavior patterns accepted by the parent may differ and perhaps conflict with those expected by the teacher. Consider the case of a four-year-old child who was from a one-parent home where the parent worked 16 hours each day. Deborah's responses puzzled the nursery school teacher. Upon the "suggestion" that she should engage individually in a simple learning task, her response was attentive but without movement toward the activity or facial indication of the degree of understanding. However, the child responded to activities which were required of all the children, such as standing in line, forming a circle, sitting, preparing to eat. Despite elaborate coaxing, exposure to a variety of interesting activity choices, enthusiastic adults, and spontaneous peers, Deborah made no self-initiated move to engage in a learning task.

One day, the teacher became a bit impatient and gave Deborah a "direct," firm, but kindly spoken, command. The child hesitantly made a move toward the activity. The teacher smiled, nodded approval and repeated the command firmly. Deborah followed the direction and received a rewarding verbal response and friendly pat from the teacher. She smiled, the first time since she had entered nursery school four months previously.

CONFLICT BETWEEN SYSTEMS OF BEHAVING

The responses of this child imply that the dominant pattern of verbal interaction between parent and child was parent's direct (definite and simple) command—child's positive reaction—parent's approval, whereas the pattern of verbal interaction between the teacher and child was customarily teacher's suggestion (indefinite and complex)—child's positive reaction—teacher's approval.

Apparently the child had had little, if any, association with the indefinite direction. Opportunities for choice were practically nonexistent prior to her preschool experience. The classroom teacher should be sensitive to such differences in systems of behavior and be able to function within various systems, gradually giving the child experience with generally accepted adult-child interaction patterns.

Deborah's case as well as others indicate that the degree of educational progress made by a child is significantly related to the degree of progress expected by the teacher. Rosenthal and Jacobson [3] investigated the assumption that poor children often fail in school because that is what is expected of them. In a school where most of the children were from low-income homes, it was found that the children from whom teachers expected greater intellectual gains showed such gains.

Furthermore, these children were described by their teachers as having a better chance of being happy and successful in later life; showing a greater degree of curiosity and varied interests; appealing socially to other children; and being better adjusted emotionally. Ironically, the children involved in the experiment were chosen randomly from a group of average achievers for that school. The treatment involved nothing more than labeling the sample as potential intellectual "spurters" and giving their names to the teachers.

Additional data were collected on the children who were placed in low-ability classrooms. Of this group, those who made the greatest intellectual gains were given the most unfavorable ratings by their teachers. In other words, it is unlikely that a child who has been labeled "low," "slow," or perhaps "poor," even if his IQ is rising, will be seen by his teacher as well adjusted and successful.

From the preceding example, it appears that the perception that the teacher has of the child's potential, whether it is negative or positive, may be an additional, pertinent influence on the degree of intellectual and social-emotional gain that the child will experience. The teacher must develop technical skills that will allow him more objectively to view the child and evaluate his learning progress as a basis for constructing curriculum and setting the conditions for learning.

Although the term "reinforcement" is not generally used by teachers, it describes a widely acceptable technique which most teachers utilize in the teacher-child relationship. Characteristically, reinforcement is applied through variations of approval-disapproval. For many purposes—giving a child a measure of self-security and confidence, enhancing his productivity and creativity, helping him eliminate unacceptable behaviors—teachers traditionally use verbal praise or disapproval, friendly physical contact or a good shaking, negative or positive nods, smiles or frowns, and more subtle ignoring or accepting behaviors.

REINFORCEMENT NEEDED

Some teachers use isolation and other punitive techniques as the most "expedient" means of eliminating unacceptable behaviors. In fact, it is common to find a frequently used "baby corner" in the kindergarten and a comparable "kindergarten corner" in the first and second grades. Having the child stand just outside the classroom door or sit in the principal's office for a period of time can be categorized as additional isolation practices. When Bereiter and Engelmann [4] came forth with their statement that isolation is effective under certain conditions, many teachers were shocked and claimed that such ideas were totally inhumane. These same people may not have considered the feelings of the child in the "baby corner." In other words, many teachers may be quite unaware of the types of reinforcement which they normally use and, particularly, the effects of that reinforcement on children.

Although teachers generally agree that reinforcement, particularly in the form of praise, is an effective motivator, the basic understanding should be that of what types of reinforcers are most effective for certain children. In recent years, many researchers have attempted to answer questions about the appropriateness of reinforcement techniques in classroom situations. For example, Zigler and Lanzer, from a study of various verbal reinforcers, found that middle-class children respond more to verbal feedback indicating "correct" and "right," while lower-class children respond more to personal statements of "good" and "fine." [5] This finding implies that, as a child becomes more self-confident as a learner, reinforcers of attention and praise decrease in importance and are replaced by the knowledge that one is correct and achieving.

O'Leary and Becker [6] found that a teacher will be more effective at helping children control their deviant behaviors if he employs a token or concrete reinforcement program. It may be assumed then that a more tangible means of reinforcement is necessary to elicit the desired responses from some children.

The teacher must also take into consideration the motivating influence of negative reinforcement. Kelly [7] found that children who receive simple negative reinforcing statements ("That's slow—not too good"), while performing a learning task, will show the highest response rate. Notice that rate of learning rather than quality or depth of learning was the desired response. There are times in the regular classroom when speed and efficiency as well as quality are expected.

OBSERVATION

Reinforcement procedures may be more effectively used by the teacher who remembers that the child will work to obtain something that is meaningful to him. Rewards that attract the child seem to stimulate learning to the degree that they relate to the following levels of need: tangible knowledge of success, other-oriented knowledge of success, and self-knowledge of success.

To discover the child as a unique being, the teacher must first be careful *not* to apply the authoritative generalizations about how children learn to the individual who sits in his classroom. He must be especially sensitive to unexpected influences which may prove to be major determinants in the child's educative process. Each time he observes or thinks of "Debby," the individual, he will evaluate his own behavior in terms of the child's needs and expectations. His extensive knowledge of child development and education will help him understand that *all* children learn, and that learning rates and levels may be circumscribed by stifling influences which originate from various sources, some of which may be the techniques, curriculum, and expectations imposed by the teacher.

A second challenge for the teacher is to discover ways to detect differences among children and provide for individuation. One old but promising technique of detecting differences is the observation method. For example, a teacher may conduct a thorough observation of one child each day. As the child moves through a series of learning situations, the teacher may choose to record the child's approaches, reactions, and successes for a duration of five or ten minutes while he is engaged in selected activities. On the other hand, the teacher may choose to study random samples of the child's behavior as it is presented in response to randomly selected learning tasks. This technique should facilitate observation of more than one child each day in a shorter length of time and for a specific purpose.

Among the children in his classroom, the teacher should discover variations in learning rates and levels, interests, and systems of behaving. As a result, the teacher may even find it possible to make some assumptions about the types of influences which have an impact on the child's learning process. Consistent evaluation of rates and levels of learning will allow the teacher to construct a realistic curriculum for each child—presenting to him learning tasks which are appropriate to him as an individual learner. Each day, the teacher learns more about the child, the person who goes to school.

NOTES

1. John R. Hurley. "Parental Acceptance—Rejection and Children's Intelligence." *Merrill-Palmer Quarterly* 11: 19–31, 1965.
2. William Itkin. "Relationships Between Attitudes Toward Parents and Parents' Attitudes Toward Children." *Journal of Genetic Psychology* 86: 339–52; 1955.
3. Robert Rosenthal and Lenore F. Jacobson. "Teacher Expectations for the Disadvantaged." *Scientific American* 218: 19–23; 1968.
4. Carl E. Bereiter and S. Engelmann. *Teaching Disadvantaged Children in the Preschool.* New York: Holt, Rinehart and Winston, Inc., 1965.
5. Edward Zigler and Paul Lanzer. "The Effectiveness of Two Classes of Verbal Reinforcers on the Performance of Middle and Lower-Class Children." *Journal of Personality* 30: 157–163; 1962.
6. K. Daniel O'Leary and Wesley C. Becker. "Behavior Modification of an Adjustment Class: A Token Reinforcement Program." *Journal of Exceptional Children* 33: 637–42; 1967.
7. Richard Kelly. "Comparison of the Effects of Positive and Negative Vicarious Reinforcement in an Operant Learning Task." *Journal of Educational Psychology* 57: 307–10; 1966.

FIRST YEAR TEACHER?
TRY INSTRUCTIONAL OBJECTIVES

M. Bruce McLaren

Unlike the proverbial new broom, teachers rarely arrive as educators at the peak of efficiency. After their four years of college education most beginning teachers can often do little more than struggle through their new world of pupil personalities and unfamiliar subject matter. The security they seek usually takes shape in the solidness of textbooks, workbooks, and objective examinations.

So as not to imply a complete criticism of the preservice education, it should be hastily added that all the intricacies involved in the art of teaching cannot be completely learned in advance. Each new combination of students creates problems which could not have been anticipated in the most advanced methods course.

If we agree to the assumption that the first year teacher is less than perfect, then we must also assume that improvement in teaching is neither inevitable nor automatic. Just being a teacher year after year cannot automatically ensure improvement.

There are, however, means by which we can assist the beginning teacher tackle at least some of the insurmountable problems he faces. A continuous program of inservice education to help ensure that all, including the beginning teacher, will change in ways that will make them increasingly effective in their work is vital. For the first year teacher, an intensive inservice program prior to the start of the school year might be given. New teachers coming into a

Reprinted from *Audiovisual Instruction,* 15: 64–66 (May, 1970), by permission of author and publisher.

district during the school year would also be given the inservice program before they entered the classroom. This training would deal with assisting the first year teacher by translating course objectives and goals into stated instructional behavior; this would explicitly define what the student should be able to do at the end of the course. The content of each objective, then, would contain the following:

(1) A specification of behavior that would be accepted by the instructor as evidence that the student had met the objective. This could be referred to as an observable act. (2) A description of any conditions under which the observable act would have to occur. These could be referred to as conditions of performance. (3) A specification of the criteria of performance which, to be acceptable, would describe how well the student must perform the specified observable act with its set of conditions of performance. These could be referred to as criteria of acceptable performance.

To further examine the problem the first year teacher has in specifying goals and objectives examine the experience of a beginning speech teacher whose students could not learn to "speak with greater expression." The overall objective she set was one which was open to many interpretations. The objective gave no means for evaluation or exact statement of that which was expected of each student. Until the class could hear significant differences in rate, volume, and pitch as amplifiers of meaning and feeling in oral reading, they could not demonstrate these uses in interpretive speaking. The objective offered only a vague statement of intent which, left open to a wide range of interpretations, led to confusion by both the class and its instructor.

As a result of participating in the inservice session, the speech teacher would first have taken the overall goal "learn to speak with greater expression," and broken it down into a series of related objectives in steps to achieve the overall goal. Each individual objective would have contained an intended outcome rather than a description or summary of content. In other words, each behaviorally stated instructional objective would have contained an observable act, conditions for performing of that act, and a form of measurable criteria of acceptable performance of the act. All of these individual objectives would lead to successful accomplishment of the overall objective or terminal behavior which was "to learn to speak with greater effectiveness."

A method of classifying the goals and objectives of an instructor is to express them in terms of the behaviors to be acquired or developed. Although the new teacher might find it difficult to understand behaviorally stated objectives at first, he will soon discover them to be important aspects of student performance and growth. With this in mind, the teacher will also know that the competence of both the student and himself will not be able to develop or be demonstrated accurately without a clear and functional understanding of what behaviorally stated instructional objectives are and how they are prepared and used. As he becomes more skillful in preparing instructional objectives, the instructor will find that he teaches with less wandering, laboring of points and issues, dealing in trivias and being sidetracked by irrelevancies.

Those who are in a position to observe the performance of beginning teachers, recognize quite often that the breaking down of course and unit specifications is one of the major problems in learning to prepare instructional objectives for teaching. In this sense, much like the problem the beginning speech teacher faced, a student teacher still in college will occasionally, upon misstating an objective, say that he knows what he means but just isn't able to make it into an expression which others will understand. A fallacy of this contention will occur when his supervisor asks him to try the same situation over several times. Often, it will become obvious that there is considerable differences in the objective between a vague notion and a clear concept. Furthermore, an individual in such a predicament will soon discover that his meaning is apt to be limited or even twisted by the very words used in building his thought and presenting it. Where and how does the inexperienced teacher find out what he should teach? With experience one learns that the starting point in directing learning is a decision as to exactly what changes in behavior are desired. The need for determining clear instructional objectives at the onset is a truth not always heeded. In teaching the new teacher must determine what it is he is expected to teach and he must synthesize this with what he thinks he should teach.

Teachers must be able to translate goals and objectives into behavior. The use of the instructional objective should describe an intended outcome rather than a description or summary of content. This behaviorally stated instructional objective should refer to any visible activity displayed by a learner with certain imposed conditions of performance under which the behavior is to occur. Within its framework, the behavioral objective should contain a criterion standard or test by which the achievement of the objective is to be evaluated. Since the objective the instructor is translating evolves from goals which relate just to that particular course, a reference to terminal behavior or the behavior we would like the student to be able to demonstrate at the time his influence over him ends is predominant in his thinking. By translating goals into behaviorally stated objectives, the teacher will set positive goals for himself and the class to follow.

If a beginning teacher or a seasoned professional wants to teach information effectively, he will have to become fluent at translating objectives into specific behavior. A meaningfully stated instructional objective should be one which succeeds in communicating your specification. The best objective would exclude the greatest number of potential alternatives to your goal. Unfortunately there are many words, such as: "To know, to understand, to really understand, to appreciate," that are open to a wide range of interpretation. To the extent that the teacher can use only those kinds of words, he leaves himself open to much misinterpretation and misunderstanding.

There are four steps which are suggested to follow in preparing behaviorally stated instructional objectives.

First, specify the terminal behavior by name; an identification of the Observable Act is given as to that which will be accepted as evidence that the student has achieved the objective. Second, further define the desired behavior by describing the Condition of Performance under which the behavior will be expected to occur. Third, by explaining how well the student must perform within the objective to be considered acceptable, describe the Criteria of Acceptable Performance. Fourth, write a separate statement for each objective. The more specific you become, the better chance you have of accomplishing your goal.

A good test to use in examining the potential effectiveness of objectives is if they can answer the following questions:

What will the student be allowed?

What will the student not be allowed?

What are the conditions under which you will expect the final behavior to occur?

Are there any particular skills, routines, learning experiences you are specifically *not* trying to develop? Do your objectives exclude these items?

It is desired that the teaching done will result in a change or changes in student behavior. The instructor, therefore, would be advised to state goals in terms of the terminal behavior he desires and not as a list of facts to be memorized.

Behaviorally stated instructional objectives indicate the type of evidence that can be observed or collected. In applying this, the teacher will need to identify those elements of behavior that will tell whether attitudes have changed or if facts and concepts have been clearly acquired. When a list of specific behaviors for a lesson or a course is used, it should suggest the types of evidence that will be needed to appraise performance in terms of individual capacities. Such was not the case, initially, of the speech teacher. The only item she indicated was that, in terms of overall performance, the student would learn to speak with greater expression. There was no indication of how individual appraisals of performance would be made or evaluated. Until she became aware of the above techniques, no listing to suggest how rate, volume and pitch as amplifiers of meaning and feeling in oral reading would be apparent as part of her instructional goal. After going through the inservice unit, the speech teacher prepared a list of specific behaviors desired as outcome to her original goal and within that framework she prepared a series of progressing instructional objectives which each student would have to successfully accomplish, based on evaluative criteria, before they could achieve the overall goal of "learning to speak with greater expression."

Teachers are faced with a large number and type of students. Knowledge within the various disciplines and technology within the teaching and learning processes is in a state of continual revision. The teacher must be aware of these developments so that a value can be placed on one or another, especially in his own field. While not every new development is necessarily better than a preceding one, beginning teachers should be open to these developments if they are to grow professionally. There are several choices to stimulate this awareness. A return to the college campus for refresher courses or a second degree program would be one such possibility. A selfpacing program in reading with emphasis on advancements and innovations in education offers another approach. Probably the most significant development in encouraging professional growth right in the local school district is inservice education. Activities of an inservice nature play a vital role in creating interest and enthusiasm, in keeping teachers abreast of recent developments, and in refreshing their knowledge of past ideas which have proven to be of value.

The importance of instructional objectives and their relation to the role of the beginning teacher led to the development of a related inservice activity geared specifically to the preparation of behaviorally stated objectives of instruction. The design model of this instructional system underwent a preliminary presentation and testing at a PACE Project to Advance Creativity in Education (Title III ESEA Seminar), with a group of 41 teachers of language arts at Oakland Schools, Pontiac, Michigan in January of 1968. They proceeded through the unit and at certain points took tests to evaluate their progress.

At the conclusion of the PACE Seminar, a program evaluation was given to all participants to complete before they left. This was done to capture responses and opinions which otherwise might have been forgotten by the time the major evaluation form reached them in the mail. Also, the intent of this brief evaluation was not to evaluate the seminar in light of its effectiveness as a unit of inservice instruction for beginning teachers, but on its informative nature to the members of the PACE Project regarding the preparation of behaviorally stated instructional objectives. This latter goal, the references to behaviorally stated instructional objectives, met with a very favorable reaction, although many of the members felt it was something which would have been of even greater value had it been a part of their practicum a year or so prior to this seminar. The remarks of one teacher sum up the immediate reactions of the group, in that he or she felt that it is never too late for an educator to learn that a goal is only a statement of intent, a "glittering generality," unless there is some indication of how that goal will, when met, result in a change in an individual's behavior.

The seminar evaluation which was mailed to the participants who indicated, in the mean scores, a continued enthusiasm on the part of the participants regarding its usefulness as a unit of inservice instruction, especially for first year teachers as indicated by a score of 1.95 (1 = very effective, 2 = effective, 3 = somewhat effective, 4 = not effective) for question 11 which dealt with the use of the seminar as a possible inservice workshop for first year teachers.

Inasmuch as this particular seminar was brief, born out of the need for a unifying attempt to give an additional shot-in-the-arm to the 41 PACE participants who were in the final phases of their Title III ESEA program, their acceptance of the unit in which they participated and how many of them spoke to the instructor and members of the PACE staff afterwards in regards to the effectiveness this unit would have on them in future preparation of instructional objectives and how it surely could relate, also, to beginning teachers just out of college looking for some usable form of security to latch onto as they entered the teaching profession, was most rewarding.

A second use of this unit of inservice instruction was implemented during the week of August 19–23, 1968 by the staff of the Okemos (Michigan) public schools as a part of a two-week pre-school inservice workshop program for both experienced and beginning teachers.

With the acceptance of this unit of inservice instruction by the initial test group and the further adoption of it into a pre-school teachers' inservice program by a school district, it is evident that by following the unit of instruction suggested, the beginning teacher will be able to develop clear and workable behaviorally stated instructional objectives rather than vaguely proposed prescriptions of intent.

USING CURRICULUM GUIDES

Kopple C. Friedman

Educators probably will not agree on a common interpretation for the proper use of the curriculum guide by teachers. This may often be perplexing to beginning teachers, let alone experienced ones. The purpose of this article is to state a point of view about the role of the curriculum guide, and to concede that there may be opinions that differ from it.

Just what is a curriculum guide? Basically, it sets forth a framework which furnishes guideposts to the teacher for the development of learning experiences. It does not prescribe a particular method of instruction nor does it outline a detailed pattern of content which must be followed rigidly. It is a document which should give the teacher the security of knowing definitely what is to be taught, and yet leave him with a feeling of independence on how to approach the job.

A guide may consist of an outline of objectives, content, understandings, skills, and attitudes. It may further include sections on such topics as the characteristics of children at various age levels, the nature of the learning process, modern methodology, the selection and utilization of various in-

Reprinted from *Education*, 82:215–217 (December, 1961), by permission of author and publisher, The Bobbs-Merrill Company, Inc.

structional resources, suggested teaching and learning activities, reference lists, and illustrative teaching units.

Although the outline of content need not be followed rigidly, there are certain major areas that must be included in the year's study. The curriculum guide is not just an optional document on a take-it-or-leave basis. It should be understood that it is to be followed.

There is a difference between a curriculum guide and a resource unit. A resource unit is suggestive; it indicates many ideas for the organization of content, activities, and resources. There is a difference, also, between a resource unit and a teaching unit. Usually a teaching unit is only provided for illustrative purposes. It is the blueprint of what one teacher has planned and carried on for a particular class. In this sense it is more specific than a resource unit. Other teachers may use it for whatever good it does them.

CONSTRUCTION OF A GUIDE

It is generally thought that if curriculum guides are constructed by the total body of teachers, they are more apt to be used by them. There are both fact and fiction in this assumption. For one thing, the development of a curriculum guide by many people of varying opinions must necessarily represent a certain amount of compromise. Whether or not these compromises are actually implemented in individual classrooms is open to question.

Again, in large school systems it is difficult to have direct participation by every classroom teacher in a particular subject matter field. Then, too, new teachers are always entering the school system who have not had a part in a guide developed in previous years.

While these limitations exist, it is nevertheless reasonable to assume that when teachers have had a hand, in varying degrees, in establishing curriculum policy they are more apt to feel that the instructional program is one that they believe is good.

Perhaps a sound course of action might be to have a limited number of teachers engaged in the actual production job. During this process the total staff should react to the small committee's efforts and thus guide in a general sort of way the direction that the curriculum takes.

This proposed course is based on the following reasons: (1) many teachers do not have the time for curriculum work because of other responsibilities; (2) all teachers are not equally interested in curriculum work; and (3) some do not have the background to participate actively in a production job of this nature.

Effective participation in curriculum development requires a breadth of experience and training in viewing a total program beyond the segment the teacher teaches in his classes, an interest in studying current developments in the particular area of concern, and the ability to write clearly and to organize material effectively.

PITFALLS AND THEIR AVOIDANCE

It is in the utilization of the curriculum guide that pitfalls confront the teacher. Too frequently the teacher plans daily lessons without thinking in terms of "wholes" or units spread over a block of time during which a "bundle" of content and classroom activity is handled. Too frequently the teacher may get bogged down in a mass of detail and lose sight of major and underlying purposes.

In handling a larger unit of work the teacher must take the needed time to motivate and to initiate. The class must study the unit as far as it can in depth during the period allotted and then move on to another "whole."

During the course of the year a limited number of these "wholes" or units is selected for intensive study. This saves the teacher from spreading his instruction thinly over "everything" and then becoming frantic when he is not able to cover all of the desired content. By selecting and planning a limited number of studies in depth, the teacher can maintain a balanced program for the year.

A pitfall that the beginning teacher, in particular, often meets is to start teaching the way he has been taught in college, namely, through the lecture method. Too many teachers plan to use their college class notes as the basis for their instruction. They would be far better advised to throw away these old notes and start from the first day of school by getting to understand their students and learning how their interests, needs, and abilities can shape what ought to be taught. They will soon find that many of their students don't share their enthusiasm for learning or their love of subject matter.

Another pitfall is to confuse the textbook with the curriculum. The basis for determining the learning activities is the curriculum guide. The textbook, in whole or in part, is used only as it fits the framework for the year. Pity the poor class that has to plod through the textbook chapter by chapter, paragraph by paragraph, line by line, getting bogged down in details instead of focusing on understandings. Pity all the more when the class wearily outlines the chapter or writes answers to the questions at the end of the chapter as the chief basis for a so-called instructional program during the whole year.

TEACHING BY UNITS

It has already been stated that the selection of a limited number of units for study in depth is preferable to trying to "cover" everything. This selection, based on the framework of the curriculum guide, should provide a good balance in the year's work. It has also been stated that the unit is a bundle of content together with the activities that are used to develop that content.

It is frequently desirable for the teacher to let the students participate in planning the general organization of the learning activities for the unit. Unfortunately, too many teachers hesitate to do this because they associate it with the "Now, class, what shall we study?" school of thought. By all means the pupil-teacher planning situation should not be conducted until the teacher has adequately warmed the class up to the importance and scope of the unit.

This is in contrast to the teacher-dominated situation where there is mostly "telling" going on by teachers. Here the students do not get enough chance to be active learners. The teacher is doing too much talking and the students are not doing enough learning.

In a pupil-teacher planning situation, it can be determined just what everyone is going to study in common and what everyone, individually or in groups, is going to work on in specialization. This specialization is important, because it must be recognized that every student does not come to school each day expecting or needing to learn things in exactly the same way as every other student.

Failure to provide for such individualization, whether it be for the able, the average, or the slow learner, is indicative of failure to take account of what is known about child growth and development and the psychology of learning.

Some teachers in the secondary school may assert that a pupil-teacher planning situation works in the elementary classroom but not in their high-school class. Others may say that it works only in a class of more able youngsters. The fallacy of these statements is shown by the fact that many secondary teachers use this technique successfully.

THE TEACHER AND THE GUIDE

In conclusion, it might be said that the curriculum is not so much what is found in the printed guide as what the teacher actually makes of it in the classroom. It is his adaptation of it to meaningful learning experiences that really counts. The teacher should use the guide as a framework and must feel free to express his teaching methods in the way that can best help make him a success in the classroom.

The teacher must not be kept from being resourceful and inventive. By all means he should not permit the textbook to determine the curriculum. He should only use the textbook or parts of it in such ways as to achieve the major objectives of the unit and of education in general.

Chapter 3

PRESENTING THE LESSON AND GUIDING PUPIL DISCUSSION

INTRODUCTION

Student teachers frequently attempt to imitate the teaching techniques of instructors who seem to be effective. Very often these student teachers are disappointed with the lack of success they achieve using these duplicated methods. However, greater success will be realized when the student teachers personalize their own teaching techniques.

The editors of this book believe that there is not a "best" way to present a lesson. Rather, the planning of any lesson should be a conscious effort on the teacher's part to choose the most appropriate teaching methods, considering the objective for the lesson, the learner, and the learning environment.

Past experience seems to indicate that some teaching techniques have been found to be more effective than others. In this chapter we will present some of these methods, knowing that not all suggestions which are made will be effective for all student teachers.

John Holt stresses that teachers who talk most of the time are not necessarily communicating with their students. He suggests that teachers should do less talking and allow students to ask questions and satisfy curiosities which they have.

Two of the articles deal specifically with techniques of questioning. Francis Hunkins suggests that instead of using queries for testing the pupils' knowledge we should be asking questions which stimulate pupils' thinking. Albert Klevan points out ways in which teachers may raise questions which help the students clarify their own valuing and thinking.

Ruth Ellsworth makes a plea for teachers to encourage critical thinking while Ross Coxe indicates that classroom instruction, particularly in the social studies, can be strengthened through integration with other subjects, individualizing instruction, and the use of multiple resources as opposed to one textbook.

Classroom discussion generally is recognized as an effective teaching technique. Ruth Litchen emphasizes the need for classroom discussion and offers practical suggestions for using this technique in presenting a lesson.

Learning centers recently have been gaining in popularity in American schools. R. V. Allen suggests that grouping through learning centers is an effective presentation technique.

136

Frank Riessman points out that children differ in their learning styles, and contends that teachers who adjust their teaching techniques to meet the different styles of learning exhibited by the group will meet with more success than those who ignore this fact in their classroom presentations.

Arthur Combs exhorts teachers to strive to produce self-directed students, and offers suggestions for teachers who are desirous of encouraging self-direction in their students.

DO TEACHERS TALK TOO MUCH?
John Holt

Do teachers talk too much? I'm afraid we do. Much too much. From the time we enter the school in the morning till we leave it at night, we hardly stop talking. We only realize how much we talk when we come to school with a sore throat.

What do we talk about? Some of the time we hand out information. Perhaps we read something from a text. Or we tell students something we think they ought to know—certain rules of grammar, facts about a place or an event, what a poem means, why this book is important, and so on. We like handing out information. It's our pleasure as well as our business.

Other times we demonstrate, or explain, or criticize, or correct: This is how you do long division. This is how you factor quadratic equations. This is how you do this experiment. This is how you are to write your book report. This is why you got that problem wrong. This is what you should be doing with that picture. The last may seem surprising, but in my limited experience with them I have not found that art teachers are noticeably more silent than others.

DOMINANT IN DISCUSSION

Sometimes we run what we like to call discussions. Even then, we usually talk as much as all the students put together. Not long ago I saw a video tape of an expert teacher running a discussion in social studies. His high school class talked freely, but he outtalked them. However much they managed to say, answering his questions, he managed to say more in commenting on their answers and setting up his next question.

Most discussions are pretty phony, anyway. Look through almost any teacher's manual. Before long you will read something like this: "Have a discussion, in which you bring out the following points. . . ." Most teachers begin a discussion with "points" in mind that they want the students to say.

Reprinted from *The PTA Magazine*, 62:2–4 (October, 1967), by permission of author and publisher. Copyright © 1967 by John Holt.

The students know this, so they fish for clues to find out what is wanted. They say, "I don't get it." "Would you please repeat the question?" "I don't quite know what you mean by. . . ."

The teacher's questions get more and more pointed, until they point straight to the answer. When the teacher finally gets the answer he was after, he talks some more, to make sure all the students understand it is the "right" answer, and why it is.

Once I was teaching a fifth-grade math class and was very much pleased with myself because, instead of "telling" or "showing" a youngster, I was "making her think" by asking questions. But she didn't answer. I followed each question with another that was easier and more pointed. Still no answer. I looked hard at my silent student and discovered she didn't even look puzzled. Just patient. Then it dawned on me: She was just waiting for that really pointed question—the one that would give her the right answer.

So-called discussion often goes that way. Students know that teachers have answers in mind. They know, too, that if they patiently persist in fishing for clues, most teachers will rise to the bait.

This is a really harmful thing. As I pointed out in my book *How Children Fail,* "When a child gets right answers by illegitimate means and gets credit for knowing what he doesn't know, and knows he doesn't know, it does double harm. First, he doesn't learn, his confusions are not cleared up; secondly, he comes to believe that a combination of bluffing, guessing, mind reading, snatching at clues, and getting answers from other people is what he is supposed to do at school; that this is what school is all about; that nothing else is possible."

Much of teachers' talk, maybe most of it, is just classroom management—keeping the kids in line. Somewhere we got the crazy notion that a class would learn most efficiently if everyone was learning the same thing at the same time. As if a class were a factory.

So we have these flocks of school children, twenty-five or more of them, that we are trying to lead or drive down a chosen road. They don't all want to go down that road; maybe none of them do; they have other things they would rather do or think about. So we continually have to round them up and move them along, like a sheep dog herding sheep. Only, our voice is the dog.

"Now, children, take out paper and pencil, and turn to page thirty-four in your book. We're going to work on—Tommy, where is your pencil? What? Well, why don't you? I've told you enough times you should come to class ready for work. Everyone else is waiting for you. Come up here and I'll give you another.

"Mary, stop whispering to Helen. Is your book open to the proper page? Well, you would have heard me if you hadn't been so busy talking to each other."

And so on. We talk to get children ready to do what they are supposed to do, and then we talk to make sure they are doing it. We ask about yesterday's homework or tell about tomorrow's. We talk to keep everyone's attention focused on the front of the room.

Not long ago I saw an expert teacher, who had good rapport with his class, using a slide-film projector to do an arithmetic lesson. I began to wonder how many of the words he was speaking had to do with the actual work and how many had to do with sheep-dogging—keeping the class together. It was clear after a while that there was much more sheep-dogging than work—two or three times as much. This is not unusual.

TUNING OUT

One result of too much teacher talk is that children who, when they were little, were turned on full all the time, learn to turn themselves off or down. They listen with only a small part of their being, like any adult listening to boring talk. If this goes on long enough, they forget how to turn themselves up, to listen with all their attention. They lose the knack of it and the taste for it. It is a great loss.

Teachers are not unaware that children tune them out. I once watched an experienced teacher showing how some problems should be worked. His method of keeping students' attention was to call on a student and ask, "Is this right?" as he finished putting each step of a problem on the blackboard. The student who was called on would answer, "Yes," and then the teacher would go on to the next step. It was all very dull, and my mind was wandering off to other things when suddenly my attention was jerked back to the classroom.

The boy who had been asked if the answer was right was saying, "No, sir, it isn't. It ought to be so-and-so." The teacher agreed, made the change, and went on as before. Talking after class, the teacher said to me, "You notice that I threw them a little curve ball there. I do that every now and then. Keeps them on their toes." What the teacher hadn't noticed was that when he threw his curve ball his voice changed, so that the children had a signal that it was time to turn up and tune in.

Yes, teachers know that children turn them off, and they have their little tricks to try and keep the children tuned in. But the children learn the little tricks that various teachers use, and low-powered listening becomes a substitute for high-powered attention. This is too bad.

But more important is the fact that while teachers talk all they want, the children get hardly any chance to talk at all. In most schools the rule is still that children may speak only when called upon by the teacher. Many schools prohibit talking between classes, more than a few prohibit talking at lunch, and I have even heard of some where children were not allowed to talk during recess.

Some will say, "What's wrong with that? Children come to school to learn, not talk." As if learning were a passive process, like a kettle being filled at a faucet.

The trouble is that when we treat children this way, we make them bad learners. For real learning takes place only when the learner plays a dual role, when he is both learner and teacher, doer and critic, listener and speaker. The student who tries only to remember what is in his book will not even succeed in doing that. The skillful learner talks to, even argues with, the book. He asks himself questions and checks his understanding as he goes along. Your poor student never knows what parts of a lesson he understands and what he does not. He leaves it to the teacher to find out.

Even in learning a skill—painting, or music, or a sport—the learner, as he performs, must continually judge his own performance, be aware of his mistakes. Am I in tune and in rhythm? Am I watching the ball? Little children learning to walk, talk, and do a hundred other things are good at this. Too often, it is school and nonstop talking teachers that turn them into inert and passive learners—targets for verbal missiles that injure initiative.

TALKING TAKES PRACTICE

Moreover, when a child gets little or no chance to talk, he does not get better at talking. Most of the fifth-graders I have known were no more articulate than many five-year-olds of comparable background; many of them were less so. This affects all their work in English. The child who is not used to putting his thoughts into words will not be able to put them into writing. He will say that he can't think of anything to write about. When he does write, he will find it hard to tell whether his writing is good or not. For the test of good writing, after all, is not whether it conforms to rules of grammar—some of the worst writing around does that—but whether it sounds good. The only way a child can become skillful in the use of language is through trying to say, in speech or writing, things that he wants to say, to people that he trusts and wants to reach.

But there is a still more important reason for having teachers talk less and letting children talk more. A child first comes to school full of thoughts, ideas, curiosity, wonder. But he soon finds out that nobody is interested in what he knows, what he is curious about, what he cares about. School is not a place for him to ask his questions, share his concerns, satisfy his curiosity. Before long he comes to doubt the worth of his own thoughts. He begins to feel, like his teachers, that the things that worry or please him or that he needs to find out about are unimportant, a waste of time.

He does not develop a sense of his own identity and worth. He does not think of himself as a unique and valuable person, with ideas to express and share, with interests and skills he would find joy in pursuing and developing. He comes instead to feel that he can find satisfaction in life only by pleasing the authorities or the crowd. He loses his taste for independence and freedom, and is ready to follow anyone, or any group, that will make him feel like a somebody instead of a nobody.

Is this what we want? Haven't we learned by now how much harm such people can do? Do we need still more lessons?

Let me repeat what I have said in *How Children Fail:*

> It is not subject matter that makes some learning more valuable than others, but the spirit in which the work is done. If a child is doing the kind of learning that most children do in school, when they learn at all—swallowing words, to spit back at the teacher on demand—he is wasting his time, or rather, we are wasting it for him. This learning will not be permanent, or relevant, or useful.

> But a child who is learning naturally, following his curiosity where it leads him, adding to his mental model of reality whatever he needs and can find a place for, and rejecting without fear or guilt what he does not need, is growing— in knowledge, in the love of learning, and in the ability to learn. He is on his way to becoming the kind of person we need in our society. . . . All his life he will go on learning. Every experience will make his mental model of reality more complete and more true to life, and thus make him more able to deal realistically, imaginatively, and constructively with whatever new experience life throws his way.

Are we ready to start doing less talking and more listening, to treat children so that they will grow up feeling, not like slaves and puppets, but like free and valuable men?

USING QUESTIONS TO FOSTER PUPILS' THINKING

Francis P. Hunkins

Teachers are urged to utilize classroom methods which will enable pupils to become effective thinkers. New materials are being constructed; workshops are conducted to suggest ways to achieve this goal. Pupils, it is commonly asserted, should not be developed as mere possessors of knowledge, but, rather developed into individuals capable of thinking—individuals who can utilize knowledge.

Developing thinking individuals has become the slogan of the schools and the selling-point of educational materials, whether they be textbooks or tests. Some aspect of this goal of developing thinkers is mentioned in our lesson-plan objectives. Means of achieving this objective are listed. However, one procedure which is usually *not* mentioned in lesson plans, or in school slogans, or in educational materials is the effective use of the *question*.

Questions in teacher-talk and instructional material are significant in the guidance of/or guiding the teaching-learning situation toward the achieve-

Reprinted from *Education*, 87:83–87 (October, 1966), by permission of author and publisher, The Bobbs-Merrill Company, Inc.

ment of objectives. Questions which teachers ask substantiate stated objectives and reveal unverbalized aims. They may stress, for example, increasing pupils' knowledge of facts, increasing pupils' understandings and concepts, or increasing pupils' skills at interpreting materials. Yet, from current research, the predominant emphasis of teachers' questions seems to be on knowledge of facts—not thinking.

SOME TYPICAL TEACHER QUESTIONS

An excerpt from a tapescript made in a fifth-grade social studies class is presented. It gives evidence of the poor quality of teacher questions and testifies, also, to their emphasis upon factual knowledge. The tapescript also reveals that teachers' verbal utterances are many times inappropriate to the subject area being discussed. This "bit" of dialogue should not suggest sweeping generalizations, but, rather, should give the reader an instance of discourse to stimulate his thinking.

> T.　(pointing to map): Is there anyone here who could not tell how we got all those chunks? (Chunks refers to the first states.) Well, let's go over them very briefly. Ah, what happened first, there?
>
> T.:　What was the first addition?
>
> T.:　The first, we started with what?
>
> T.:　Let's change our question.
>
> T.:　We started with what?
>
> T.:　What did we, our country, start in 1789 when we were first organized as a country?
>
> T.:　When we first started to be a country?
>
> P.:　Thirteen colonies were made into thirteen states.
>
> T.:　And their western boundaries were to be what?
>
> P.:　The western boundaries of these thirteen states that grow out of the ocean, they were to go west to the Mississippi.
>
> T.:　All right, then when and where and how was it that we acquired this?
>
> P.:　We fought a war with England. And that is the beginning of our country, this chunk right through here.
>
> T.:　And what was our first addition to this state?
>
> T.:　And how did we get Florida?
>
> T.:　And at that time if you will look in the book, Florida was clear over here. All right, what was the next big chunk we got?
>
> P.:　The Louisiana Purchase.
>
> T.:　And from what country did we buy it?

If nothing else is gained from reading this discourse, one can see that the questions did not really demand that pupils think. The teacher had not carefully contemplated the wording and emphasis of her questions; the questions had a spontaneous birth in the atmosphere of classroom discourse.

QUESTIONS CONCERNED WITH FACTS

Teachers stress thinking, yet their classroom questions contradict their claims. Over the years, their questions have been primarily concerned with the same thing—memory of facts—specific facts.

Over fifty years ago, Stevens (9) noted a dominant emphasis on memory questions in both English and social studies classes, with social studies sections stressing this type of question more. Consequently, Stevens called for intelligent use of questions as instructional devices and stated that questions should stimulate reflective thought in addition to mere memorization of facts. Stevens' plea has been greatly ignored.

Recently, Floyd (5) studied questions asked by primary teachers and concluded that there existed a poor balance of question types with memory questions dominating the class activity.

Adams (1), developing a system of categories by which he classified the questions asked by secondary school English and social studies teachers, discovered a similar dominating emphasis of memory questions, although the overall proportion, when compared with Stevens' study, was somewhat less. Even so, the overall emphasis on memory questions proved memory to be still the cognitive objective receiving the most emphasis in the teaching situations of both groups of teachers.

Davis and Hunkins (4) discovered that questions in fifth-grade social studies textbooks reflected this emphasis on memory. Pfeiffer and Davis (8), in analyzing teacher-made examinations found a similar factual emphasis.

AN EFFECTIVE TEACHING DEVICE

Even though actual practice has shown misuse of the question to emphasize knowledge, many books and articles have been written which extol the merits of the question as a device of effective teaching. For example, Loughlin (7) stated that effective questioning is effective teaching. Klebaner (6) adds agreement to Loughlin's claim by stating that the carefully thought out question used effectively is vital to achieving the purposes of education.

Wellington and Wellington (10), while differing in their definition of teaching, advocate more effective use of questions in the teaching situation. Teaching, they stress, is not the teacher asking questions, but rather the teacher guiding the pupils so that they ask effective questions.

Carner (3) took somewhat the same emphasis in stating that teachers must be cognizant of the types of thinking required before they can frame effective questions to assist children in such cognitive development. Teachers need to be aware of the level, concrete or abstract, of questions which is most suited to a particular learning situation. Carner stated that present teacher-emphasis is on questions which are supported by facts.

QUESTIONS HAVE MANY USES

The evidence of the past points accusingly at teachers' uses of questions. Teachers have been and are hampered in their use of questions by considering them primarily as instruments of testing what facts pupils have learned. But they need not rest on this misconception. Questions have other uses: as tools to assist in diagnosing pupil difficulties and as motivators to learning. Too, questions may be tools to foster thinking to guide learning of higher cognitive processes. Questions which stimulate thinking are difficult to construct; they demand of the teacher careful planning with respect to the goals of the lesson or unit. These questions should be as carefully thought out as are the objectives, for if the questions are poor the objectives will not be achieved.

MANY FORMS AND EMPHASES

Questions have varying forms and varying emphases. An extremely helpful guide was issued ten years ago (2). This guide, *Taxonomy of Educational Objectives: Cognitive Domain,* presents six hierarchically-arranged categories: knowledge, comprehension, application, analysis, synthesis, and evaluation.

Most classroom questions seem to get bogged down in the knowledge category. The *who, when, where, what* questions ably represent this category —the necessity of learning facts. Teachers must not hastily, and unwisely, conclude that our present plight may be remedied simply by de-emphasizing the *who, when, where, what* questions and by bringing in the *how* and the *why* questions. The form of question does play a major role in determining its emphasis or emphases, but the purpose of the question must also be known in relation to context.

If the question's form is employed as the sole rationale for judging questions, misinterpretation will result many times. To exhort teachers to use more *why* than *what* questions without an understanding of the relation of form and purpose would be, in substance, no change at all. For example, "Why are olives grown in this particular part of California?" might well be expected to call for "thinking" rather than "memorization." But if one considers the question in relation to its context in a particular book, he might discover that this question is just asking for a listing of specifics which support the fact that olives are grown in this particular geographic region.

To judge questions with regard to form without consideration of their relation to context is only half the picture. Questions neither stand alone in materials, nor can they be judged alone according to a single criterion of form. Also, the cognitive response which a question elicits depends to a great extent upon the information which an individual brings to the question. A pupil, lacking some particular information, may be stimulated by a question to analyze information. However, if the pupil already knows the information, the cognitive response might be only in the realm of knowledge.

FORM NOT ONLY CUE TO EMPHASIS

The examples of questions below give evidence that form of question is not the sole cue to its emphasis. These questions also show that one must make certain assumptions about the prior information which pupils bring to the questions.

1. What was and is today the major factor in determining a man's standing in the herding community? (knowledge)

2. Why didn't the Africans of the past produce much of their own food? (knowledge—specific facts in book)

3. Why were iron tools and weapons valuable? (comprehension)

4. How did the Africans make iron? (comprehension)

5. Locate on the map the two capitals of South Africa. (application)

6. Look at your map and determine the major landscape type of Ethiopia. (application)

7. The author states that Africa is a land of contrasts. Does the author present enough information to support this statement? (analysis)

8. Explain why the major trading cities in Western Africa were located along the western edge of the Sahara. (analysis)

9. Australia needs additional water. Describe as many ways as you can which will supply water more efficiently to this country. (synthesis)

10. Describe several plans which you propose to assist in bringing peace to the world. (synthesis)

11. Do you feel that the type of farming practices carried on by these people was efficient? (evaluation)

12. What do you think of our foreign policy? (evaluation)

These examples illustrate that questions can have either simple or complex form. There are no "pat" questions which immediately inform the teacher that he has constructed an analysis question to stimulate his class to the heights of thinking.

The difficulty of constructing good questions should not deter us in attempting improvement. Questions can be effective in fostering pupils' thinking. The time is propitious to convert our slogans about thinking into deeds and actually stimulate our pupils.

REFERENCES

1. Adams, Thomas Howard. *The Development of a Method for Analysis of Questions Asked by Teachers in Classroom Discourse.* Doctor's thesis (New Brunswick, New Jersey: Rutgers, The State University, 1964).

2. Bloom, Benjamin S., Ed. *Taxonomy of Educational Objectives, The Classification of Educational Goals: Handbook I, Cognitive Domain* (New York: David McKay Co., Inc., 1956).

3. Carner, Richard L. "Levels of Questioning." *Education,* Vol. 83 (May 1963), pp. 546–550.

4. Davis, O. L., Jr., and Hunkins, Francis P. "Textbook Questions: What Thinking Processes Do They Foster?" *Peabody Journal of Education,* 43:285–92 (March 1966).

5. Floyd, William D. *An Analysis of the Oral Questioning Activity in Selected Colorado Primary Classrooms,* Doctor's thesis (Greeley, Colorado: Colorado State College, 1960).
6. Klebaner, Ruth Perlman. "Questions That Teach." *Grade Teacher,* Vol. 81 (March 1964), pp. 10, 76–77.
7. Loughlin, Richard L. "On Questioning." *The Educational Forum,* Vol. 25 (May 1961), pp. 481–482.
8. Pfeiffer, Isobel and Davis, O. L., Jr. "Teacher-Made Examinations: What Kind of Thinking Do They Demand?" *NASSP Bulletin,* Vol. 49 (September 1965), pp. 1–10.
9. Stevens, Romiett. *The Question as a Measure of Efficiency in Instruction.* (New York: Teachers College, Columbia University, 1912).
10. Wellington, Jean, and Wellington, Burleigh. "What is a Question? *The Clearing House,* Vol. 36 (April 1962), pp. 471–472.

CLARIFYING AS A TEACHING PROCESS

Albert Klevan

Much has been written recently by Louis E. Raths and his students concerning their work in the areas of valuing and thinking. Their work suggests four areas of competence needed by teachers if they are to help children develop into valuing and thinking individuals.

The first area deals with the skill of the teacher in creating a climate favorable for valuing and thinking.[1] Competency in evoking valuing expressions and in giving invitations to think is the second skill needed by teachers. If a climate of psychological safety has been created by the teacher, then invitations to think may be more effectively tendered to the children.[2] Under conditions of safety, it is more likely that children will express prizing and cherishing.[3] Third, the teacher needs to be sensitive to thinking and valuing when these do occur. Special sensitivity training is needed to develop this competency. It is dealt with in Raths' books on valuing and thinking.

The fourth competency, the one with which this paper is concerned, deals with the question, "What does the teacher do when children are expressing their valuing and giving evidence that thinking may have occurred?" Raths and his students say, "Engage in clarifying procedures with the student."

Following are a few ways the writer has found that teachers use when they are engaged in raising some clarifying questions [4] with students. It is not meant to be a complete list; it could not be. Teachers are discovering new ways of working with students, using clarifying procedures each day. It is meant to provide a simple collection of devices for those who would like to use them.

The reader will note that the clarifying procedures have been divided into

Reprinted with permission of the Association for Supervision and Curriculum Development and Albert Klevan. Copyright © February, 1968 by the Association for Supervision and Curriculum Development, Vol. 25:454–458.

two modes, *reflective* and *dissonant*.[5] Some research has been done to study the relative effects [6] of these modes; yet more needs to be done since the findings are inconclusive.

REFLECTIVE MODE

1. Repeating exactly what the student has said but with an inflection indicating a question is being raised.

2. Paraphrasing the student's remarks with an inflection as in "1." Teacher says, "Did I understand you?", followed by the paraphrased comment.

3. Asking for a definition of terms when appropriate. Teacher says, "How much appreciation of American History is an adequate appreciation?"

4. Raising the question concerning the degree of certitude with which an idea is held. Teacher says, "How sure are you?—Would you bet *all* your money on it?" This could be used when the student expresses either extreme certainty or uncertainty.

5. Asking the "How do you know?" question with a focus on the data to support a stated belief. Teacher says, "Can you cite some data to support your notion?"

6. Asking the "How do you know?" question with a focus on the origins of a belief. Teacher says, "Who else would agree with you?" or "I wonder where that idea got started?"

7. Requesting the student to expand his views. Teacher says, "Tell me more," or "Uh-huh?"

8. Inquiring into the longevity of a belief. "Have you felt this way very long?" the teacher says, or "Is this an idea that you have thought about only recently?"

9. Raising the question of the critical incident. Teacher says, "Tell about an incident that was crucial to you in forming your opinions."

10. Asking a student to anticipate consequences by completing an "if . . . then" statement. The teacher says, "If we were to implement your proposal, then tell about the consequences you anticipate." "If we were all more humane to each other, what do you expect would result?" the teacher asks.

11. Soliciting statements of immediacy. Teacher says, "Is this close to your life right now?" or "Does this idea affect your life today?"

12. Looking for likenesses or differences in ideas expressed by others. Teacher says, "Where do you differ with (insert a political figure)?" or "Where do you agree with (same politician)?"

13. Asking the student for examples. Teacher says, "Can you give a 'for instance'?"

14. Focusing on the facts. Teacher says, "Would you summarize the data that bear on the problem?"

15. Evoking expressions of feeling. Teacher says, "Are you happy that you believe this?"

16. Eliciting value-type expressions. Teacher says, "Do you prize your belief?"

17. Raising the question of the utility of an idea. Teacher says, "Would your idea be helpful to someone else to hold?"

18. Anticipating a more encompassing notion. Teacher says, "Where do you think this idea is taking you? Eventually, where is it leading you?"

19. Finding a point of difficulty. Teacher says, "You seem to have followed the notion up until we started looking for the assumptions. At what point after that did you find you were not following the discussion?"

20. Relating feelings and behavior. Teacher says, "Tell how you felt when you were (insert specific behavior)."

21. Inquiring into purpose. Teacher says, "What was your goal (in a specific action)? What were you trying to accomplish?"

22. Asking for retrospection into process. Teacher says, "When you started the painting, did you have the finished product in mind?" or "Tell me what you were thinking about as you worked out your present beliefs. If you had it to do over again, would you change what you have done in any way?"

23. Focusing on choices others have made. Teacher says, "Tell about the choices you think (insert name) has made. What alternatives did he have?"

DISSONANT MODE

1. Distorting what the student has said with an inflection indicating a question. Extreme words may be added to the student's remarks. Teacher then says, "Is this what you meant?"

2. Stating assumptions for the student that have a negative connotation. Teacher says, "Are you assuming that Man is an animal?" (The teacher must be careful that the inflection of his voice does not communicate judgment.)

3. Raising moral or ethical questions. "Are you stating that it is ethical for one person to control the thoughts of another?" (The same caution mentioned in "2" above applies to this one also.)

4. Shifting the focus of the student's remarks to an implication that may be drawn from the statement. Student says, "The man who immolated himself was a hero because he was committed to an idea." Teacher says, "Maybe he was committed to self-destruction."

5. "Can you think of other explanations that somebody might hold?" This method focuses attention on alternatives. It is especially applicable to situations involving causal relationships.

6. Teacher says, "Tell us about some of the alternative explanations that you have rejected." Getting the student to look back on the choices he made in arriving at his present beliefs or conclusions.

7. Looking at alternatives. Teacher says, "What are some of the alternatives?" or "What other solutions do you see?" or "What solutions do other people propose?" or "What are some other suggestions?"

8. Taking a generalization a student has made and applying it to a new or extreme situation. "You say Democracy is the best way man has found for

establishing decent human relations; would you say it is applicable to other institutions such as the army, the military, the family, or even education?"

9. Testing for the universality of a personal belief. Teacher says, "Do you think everyone ought to agree with you?" "Are there some whom you would expect to see things differently?"

10. Giving counter-examples. Students say "Hippies take LSD." Teacher says, "I know two hippies who do not."

11. Finding apparent inconsistencies in a student's remarks. Teacher asks a student to reconcile two statements he made previously that may be inconsistent; or to explain his behavior which may be inconsistent with an earlier exhortation.

12. Waiting for the student to draw an inference or state a conclusion. When the student finishes a statement that lacks a conclusion, the teacher says, "And therefore . . . ?"

13. Eliciting of counter-evidence. Teacher asks, "What data would you need to see before you would change your mind?"

14. Eliciting of counter-examples. Teacher says, "Are there some exceptions you can think of to your generalization?"

15. Examining the limitations of a belief. Teacher says, "Can you think of the conditions that might exist under which your belief would not be true?"

16. Raising the question of credibility of data. Teacher says, "Can you trust your source of information?" or "Can you trust your perceptions?"

17. Focusing on the extreme words used by the student, the teacher says, "Did you mean *all*?" or "Never" or "Continually" or "Always," etc.

18. Paying attention to indeterminate phrases. Teacher says, "Does it merely *seem* so to you?" or "Do you really just *think* so?" or "Is such an eventuality only a *possibility* to you?"

Two characteristics of the clarifying question that should be noted by the reader are (a) they are questions to which only the student could know the answer and (b) they include the word "you" in the question.[7]

The teacher who tries this method of instruction even for a very small portion of each day is likely to be rewarded by some relatively profound changes that take place in his classroom. Wouldn't it be wonderful if we could say each day, "I really helped my children today. I could see them developing commitments, thinking more clearly."

NOTES

1. Suggestions for creating such a climate are described by: Louis E. Raths. *Understanding the Problem Child*. West Orange, New Jersey: The Economics Press, 1963.
2. Louis E. Raths *et al. Teaching for Thinking*. Columbus, Ohio: Charles E. Merrill, 1967.
3. Louis E. Raths *et al. Values and Teaching*. Columbus, Ohio: Charles E. Merrill, 1966.
4. The writer has drawn from papers written by Louis E. Raths, Laurence Hopp, Sidney Simon, James Raths, and others.
5. Leon Festinger. *A Theory of Cognitive Dissonance*. Evanston, Illinois: Row, Peterson, 1957.

6. Margaret D. Barnes. "The Relationship Between Reflective and Dissonant Forms of Clarifying Process." Unpublished research paper. College Park: University of Maryland, 1966.
7. Suggested by Sidney B. Simon, Temple University, Philadelphia, Pennsylvania.

CRITICAL THINKING

Ruth Ellsworth

When Tom brought his new whistling ring to school to show his third grade classmates, it was much admired and he was envied. The natural, immediate reaction of many children was to want a whistling ring for themselves, so a first question was, "Where did you get it?" Tom explained that he had sent a box top and ten cents to a company for the ring. Several children thought that was cheap, and one asked, "How can a company afford to do that?" The ensuing discussion brought forth many ideas, including the thought that the advertising involved led to increased sales and sufficient profits to cover much more than the cost of the whistling rings. From their initial attitude of wonder, the children moved to analyze the economics of Tom's exchange. They raised questions and used their knowledge of buying and selling and prices to help answer them.

The attitudes displayed by third graders—the attitudes of wondering, of questioning, of suspending judgment until facts and propositions have been examined—are important factors in critical thinking. They are basic to propaganda analysis, which involves many abilities included in the complex process commonly termed "critical thinking."

Advertising is only one of the forces today demanding children's money, time, attention, and allegiance. They are also besieged by Little Leagues, clubs, the Scouts, religious groups, neighborhood gangs, television and radio programs, hobbies, stepped-up homework, school activities, and occasionally the family. Children feel the impact of these varied stimuli through conflicting demands and points of view.

Schools can help children sort out the forces operating on their lives and can guide them to ponder their choices and decisions. They can assist them in studying their world, including its people and cultures. This is the area of the social studies.

Samuel McCutchen, in his presidential address to the National Council for the Social Studies, November 1963, said, "Our program must induct young people into today's society, help them to understand it, to find meaningful places in it, and make it more livable; that is, move closer to its ideals. This task identifies these four elements of the discipline of the social studies:

A. The societal goals of America

B. The heritage and values of Western civilization

C. The dimensions and interrelationships of today's world

D. A specific process of rational inquiry and the tenets of good scholarship." [1]

A recent investigation of the social studies interests of 715 elementary school children indicates that they "center about the current problems that dominate the local, national, and international scene—the problem of the integration of the races, of the cold war. . . . Social studies interests of elementary school children appear to be elastic and to move from the community to the world scene as easily in the first grade as in the sixth." [2]

Indeed, children as well as adults are enmeshed in the problems of people. They experience the gamut of human dilemmas: poverty, anxiety, boredom, crowded conditions in home and school, inadequate play space, conflicts with playmates, loneliness, overstimulation, pressure to succeed, the segregation of the suburbs or the inner city. They want to understand why they, their parents, their city, their world are troubled and what *they* can do to remove the obstacles to a satisfying life.

The social studies program offers experiences through which children inform themselves about their world, begin to find answers to their questions and formulate positions on problems, and in some cases, do something about problems.

For example, a group of sixth graders in an inner city school, wanting to keep their neighborhood a good place in which to live, made a comprehensive study of the neighborhood conservation program of their city to find out what they and their parents could do. They secured as resource people the president of the neighborhood council who lived next door to the school and the executive secretary of the Committee on Neighborhood Conservation. They surveyed an alley near their school to find out if refuse was being cared for properly. They secured pamphlets and legal codes which, although written at the adult level, they read eagerly—because they wanted to learn and the material had meaning to them.

Observation of these sixth graders at work revealed several reasons for the satisfaction they felt in their study. They had a concern, they formulated their initial questions clearly, they had wise guidance in selecting and using instructional resources. As they studied, new questions arose and problems were seen in somewhat different contexts. The expressway which had cut many of the children off from some of their friends appeared in a different light when they learned how many cars used it daily and when they realized that it relieved local streets in their neighborhood of through traffic and thus made them safer to cross. The children had more to think about with each experience. They asked why the city did not pay for sidewalk repair and learned that when property owners had to pay the bills, fewer sidewalks were damaged. This information led them to wonder how people learn to feel responsible for property commonly owned through government. Thus the answering of simple questions led the class to consider more complex and comprehensive problems.

Usually in the initial study of a problem or area of interest, there is a period of exploration stimulated by curiosity rather than by clearly defined questions. Some free-wheeling occurs. Children question and requestion, becoming increasingly purposeful. It is good to encourage and accept this process rather than to force precise questions in the beginning or to seek answers prematurely. Often children are not ready to determine answers because the questions have not been clearly enough defined or the most significant questions have not been raised.

Many people have studied the problem-solving process and analyzed its steps. Although the descriptions differ, there is basic agreement on what must be done. The problems must be sensed and defined and the questions or hypotheses formulated. Procedures for answering the questions or testing the hypotheses have to be worked out and data gathered and interpreted. Answers to the questions must be decided upon or a conclusion drawn. Action must stem from the decision. It all takes time.

REQUISITES FOR CRITICAL THINKING

What does a child need to learn in order to think critically, to be an effective problem solver?

Questioning attitude: First, a sensitivity to problem situations and a feeling that he can do something to resolve them trigger a child's thinking. A willingness to think and a degree of self-confidence are essential. If children are too long told what to do and when and how to do it, they tend to find this an easy way of life. Then having to think becomes a chore. A questioning frame of mind or a look-again attitude starts a child investigating. "Why" and "how" questions are especially valuable.

Creative search for information: Second, in a rapidly changing world marked by the development of new communication media, a child who has learned to think creatively about sources of information is likely to find more significant and pertinent facts than one who relies upon traditional sources. Educational listening and viewing opportunities present themselves in a vast array of radio and television programs, films, filmstrips, slides, and pictures. Numbers of people have their own extensive picture records of life in many parts of the world. Americans are a mobile people so that most children come in contact with new acquaintances constantly, people whose firsthand experiences may differ greatly from the child's. Contact with such people helps the child to start building some new concepts through vicarious experience—for example, concepts about different geographic locations and phenomena or cultural groups, institutions, and traditions.

Data-gathering: A third requisite for critical thinking is good data-gathering skill. This includes the disciplined ability to observe behavior and situations accurately. Much uncritical thinking results from careless observation. For example, a student may be using a group of maps to study the life of people in a given area. He will be able to envision their life more realistically if he carefully observes relationships between data on the rainfall and temperature maps for the area. A group of children trying to improve the use of reference materials in the school library can be effective to the degree that they observe accurately the students at work in the library, the materials they use and the length of use, the relative location of various items used by the same persons, the questions asked by users, conversation between users, and so forth. Such observations spur creative thinking—in this case, ways to organize the library for better use.

There are other important data-gathering skills. Children should learn the differences between primary and secondary sources of information. A field trip to a newspaper office may enable them to observe reporters, layout men, and typesetters at work and to see the presses roll. Back at school, secondary sources such as films, pictures, and books enable them to continue their study.

They can become familiar with the complete but unselective record made by the camera and the tape recorder and recognize that their own eyes and ears are selective in what they record. They learn that what they see depends upon what they have been taught to look for by past experiences. For example, children who have had experience with crops on a farm notice the kinds of grains growing in the fields they pass on a trip.

It is also important for children to recognize when they are observing facts, when they are drawing inferences from facts, and when they are applying their own value judgments to a situation. For example, they may observe children with swollen stomachs. They infer that the children are undernourished. They judge that people in a world of plenty are wicked to allow children to go hungry.

Pupils should also learn to interpret other people's statements in the light of the speaker's or writer's purpose. Sometimes the purpose is stated directly, but at other times it must be inferred from what is said or written. Teachers can also help students learn to investigate the background and experience of people whose statements they consult.

Selectivity: Wise selection of ideas and information is a fourth crucial ability to develop. There is evidence that many children who score well on reading comprehension tests are not able to select from a paragraph those statements which relate to a particular purpose. Yet this ability to be selective is essential when trying to think through an issue. Any effort to test a hunch or to answer a question necessitates selecting pertinent facts. Careful pupil-teacher planning of objectives makes children more sure of what information they are seeking. Frequently when each child makes a simple study guide listing his own immediate questions to be answered, it is easier for him to keep the objectives in mind as he observes, reads, listens, or conducts an experiment.

Recognizing relationships: A fifth mark of good thinking is the ability to use new data and to reorganize previously acquired knowledge for new purposes —to solve new problems and to form new conclusions. Relationships between facts are important, recognizing main and subordinate points. Children can learn to ask themselves: What are the main points contributing to an answer to my questions? What other facts help to explain these main points? What more do I need to know to have a complete picture?

Assigning cause and effect relationships is tricky business. Students can be helped to avoid the common pitfall of assuming that simply because events follow one another, there is a cause and effect relationship. Such a mistaken idea leads to the erroneous belief that there is a simple cause for complex events and, hence, to conclusions based upon inadequate evidence. In reality, most situations stem from a complex of causes. Understanding this, students realize that frequently several actions are needed to change a situation. They then avoid the faulty thinking of single causation and single remedy. For example, usually a chain of events and circumstances brought about the continuous growth of a city—not just the location of the city at the meeting of two rivers or the selection of the site for a hostelry on the post road. Some well-situated settlements lose inhabitants and are abandoned because the market for their goods shifts or the major product is supplanted by a new invention. In studying a community, children may be helped to think beyond the obvious and avoid oversimplification. It is important to be aware of both geographic and cultural influences on a people. Mead establishes this concept clearly in describing the substantial cultural differences in the lives of several groups of people living within the Arctic Circle under quite similar geographic conditions.[3]

Testing ideas in action: A sixth mark of good thinking is continuous testing of ideas in action. Failure to do this leaves thinking at the "knowing about" stage rather than at the true knowing-in-action level. Failure to test in action leaves children in the role of spectators watching society operate, instead of participants learning the operation. Children are not candidates for their culture. They are members of it. To illustrate, the critical thinking involved in making decisions in a school election needs to be tested by watching the results. What are the effects? Does the school council member really represent the class who elected him? Does he report satisfactorily to his constituents? Is he inventive in finding ways to further the work of the council? Was the choice of representative a wise one? Solving real problems stimulates children's motivation, gives direction to their thinking, and enables them to see the results of their decisions. It also helps them avoid the apathetic thinking so common among adults who comment, "What can one person do about it?" or "I don't know what to do, but I guess it will all work out somehow."

Teachers render children a great service when they help them learn to ask, "What can I do about it?" and then guide them to do something. This commits teachers, of course, to letting children try their ideas without always attempting to substitute others. It means avoiding the behavior of the football coach who in his pep talk said to the quarterback: "Now it's entirely up to you. Get into the game. Use your brains and use your ingenuity, and do exactly what I signal from the bench."

Incidentally, participation in the solution of problems through carrying ideas into action serves two further purposes: it relieves the tensions which develop in children when they have problems and helps them to feel that they belong and are accepted. Participation also may lead to an effort to avoid creating more problems. For example, a child who has helped think through and carry into action a program to reduce accidents on the playground is likely to think twice before doing anything to cause an accident.

These learnings are significant in social education. They tend to help a child appreciate the work that goes into making a school or a community a good place to live. He appreciates this cultural heritage and the need for continuous, constructive change and improvement in the school and in the larger community.

HELPING CHILDREN TO THINK CRITICALLY

Sharing responsibility: What are some of the things that teachers can do to help children learn to think critically? Teachers who can help students learn to think critically trust them. They share many responsibilities with them. They also plan which jobs students can safely and profitably perform by themselves. Then when they agree that children may make the decisions involved, they let them carry the responsibility their way. Teachers who are not willing to do this should not give away the responsibility. However, teachers who do share responsibility with children do not withdraw from the group. When their ideas are sought, they contribute to group planning, but the teacher's suggestions are allowed to stand on their merit along with the children's ideas.

Faith in children: Second, teachers who help children think have faith in them and let them earn ever more freedom. They have faith in children's ideas and free them from the kind of classroom instruction which is really a guessing game in which the teacher asks questions and children guess what answers the teacher wants. Recent research has indicated that much instruction is of this quality.[4] Children do not learn to develop ideas this way.

A teacher who has faith in children also believes in their ability to direct themselves. He stimulates interests, makes the classroom an instructional laboratory full of challenging resources, guides children in planning promising learning experiences, and then assumes that the children will work. Most healthy children learn to respond to this faith by keeping constructively occupied at all times. When one job is finished, they start another without a reminder from their teacher. Children who have never experienced such faith do not usually respond to it overnight. It takes time to learn self-direction.

Use of current issues: Third, experiences with the real world are the stuff from which thinking is learned. Current affairs must be studied—questions for which there are no answers on the "answer sheet." An illustration of such a study is the project one class carried out during a millage campaign for school funds. The children thought through the issue carefully and studied school needs. Their school building was a good one, but some old schools needed to be replaced. They visited one such school, observed children using it, talked with them, and gathered information about the school. Then they wrote a booklet on the millage and bond issues and distributed it to their parents and other citizens of the community. They included simple information, beginning with the meaning of a mill and continuing with a presentation of school needs in the community. This real current issue in the field of taxation, in which they as school children had a vital stake, helped them improve their thinking abilities.

Exposure to different views: A fourth help which teachers can give children is to expose them to different points of view. In their families and churches, children often have experience with only one side of many issues. The school is the institution, established by the citizens in our free society, in which children from all kinds of homes come together to learn. The presence in a school group of children of different national origin, color, religious beliefs, political heritage, vocational expectations, and moral values makes the group a tremendous source of different points of view. More homogeneous school groups offer limited resources in this respect and people with different ideas and backgrounds should be brought in to share their thinking. It is important for teachers to help students avoid or break down stereotypes not only about religious, political, racial, ethnic, and vocational groups but also about slow and fast learners and the talented and untalented.

Unfortunately, the migration of people into cities and the later movement to the suburbs has tended to segregate people by socio-economic groups and also by color groups. As a result, school populations are increasingly more homogeneous in many ways than they were in small towns.

In compensating for this segregation, teachers need to bring in varied people, films, printed materials, and other resources to broaden children's experiences. I pay tribute to my own seventh grade teacher who provided her students with history books by both Canadian and American authors for the study of the period of the French and Indian and Revolutionary Wars. Accounts of an event from several newspapers frequently bring out varied viewpoints. One group of students, exploring the possibilities of seaport development in a city on the St. Lawrence Seaway, benefited from talking with both the manager of a private port facility and a representative of government who was working for public port facilities. The students discovered that they tended to favor the ideas of the more personable gentleman. The more they learned about the highly controversial issue, the more they realized that they needed to know still more and the less ready they were to take a firm stand for either a private or a public port.

Communicating ideas: A fifth help teachers can provide children is to encourage them to communicate their ideas. Asking children to describe their perceptions and share their thinking produces at least three benefits: 1) it enriches learning experiences for the class group; 2) it helps each participant clarify his perceptions and generalizations by having to formulate them into language or into a picture, diagram, or model; and 3) it enables the teacher to identify weak spots in the child's perception or reasoning.

Individualization: Sixth, teachers do well to recognize that learning is an individual matter. Even though great benefits accrue from exchange of ideas and from cooperative study, each child is called upon to apply many ideas and make many decisions as an individual. Indeed, the person he is interested in testing in action constantly is himself. Many mass procedures could well be abandoned. For example, much more individual use of books would enable each child to pursue his own study at his own rate. Frequently, the need to interview a resource person without a helping partner, when he is able to do this, forces a child to stand on his own feet. And even the business of getting into and out of his school building and classroom without being marched in a line helps him to learn to think about his own controls.

Better study of history: Seventh, teachers need to face the problem of how to teach history effectively. True, it is frequently more entertaining to read history for pleasure than to read fiction. But history has something more to offer. In order to better understand the present and to predict and live in the future more intelligently, we may need to start with the present and probe accounts of past events for clues to the origin of present-day problems and for an understanding of cultural problems. An understanding of the problems and behavior of American Indians is dependent upon a knowledge of the history of their confinement in reservations, the handling of civil rights, and a multitude of other factors. Or an understanding of relationships between police and newcomers to a large city depends upon tracing the experiences the people had with the police in another setting where the law enforcement pattern was radically different.

Making thinking exciting: Finally, teachers who think critically themselves and find the process exciting tend to encourage their students to find the experience exciting. Education is, in many ways, a process of contagion. It is easy for adults to fail to recognize this and to concentrate on admonishing children about their behavior rather than devoting major effort to providing in themselves models of critical thinking.

A present challenge to teachers is the need for more knowledge of how people think. The research about thinking processes is meager. At present, educators rely largely upon intuitive truths—the findings from experience. There is great hope, however, that studies now in process will provide teachers with more tangible assistance in the essential task of teaching children to think critically.

NOTES

1. McCutchen, Samuel P. "A Discipline for the Social Studies." *Social Education* 27: 61–65; February 1963.
2. McAulay, J. D. "Interests of Elementary School Children." *Social Education* 25: 407–409; December 1961.
3. Mead, Margaret. *People and Places.* Cleveland, Ohio: World Publishing Co., 1959. 318 pp.

4. Hughes, Marie M., and associates. *A Research Report. Development of the Means for the Assessment of the Quality of Teaching in Elementary Schools.* U.S. Office of Education Cooperative Research Project No. 353. Salt Lake City: The University of Utah, 1959.

STRENGTHENING CLASSROOM INSTRUCTION IN THE SOCIAL STUDIES

Ross M. Coxe

"What Rome was to the ancient world, what Great Britain has been to the modern world, America is to be to the world of tomorrow. We might wish it otherwise. I do. Every man who was young in the easier America of the pre-war world must long for it at times. But our personal preferences count little in the great movements of history, and when the destiny of a nation is revealed to it, there is no choice but to accept that destiny and to make ready in order to be equal to it."

These words, written by Walter Lippmann in 1939, are as significant now as they were then. The intervening years have brought America to the almost overwhelming responsibilities of world leadership. Prophecy has become reality, and we have no alternative but to exercise our responsibilities with all of the intelligence and vision we can muster.

Today, our nation is in desperate need of a citizenry that is capable of acting responsibly on the host of issues that confront us. We need citizens who possess social literacy and a sense of social responsibility, who can intelligently grasp the complex problems of our social order and wrestle with them productively.[1]

Sophisticated social skills are indispensable. We will not fulfill our responsibilities as the leading free nation or win our war against communism without them. It is not just through technology and the physical and biological sciences that we will prevail; we must also seek to prepare ourselves through the social sciences—and through the fine arts and the humanities.

The social studies should hold a position of the highest importance in the total school curriculum. The social studies are considerably more than history, geography, and civics. They are the learning experiences drawn from all of the subject-matter areas that are concerned with man and his interactions with his social and physical environment. So conceived, the social studies are manifestly essential to the development of a citizenry able to deal intelligently with the problems of man.

Reprinted from *The National Elementary Principal,* 42:30–34 (May, 1963), by permission of author and publisher.

Regrettably, many school systems do not accord the social studies their proper emphasis. In numerous cases, the sciences and mathematics are considered to be the most important areas of the curriculum, and school systems have devoted much time and money to their revision and improvement. This is important, to be sure. But now we need to direct our attention, our energies, and our resources to the problem of revising and upgrading the social studies.

Improvement of the social studies must necessarily come through many approaches and through the efforts of many people. The content of the social studies curriculum must be rigorously evaluated and then planned to serve the social objectives we seek. The ideas of academic scholars and specialists in learning, of classroom teachers and administrators, of parents and community leaders must all be given an audience. But improvement of the social studies cannot be effected unless classroom instruction is strengthened. It is in the everyday, practical ways a teacher works with children that the social studies are made vital.

Let us look now at three major aspects of social studies instruction and examine some of the ways teaching and learning can be improved.

INTEGRATION WITH OTHER SUBJECTS

If we look at the definition of social studies—the learning experiences drawn from all of the areas concerned with man and his interactions with his environment—it is apparent that every teacher is a teacher of social studies and that every area of the curriculum is related to the social studies. Good teaching does not compartmentalize knowledge or set up artificial divisions between subject-matter fields. And good teaching is based on conscious efforts to relate one idea to another, to generalize and interpret.

Science and social studies, for example, should be closely related in the elementary school. If a group of children were studying a science unit on climate, they would immediately get into an investigation of how climate affects man—how it affects his dress, his home, the food he raises, the occupations he pursues. As they related the study of climate to the social studies, the children would discover some of the reasons why people live in different ways.

As another example, if a class were studying automation as part of their science program, they would very naturally need to consider the effects of automation on man. If an industry in their community were automated and half of the working population were thrown out of jobs, how would this affect their fathers and the community in which they live? This is social studies —and social studies of a very vital kind.

By relating social studies with the basic reading program, a primary teacher might help her group of learners to understand another country and its people better through reading stories of other cultures. This would be an opportunity to use the globe and maps and talk with the children about the country's location. At this level, the children have a very limited understanding of space and direction, but they can begin to learn that the earth is round and the meaning of north and south, east and west.

Consider the relationship between mathematics and the social studies. The teacher has a wonderful opportunity to teach some basic social studies concepts and skills through math. In the first grade, for example, a class might be working on an arithmetic unit on telling time. As part of their study, they can learn something about time zones (geography) and about sundials (history and cultural anthropology).

Or the language arts. If we define the language arts as the communication skills of reading, speaking, writing, and listening, the social studies become an important avenue for instruction. You cannot teach reading in a vacuum. You cannot teach children to listen unless you say something for them to listen to. Drawing upon the content of the social studies, we can develop the communication skills, and these skills, in turn, are important to learning in the social studies.

Good social studies instruction, then, must be related to good instruction in other areas of the curriculum. The study of man and his relationships to his environment should be broadly conceived. And it is precisely because the social studies are so encompassing that they should be central to the elementary school curriculum.

INDIVIDUALIZING INSTRUCTION

One of the greatest problems we face in the social studies is individualization of instruction. The idea that people are different, and that these differences should be taken into account in education, is not new. Plato, for example, recognized human variability when he said, "For it comes into my mind when you say it that we are not born all exactly alike but different in nature for all sorts of different jobs." Comenius treated individual differences at length. He besought teachers to accept nature, to adjust methods and materials accordingly, and to start instruction at the pupil's level. Rosseau, too, recognized variation both among and within individuals, almost advocating a tutorial system.

We all believe that each human being is unique, that he is different from his fellows. Yet when one looks at school organizations and practices today, he wonders. Generally, the social studies curriculum is planned for the group rather than for the individual. One of our biggest tasks, then, in improving social studies instruction, is to examine our organizational plans and instructional practices and seek better ways to meet individual differences. We need to develop programs that will help each individual to develop his potentialities and achieve his goals.

We should begin by making sure that we understand what we mean by individual differences. Teachers, principals—all educators—need to have a thorough understanding of individual differences in childhood and adolescence. We need to recognize the physical, social, emotional, and intellectual behavior of different children at various stages of development. We need to be aware of the individual differences that exist in reading achievement and reading interest, in hobbies, in extent of travel, in the amount of stimulating conversation at home, in interests and talents, in intellectual curiosity, in study skills, in written and oral expression. Unless we are aware that all of these individual differences exist, how can we truly make instruction fit the pupil?

Let us look now at a number of ways in which instruction can be individualized in the social studies program.

Individualizing units: The unit method of teaching is valuable if we understand and apply two basic concepts. First, a unit does not have to be of any specific duration. One unit might last for a day; another, two weeks; another, three months; yet another, the entire school year. Second, a unit does not need to produce uniformity of instruction; all of the children do not have to study the same materials in the same way at the same time. This second point, in particular, merits some explanation.

Let us say that a group of fifth graders are organizing for a unit of work on the New England states. The program of work can and should be planned to take into account individual differences. The slowest learning youngster in the class might only be capable of studying and making a map of the New England region by tracing from an atlas or by use of an overhead projector. At the same time, the average youngsters are also doing research and practicing their work study skills of locating, interpreting, organizing, and utilizing information. But in keeping with their particular abilities, the average youngsters are studying the occupations of people in the New England states and the area's geography, history, and resources. The rapid learners in the class will very quickly grasp all of these phases of the unit. They can go into depth and study the role that the New England states play in the nation's economy; they can learn something about the interdependence of New England and other regions of the country. At times, the entire class can work together—for example, viewing a film or taking a field trip.

By organizing a unit in this way, social studies instruction can be individualized. Each child works according to his abilities and interest. Yet, at their own levels of comprehension, all are learning to do research. All are having an opportunity to discover and utilize information. All are learning something about the New England states. The teacher's role is to help each child achieve ever higher levels of competence and understanding—to work with the slow learning youngster, who at first is only able to make a regional map, so that he can move on to the next higher level of activity.

Invariably when this kind of an approach to unit study is proposed, the question is raised of how you can be sure that the curriculum guide or textbook will be covered. We would do better to attend to the business of making what we do teach valuable. Every teacher has a responsibility to help children uncover material—not to cover it. Content is a means to an end and not an end in itself. There is little merit to covering a voluminous amount of material without understanding it. There is little merit to covering the curriculum guide or textbook if instruction is not individualized to help each child acquire the values, concepts, and skills which the material was designed to develop.

Individualizing through school organization: All schools are organized on both a vertical and horizontal plan. The vertical organization of the school should provide for the continuous, unbroken, upward progression of all learners.[2] The horizontal organization of a school is a system of dividing the learners into instructional groups and assigning them to teachers. This might be the self-contained classroom, departmentalization, platoon or team teaching. We need to develop criteria against which to screen present and proposed practices. For example:

Do current or proposed practices provide for individual differences?

Do current or proposed practices provide motivation for continued learning?

Do current or proposed practices provide for the development of skills, concepts, and values?

Do current or proposed practices provide for the development of independent and critical thinking?

Do current or proposed practices develop an understanding of the interrelationship of the various areas of knowledge?

Another way to individualize instruction, organizationally, is through a block program. When a substantial amount of time is available for an integrated learning experience, it is usually easier to diversify activities and to provide for individual differences. However, it should be noted that a block program will not accomplish its objectives if it becomes nothing more than a sequence of unrelated periods of instruction. If a school sets up an hour-and-a-half block to teach the language arts and social studies, and teachers spend 15 minutes on history, 15 minutes on geography, 15 minutes on civics, 15 minutes on spelling, 15 minutes on writing, and 15 minutes on grammar, this is not a real block program. It is simply a separate subject-matter approach.

Individualizing through classroom organizations: There are many ways to individualize instruction in the classroom—among them, by grouping, by enrichment, by acceleration, and by independent work.

As was pointed out in discussing social studies units, ability grouping offers one means of individualizing instruction. Groups, of course, can be established on the basis of other criteria as well—on the basis of interests, for example. Taking into account the many variables that comprise individual differences, a teacher might divide a class into groups to do specific jobs in relation to a unit of study. If a class were studying their community, one group of youngsters might investigate the community's government. Another group could study local industries. Another might make a mural depicting the history of the town. Another might find out about the cultural resources of the community. Still another could study the town from a sociological standpoint.

Each group's findings would be reported back to the total class so that all the children would benefit from each of the studies.

Enrichment is another means of providing individualized instruction. Too many teachers think that enrichment is just more of the same. It isn't. Enrichment provides learning experiences outside of the regular course of study that take children into depth and broaden their understanding and concepts. Properly conceived, enrichment can be used to provide each pupil with experiences beyond the regular classroom fare which are uniquely fitted to his abilities and interests.

Acceleration is a third way to individualize instruction in the classroom. Most of us think of acceleration as skipping a grade. In the context in which it is used here, acceleration refers to the repositioning of content, keeping the youngster with his class and repositioning content as he is ready for it. In this context, acceleration obviously can help to provide for individual differences.

A fourth method by which a teacher can individualize the program is through independent study. There are times when every child should have the opportunity to work alone—perhaps in the classroom, perhaps in the library with the guidance of the librarian, or perhaps in the community. This is an excellent technique for individualizing instruction, especially for rapid learners.

In all of these ways—through the organization of units, through school organization, and through classroom organization—teachers and principals can develop practical ways to accommodate the individual differences in every class group. There is no one best way to individualize. The important thing, if we are to improve the social studies program, is to be sure that we do it.

USE OF MULTIPLE RESOURCES

One of the most important ways in which teachers and principals can practically improve the teaching of social studies is through the use of multiple resources.

The day of the single textbook has passed. A really vital social studies program cannot be taught "by *the* book." Why? First, we cannot rely on any single textbook to give us all of the information we need on a given subject. Second, no one textbook can meet the wide reading range in any class of children. Third, if we really want to help children to learn the techniques of research, we must encourage them to use a variety of materials. Fourth, a textbook usually reflects one person's opinion or, in the social studies, is slanted to geography, or history, or economics, or civics to the exclusion of other social science disciplines.

Three of our major goals in the social studies are to teach critical thinking, to teach children how to solve problems effectively, and to help them generalize and draw their own conclusions. If we are to achieve these goals, we must use multiple learning materials. Pupils must have resources available which give many points of view on an issue, which discuss a problem from the perspective of several disciplines. Only then do they have a basis from which to analyze, generalize, and come to their own conclusions.

We do, of course, need to use textbooks. They help us organize our teaching. They can serve as a common point of departure from which children can move into supplementary texts and reference books, maps, globes, and charts, films, filmstrips, and records, tradebooks and pamphlets, and community resources—both natural and human. But this kind of use of a textbook is entirely different from the narrow page-by-page approach of previous years.

The creative use of multiple resources is being supported currently by the development of materials learning centers, in which a school system houses all of its instructional materials in a central location. Under this arrangement, teachers can go to the center and select from a large collection those materials which fit the needs of her class. Each teacher has a much wider range of resources available than she would under a classroom-by-classroom or school-by-school allocation of learning materials.

Whether or not there is a central materials center, the important thing is that teachers have available and use a variety of resources in teaching the social studies. When we do this, and do it creatively, we will have taken a major step toward the strengthening of the social studies program in the elementary school.

THE PRINCIPAL'S ROLE

We have discussed three specific ways in which classroom instruction in the social studies can be improved—through integration with other areas of the curriculum, through greater individualization of instruction, and through the use of multiple resources. The degree to which these things are done depends considerably upon the leadership of the principal.

As the educational leader of the school, the principal plays an important role in any effort to strengthen the social studies. It is the principal who helps teachers to become more aware of the importance of the social studies and of making them an integral part of the curriculum. And once this awareness exists, it is the principal who helps the faculty to organize into work study groups. He procures resources. He creates a climate for learning, for study, for change in the social studies program. He helps teachers to gain the enthusiasm and the security which will send them back into the classroom ready to experiment and to seek better ways of teaching the social studies.

Without the active and informed leadership of principals, the elementary school social studies program cannot be substantially revitalized. And without improvement of the social studies, there is a serious question of how well our country will be able to meet the complex problems of world leadership.

NOTES

1. Preston, Ralph C. "The Role of Social Studies in Elementary Education." *Social Studies in the Elementary School*. Fifty-Sixth Yearbook. National Society for the Study of Education. Chicago: University of Chicago Press, 1957. pp. 4–26.
2. John Goodlad. Unpublished paper for the NEA Project on Instruction.

HOW TO USE GROUP DISCUSSION

Ruth E. Litchen

DISCUSSION: A DEMOCRATIC FORCE

The need for group discussion in contemporary American life is clearly recognized. Critical issues on both domestic and international fronts demand the use of effective, democratic procedures which will bring group intelligence to bear on problems.

Labor groups, international and national clubs, consumer and educational organizations, churches and other groups—all agree to the need for open discussion whether the issues are of world import or only pertinent to their particular needs.

But with this growing feeling that discussion is a necessary force in the democratic way of life comes the realization that numerous citizens lack adequate training and experience in discussion, and thus are not able to make real contributions to problem solving. We are a literate people for the most part. We read about our social, economic, and political life both to understand the present-day world and to learn about the past. But as in the realm of sports, music, theater, motion pictures, and television, we have become victims of "spectatoritis." As we have developed as individuals and as a national group, we have been taught to listen and in large measure to accept. Too often rather than trying to solve our own problems we wait for someone else to solve them for us.

In a democracy, the use of group processes and of group problem solving is essential. Unless we learn to cope intelligently and effectively with common problems democracy cannot survive.

Communication is necessary for cooperative enterprise. Of the several ways man has devised for communicating thoughts to his fellows, the oldest and most common is that of face-to-face exchange through speech. There are several advantages in this personal situation. An interchange of ideas stimulates interaction in such a way that something extra is generated— something more than the sum of the thinking of its members. Further, the individual develops and grows when he comes before a group to express himself. The very fact that he has learned to put his thoughts into words makes a difference in that person.

The process may develop somewhat in this manner: One member will make a suggestion about the problem; another may react to it by adding new evidence; a third objects by bringing out another side; a fourth sees a way of reconciling the original suggestion and the objection. The result is that the

Reprinted from *How to Do It Series—No. 6,* National Council for the Social Studies, by permission of author and publisher.

solution belongs not to any one individual but to the group itself. This example is oversimplified, of course, but almost everyone can recall a similar incident from his own experience. "Give and take" of this kind does much to create the group morale which is evidence of a well-integrated group; even more important, better solutions are the result.

DISCUSSION AIDS THE INDIVIDUAL

Certain individual as well as group values can result from the discussion method. These are some that will accrue to the participating individual:

1. Increased ability to express oneself before a group. 2. Added power to do critical thinking. 3. Greater knowledge through shared experience. 4. Increased tolerance for views of others. 5. Better skills for critical evaluation of one's own and others' points of view. 6. Realization that "truth" is often complex and many-sided. 7. Increased ability to become a participating citizen on the basis of knowledge.

Note that these values come for the "participating individual." Not the one who only sits in on a discussion group, but the one who joins in their thinking and expresses himself, learns and grows through the experiences of group discussion.

HAS TWOFOLD PURPOSE

Two general purposes of discussion are policy making or planning for immediate action based on accepted values, and learning or resolving value conflicts for deferred action. These purposes function in almost every group situation, at all levels of maturity. The kind and amount of discussion will depend upon the many variables; among them, the purpose of the discussion, the nature of the problem, the amount of basic information on the problem which the participants have, the emotional reaction to the problem, and the age and experience of the discussants.

Many of the problems leading to policy making in classroom discussions arise as parts of larger units of work. For example, a first grade class is planning a trip to a fire station. Group planning is essential to provide for good conduct en route as well as during the visit. Later, as an outcome of the trip, the question may be raised: "How can we help the firemen?" From such a query another policy-making discussion might ensue.

Perhaps a majority of classroom discussions occur in order to learn about or resolve value conflicts. For example, a class in American Problems considers the question: "What is the fairest system of taxation that can pay for the protection and services we receive from national, state, and local budgets?" The action that follows may establish values which will be the basis for deferred action. On the other hand, it may lead to immediate action through a community service project such as providing interested civic groups with information on taxation. As the result of buying food for a party, a group of elementary children might raise the question: "Why must we pay a tax to the government on things we buy?" The less complex concepts involved here might be discussed and understood as a basis for deferred action.

Action, whether immediate and direct or deferred and indirect, should be the ultimate goal of all problem solving and thus of discussion.[1]

SEATING THE PARTICIPANTS

The seating arrangement of the group can contribute materially to a successful discussion. To get attention and maximum participation, seats should be arranged to face one another. In the classroom, desk chairs may be placed in a circle, semicircle, or oval. Teachers and pupils can try out these groupings to see which is most satisfactory. Sometimes tables can be placed to form a hollow triangle, with pupils and teacher all seated around the outside facing one another. Probably best of all is the conference table arrangement. Here, as in adult conference groups, pupils in the classroom can meet around the table, discuss with one another and with the teacher the problem at hand, and arrive at generalizations of real value. In all cases, the teacher or group discussion leader will get more successful participation if he becomes a part of the group. Any arrangement of seats which puts the teacher in a dominant position or holds him apart is apt to act as a deterrent to discussion because the group may develop the attitude that it will be told all of the answers.

GUIDE TO STRAIGHT THINKING

Although the seating may be an aid or hindrance to good discussion, it is after all only one factor. Excellent discussions have been carried on in rooms with seats screwed to the floor and everyone facing the front. What matters most is the quality of thinking.

It is commonly conceded that good group thinking follows the same general pattern as good individual thinking. John Dewey analyzed the thought process and broke it down into five steps, sometimes known as the scientific method or the process of "straight thinking." They are:

1. A felt difficulty, a recognized problem. 2. Location, definition, and analysis of the problem. 3. Suggestion of possible solutions. 4. Development, by reasoning, of the consequences of the solution (intellectualized development of the suggested solutions, action). 5. Further observation and experimentation (verification).[2]

No discussion need adhere to these steps in precise order. But they are excellent guideposts by which to check the "straightness" of the group's thinking.

THE PROBLEM

The problem, or felt difficulty, is the center of the discussion. Therefore, it must be one of concern to the group and within the experience of the individuals participating in its solution. The truism that "the discussion belongs to the group" must be kept in mind in choosing a problem. Special enthusiasm of the teacher or a small group of students should never be allowed to dominate the selection. If they do, the rest of the group will have only a nominal interest in the solution and the discussion will probably bog down.

A problem for work or discussion need not be a "difficulty"; it may be a "concern" or an "interest." It need not be "controversial" in the common usage of that term, but it must be of sufficient importance and interest to warrant group consideration. However, it should not be so complex that the group cannot make headway toward its solution, and its scope should be limited enough that progress toward solution can be made in the time available. An elementary school class, for example, can scarcely deal adequately with the problems of what should be done with minority nationalities in Europe, but they may make progress with a problem involving minorities in their own school or community. Through success in considering limited phases of problems, they can better understand remote situations.

Among the various approaches that can be used to arouse interest in a problem area is the shared experience. This might be a field trip to a place of interest such as a government agency, distribution center or museum. Another possibility is the laboratory situation—using pictures, models, movies, radio, television, stories, and printed materials to stimulate discussion. Stating the problem in question form is perhaps the most effective way to point up the issue to be studied.

THE SOLUTION

The solution should not be proposed prematurely, that is, before most of the facts are in. Superficial reporting of authority or opinion is not enough; the thinking of the group must be based on specific facts resulting from adequate research. Sometimes skilled questioning will help the group see whether or not they are ready to consider solutions, and illustrations will show where a proposed solution might lead. These techniques encourage critical thinking by pointing up further issues involved in the problem. They may have to be suggested by the teacher at first; but as the group becomes more experienced in group discussion and more conscious of techniques of scientific thinking, individual members will gradually accept the responsibility. Care must be exercised, however, that the discussion does not degenerate into noisy argument, nor into conflicts based on personal animosities. It should be clearly understood that discussion is a cooperative enterprise for a common purpose, where the aim is consensus of the group on the best available solution.

Too often democracy is conceived solely as majority rule. True, a majority decision must be accepted when an issue comes to the test; but the ideal is to lead group thinking to the point of consensus as often as possible. Taking an early vote to see how the issue stands is not always a good policy; it may crystallize an unreasoned opposition and thus make a common solution more difficult. As the group becomes more proficient in discussion, and as each individual develops willingness to consider all relevant materials, consensus will become increasingly important to the group itself.

COMMON PITFALLS

Any socialized discussion group regardless of age level or experience is likely to encounter certain persistent difficulties. They must be recognized by group members (including the teacher), and attempts must be made to resolve them with fairness to each participant. The method of dealing with them must vary with each situation, since the difficulties take different forms in different groups. These common pitfalls include:

The problem of domination by a minority. Often a few participants are inclined to dominate the situation—to do all of the talking. The leader can encourage the less loquacious to enter the discussion by putting a question to them or asking their opinion. With wider participation, there will be less chance of domination by the few. The teacher may encourage participation through casual conversation outside of class, or by asking the reticent pupil to repeat something which he has said at another time. Sometimes the teacher may even quote him. After a pupil has made a contribution which is accepted and appreciated, he becomes more willing to make additional ones. Real interest in the problem on the part of both teacher and pupils will do much to draw out the timid.

The problem of holding to the issue. Another problem is that of keeping the remarks relevant to the subject at hand. Here the teacher or discussion leader must use careful judgment. The point raised may not be so irrelevant as it first appears to be; it may have a real relationship to the problem which does not appear on the surface. When the discussion gets obviously out of line, the leader can, by careful steering, bring the major point into focus again. He may give a brief summary of the main points in the discussion thus far or call on one of the other participants to do so. A blackboard listing of major points will help to hold the discussion to the issue. Questions directed to various participants will bring them back to the topic.

It is particularly important to keep to the subject if the discussion involves policy making, that is, if certain issues must be considered and settled in order to clear the way for further action. The discussion leader need not work alone. Children and young people are quick to recognize irrelevancy, and if the subject is one in which they are genuinely interested, they will not want to see it discarded or passed over lightly. They will often bring in ideas themselves or raise questions which will again set the course of discussion in proper channels. Children as well as adults need to learn through experience that keeping a discussion on its proper course is a matter of judgment and guidance, not of sarcasm or outspoken criticism.

If the purpose of the discussion is to build informational background, the group may wish to pursue the digression for a time, finding it more profitable than the subject under discussion. If so, they should be allowed the opportunity but all members should recognize that they have temporarily left the main issue.

The problem of lagging discussion. Sometimes discussions seem to stall. The thinking or talking goes in circles and no progress is evident. Inadequate information upon which to base a tentative solution is often the cause. In this case the teacher or some other participant needs to point out the difficulty, and the discussion should be postponed until the needed evidence can be gathered. Sometimes the issues need to be sharpened; this is often done best by summarizing what has been said and pointing out what needs to be decided. Many discussion groups fail to use the summary to its fullest advantage. Every group needs to stop occasionally in the course of discussion to take stock of what has been done and what remains to be accomplished. Sometimes contributions become repetitious. The leader, teacher or student, has an obligation to move the discussion along to the next point when it is clear that the one at hand has been exhausted. Again the summary is a useful technique.

VARIATIONS WITHIN

Groups vary as do individuals. The problems mentioned above will be somewhat different from group to group, and from day to day within the same group. Factors which condition the nature of the group include: (a) the size of the group, (b) the maturity of its members, (c) the types of experiences of the individuals within the group and of the group itself, (d) the amount of practice individual members have had in democratic group problem-solving situations, (e) how long they have been in close association, (f) the intensity of interest in the problem, and (g) the leader's skill and understanding of discussion techniques. There are levels of development in the integration of groups as well as of individuals.

An aggregation of people brought together to solve a common problem is seldom a well-unified group until it has worked together for some time. The common problem becomes the unifying force. This is as true in an elementary or secondary school classroom as in an adult organization.

Initial lack of integration makes desirable some type of leadership, temporarily appointed or elected, to help develop group action. In the classroom, the teacher usually provides it in this initial stage. As soon as the group can work together relatively well, however, students may take over as discussion leaders and may be expected to develop real skill.

In the earlier stages the teacher may need to choose leaders from the group. As soon as students begin to understand the purpose and pattern of discussion and to know each other well, it is both "safe" and democratic to turn selection over to them. Their sense of fitness will usually guarantee that the leadership is passed to pupils particularly interested in given materials.

Leadership within the group should shift as often as is practicable or necessary. Each member has some special ability or knowledge which qualifies him to direct certain activities. These potentials should be recognized and used whenever possible. There appears to be a positive relationship between successful group integration and the ability to arrive at higher levels of thinking and discussion when interests and intelligence levels are similar. Background homogeneity and similarity of interests are factors that contribute to the solidarity of the group.

The leader's function is to direct cooperative activity so that the group is able to realize its fullest potentialities in the thinking process. He must remember, however, that the discussion belongs to the group. No individual (not even the teacher) should exploit the discussion for his own ends at the expense of the class, no matter how worthy the goal. The leader needs a variety of techniques, such as the following:

Write on the blackboard the question to be discussed; call attention to its phraseology when the discussion threatens to wander.

Phrase questions so that a "discussing" answer, rather than "yes" or "no," is required. "Why" and "how" questions tend to bring out discussions better than do "what?" "when?" or "where?" The last three often stifle discussion, because the answer to any one of them may seem to settle the problem.

However, yes or no questions may be used to draw timid persons into the discussion.

Phrase questions impartially, so that they are not leading questions.

Never answer questions; rather, refer them to a member of the group.

If no one offers to answer a question, rephrase it.

Sometimes refer a question to the whole group, asking for a volunteer response.

Sometimes refer a question to a member of the group who has not taken an active part, but only if there is good reason to believe he can contribute.

Follow a participant's comment by two or three questions growing out of it.

Use summaries, as suggested above.

In summarizing, give credit for major points and opinions to the individuals who contributed them.

Ask another participant, perhaps a reticent one, to summarize.

Accept each contribution as worthy of thought.

If a contribution is to one side of the main point, make a note of it and say, "That is an important factor. May we come back to it when we reach that part of our problem?"

If a contribution seems irrelevant, ask the contributor to explain his point a bit further, to clarify its relation to the topic at hand.

Use a blackboard to list the arguments on different sides of the question; advantages and disadvantages of a course of action; probable results of a course of action.

The leader may profit from a checklist which he can use as a guide before the discussion and afterwards as a means of self-evaluation. The following is a sample.[3]

1. Was there any evidence that the conference leader knew what he was trying to accomplish?

2. Was the leader able to handle the discussion so as to avoid confusion of thinking either on the part of the group or on his own part?

3. Was the leader's background work effective in assisting the group to organize and clarify their thinking?

4. Did the leader try to force his ideas on the group?

5. Was the leader able to keep still and let the group talk?

6. Did the leader allow time for the group to think it out for themselves?

7. Did the leader show good judgment as to the proper time for summarizing or crystallizing the discussion?

8. Did the leader avoid being sidetracked and demonstrate ability to hold the discussion to the main topic under consideration; did he know when and how to get back to the main question after being sidetracked?

9. Did the leader throw questions back to the group in accordance with good conference procedure?

10. Was good distribution of discussion secured or were a few individuals permitted to monopolize it?

11. Did the leader maintain control of the group without appearing to dominate?

12. Did the leader exhibit resourcefulness in the use of suitable and effective devices to stimulate and clarify thinking?

13. Was the leader able to sense "dynamite" situations and handle them effectively?

14. Did the leader guide the group thinking through the steps of the conference procedure?

SIZE AND PROGRESS

It may be well to add a word at this point about size of discussion groups. There is no fixed minimum or maximum that can be set because the other variables already mentioned must be considered. However, two general statements seem possible. First, the group should be large enough to provide stimulation. Second, if the group is large, procedure will need to be more formal; in other words, it will take longer to reach the higher levels of integration.

As the level of integration increases within the class group, the leadership moves from teacher to pupil leader, from pupil leaders to group. The third level requires a high degree of group cohesiveness and should be the goal toward which all groups strive. At this level leadership is not centered in any one individual except as he temporarily functions because of his unique ability to give a bit of evidence, suggest a possible solution, or raise a pertinent question. Each person is allowed freedom to present his own ideas honestly in the discussion. Speakers do not need to be recognized; hands are seldom raised for permission to speak. When a pupil senses that he has a worthwhile addition to make, feels that a summary is needed, or wishes to raise a question or challenge a point, he does so, carrying his share of the group responsibility in solving the problem at hand. This kind of procedure means that interrelationships in the group have been developed on a sound basis of respect for the opinions of one's fellows, on sportsmanship in awaiting one's turn, on desire to get the job done in the best way possible, and on a feeling of group morale in the classroom developed through real activities.

THE TEACHER'S PLACE

The teacher must be cognizant of the dynamics of group development if discussion is to flourish and grow into a democratic technique under his guidance. He must be sensitive to the total situation, knowing when to take the lead; when to wait and watch. This writer's concept of the teacher's role has been one of guidance and counsel, not of authority or dictatorship. Real group discussion is never found in an authoritarian situation.

The teacher has certain responsibilities for maintaining a learning situation in the classroom. He must have a sense of direction for himself and his students and have sound ideas about methods by which they may arrive at their goals. He must always be a responsible member of the group whether there is an acting discussion leader or not. His job is to aid the individual and the group in its growth and development. As the adult leader he can never shunt these responsibilities onto students.

Listed below are some of the most important among the teacher's manifold responsibilities. He should:

1. See that all of the really important facts bearing on the problem have been considered, perhaps pointing out material that has been forgotten or ignored.

2. Make sure that the process of group thinking is based on the scientific method which means "straight thinking." (On all levels the teacher should try to help students learn to recognize and analyze that process for themselves.)

3. Be certain that the important and appropriate concepts or generalizations have been drawn from the discussion.

4. Help each member of the group to develop respect for his fellows and recognize his own responsibility to the group.

5. See that the discussion remains focused on the solution of the problem and that it never becomes personally directed toward an individual or group of individuals.

6. Plan so that the group is steadily advancing to a higher level of development in problem solving.

7. Be aware of the need for adaptation to individual differences in terms of abilities, skills, knowledge, experiential background, and interests of participants in the discussion.

8. Be alert to maintain a learning situation if the self-discipline of the group breaks down badly.

EVALUATION OF THE METHOD

Occasionally the teacher (and the discussion leaders of more mature groups) needs to pause to see what direction progress is taking in group discussion. The following questions might serve as guides:

1. Have the discussions really belonged to the group; have the topics been chosen along the lines of pupils' interests and have they been built on their experience?

2. Has sharing experiences helped to push and clarify pupils' thinking?

3. Has it made pupils realize that there are many ways of thinking about a problem; that there are no formulas for solving problems, but that each must be carefully considered in its particular setting?

4. Has it made the pupils more willing to participate and carry through?

5. Has it made the pupils more discriminating but also more tolerant of varying points of view?

6. Have the discussions followed the five steps for "straight thinking"?

7. Have the pupils increased their proficiency in group problem solving; have the discussions helped build *esprit de corps?*

8. Have attitudes been developed which will express themselves in action, *i.e.,* in terms of better citizenship and democratic behavior?

9. Many discussion leaders, among them alert teachers, have found it helpful to have participants fill out a brief questionnaire after the discussion. The forms should be unsigned, and should urge the participant to be frank. A few sample questions are:

(a) Was the discussion very interesting? Mildly interesting? Not at all? (b) Did you learn something new about the subject? Much? A little? Nothing? (c) Has your understanding of the subject grown? (d) How much did the leader talk? Too much? Just enough? Too little? (e) Did you participate in the discussion? Once? Often? Not at all?

Similar questions fitting the need of the particular group or point of discussion, or both, would give the leader insight in planning for further discussions.

As teacher and pupils become more skilled in discussion techniques and continue to grow in problem-solving ability, changes should become perceptible. Attitudes based on value concepts should begin to change. Active participation in school and community projects for the common good should follow. Unless something definite happens as a consequence of discussion, it becomes a hollow, meaningless form of verbal exercise for those who engage in it. However, action is sometimes deferred and attitudes and their changes are difficult to measure. This should not be cause for teachers to despair. It should stimulate them to renewed vigor in searching for effective techniques and evaluation instruments to measure them. Certainly group discussion in social studies instruction is of key significance and worthy of further study, practice, and research.

NOTES

1. For teaching materials which directly relate the discussion method to community and civic action programs on specific issues see National Association of Secondary-School Principals, *Operation Atomic Vision;* and Association for Supervision and Curriculum Development, *Toward Better Teaching.* 1949 Yearbook. Chapter 6.
2. Dewey, John, *How We Think.* Boston: D. C. Heath and Co., 1910. p. 72.
3. Klinefelter, C. F., and Battin, Charles T. *Social Leadership.* U.S. Office of Education, Federal Security Agency, Bulletin 1945, No. 231. Washington, D.C.: Superintendent of Documents, Government Printing Office, 1945. pp. 13–14.

GROUPING THROUGH LEARNING CENTERS

R. V. Allen

GROUPING MYTHS THAT LEAD TO GROPING

A popular myth among educators is that "a group can learn something." *No group ever learned anything—only individuals learn!*

To assume that one can find the "achievement levels" of individuals and place them in "alike groups" is another popular myth. *Children with the same achievement scores on any given day are not alike, and excellence in teaching will increase the already existing differences!*

A myth gaining in popularity is one that proposes that it is "good" to move "the same curriculum content" from a teaching format of mass instruction with one child answering questions as a representative of many children to one of procedures and materials that require every child to answer every question. The myth implies that the ability to answer an endless round of questions is to gain an education. *Asking valid questions and having available a variety of resources, including human resources, to find answers that are valid for the individuals asking them is the true pursuit of education!*

Rather than grope for *the right way* to group children, many teacher groups are abandoning grouping mythology and are seeking a measure of flexibility in managing class groups, made possible by new curriculum ra-

From *Childhood Education*, December, 1968, Vol. 45, pages 200–203. Reprinted by permission of R. V. Allen and the Association for Childhood Education International, 3615 Wisconsin Avenue, N.W., Washington, D.C. Copyright © 1968 by the Association.

tionales, materials and equipment. They are finding grouping procedures that highlight success rather than lack of it. They are realizing that, to be successful, goals of providing opportunities and experiences for the most number of children are met with flexible groupings that emphasize *each child's success;* and they are accepting the fact that every child individualizes his learning whether we want him to or not.

LEARNING LABORATORIES PROMOTE SUCCESS

Classrooms are operated as learning laboratories that extend throughout the day and include learning centers in all curriculum areas. The concept is in sharp contrast to the arrangement of interest centers that provide children with attractive places to spend their time when they have finished their work. *In learning centers, the children work.*

The laboratory might be characterized by two major streams of organization: (1) teaching activities, in which the teacher assumes responsibilities for identifying and extending concepts and leading children to formulate questions for further study and investigation; and (2) learning centers, where children can go by choice or by assignment to engage in self-expression or to contact and interact with the ideas of other people who have communicated in many ways—through tapes, recordings, films, filmstrips, picture sets, books, art prints, riddles, sculpture, and friendly conversation.

The two major streams of organization are interwoven in actual practice because one is impossible without the other. For example, introduction and demonstration of a set of skills by the teacher should usually be extended and exercised in one or more of the learning centers. On the other hand, observation of student performance in the learning centers will often suggest skills and abilities that need to be called to the attention of the whole class or a small group. Individual and small group work, necessary for success for most children, is possible only in an environment that provides for ongoing learning centers where children work when not in the more organized teaching-learning experiences.

LEARNING CENTERS PROVIDE FLEXIBLE GROUPING

Children and teachers plan ways of using the learning centers efficiently and effectively. Some of the day may be devoted to work in assigned centers. This assures that every child has a variety of experiences in all curriculum areas. Some of the day may be devoted to work in self-selected centers, with controls being placed on the number of children who can be accommodated in any one center. This assures that each child can pursue his personal interests and explore new ones in an atmosphere free from the pressures of testing and reporting. Some of the day may be devoted to large group activities, with the teacher or children in charge. This assures a degree of unity in the group, regardless of the range of ability or age. It also assures that the teacher can expose children to skills and abilities with increasing challenge and introduce new materials and ideas that are being placed in the learning centers for independent work.

Some learning centers are established as continuing centers for the school year and others as temporary centers for a special study or season. Some that might be used most of the time are:

Book Center for Browsing and Reading: This collection should contain books for recreational reading, books for information to serve all curriculum areas, and books that help children to be better readers. It should contain books and magazines published in the classroom by groups of children and by individual authors.

Communications Resource Center: This center should provide a place where children can choose writing and language study as a recreational activity and as a means of increasing language skills—especially writing skills. It should be as available for all children as book centers have been in the past. This center might contain motivators and stimulators to help children decide upon something to write; resources for words children use as references for spelling; a variety of dictionaries; categories of words used frequently in descriptive writing—color, size, shape, texture, action, weather; and language study folders that might be used as follow-up activities from group presentations by the teacher.

Viewing Center: A few individual viewers for filmstrips and a collection of filmstrips for browsing and reading add one other means for children to come in contact with the ideas of other people. Motion picture projectors with listening headsets provide multisensory materials in all curriculum areas, including recreational and enrichment of life.

Listening Center: A collection of records and tapes adds a dimension to the class that can be recreational in nature and supplement the direct teaching of skills. Books with accompanying recordings give children a chance to hear the voices of many excellent readers as they follow along in the books. In low reading groups, poor readers are freed from the boredom of always hearing poor readers read.

Art Center: Multiple materials for self-expression must be available to children. Ideas germinate as children explore painting and manipulate materials. From these ideas language grows and ideas are extended. Materials must be available for illustrating books and binding them attractively. It is imperative that this center be available to all children and not be used as a reward for those who perform and conform.

Game Center: Games that review and practice skills should be available for children to play individually or in small groups—commercial games or games developed by children and teachers from classroom learning experiences.

Science Center: Children must have a place in the classroom that invites them to see the world in which they live in new ways and to have new words to express themselves as they observe, hear, feel, taste and smell the "newness of life."

Role-Playing Center: A place and materials must be provided that permit children to act out roles of many people—real and imaginary. Young children might engage in dramatic play, while older children might prepare and present dramatic productions. Regardless of age, children have need to try out roles of other people and view themselves in situations that have never been possible in real life.

LEARNING SITUATIONS
PLACE VALUE ON UNIQUENESS

Learning situations are organized in ways that permit each child to view himself as worthy and able to succeed in learning tasks of increasing difficulty and complexity. The child feels the success of working alone, of working with children of like ability and age, of working with those whose ability and age are significantly different from his, and of working as a contributing member of a large group.

A classroom organized around learning centers gives all children a chance to grow in unique ways, to maintain their personality differences in a climate of warm understanding, and to extend their personal interests. At the same time, learning center groupings give the teacher a chance to guide children to questions that are significant to them and to encounters with skills and abilities that need to be extended, at the same time encouraging self-expression in many forms and with independence from direct instruction.

Individuals learn in learning centers.

STYLES OF LEARNING

Frank Riessman

In any classroom, probably no two pupils learn the same things in the same way at the same pace. Some learn most easily through reading; others through listening; still others through doing things physically. Some prefer to work under the pressure of deadlines and tests; others like a more leisurely pace. Some learn by being challenged by people ahead of them; others learn best by helping people behind them.

Everyone has a distinct style of learning, as individual as his personality. These styles may be categorized principally as visual (reading), aural (listening), or physical (doing things), although any one person may use more than one. Some persons, for example, find it much easier to pace the floor while reading an assignment than to sit perfectly still at a desk. Their style may be more physical.

Reprinted from *NEA Journal,* 55:15–17 (March, 1966), by permission of author and publisher.

A common characteristic of the disadvantaged child is his physical approach to learning. He has been exposed to very little reading because his parents rarely have the time to read to him. For this reason, it may be easier for him to learn to read by acting out the words than by hearing them spoken by his teacher. This is borne out by the fact that children at a school in one of New York City's poorest neighborhoods are learning to read effectively by singing and dancing to the words. Since songs and physical movement have been incorporated into the teaching of reading, the percentage of retarded readers in the school has reportedly been cut in half.

For a long time now, teachers and guidance workers have tended to ignore the concept of different styles of learning. They have, instead, focused their attention on emotion, motivation, and personality as causes for learning or failure to learn. When confronted with an intellectually able student whose learning fails to measure up to his learning potential, they have tended to attribute this failure to an emotional block or personality conflict. Little attention has been given to how a pupil's learning could be improved simply by concentrating on the way he works and learns.

I believe that a careful analysis of the way a child works and learns is of greater value than speculation about his emotional state. He may indeed feel sibling rivalry or certain irrational fears, but these conditions may not affect his learning as much as the methods his teacher uses to teach him. The important consideration, in my opinion, is whether the methods of learning imposed by the teacher utilize sufficiently the strengths in a child's style of learning.

Most teachers, unfortunately, have been trained to look upon learning in a general way. Their preparation, which may include no more than a few survey courses in educational psychology, neglects the idiosyncrasies involved in learning.

For example, most teachers probably assume that the best way to study a reading assignment is first to survey the chapter. This is what they have been taught from the early grades through college because it is the way most people learn best. Some students, however, become so anxious and disturbed at being told to take an overall view of a chapter that they cannot function. Their style calls for reading a chapter slowly, section by section. Requiring such a person to skim the entire chapter first makes no more sense than telling a person who can't resist peeking at the last chapter of a mystery that he must read the book straight through.

The general recommendation that one must have a quiet place to study may be equally lacking in validity. Strangely enough, some people do their best studying in a noisy place, or with certain sounds such as music or even traffic in the background. The textbooks do not talk about this because, for the "average" person, peace and quiet are more conducive to learning.

Style is also very much involved in taking tests. For some individuals, the prospect of a test operates as a prod that stimulates them to absorb a great deal of material they need to master. On the other hand, being faced with a test causes many people to become disorganized, overanxious, and unable to work. After a test, some pupils are so upset over their mistakes that they develop an emotional block about remembering the correct answers to the questions on which they erred. Consequently, they repeatedly miss the same questions. For others, finding out that they gave wrong answers aids recall and challenges them to master the problems.

Each classroom is likely to include students whose styles of learning vary widely. Although the teacher cannot cater completely to each student's particular style, he can attempt to utilize the strengths and reduce or modify the weaknesses of those in his classes.

An individual's basic style of learning is probably laid down early in life and is not subject to fundamental change. For example, a pupil who likes to learn by listening and speaking (aural style) is unlikely to change completely and become an outstanding reader. I am not suggesting that such a pupil will not learn to read and write fluently but rather that his best, most permanent learning is likely to continue to come from listening and speaking.

Since the student is the person most vitally concerned, the first step is to help him discover his particular style of learning and recognize its strengths and limitations.

In identifying a style, it is extremely important to ascertain the person's work habits as precisely as possible. If a youngster is in despair because he cannot get any work done during the study time allowed in class or in the study hall, teachers should question him carefully about his routine. What does he do first when study time is announced? How does he try to make himself concentrate? What disturbs him?

Perhaps his answer will be: "At first I'm glad we have time to do the work at school so that I will be free when school is out. I open my book to the assignment, but it's noisy because kids are asking the teacher questions or flipping through their books or whispering. I go sharpen my pencils while I'm waiting for it to get quiet.

"By the time things settle down, I know I don't have too much time left and that I have to hurry or I won't get done. I try to read fast, but the words all run together and mean nothing. Some of the smart kids are already through, and I haven't even started. I usually give up and decide I may as well do it all at home like all the other dumb bunnies do."

A number of things may be involved in this boy's problem. Possibly he is a physical learner (sharpening the pencils may show some need for movement) who has difficulty with visual learning. Apparently he warms up slowly and works slowly, for when he tries to hurry, he finds he can do nothing.

The physical learner generally gets his muscles into his work, and this takes time. Such a student must realize that attempts to rush himself are of no avail, but that this does not make him a "dumb bunny." Once he gets past his warm-up point and begins to concentrate on his work, he may work very well for long periods of time.

If this student is made aware of the way he learns, he can schedule any work requiring concentration for longer periods of time, and use short periods for something less demanding, perhaps a review of the day's schoolwork. Probably his warm-up period will gradually decrease as he becomes less anxious about failing to keep pace with his fellow students.

A pupil can take advantage of the strengths inherent in his style of learning to balance his weaknesses. For example, consider the pupil who has to learn to read, although his learning style is physical rather than visual.

In order to teach reading to a youngster for whom reading is stylistically uncongenial, the teacher may want to try role playing, which is related to a physical style of learning. The pupil is more likely to be able to read about something that he just role played.

By teaching reading in this way, the teacher is not helping the pupil develop a reading style; he is helping the pupil develop a reading skill.

In a sense, the teacher is overcoming the pupil's difficulty with reading by making use of the pupil's strength, whether it be physical, aural, or whatever.

The challenge to every teacher is first how to identify the learning strengths in his pupils and then how to utilize them to overcome weaknesses. This is the central problem in the strategy of style.

FOSTERING SELF-DIRECTION

Arthur W. Combs

Schools which do not produce self-directed citizens have failed everyone—the student, the profession, and the society they are designed to serve. The goals of modern education cannot be achieved without self-direction. We have created a world in which there is no longer a common body of information which everyone must have. The information explosion has blasted for all time the notion that we can feed all students the same diet. Instead, we have to adopt a cafeteria principle in which we help each student select what he most needs to fulfill his potentialities. This calls for student cooperation and acceptance of major responsibility for his own learning.

As Earl Kelley has suggested, the goal of education in the modern world must be the production of increasing uniqueness. This cannot be achieved in autocratic atmospheres where all decisions are made by the teachers and administration while students are reduced to passive followers of the established patterns. Authoritarian schools are as out of date in the world we live in as the horse and buggy. Such schools cannot hope to achieve our purposes. Worse yet, their existence will almost certainly defeat us.

The world we live in demands self-starting, self-directing citizens capable of independent action. The world is changing so fast we cannot hope to teach each person what he will need to know in twenty years. Our only hope to meet the demands of the future is the production of intelligent, independent people. Even our military establishment, historically the most authoritarian of all, has long since discovered that fact. For twenty years the armed forces have been steadily increasing the degree of responsibility and initiative it expects of even its lowest echelons. The modern war machine cannot be run by automatons. It must be run by *thinking* men.

Much of the curriculum of our current schools is predicated on a concept of learning conceived as the acquisition of right answers and many of our practices mirror this belief. Almost anyone can pick them out. Here are a few which occur to me:

Preoccupation with right answers; insistence upon conformity; cookbook approaches to learning; overconcern for rules and regulations; preoccupation with materials and things instead of people; the solitary approach to learning; the delusion that mistakes are sinful; emphasis on memory rather than learning; emphasis on grades rather than understanding and content details rather than principles.

Meanwhile, psychologists are telling us that learning is a *personal* matter; individual and unique. It is not controlled by the teacher. It can only be accomplished with the cooperation and involvement of the student in the process. Providing students with information is not enough. People rarely misbehave because they do not know any better. The effectiveness of learning must be measured in behavior change: whether students *behave differently* as a consequence of their learning experience. This requires active participation by the student. So learning itself is dependent upon the capacity for self-direction.

TOWARD SELF-DIRECTION

What is needed of us? How can we produce students who are more self-directed?

1. *We Need to Believe This Is Important.* If we do not think self-direction is important, this will not get done. People are too pressed these days to pay much attention to things that are not important. Everyone does what seems to him to be crucial and urgent. It seems self-evident that independence and self-direction are necessary for our kind of world. Why then has self-direction been given such inadequate attention? It is strange we should have to convince ourselves of its importance.

Unfortunately, because a matter is self-evident is no guarantee that people will really put it into practice. It must somehow be brought into clear figure in the forefront of our striving if it is to affect behavior. Everyone knows it is important to vote, too, yet millions regularly fail to vote. To be effective as an objective, each of us must hold the goal of self-direction clear in our thinking and high in our values whenever we are engaged in planning or teaching of any kind.

This is often not easy to do because self-direction is one of those goals which *everyone* is supposed to be working for. As a result, almost no one regards it as urgent! For each person, his own special duties are so much clearer, so much more pressing and his derelictions so much more glaring if he fails to produce. The goals we hold in common do not redound so immediately to our credit or discredit. They are therefore set aside while we devote our energies to the things that *really* matter to us.

To begin doing something about self-direction we must, therefore, begin by declaring its importance; not as a lofty sentiment, but as an absolute essential. It must be given a place of greater concern than subject matter itself, for a very simple reason: It is far more important than subject matter. Without self-direction no content matters much. It is not enough that it be published in the handbook as a "Goal of Education." Each of us at every level must ask himself: Do I really think self-direction is important and what am I doing about it?

2. *Trust in the Human Organism.* Many of us grew up in a tradition which conceived of man as basically evil and certain to revert to bestial ways if someone did not control him. Modern psychologists tell us this view is no longer tenable. From everything we can observe in humans and animals the basic striving of the organism is inexorably toward health both physical and mental. It is this growth principle on which doctors and psychotherapists depend to make the person well again. If an organism is free to do so—it can, will, it *must* move in positive ways. The organism is not our enemy. It wants the same things we do, the achievement of adequacy. Yet alas, how few believe this and how timid we are to trust our students with self-direction.

A recent best selling book, *Summerhill,* by A. S. Neill has fascinated many educators. In it Neill describes the absolute trust he placed in the children under his care. Many teachers are shocked by his unorthodox procedures and the extreme behavior of some of the children. But whether one approves of Neill's school or not, the thing which impressed me most was this: Here was a man who dared to trust children far beyond what most of us would be willing to risk. Yet, all the things we are so afraid might happen if we did give them such freedom, never happened! For forty years the school continued to turn out happy, effective citizens as well as, or better than, its competitors. It is time we give up fearing the human organism and learn to trust and use its built-in drives toward self-fulfillment. After all, the organism has had to be pretty tough to survive what we have done to it through the ages.

Responsibility and self-direction are learned. They must be acquired from experiences, from being given opportunities to be self-directing and responsible. You cannot learn to be self-directing if no one permits you to try. Human capacities are strengthened by use but atrophy with disuse. If young people are going to learn self-direction, then it must be through being *given* many opportunities to exercise such self-direction throughout the years they are in school. Someone has observed that our schools are operated on a directly contrary principle. Children are allowed more freedom of choice and self-direction in kindergarten (when they are presumably least able to handle it) and each year thereafter are given less and less, until, by the time they reach college, they are permitted practically no choice at all! This overdraws the case, to be sure, but there is enough truth in the statement to make one uncomfortable. If we are to produce independent, self-starting people we must do a great deal more to produce the kinds of experiences which will lead to these ends.

3. *The Experimental Attitude.* If we are going to provide young people with increased opportunity for self-direction, we must do it with our eyes open *expecting* them to make mistakes. This is not easy, for the importance of "being right" is in our blood. Education is built on right answers. Wrong ones are regarded as failures to be avoided like the plague. Unfortunately, such attitudes stand squarely in the way of progress toward self-direction and independence.

People too fearful of mistakes cannot risk trying. Without trying, self-direction, creativity and independence cannot be discovered. To be so afraid of mistakes that we kill the desire to try is a tragedy. Autonomy, independence and creativity are the products of being willing to look and eager to try. If we discourage these elements we do so at our peril. In the world we live in, victory is reserved only for the courageous and inventive. It is possible we may lose the game by making mistakes. We will not even get in the game if we are afraid to try.

Experimentation and innovation must be encouraged everywhere in our schools, in teachers as well as students. Each of us needs to be engaged in a continuous process of trying something new. The kind of experimentation which will make the difference to education in the long run is not that produced by the professional researcher with the aid of giant computers *but by the everyday changes in goals and processes brought about by the individual teacher in the classroom.*

To achieve this, teachers need to be freed of pressures and details by the administration for the exercise of self-direction and creativity. In addition, each of us must accept the challenge and set about a systematic search for the barriers we place in the path of self-direction for ourselves, our colleagues and our students. This should suggest all kinds of places for experimentation where we can begin the encouragement of self-direction. One of the nice things about self-direction is that it does not have to be taught. It only needs to be encouraged and set free to operate.

4. *The Provision of Opportunity.* The basic principle is clear. To produce more self-directed people it is necessary to give more opportunity to practice self-direction. This means some of us must be willing to give up our traditional prerogatives to make all the decisions. Education must be seen, not as pro-

viding right answers, but as confrontation with problems; not imaginary play problems either, but *real* ones in which decisions count.

Experiences calling for decision, independence and self-direction must be the daily diet of children, including such little decisions as what kinds of headings and margins a paper should have and big ones like the courses to be taken next year. They must also include decisions about goals, techniques, time, people, money, meals, rules, and subject matter.

If we are to achieve the objective of greater self-direction, I see no alternative to the fuller acceptance of students into partnership in the educative endeavor. Our modern goal for education, "the optimal development of the individual," cannot be achieved without this. Such an aim requires participation of the student and his wholehearted cooperation in the process. This is not likely to be accomplished unless students have the feeling they matter and their decisions count. Few of us are deeply committed to tasks imposed upon us; and students are not much different. Self-direction is learned from experience. What better, more meaningful experience could be provided than participation in the decisions about one's own life and learning?

The basic belief of democracy is that when people are free they can find their own best ways. Though all of us profess our acceptance of this credo, it is distressing how few of us dare to put it to work. Whatever limits the capacity of our young people to accept both the challenge and the responsibilities of that belief is destructive to all of us. It is time we put this belief to work and to expression in the education of our young as though we really meant it.

Chapter 4

MOTIVATION

INTRODUCTION

It is recognized generally that motivation of the learner is one of the most difficult and important tasks of the teacher. The motivated student frequently will surprise his teacher with how long he will stick to a task or how much he will learn. The unmotivated student frequently is the cause of most classroom behavior problems; besides being the cause of frequent classroom disruptions he probably is learning very little in school.

For many student teachers the task of motivating individual learners is especially difficult. Such factors as the short tenure in the classroom, the lack of understanding of individual problems within the class, and limited background involving motivational techniques make this one of the most challenging areas of the student teaching experience. Articles in this chapter were chosen to help student teachers understand the significance of classroom motivation and the various strategies that may be used in motivating children to learn.

David Ausubel's article points out that although some learning may occur in an unmotivated learner, it usually cannot be used by the student to form an adequate foundation for sequential learning.

John Ohles shows the relationship of interest to motivation. He implores teachers to create attractive environments where every student can feel accepted and achieve success. He believes this success must be in both personal relationships and learning achievement.

Two selections discuss specifically the topic of external motivation. Don Reggins points out that in most cases children need external motivation to learn and it is the teacher's job to provide the motivation that will enable the child to become an active learner. Edward De Roche offers many practical suggestions for motivating students to learn.

Jack Frymier suggests that motivation of students will come about as we apply different teaching strategies tailored to fit each individual student's learning needs. He emphasizes that the ultimate goal for the teacher should be to help all students move to an optimal level of individual motivation.

Two articles deal with specific areas of concern within the field of motivation. Nicholas Criscuolo discusses motivation as an absolute necessity for problem readers, and he offers several suggestions for achieving this motivation. Ruth Strang's article will be especially valuable to students who are student teaching in the upper elementary grades.

186

MOTIVATION AND CLASSROOM LEARNING

David P. Ausubel

After fifty years or more of research on motivation, perhaps the most striking conclusion that emerges from consideration of the staggering mass of research data and theory in this area is how little we *really* know about it and its role in learning, and how much is still a matter of conjecture and speculative preference. In most instances, the same data can be used to bolster widely divergent theoretical positions.

This brief review, which focuses on motivational aspects of classroom learning, and which, because of limited space, can consider only some of the more salient issues, and offer only selectively illustrative research evidence relating to these issues, is obviously no exception to the latter generalization. However, this unavoidable limitation need not necessarily give rise to misleading impressions as long as the reader appreciates that the purpose of this review is more to raise pertinent questions from a particular and unambiguously stated set of theoretical biases than to provide definite answers to these questions.

One of the theoretical biases that should be made explicit at the very outset is the assumption that both the role and relative importance of different kinds of motivations (e.g., cognitive, ego enhancing, and affiliative) vary depending on the type of learning involved and on the species membership and developmental status of the learner. It is further assumed that classroom learning, the primary object of our motivational concern in this paper, consists of the long-term, meaningful acquisition and retention both of intellectual skills and of large bodies of subject matter; typically involves the learning of didactically presented material (reception learning) rather than the discovery of the content of what has to be learned; and occurs in an interpersonal and group setting.

Hence, it would be anticipated that the role and relative importance of these various kinds of motivations in classroom learning are quite different than in short-term and fragmentary varieties of rote, instrumental, motor, and discovery learning. Additional differences in these same respects would also be anticipated depending on the use of human or animal subjects and on age level variability within each of these latter categories.

Reprinted from *Education*, 86:479–483 (April, 1966), by permission of author and publisher, The Bobbs-Merrill Company, Inc.

IS MOTIVATION INDISPENSABLE?

Unmotivated learning of a sort, particularly of an unorganized and short-term nature (1), undoubtedly occurs. It is more likely to take place in the classroom than elsewhere, inasmuch as meaningful reception learning requires much less effort, for example, than rote learning (2) or problem solving. Such unintentional learning, however, is less effective and precise than when learning is deliberate or occurs in response to explicit directions (2, 3). Available evidence (4) suggests that this facilitating effect of intention to remember on classroom learning is restricted to the learning phase of acquiring subject-matter knowledge, and has no direct influence on the retention process per se.

But even though any *particular* instance of meaningful reception learning may be largely unmotivated, it seems reasonable to suppose that large bodies of organized subject matter, or complex intellectual skills (e.g., reading, arithmetic computation), can be mastered on an integrated, precise, and long-term basis only if their mastery becomes a matter of concern to or constitutes a felt need in the learner. Learners who have little need to know or understand quite naturally expend relatively little learning effort; do not exhibit sufficient concentration, attentivity, and persistence; fail to reconcile new material with previously learned concepts or to reformulate new propositions in their own terms; and do not devote enough time to practice and review. Knowledge is, therefore, never sufficiently consolidated to form an adequate foundation for sequential learning.

The causal relationship between motivation and learning is typically reciprocal rather than unidirectional. Both for this reason, and because motivation is not an indispensable condition of learning, it is unnecessary to postpone learning activities until appropriate interests and motivations have been developed. Frequently, the best way of teaching an unmotivated student is to ignore his motivational state for the time being, and to concentrate on teaching him as effectively as possible.

Some degree of learning will ensue in any case, despite the lack of motivation; and from the initial satisfaction of learning he will hopefully develop the motivation to learn more. In some circumstances, therefore, the most appropriate way of arousing motivation to learn is to focus on the cognitive rather than on the motivational aspects of learning, and to rely on the motivation that is developed *retroactively* from successful educational achievement to energize further learning.

INTRINSIC VERSUS EXTRINSIC DRIVES

It is becoming increasingly more apparent that the reduction of extrinsic and aversive drive states (e.g., hunger, pain, anxiety) plays a relatively minor role in learning at the primate level. Such drives are not only quickly satiated, but also disrupt learning when accompanied by intense affect (5).

The trend of recent research and thinking has been to place greater emphasis on the motivational power of such intrinsic and positive motives as curiosity (6), exploration (7), activity (8), manipulation (9), mastery or competence (10), and the need for stimulation (11). In addition, these latter drives have been elevated to the status of primary drives in their own right.

At the human level, cognitive drive (the desire for knowledge as an end in itself) is more important than in rote or instrumental learning, and is, at least potentially, the most important kind of motivation in classroom learning. This is so, both because of its inherent potency, and because meaningful learning, unlike these other kinds of human learning, automatically provides its own reward. That is, as in the case of all intrinsic motives, the reward that satisfies the drive inheres in the task itself.

Cognitive drive is probably derived in a very general sense from curiosity tendencies and from related predispositions to explore, manipulate, understand, and seek stimulation from and cope successfully with the environment. These latter predispositions, however, originally manifest *potential* rather than actual motivating properties, and are self-evidently nonspecific in direction. Their potential motivating power is actualized in expression and particularized in direction as a result of successful exercise and the anticipation of future satisfying consequences from further exercise. Far from being largely endogenous in origin, therefore, specific cognitive drives or interests are largely acquired and dependent upon particular experience.

Despite the potential centrality of cognitive drive for classroom learning, it is nevertheless true that in our utilitarian, competitive, and achievement-oriented culture, such extrinsic considerations as ego enhancement, anxiety reduction, and career advancement become, with increasing age, progressively more significant sources of motivation for school learning. Beginning with the first four years of school life, ratings of achievement and recognition-seeking behavior tend to remain quite stable, and are reasonably predictive of analogous behavior during adolescence and early adult life (12). Even material rewards tend to become less ends in themselves than symbols of academic status, achievement, and competitive advantage.

Eventually, of course, the viability of the cognitive drive as an intrinsic, task-oriented type of motivation is impaired as a consequence of the increasing, almost exclusive, association of intellectual interests and activities with ego-enhancing and anxiety-reduction motives. If the desire to learn and understand is almost invariably exercised in the context of competing for grades, obtaining degrees, preparing for a vocation, striving for advancement and reducing the fear of academic and occupational failure, there is little warrant for believing that much of it survives as a goal in its own right.

This trend is reflected in the progressive decline in school interests and intellectual enthusiasm as children move up the academic ladder (13). Theoretically, of course, it is true that some cognitive drive may be developed as a functionally autonomous by-product of successful learning, even though the intellectual activity in question is originally motivated by extrinsic considerations.

EFFECTS OF ATTITUDES ON LEARNING

Only relatively recently has it been recognized that cognitive as well as affective factors account for the differential effects of positive and negative attitudinal bias on the learning of controversial material. This recognition was largely an outgrowth of Peak's theoretical formulation of attitude structure as consisting of an interrelated group of ideas organized around a conceptual nucleus and manifesting affective properties (14). How the influence of the affective component of attitude is manifested is clear enough: when the learner's attitude toward the controversial material is favorable, he is more highly motivated to learn it, and he accordingly puts forth more vigorous, persistent, and concentrated learning effort.

This same positive affect, however, is accompanied by a corresponding group of supportive general ideas which provide ideational anchorage for incorporating more detailed controversial learning material congruent with the attitudinal bias. When, on the other hand, the learner's attitude toward the learning material is unfavorable, both motivational and cognitive variables operate in precisely the opposite direction, and induce corresponding negative effects on learning.

The influence of the cognitive component of attitude structure has been demonstrated experimentally by showing that the learning differential between Northern high school students favorably and unfavorably disposed, respectively, to a learning passage presenting the Southern viewpoint about the Civil War, was greatly reduced when the effect of relevant background was statistically controlled (15). Jones and Kohler (16) similarly found that controversial material is learned *least* well when it is least relatable to the prevailing ideational component of the learner's attitude structure, that is, when favorable material is implausible and unfavorable material is plausible.

Another manifestation of the same phenomenon is the fact that the emerging new meanings that learners acquire in reading controversial material tend to be consonant with their individual attitudinal biases (17), because a corresponding set of congruent propositions, in each learner, serves as the idiosyncratic, relevant, and established ideas in his existing structure of knowledge to which the new material can be related in the process of meaningful learning.

In the case of retention, however, cognitive factors mediate most of the effects of attitude structure, because, contrary to the situation in learning, there is no way in which affective factors can influence the retention process per se. In only relatively rare instances does the degree of negative affect associated with a given degree of attitudinal bias produce enough anxiety to raise the threshold of availability sufficiently to inhibit (repress) the elicitation of retained and otherwise evocable controversial material. More typically, positive and negative attitudinal bias affect retention differentially as a result of the continued operation on the availability of the material, during the retention interval, of the same cognitive factors that account for the original difference in learning. Thus, when the influence of the cognitive dimension of attitude structure was eliminated in the aforementioned study using a Civil War passage (15), the residual affective dimension of this structure (attitudinal bias per se) had no differential effect on retention.

REFERENCES

1. Stevenson, H. W. "Latent Learning in Children." *Journal of Experimental Psychology*, Vol. 47 (January, 1954), pp. 17–21.
2. Bromer, J. A. "A Comparison of Incidental and Purposeful Memory for Meaningful and Nonsense Material." *American Journal of Psychology*, Vol. 55 (January, 1942), pp. 106–108.
3. Reed, H. B. "Factors Influencing the Learning and Retention of Concepts." *Journal of Experimental Psychology*, Vol. 36 (February, 1946), pp. 71–87.
4. Ausubel, D. P., Schpoont, S. H., and Cukier, Lillian. "The Influence of Intention on the Retention of School Materials." *Journal of Educational Psychology*, Vol. 48 (February, 1957), pp. 87–92.
5. Marlow, H. F. "Motivation as a Factor in the Acquisition of New Responses," in *Current Theory and Research in Motivation* (Lincoln: University of Nebraska Press, 1953), pp. 24–49.
6. Berlyne, D. E. *Conflict, Arousal, and Curiosity* (New York: McGraw-Hill Book Co., 1960).
7. Montgomery, Kay C. "The Role of the Exploratory Drive in Learning." *Journal of Comparative and Physiological Psychology*, Vol. 47 (February, 1954), pp. 60–64.
8. Hill, W. F. "Activity as an Autonomous Drive." *Journal of Comparative and Physiological Psychology*, Vol. 49 (February, 1956), pp. 60–64.
9. Harlow, H. F. "Learning and Satiation of Response in Intrinsically Motivated Complex Puzzle Performance by Monkeys." *Journal of Comparative and Physiological Psychology*, Vol. 43 (August, 1950), pp. 289–294.
10. White, R. W. "Motivation Reconsidered: The Concept of Competence." *Psychological Review*, Vol. 66 (September, 1959), pp. 297–333.
11. Butler, R. A. "Incentive Conditions Which Influence Visual Exploration." *Journal of Experimental Psychology*, Vol. 48 (July, 1954), pp. 19–23.
12. Moss, H. A., and Kagan, J. "Stability of Achievement and Recognition Seeking Behavior from Early Childhood Through Adulthood." *Journal of Abnormal and Social Psychology*, Vol. 62 (May, 1961), pp. 504–513.
13. Jersild, A. T., and Tasch, Ruth J. *Children's Interests* (New York: Bureau of Publications, Teachers College, Columbia University, 1949).
14. Peak, Helen. "Attitude and Motivation," in *Nebraska Symposium on Motivation* (Lincoln: University of Nebraska Press, 1955), pp. 149–188.
15. Fitzgerald, D., and Ausubel, D. P. "Cognitive versus Affective Factors in the Learning and Retention of Controversial Materials." *Journal of Educational Psychology*, Vol. 54 (May, 1963), pp. 73–84.
16. Jones, E. E., and Kohler, Rika. "The Effects of Plausibility on the Learning of Controversial Statements." *Journal of Abnormal and Social Psychology*, Vol. 57 (November, 1958), pp. 315–320.
17. McKillop, Anne S. *The Relationship Between the Reader's Attitude and Certain Types of Reading Response* (New York: Bureau of Publications, Teachers College, Columbia University, 1952).

INTEREST AND LEARNING

John F. Ohles

The complexity of life rests in the most simple solutions. Yet the fulfillment of life goals proves frustratingly elusive because of the complexities hidden within the mundane. The theologian seeks the millennium in love, the humanist seeks it in man's intelligence, the materialist seeks it in proper distribution of goods. Similarly, in education the ultimate goals are simply expressed in teaching that stimulates interest and learning that follows interest patterns.

Just as love, intelligence, or distribution of goods may singly or in concert solve problems of man to man or man to nature, interesting teaching and interested learning may solve the difficulties of educating today's and tomorrow's generations. But all these simple truths become mired in the complex nature of love, intelligence, distribution, and interest. The human engineer and educational technician fail because of inabilities to fathom their simple truths.

INTEREST AND MOTIVATION

In education interest is related to motivation, and this is a correct association. Often, however, interest is equated with motivation and this is a basic error. John Dewey, who more than any other individual sold the truth that interest more than discipline is a key to educational success, knew the basic nature of interest. In *The Child and the Curriculum,* he noted: "Interests in reality are but attitudes toward possible experiences; they are not achievements; their worth is in the leverage they afford, not in the accomplishment they represent." [1]

The relation of interest to motivation is that of any other attitude—no more, no less. An attitude is generally defined as a condition prior to behavior, a readiness or predisposition to action. Motivation evolves from an internal condition, in this instance attitude, and is a force that results in action.

INTERESTS ARE ATTITUDES

To understand, discuss, utilize interests toward school, a subject, a particular educational experience, interests must be treated as unique attitudes, as those with which the school, the teacher, information, and experiences have a particular role in the molding. Proceeding on the assumption that the simple matter of relating education to interests or interests to education is

Reprinted from *Education,* 89:249–252 (February–March, 1969), by permission of author and publisher, The Bobbs-Merrill Company, Inc.

the way out of an educational dilemma leads to a commitment to allot this attitude formation a high priority in the educational scheme.

To operate effectively in structure or restructure of attitudes demands recognition of polarity and continuum of an attitude along extremes toward or from a relationship. It does not suffice to speak of "good" or "positive," of "bad" or "negative" attitudes, for individual orientation assesses a value judgment. Attitudes toward race and color differ in value judgment as seen from integrationist, segregationist, or "moderate" positions. To assess a "poor" attitude is an evaluation of the appraiser, not of the appraised.

To the Dewey definition of interests as "attitudes toward possible experiences," must be added their structuring from the previous. While attitudes are structured from a first experience and are anticipatory toward future experience, they are as well subject to modification by each subsequent experience.

Attitudes are an ego-fulfillment emerging from an ego-involvement. Attitudes toward race and color need not arise from contact with the minority group; may, in truth, be more polarized when isolated from the group, may be dependent instead on ego involvement, on identification with peers, with an author or even with a political figure. It may be axiomatic that polar positions coincide with lack of experience, that subsequent and varied experiences must modify the attitude, excluding as a matter of course the irrationalist.

Interest in school, then, is an attitude toward school based on experiences prior to enrollment in school, slanted by ego involvement within a family, group, gang, society. The youngster from the suburban home may play "school," may stay glued to "Auntie Jane" on a morning television program while the slum youngster is as earnestly running from imaginary cops or watching the afternoon soap opera.

SECURING INTEREST

The challenge for interest in school, then motivation, then learning is obvious, if beclouded. Whatever the preschool interest in school and schooling, experiences at school modify the attitude. The school-eager youngster may have the excitement, the interest, dulled by experience, although this is yet tempered by positive attitudes toward education from the home. The school-reluctant child may experience a modification of attitude toward greater interest in school—or toward a continued revulsion.

It is obvious that the quality of the school experience fashions school interest. It is also true that sequence of experiences is likely to affect interest in school. The normal pattern of school life follows, even though unconsciously and incidentally, the sequence of happy and rewarding experiences in school. Initial school contact, kindergarten and first grade, is generally satisfactory. But occasionally, it could seem, do we find bitter and negative teachers at the earliest school level. Most youngsters are likely to experience success in the educational initiation.

Assuming that youngsters from the "wrong side of the tracks" do not feel rejection as forced undesirables upon neat and scrubbed teachers, failure is likely to start with reading instruction and to thus persist through learning-by-reading experiences and eventually move to rejection by teachers who have little patience with "stupidity" and "laziness." The positive foundation of school interest by most youngsters is dulled for many by failures experienced as instruction outruns them. On the other hand, the highly successful pupil may show a slackening of interest when success comes too easily, when deliberate pace and repetition take the edge off excitement of the new and unknown.

The answer to "making school interesting" is to create in every school, and more importantly in those schools serving slum areas, the depressed or lower classes, attractive environments where every youngster can feel accepted and may achieve success. On the most obvious level this means neat and attractive (not necessarily new) buildings, abundant teaching materials, and skillful and understanding teachers. Whatever deviations there may be from the ideal are best tolerated in privileged neighborhoods.

Creating or sustaining or exploiting an interest in subject matter demands especial attention to the avoidance of boredom from failure to challenge, thus stimulate, brighter youngsters to the bypassing of learning levels of slow learners. If interest is essential to learning a subject or relating to a classroom, the youngster must find acceptance and success. Acceptance is found in teachers and peers. Success rests both in personal relationships and learning achievement. Success in the subject does not result from receiving passing grades for failing work—or, indeed, in grades at all. If there is an interest in grades, it is no more than that and cannot be equated with an interest in knowledge.

The "interesting" classroom is a place where exciting things happen, where the attitude that is interest is stimulated and reinforced toward an acceptance of the classroom and what it represents. In concrete terms this means a variety of learning experiences so that the particular attitudes, values, abilities, of every individual are positively exercised. It means an environment, physical and interpersonal, that is not only satisfactory but satisfying. Implicit in this environment is the acceptance of each individual by every individual, most importantly by the teacher.

"Interest in subject matter" means the structuring of attitudes of acceptance by youngsters of academic materials as a minimum, eager involvement as the optimum. It presupposes the ability to first understand, then appreciate, subject content. Selectivity in this framework is not directed toward admission of students to academic experiences as much as tailoring learning to the individual. Every youngster may find mathematics rewarding but not in the rigidity of the quadratic equation on a given day in a given week in a given month for a particular age level. The reward, the stimulation, the interest come not in exposure but in meaningful exposure, in learning.

MEASURING INTEREST

Measure of an "interesting" experience is positive reaction of students. It would be unrealistic to assume that every positive reaction to an educational experience is a direct reflection of interest in the subject or in the learning process. It should be obvious that many a movie, field trip, committee assignment initiates positive reactions in a change of procedures, in the opportunity to engage in an activity that breaks a routine. A film that is welcomed for the opportunity to watch any movie, to escape from the pressure of a recitation or the boredom of a lecture, may result in little learning.

For many youngsters, school is an "interesting" environment the day before a homecoming football game when a pep fest feeds the aura of excitement. Similarly, the day before the Christmas recess may be interesting because of a relaxed atmosphere in carol singing and class parties. Interest may be in the anticipation of a vacation from school.

The only valid test of "interesting" experiences in a classroom is a reinforcement of that for which the situation was structured. Certainly, it is a play on negativism to assume that engagement of students in numerous recreational activities in the school to make instruction palatable actually transfers to interest in subjects and increased efficiency of learning.

That simple answer that is interest in a subject involves the complexity of individualizing of instruction. Old techniques and recent and those yet-to-come must combine into an educational program that meets the needs of every youngster—not on the theoretical or purely verbal level, but on the operational level.

CONCLUSION

If these suggestions for making learning interesting and relating learning to interest seem to be demanding the ideal—why not? Efficiency in farming demands rich soil, controlled seed (and, sometimes, transported moisture), skill and knowledge of the technical and workable and working machinery. The merchant seeks superior location, quality merchandise, marketing research and sales techniques. If the neighborhood school is to seek the efficiency of farm or shop, it must no less obtain the raw material from which the full cloth is spun.

To speak in terms of interest and learning, to seek or demand their marriage and natural offspring requires creation of reasonable conditions for success. To be unwilling to go the full route is to settle for a half-educated, half-ignorant society and all that unpromising situation portends.

To make real the truth that learning and interest are essential and compatible for success in the educational process demands going beyond vague generalizations. Educators desperately need to take an interest in (form attitudes toward) interest itself, for itself. There must be a step down from generalities to specifics, else discontinuance of the questionable blessings of unfettered speech and unfulfilled promises. Interest in interest leads to learning about interest, understanding its complexities and pursuing this understanding to a restructure of the educational process.

NOTE

1. *The Child and the Curriculum and The School and Society* (Chicago: The University of Chicago Press [Phoenix Books], 1956), p. 15.

MOTIVATION AND TEACHING

Don Reggins

A successful teacher influences the thinking, behavior and attitudes of pupils. He fights against ignorance and misunderstanding and shares with the pupils the rich experiences of his life. Every teacher should seek methods to fulfill this challenge.

There is not just one way to teach a class of elementary or secondary school children. Among the many possible techniques of teaching there are numbers of good approaches.

Which of these approaches a teacher will use depends upon the individual pupil in the classroom plus the training of the teacher, the goals established by the school district, the materials available in both the school and community, but perhaps equally important, the teacher's personality and skill.

The teacher and the learning process are very closely related. But the teacher cannot do the learning for a pupil. Successful teaching is pupil guidance.

In most instances the pupil needs motivation and it is the teacher who provides the type of motivation that will enable the pupil to become an active learner.

Motivation involves a two-way responsibility which rests with both the teacher and the pupil. The teacher must be willing to search for the methods and materials which will stimulate the pupil and cause those pupils to want to learn and seek new experiences.

The teacher should fully realize that all pupils are different. They have had different experiences and have different needs. We are to teach the child and not subject matter. In order to teach the child, individual attention must be given in terms of the individual's learning capacity and interests. The teacher

Reprinted from *School and Community*, 51:15, 18 (September, 1964), by permission of author and publisher.

should become aware of the pupil's background, his interests, aspirations and his personality.

The lower the pupil-teacher ratio the more individualized attention can be given. The teacher has the time to find out more about each child. As much motivation as possible should be used in both the elementary and secondary schools.

We say that the purpose of teaching is to satisfy the needs of the pupils, but many pupils are unaware of their needs. In these situations, it becomes the teacher's responsibility to help the pupils recognize that the skills and knowledge being taught are useful and worthwhile. It is his duty to show immediate rewards to keep the pupils working toward the long-range goals. He must motivate pupils to want to learn.

Many times in the classroom there develops a spontaneous or natural motivation derived from the natural interests of the pupils. Little has to be done on the teacher's part to stimulate interest or study. Most often, however, the teacher must stimulate interest in learning skills and information that will be directly useful in bettering the lives of pupils.

We must always keep in mind that we are preparing boys and girls for the future. We must present learning experiences which will help them when their school days are over. The school should be a training ground for the future.

New ideas, units of study, and information may be introduced in novel ways. Some devices used in motivating pupils are: field trips; a current events item; a movie or television program; a display, exhibit or other art projects; a visual or audiovisual aid; games, songs and stories; personal experiences; experience charts.

The teacher should arouse the pupil's interest by giving him individual attention and by adapting methods and materials so they motivate the pupil to gain satisfaction from learning activities.

Certainly the teacher is not to reduce study to the play level, but he can introduce some of the play attitude into the learning situation. Learning is serious business but it can be undertaken with enjoyment and interest without losing sight of its main purpose.

Motivation bridges the gap between the pupils' background experiences and new experiences. Whatever is done to arouse interest must have a functional relationship to the problem under consideration. Since all learners do not react similarly, the stimulation of learning must be varied for different individuals.

The ultimate goal of all facets of motivation is to help each boy and girl to develop self-motivation, a curiosity and desire to learn which will carry over into adult life.

Teachers can utilize motivation in all subject areas from reading, science, social studies and the fine arts to arithmetic. Motivation makes learning possible and successful teaching probable.

MOTIVATION: AN INSTRUCTIONAL TECHNIQUE

Edward F. DeRoche

Motivation is not something a teacher does next week or during the fourth period on Friday. Educational psychologists agree that motivation is an integral part of the learning process. As such, it must become for the teacher a "teaching habit." The success or failure of a learning task partly depends on how the learner is motivated toward the task. Briefly, the learning process involves the following categories: readiness, motivation, goals, exploration, action, and reaction to consequences.[1]

Jack Frymier has found that the learner focuses upon the teacher as a major factor in motivation. The teacher's influence as a motivating factor seemed to increase in importance as one progresses from grade to grade. For example, whereas in the fifth grade only 20 per cent of the students place great importance on the teacher, 31 per cent of the eleventh grade students place the teacher first in importance.[2] Thus this article presents some ideas about motivation as a *teaching technique.*

MOTIVATION DEFINED

The root word for motivation is "motive"—that condition that makes one do something. Since motives are the drives, desires, feelings, interests, and needs of our students, they provide teaching clues usable to encourage the learner. Thus, in a teaching sense, motivation can be defined as "activating a desire to learn."[3] In terms of the learner, it means "to be impelled to seek a goal that seems to have personal value."[4]

I like to define motivation in terms of an instructional technique as anything the teacher does to cause a student to have interest in an excitement about a particular learning task. *Interest,* in this definition, means the amount of attention demonstrated by a student to the learning task at hand. *Excitement* refers to the degree of follow-up exhibited by a student after he has become exposed to and/or interested in the learning task. For example, a student may become very interested in the science experiment a teacher is demonstrating. For the entire class period the student sits there absorbed in what the teacher says and does. He even participates when requested to do so. However, when it is his turn to follow up on what is being taught, his interest wanes. The excitement which the teacher hoped to initiate doesn't materialize. This is evidenced by the student's failure to do his assigned read-

Reprinted from *The Clearing House,* 41:403–406 (March, 1967), by permission of author and publisher.

ing or his written homework, or in his doing it haphazardly. In other words, like television or movies, the teacher did little more than capture interest for the moment. "To motivate or not to motivate" is the question. The answer to which is best expressed by Cutts and Moseley: "The art of pedagogy is the art of discerning how best to motivate your pupils to achieve the objectives you think worthy." [5] Thus, motivation is viewed as an instructional aid, not as an end, but as a means of promoting learning.

MOTIVATIONAL TECHNIQUES

Interests. A student is motivated by what interests him. The teacher can capitalize on existing interests or help the student develop new interests. Curiosity can be very effective in arousing interest. For example, an eighth grade science class had just completed a science unit on heat and was about to begin one on "warm and cold-blooded animals." As the students were completing a quiz on the previous unit, the science teacher went to the back of the room and brought a frog to the front. He placed the frog on the desk, saying nothing to his students. As the students looked up from behind their quiz papers, the frog jumped off the desk. The teacher calmly picked up the frog and put it in a jar of ice cubes he had placed on the desk before class began. Some students started to whisper among themselves. "What is he doing?" "Did you see that?" "He put the frog on ice!" The teacher called the class to order, reminding them about the quiz they were taking. After five or six minutes, the teacher removed the frog from the jar of ice, put it on the desk, and still said nothing to the class. Many students again noted the frog. But this time it didn't move. "It's dead," one student said in a loud whisper. The teacher said nothing. In a short time, the frog began to move again. It jumped off the desk. The science teacher picked it up and put it back into the terrarium. The bell rang, the teacher collected the quizzes, said nothing about his activities with the frog, and dismissed the class. The students were bubbling with questions, some being concerned about the teacher's sanity. The next science class, the teacher introduced the unit asking them to recall the "frog episode" the day before. Their interest was obvious. The teacher had accomplished his task. They were curious enough now to do their own learning.

Individual interests serve as a motivational force. Although it is time-consuming for the teacher, individual interests can be most helpful to the learner. For example, Clyde, who is failing mathematics, is known to be most interested in automobiles. Clyde's greatest difficulty in mathematics stems from his inability to solve word problems. The mathematics teacher knows of both Clyde's weakness and his great interest, so he designs mathematics problems that use the auto as the focal point. Thus the teacher is using an area of interest to help the student strengthen a specific weakness.

Of course, interest in subject matter itself provides motivation. Some students are more interested in science than they are in English. Others like history best. Students usually do better in a subject they like and find interesting. Thus boys usually do better in science and mathematics, while girls do better in language and social studies.

Goals. Immediate goals are more important to most students than long-range goals. To tell a student he should study Latin or chemistry because it will make him a more worthy citizen, or that it will help train his mind is, in Whitehead's words, "pedantic bunk."

A student must be able to regard a goal as readily obtainable, otherwise he may develop a "why bother" or "I don't care" attitude. Therefore, long-range goals should be divided into smaller, achievable goals. As Cronbach says, "With success in short-range plans, the person gains confidence in his ability and enough interest to sustain a longer activity. The teacher who helps pupils attain clear short-term goals assists them to develop foresight." [6]

Avoidance of frustration. If there is anything that is anti-motivational, it is attempting a learning task for which one is not ready. Many youngsters experience this problem, so each teacher must be acutely aware of the frustrating aspects of the learning process. Probably more than half of our discipline problems arise because youngsters become frustrated in the learning process. Many students have experienced nothing but failure in school, and as a result they quit at the first hint that the task may be difficult. These students need their confidence restored, need to find success, need to become aware of their abilities no matter how limited they may be. This is not to say that everything should be easy. Rather, the teacher should keep the task within the student's reach; difficult enough so th~ it will involve effort on the student's part.[7]

Success. The old saying that "nothing succeeds like success" is as solid psychologically as any cliché can be. Success is probably the greatest of motivational devices because the successful student is usually self-motivated. Self-motivation is the aim of all motivational techniques. The desire for recognition is one of the underlying causes for seeking successful experiences. Many students experience few successful school experiences because the school rewards those qualities that they find most difficult—memorizing, reading, thinking quickly, and the like.

Thus, the teacher's task is to find those elements in the subject matter that the student can do successfully, and from this point build upon these experiences carefully. In this way, the teacher helps the student become ready for ensuing learning tasks. The teacher doesn't wait for readiness to develop; he initiates the process. And, when it is obvious to the teacher and student that they are prepared to go ahead in the learning sequence, both do so recognizing that the chances for success are good.

It is rather obvious that if some successes in school were experienced by more students, our discipline problems and dropout rate would be reduced drastically. Teachers drop out of graduate school or refrain from taking needed courses for one of two reasons; they are afraid they will not be successful, or they feel that the course will have no value for them. The same applies to students in our classes.

Tests, quizzes, grades. Whether for pragmatic reasons or not, most students are motivated by tests and quizzes. This desire for a "good grade" enables the teacher to use tests and quizzes for motivational, as well as evaluative, purposes.

Grading papers has been found to provide a means for motivating students to better achievement. Ellis B. Page found that teachers who mark papers with a letter or numerical grade and make free comments of praise (encouraging, favorable comments) on their papers, caused these students to achieve higher on ensuing tests than teachers who just assigned a grade, or those who assigned a grade with just a short comment such as "Excellent! Keep it up!" [8]

Research also indicates that a learner who knows his progress as well as his strengths and weaknesses will "work harder and more intelligently." [9] As a motivational technique for the teacher, this means that students should keep records of their progress. For example, the teacher can provide a record sheet on which each student records his grades for quizzes, tests, and assignments. The teacher can also provide a chart on which each student makes a line or bar graph of his own progress. The graph and record sheet provide a quick appraisal of progress, challenge the student to compete against himself, and help the student answer his own question: "How am I doing?" This procedure also eliminates the "surprise" of report card grades.

Competition vs. cooperation. For some students, particularly the winners, classroom competition can be beneficial. For those who find learning a difficult task, competition may produce behavior problems. As a motivational technique, it may be wiser to have an individual compete against himself, unless the competitors are so closely matched that each has a chance for success. Obviously, students need experiences in competition as well as cooperation. In competition, however, the student should have the learning experience in an area in which he is capable, be it spelling, history, or physical education. Sorenson states it best, saying, "It seems, an atmosphere in which students sometimes compete in a friendly, sportsmanlike way and sometimes join in spirited teamwork is most emotionally healthful and educationally effective." [10]

Potpourri. There are many other techniques teachers use to motivate students. A few ideas are listed to help illustrate the conscious effort that must permeate teaching strategy:

1. Every lesson should have a specific objective which should be obvious to every member of the class.

2. Teacher enthusiasm for his subject may be imitated by the students.

3. Not only is "variety the spice of life," it is the hallmark of good teaching. Therefore, various teaching methods should be employed.

4. To illustrate concepts, use materials and examples that are familiar to the students.

5. The use of humor can be an effective motivational technique.

6. Conclude each lesson with a summary of what was accomplished. The summary should be stated by students in their own words.

7. Make appropriate use of newspapers, magazines, commercial television, and games and toys for motivational purposes.

8. Use questionnaires and inventories to determine students' interests.

9. Make adequate use of community resources: professional, industrial, political, and cultural (movies, plays, concerts, museums, etc.).

SUMMARY

While there is no one motivating technique that will encourage every student, teaching techniques must be employed. In our efforts to teach students subject matter, it is easy to overemphasize *what* we are teaching, forgetting at times *how* we are teaching. We have explored motivation, not in its entirety, but rather as a reminder that it, too, is part of the teaching-learning process. Self-motivation is our objective. Sound motivational techniques are the means to accomplish this objective.

NOTES

1. Robert C. Craig, *The Psychology of Learning in the Classroom*. New York: The Macmillan Co., 1966, p. 1.
2. Editor's Notes, *The Catholic School Journal* (May, 1966), p. 5.
3. Kenneth Hoover, *Teaching and Learning in the Secondary School*. Boston: Allyn and Bacon, Inc., 1964, p. 81.
4. Sterling G. Callahan, *Successful Teaching in Secondary Schools*. Chicago: Scott, Foresman and Co., 1966, p. 326.
5. Norma E. Cutts and Nicholas Moseley, *Teaching the Bright and Gifted*. Englewood Cliffs, New Jersey: Prentice-Hall, Inc., 1957, p. 139.
6. Lee J. Cronbach, *Educational Psychology*. New York: Harcourt, Brace and World, Inc., 1963, p. 471.
7. *Ibid.,* p. 480.
8. Ellis B. Page, "Teacher Comments and Student Performance: A Seventy-four Classroom Experiment in School Motivation," *Journal of Educational Psychology,* 48: 173–81 (August 1958).
9. Herbert Sorenson, *Psychology in Education*. New York: McGraw-Hill Book Co., 1964, p. 413.
10. *Ibid.,* p. 418.

MOTIVATING STUDENTS TO LEARN

Jack R. Frymier

"What makes Johnny try hard in school? What can I do with Billy? He doesn't seem to want to learn." What is motivation? Can a teacher change a young-

Reprinted from *NEA Journal,* 58:37–39 (February, 1968), by permission of author and publisher.

ster's motivation level? Will this instructional technique or that set of curriculum materials affect a student's desire to learn?

During the last several years, staff members at the Center for the Study of Motivation and Human Abilities at Ohio State University have completed a number of research studies which deal directly with questions like these. Their findings suggest some clues that may help us understand what motivation is and what teachers can do to increase children's motivation to learn.

"What is motivation?" In general terms, it is that which gives both direction and intensity to human behavior. In an educational context, motivation to learn is that which gives direction and intensity to students' behavior in academic situations. If you say that the phrase *that which* is not very helpful, you are right. However, describing and understanding motivation to learn must begin at that point.

In many ways, the problem is similar to the one we face in dealing with intelligence in an educational setting. We always infer the nature and degree of intelligence from observations of a student's behavior. No one really knows what intelligence is, so we simply watch what a student does (or study his performance on standardized tests) and then make inferences about his intellectual ability. We never actually measure his intelligence, but only how he uses *that which* he has.

We have to use the same process to understand *that which* gives direction and intensity to what young people do in school. Studies we have made of dropouts, underachievers, overachievers, medical students, delinquents, students in slum schools, students in plush suburban schools, and various other groups have led us to the following conclusions:

Generally speaking, girls tend to be more positively motivated to learn in school than boys. Also, students from more favorable socioeconomic situations are, on the average, better motivated academically than those who come from less advantaged circumstances. Further, motivation to learn appears typically as a fairly constant and stable phenomenon. It will change, but only slowly and over extended periods of time, as the result of both intensive and extensive experiences. Finally, there can be such a thing as too much motivation, and for that reason we probably should try to think in terms of optimal rather than maximal motivation. Just as extremely high blood pressure is not conducive to health so the highest degree of motivation is not necessarily most conducive to maximum achievement in school.

Motivation is so complex that we must examine it from a number of angles in order to discover its nature. From the operational angle, our research reveals that students whose desire to learn in school is positive in nature and optimal in level differ in at least four ways from those whose motivation is less desirable: self-concept, values, orientation toward time, and openness to experience.

Highly motivated students tend to have a positive self-concept: "I count. I am competent. Other people like me. I can do it." On the other hand, students whose motivation is less positive tend to have a negative self-image:

"I'm no good. Other people don't like me. I'm not sure that I can do it. I'm not as capable as others." Difference in self-concept is one of the most obvious factors research studies consistently show.

Another factor is a difference in values. Youngsters with a negative attitude toward school tend to value the concrete and specific, while optimally motivated students tend to value the abstract, aesthetic, or general. Considering the high positive correlation between social class and motivation, however, one cannot help but wonder which is cause and which, effect. That is, optimally motivated students generally come from middle- or upper-class homes, which provide them with more toys, books, and other material things than is the case with disadvantaged homes. If one were to remove these from the environment of the highly motivated, would their values change, and then their motivation? It may be that students from more prosperous homes are able to go beyond concrete concerns to the less tangible and more abstract because they already have the material things.

Positively and negatively motivated students also differ markedly in their perceptions of time. The low-motivated student is typically preoccupied with the present, obsessed with the past, or fearful of the future.

Those students who really want to learn are generally conscious of the present, past, and future, but they do not freeze on one aspect of time as do their less adequately motivated counterparts. They are more open to experience than the relatively unmotivated. Less threatened, more curious and seeking in their behavior, they exhibit a kind of perceptual energy which enables them to pursue stimuli, so to speak.

Drawing upon these patterns which have become apparent in the course of our research, the staff at the Center for the Study of Motivation and Human Abilities has begun to reconceptualize a theory of academic motivation. Two generalizations have emerged to date.

First, whatever motivation is, it is neither intelligence nor creativity.

Second, any adequate concept of motivation to learn in school must encompass the fact that it involves at least three dimensions: internal-external, intake-output, and approach-avoidance.

Motivation to learn in school is in part a function of what resides within the individual and in part a function of the external world he encounters. Some positively motivated youngsters seem to draw most heavily upon forces located within themselves to enhance their learning. They believe in learning and knowledge, for example, and the new and novel excite them. Ambiguity and uncertainty intrigue them.

Other students, equally well motivated, seem to be most positively affected by the quality and quantity of stimuli which they experience in school. Exciting lectures, fascinating movies, vivid illustrations, and intense discussions are likely to spark these students' efforts.

In terms of the intake-output dimension, some students seem moved to consume the learning world around them, while others are producers. Students who are avid readers and thoughtful listeners—who seek information in every way—are "intake" types. They are consumers of information and experiences of every kind. Other students are "output" people. They write. They talk a lot. They generate ideas and concepts. Their motivations propel them to active rather than passive learning roles.

Finally, there are obvious differences in the way some students move toward teacher approval, marks, social acceptance, ambiguity, and the like, while others move away from such things.

Although the approach-avoidance dimension is a very real part of motivation to learn in school, not all positively motivated students move toward teacher approval or high marks, nor do all negatively motivated persons move away from such phenomena. The problem is more complex than that. For example, one student whose motivation to learn in school is positive might move toward (*approach*) reading (*intake*) an exciting novel (*external stimulus*). Another youngster whose motivations are equally positive might move away from (*avoidance*) teacher approval (*external*) in order to generate (*output*) a graphic description of social equality for his history course.

The point is, *that which* causes some young people to want to learn in school is complex rather than simple and requires a sophisticated rather than a naive professional response. Let's turn now to what teachers can do.

Traditionally, most teachers have approached the motivational problem from two directions: quality of the stimulus (subject matter) and variations in stress (instructional techniques).

The first approach is obvious. Those of us who teach have generally felt that if we could provide "good" content and "interesting" experiences, motivating students would be at least partially solved. And, according to the theoretical model described above, this will help some students. The approach will fail with other students because, for them, it simply does not get at the heart of the matter.

The technique of varying stress is equally elusive. Efforts to "raise standards," "bear down," or "require more hard homework" are all illustrations of our occasional attempts to place greater stress on the learner in the hope of affecting his achievement. Our common sense tells us that if we increase the stress, we may be able to raise his motivations and thus maximize achievement. Sometimes these techniques fail, however, because we do not recognize that the relationship between motivation and achievement is an extremely complex one, containing many separate but interacting elements.

Students who are more able tend to learn more than students who are less able. It is easy to move from that generalization to one which assumes that highly motivated students will learn more than poorly motivated students. Carrying the logic further, we then tend to assume that if we can somehow raise the motivational levels of the students in our classes higher and higher, they ought to learn more and more. The generalization is neat and logical, but only partially correct.

Students who are too highly motivated focus on a very narrow segment of their educational world and miss the relationships in learning which are so important. They are less able to see the pattern of events and to make meaningful interpretations of the complexities of learning stimuli.

Students whose motivation to learn is too low are unable to focus their perceptual energies long enough or clearly enough to engage in the kinds of experiences which are personally rewarding or which will be approved of by parents or teachers or both. And without some positive internal or external feedback, motivation to learn in school will eventually die.

Motivation to learn in school is so important and so complex that those of us who teach must seek out and use teaching techniques that produce positive results. In my opinion, our only hope is for a very subjective rather than objective approach. Capitalizing on research findings, we need to sort out the nuances of motivation and the variations among our students and then employ differentiated teaching strategies tailored to fit each individual student's learning needs.

Our short-range effort must be to start with each student where he is and to vary our instructional procedures to suit his immediate learning needs. Over the long run, however, we have to work in such a way that we help all our students to move to an optimal level of motivation.

Throwing away old clichés may be one place to begin. "We must treat all children alike" is one. Nonsense. Each student is unique. Our assessment of his motivations and other abilities demands that we use differentiated teaching techniques to help him learn.

And "Why doesn't Billy try to learn?" should probably be rephrased to "What can I do to help Billy learn to try?" Helping Billy learn to try means teaching him to become better motivated to learn in school. That, in turn, means to develop a positive self-concept, a set of values which includes the importance of learning, a tolerance for ambiguity, and a curiosity which just will not quit.

In the final analysis, this means that we must consciously and deliberately work at the business of personality development and personality change. This is an awesome and frightening task, but it will never go away. If we are seriously concerned about the possibilities of excellence in education, we must assume that responsibility.

MOTIVATING THE PROBLEM READER
Nicholas P. Criscuolo

One of the most acute problems in the field of reading is how to motivate the poor reader to want to read. Sitting in the regular classroom, the poor

Reprinted from *Education,* 87:233–235 (December, 1966), by permission of author and publisher, The Bobbs-Merrill Company, Inc.

reader is restless and bored because, due to his reading handicap, he cannot cope academically with the classroom situation. Motivating the problem reader is a difficult task for the classroom teacher, who must be concerned with meeting the needs of all the pupils in his class. A remedial reading teacher may work with problem readers several times a week, but it is the classroom teacher who must provide daily instruction.

It is the low reading group, comprised of the poorest readers in the class, who concern the teachers the most. In addition to the failure to master basic reading skills, many of these problem readers evince very little desire to read. The importance of interest in learning to read was demonstrated by Witty in his study of 100 poor readers (1). Eighty-two of the children studied showed a lack of interest in reading, whereas 43 actually disliked reading. Physical factors which impeded reading progress accounted for only 14 per cent of these problem readers.

CAUSES OF READING PROBLEMS

There are many causes of reading problems, and it would be inaccurate to isolate just one factor as the sole cause of reading retardation. Pollack and Piekarz (2) divide these causative factors into four categories: physical, psychological, intellectual, and school factors, listing several causes under each factor. An interrelationship exists among these factors and frequently it is a combination of them which results in producing the problem reader.

MOTIVATION AS RELATED TO READING

The teacher functions in the classroom as a motivator of learning whereas parental interest and encouragement motivate learning at home. Smith and Dechant (3) comment that when a pupil is motivated to learn he is "set" to react to stimuli. Related to reading, the stimuli refer to adequate reading materials, instruction at the proper level, and an environment conducive to the arousal of an interest in reading.

As the teacher begins instruction with problem readers it is essential that all aspects of the pupils' development be considered. Very often these youngsters have poor self-images because they have experienced failure in reading. The initial step for the teacher is to stress the value of reading as a satisfying act and at the same time lead them to gain a better understanding of themselves and their social environment. New interests must be developed as well as a redirection of old ones.

Poor readers, because of their dependencies, need to be given easy, yet satisfying, activities which increase their ability to work independently. Cutts (4) found in his study only one personality trait that distinguished good and poor readers. The good readers were consistently more independent in their day-to-day relationships whereas poor readers displayed a dependent personality. The need for worthwhile self-directing material is apparent. Problem readers, for instance, react favorably to the S.R.A. reading laboratories because they are allowed to work on their own. The effect of material of this type will be increased reading skill as well as improved ability to work independently.

BUILDING MOTIVATION FOR READING

One of the first considerations the teacher must give to problem readers is correct group placement. Standardized reading scores should not be relied upon exclusively, but should be supplemented with informal diagnostic tests which will uncover specific areas of weakness. The teacher must keep careful records of skills which need to be taught. As they are mastered, they can be checked off on a chart. If the pupils are receiving remedial reading help, it is important that articulation exists between reading specialist and classroom teacher so that the best program possible will be offered to problem readers.

Progress should be tangible to the poor reader. Such motivational aids and devices as "Climbing the Ladder to Reading Success" or "Reaching the Moon" arouse interest as the pupil tries to reach reasonable goals set. Games that are commercially made or teacher-prepared are good ways to reinforce reading skills. Caution must be exercised in the time spent playing them so that the original purpose for using them is not lost. Reading activities should be paced properly in order to maintain variety and interest.

ACTIVITIES MOTIVATING READING

As the pupil gains skill in reading, he should be given a chance to share what he has read with the rest of the class. This form of recognition will highlight the progress he is making.

The activity "I Recommend . . ." is a good one for arousing interest in reading. The pupil, assuming the role of a salesman, shares a book read in the form of a commercial on T.V. Without divulging the entire plot, he tries to persuade his listeners to buy (read) the book. Students enjoy this activity because often the presentations made are quite humorous. Exhibits, dramatizations, and puppet construction activities also serve the useful purpose of extending and enriching reading skills and interest.

Teachers often complain that problem readers lack curiosity about books. If reading instruction is not dynamic and books are not made interesting, a lack of curiosity will occur. I once read part of a book to a third grade class with several problem readers in it. At the most exciting part, I informed the class that I would be unable to read the rest of the book and placed it on the ledge. At that point, there was a mad scramble for the book—an action which proved that if reading is made exciting, children will read!

Developing the habit of reading is essential. Reading for fun should not be reserved just for Friday afternoons. Opportunities for wide reading should be an integral part of the reading schedule.

CONCLUDING STATEMENT

The fact that "nothing succeeds like success" is an important one to consider when planning a program for problem readers. Emphasis should be on making reading a pleasurable and satisfying experience.

Instruction for problem readers should concentrate on helping them master basic reading skills not learned as well as on arousing interest in reading. The factor of motivation is a crucial one when working with the problem reader. Skills mastered should be applied to reading books which the problem reader can read independently with ease.

Progress should be made tangible by means of progress charts and records. As the poor reader gains success in reading, however small, he will gain a sense of accomplishment and satisfaction in reading. Once this happens, motivation will increase and he will make every effort to improve his reading ability.

REFERENCES

1. Witty, Paul. "Interest and Success—The Antidote to Stress," *Elementary English,* Vol. 32 (December, 1955), pp. 507–513.
2. Pollack, M. F. W., and Piekarz, Josephine A. *Reading Problems and Problem Readers* (New York: David McKay Company, Inc., 1963).
3. Smith, Henry P. and Dechant, Emerald V. *Psychology in Teaching Reading* (Englewood Cliffs, New Jersey: Prentice-Hall, Inc., 1961).
4. Cutts, Warren G. "A Comparative Study of Good and Poor Readers at the Middle Grade Level." Unpublished doctoral thesis (Syracuse, New York: Syracuse University, 1956).

MOTIVATION: AS ADOLESCENTS SEE IT

Ruth Strang

Few adolescents seem to be aware of deepseated, pervasive motivations of the type that psychologists recognize. High school sophomores and seniors in their compositions on "What Makes Me Tick" or "Why Do I Believe as I Do?" tend to account for their behavior in concrete, specific terms, rather than in terms of whole personality, self concept, or egostructure.

To understand any instance of motivated behavior, we need to know what is stimulating the individual at present, what responses he has made to similar patterns of stimulation in the past, what consequences followed, and what deprivations he has experienced. Some of them say they "just couldn't figure out why they did such a thing." However, what seems to be a spur-of-the-

Reprinted from *Education,* 86:473–478 (April, 1966), by permission of author and publisher, The Bobbs-Merrill Company, Inc.

moment response may have deep roots in the personality. One boy described his hidden motivations in this way:

"I really don't know what it is inside me, but it seems to push me to do my work. Maybe it's a 'doer' inside me that I train. Even though I don't feel like doing my work, my doer makes me do it."

In their descriptions of "critical incidents," a sampling of 100 high school sophomores have given us glimpses of the motivation process as they see it, as well as examples of specific motivation. The following is one student's analysis of the factors that motivated her in a specific situation:

"Last summer when I decided to go to work, I didn't want to. I loved the free time when I could take walks, sew, play tennis, read, and do anything I wanted to, including wasting time. I tossed the idea around for months, before I finally decided. I knew that I had to start accepting real responsibility and conditioning myself mentally for college. I realized that I was wasting so much time every day when I could be doing something beneficial to myself as well as to others.

"My parents had always told me that I didn't know how precious the second is, and for the first time I knew what they meant. I was simply staying in my bay where I was secure. I knew it was time to start crossing the ocean where I would start at the bottom and prove my every step. I loathed the idea of not being able to call my time my own, but I went to work to prove myself to myself."

Motivations may be arranged in a hierarchy. Over all are the most persistent, pervasive, and deep seated; below these stand motivations that are, in varying degrees, comparatively temporary, extrinsic, or superficial. Let us briefly examine some of the motivations expressed by adolescents.

SELF-ACTUALIZATION

The most basic motivation of all is the deep-seated desire to develop one's potentialities, to do what one is best fitted to do, to function as well as one is capable of functioning. One chooses the activities or courses of action that seem most likely to lead to self-realization or self-actualization. Though the individual may be motivated by the observed disparity between his self ideal and his present achievement, if this disparity is too great it may simply lead to frustration and serious maladjustment. None of the students clearly recognized this pervasive kind of motivation.

VALUE SYSTEM

Some adolescents did recognize that values and standards may motivate one's behavior. In some cases their values were crystallized in a sentence; one boy quoted President Kennedy: " 'Ask not what your country can do for you, but what you can do for your country.' " Or they may be personalized in a hero or a model: "My motivation is to someday carry on the work and ideas of the man I admire."

Seldom did an adolescent's value system coincide with his or her desires. However, one girl stated emphatically: "I have never had to do anything important that I did not want to do. This is the truth."

One boy decided to visit a friend in the hospital instead of going to a party. He explained his decision in this way: "I knew that my visits meant a lot to him, and I was the only one beside his parents who had been to see him. Yet the thing that made me go to see him wasn't pity. It was just that when I thought about going to the party or going to the hospital, the latter seemed more important."

LONG-RANGE GOALS

More specific motivations include certain long-range goals. A college education was the one most frequently mentioned, as in the following fairly typical quotation:

"I have never been good at math, not *even* mediocre. The truth is I cannot stand math, or shall I say, my inadequacy to learn it. However, it was imperative that I take one last course in math, geometry, this year. My reason for doing so was that more of the colleges I have written to would accept me more readily with this subject under my belt. Being accepted to a good college means practically everything to me. For, let us face facts—those facts that are forever drummed in our ears—you can hardly get *anywhere* in our world without a college education. So, regardless of my dislike for my geometry course and the poor grades which come with it, I *have* to stick with it."

In trying to analyze her reasons for doing her homework, one girl wrote: "I certainly don't do my homework because I like to. Although the ideal is to study because you want to learn all you can, I don't think that is my motive either. Maybe I am motivated by pride, a feeling that if I don't get good grades, I won't be able to go to college and I will disappoint not only my parents but myself."

For other adolescents, college is only a halfway house on the road to life-time goals. This is the way one boy expressed it: "Everyone at some time has felt a desire to do a really good job and work up the ladder—to do something worthwhile in life." Another said, "I wanted to go to college and try to make something of myself."

Daily tasks and responsibilities give rise to more immediate motivations.

OTHER PEOPLE'S EXPECTATIONS

Many adolescents feel that they must achieve goals that their parents have chosen for them. They frequently mention being motivated by their parents' expectations. If the parents really love the child and want the best for him, and if the child realizes this, he will put forth effort to live up to their expectations. However, if the child feels that he is merely a means to satisfy their ambition, he may be motivated, out of resentment, to try to frustrate their hopes. This often results in self-sabotage: the child fails to develop his own potentialities.

One youngster apparently resolved to accept her parents' plan until she got to college, and then launched out on her own:

"The biggest single thing that has motivated me all my life has been a responsibility to live up to my parents' expectations and the pattern of life they set for me—getting above-average grades, participating in worthwhile activities, making friends with acceptable people, going away to college next year to prepare for a career. All this is part of the plan my parents have had since before I was born. But soon I will have fulfilled my parents' expectations and will have to turn to myself for motivation. I plan on four years, while I'm in college, to find my direction. I then want to achieve some kind of individuality and purpose in my life."

Parental expectations sometimes become compulsions. As one girl said, "My motivation is my mother. I need a very strong motivation to do what I ought to do whether I want to or not. I guess that is what mothers are for."

PERSONALITY AND CHARACTER TRAITS

Curiosity is a prime motivation at any age; unless suppressed, it persists throughout life. Curiosity not only spurs an individual to achieve; it also increases his proficiency by heightening his interest and effort. It is alarming that so few high school students mentioned a desire to know, to discover, or to explore as the motivation for studying.

In some situations adolescents mention being motivated by fear. Sometimes this fear is physical. One boy described his motivation in a dangerous mountain climbing episode as a combination of fear and necessity:

"I feel that I was motivated by fear. The odds were against me. All I could think of was how the rock had gone crashing down. I could say I did perform the feat because it was a challenge or that I was brave, etc., etc. . . . I did it because I was scared, and at the time it seemed the only way out."

These students mentioned social fears of many types—fear of becoming involved, fear of being called "chicken," fear of failure. They less often described the motivating effect of anxiety; perhaps they did not recognize that a mild degree of anxiety facilitates learning. One may study to relieve this anxiety; relieving it becomes a goal. On the other hand, intense anxiety is inhibiting; it disrupts learning.

Some adolescents are motivated by consideration for others. This feeling is related to a value system, but its intellectual aspect is strongly reinforced by an emotional factor. One girl hated dishwashing and housecleaning. However, she wrote:

"The reason I do these things is so that my mother won't have to until she gets well. Being a mother, she feels she must do things that need to be done. So I go ahead and do them, no matter how much I hate to, so that she can get all the rest she needs."

One girl's empathy with another motivated her to go to a party she would have liked to avoid:

"The girl who invited me to her party was of a poor family, so I knew the party would not amount to much and none of my friends would be there. The night of the party I thought I would tell her I would be unable to come. I was about to call when I realized that this girl must really have wanted me to come. I thought how I would feel if I were in her place, and I felt obligated to go."

One youngster mentioned "never having learned to be rude gracefully and always feeling embarrassed when I'm impolite to anyone." Another boy broke a date he had looked forward to because his club counselor was in need of help and he was the only one who could do the job.

Adolescents are often faced with conflicting motives; their own inclinations make it hard for them to maintain consideration for others. One girl was motivated not by sympathy but by a kind of callous calculation: "I wanted to get in good with some of the popular kids and if it meant having a few really boring evenings with the dull guy who invited me, I was willing to do it."

A few youngsters admitted harboring motives that are not socially acceptable. As one said, "I am a schemer and am motivated by other feelings than kindness and sweet-little-old-lady ideals. In one instance I was motivated by pure spite with some jealousy thrown in." Another girl admitted being motivated by "selfishness": "I wasn't thinking of anybody else: I was thinking only of myself."

PRAISE AND CRITICISM

The students seldom mentioned being motivated by praise or criticism from adults. This may be because praise and blame have varying effects on various individuals. Praise may stimulate one student, but reduce the effort put forth by another. Praise given by a person whom the adolescent loves and respects will make him try harder, whereas praise given by a person whom he dislikes may have the opposite effect. Lavish, indiscriminate praise soon loses its value. It is also possible for a child to become so dependent on praise that he finds little "joy in the doing."

Some individuals respond better to blame than to praise. In other cases, being ignored may be as effective as being either praised or blamed. Neither praise nor blame is of much significance unless the student understands why his performance was good or bad.

The comments or expectations of one's peers, especially in an audience situation, seem to be more potent motivating forces than adult criticism. Comments like the following may explain much adolescent behavior:

"I wanted to be one of the fellows."

"I couldn't back out with everybody looking at me, so I dived off."

"I was afraid to do it, but everybody in the class was watching me so I got up my nerve and went ahead and did it anyhow."

PREVIOUS SUCCESS AND SATISFACTION

Success is generally motivating; it leads to further success, just as failure often breeds more failure. After one or more successful experiences, a student tends to raise his level of aspiration. However, his goal must be attainable and he must see that he is making progress toward it. He also needs to understand the process by which he arrived at his correct responses, and the reasons for his mistakes.

The individual who lacks the skills he needs for a given task, such as a reading assignment, becomes discouraged, and may soon try to "leave the field"—withdraw from the situation. On the other hand, the satisfaction that comes from increased competence is motivating. Increased confidence engenders increased confidence. Any pleasant and satisfying experience tends to motivate similar behavior when the next opportunity arises.

The underachiever is not necessarily lacking in motivation. He may be directing his efforts toward the satisfaction of needs other than the need to achieve in class. "The job is somehow to convince students that academic achievement in itself fulfills a need for self-expression." [1]

One needs understanding of adolescent motivations in working with individuals who are indifferent or resistant to learning. Take George, for instance. His reading teacher recognized the importance of discovering what is and has been stimulating him, and how he has responded to this stimulation. What is really important in his life? What has he wanted and never obtained?

Since George is antagonistic to teachers, a teacher's general praise does not motivate him. On the other hand, he responds well to specific and deserved approval from both adults and peers whom he admires. Disapproval and criticism tend only to increase his antagonism and intensify his feelings of inadequacy. If one gives criticism to George, it should be specific and constructive; it should show him just how to do better. Even slight objective evidence of improvement will spur him on to more achievement. Given sufficient experience of success, he may begin to think of himself as a more competent person.

MATERIAL THINGS

Most people work to make money. Adolescents are no exception. They often stick with unpleasant jobs in order to earn the spending money for something they want. With boys, this need or desire is most often for a car. One boy described his experience in this way:

"I think the thing that kept me working six days a week, five hours a night was that gradually my car was beginning to look nice, and I was determined to have a nice car."

Girls give up certain social events to baby-sit because, as one girl said, "Baby-sitting is my only present source of income. I certainly do not want to baby sit, but I'm forced to in order to earn necessary spending money. My motivation in this case is not avarice, but necessity."

Motivation is a complicated matter. What motivates an individual at any particular time depends upon his physical condition, his goals, his self concept, the pulls and stresses of his environment, and many other interrelated factors.

NOTE

1. William P. Wharton. "Attrition in College," *Allegheny College Bulletin*, October, 1965, p. 11.

Chapter 5
INDIVIDUALIZING
INSTRUCTION

INTRODUCTION

Much has been written in the past few decades regarding the individualization of instruction, and in fact it has become one of the major emphases in contemporary American schools. Such organizational plans as the nongraded primary program, team teaching, various forms of ability grouping, and the establishment of special classes represent attempts to teach children on a more individualized basis.

Most teachers probably would agree that individualized instruction represents the ideal toward which our schools should be striving. Teachers disagree however on the methods which should be used in individualizing instruction.

During their pre-service education student teachers are frequently exposed to many types of programs which claim to individualize instruction. These students frequently become confused about the meaning of individualizing instruction, and the techniques which have proven to be most effective in this field. In this chapter we have selected articles which give theoretical foundations for individualizing instruction along with suggestions for implementing the theory. We also have included selections which describe individualized instruction programs as they are practiced in specific schools.

The topic of individualized instruction is introduced in this chapter by Madeline Hunter. She begins by defining individualized instruction and points out several teaching practices which have been mislabeled individualized instruction. In this article she shows how individualized instruction can be effectively used in dealing with attitudes, interests, and psychomotor skills, as well as with the intellectual domain. A very important point is made regarding teachers who attempt to individualize instruction—the teacher must individualize his teaching behavior to the needs of each child rather than to the demands of a large group. Several practical suggestions are offered to help the teacher individualize instruction in different types of classroom settings.

Roach Van Allen stresses the point that merely rearranging students does nothing to improve the instructional program for each individual child. He suggests that individual learning rather than individual instruction ought to be the teacher's goal. Included in this article are basic questions about life which concern most children. He believes that these are the questions which the teacher should use in individualizing the learning for each child. Jeannette Veatch stresses the point that independent study must be a means by which a child develops his own way of solving his individual problem. She offers several criteria which will be helpful in leading to the improvement of independent study.

Dorris Lee offers specific instances where grouping is an important aspect of an individualized program. Roma Gans suggests practical techniques for giving help to students in any class.

Two of the selections describe specific programs which are committed to individualized instruction and nongraded schools. John Bolvin and Robert Glaser describe the goals of the Individually Prescribed Instruction Project at the University of Pittsburgh. They also include some of the techniques used for implementing these goals at the Oakleaf Elementary School in the Baldwin-Whitehall suburb of Pittsburgh. John Goodlad describes the nongraded University Elementary School, University of California at Los Angeles.

Bernice Wolfson discusses the basic facts supporting the need to individualize instruction. She explains the concepts that separate individualized from group instruction and also outlines the conditions necessary for the establishment of an educational climate that will foster individuality.

Alexander Frazier defines individualization of instruction in terms of lesser learnings and larger learnings. It is his contention that curriculum development must include both types of learnings with emphasis moving increasingly in the direction of the larger learnings.

TAILOR YOUR TEACHING TO INDIVIDUALIZED INSTRUCTION

Madeline Hunter

Individualized instruction is one of the most popular and most misunderstood concepts in education. Some teachers view it as the act of trying to juggle twenty-five to thirty-five child-shaped balls of different activities at the same time. Others view it as an electronic arsenal with each learner plugged into his appropriate socket. Still others perceive it as turning all responsibility for learning over to the students. None of these views is accurate.

Individualized instruction is no one way of conducting education, nor any one special program. It is the process of custom-tailoring instruction so it fits a particular learner. An individualized program is not necessarily different for each learner, but must be appropriate for each. It is based on the premise that there is no one best way for all learners, but that there are best ways for each learner, which may be different from those for another learner.

How do we achieve this "perfect fit"? An educational program has three major dimensions that can be adjusted to fit any learner: *the educational task,* or what is to be learned; *the learner's behavior,* or what the learner will do to

Reprinted from *The Instructor*, 79: 53–63 (March, 1970), by permission of author and publisher.

accomplish the learning; and *the teacher's behavior,* or what the teacher will do to make the student's learning more efficient and more predictably successful. Each of these factors will be discussed on the following pages.

It is important to note that the word "individualized" modifies "instruction," implying that the teacher's role is still a vital one.

Individualized instruction is not an end in itself, but rather a means to achieve learning successfully, economically, and predictably. It is an effective and efficient means for achieving learning goals as well as increasing student learning.

ADAPTING LEARNING TASKS

Individualization of learning tasks is based on two major premises, both of which have been validated by research. These premises are:

1. Students learn at different rates. Age and grade level are in no way guides to the appropriateness of a learning task. A task which is right for one learner will be wrong for another who has already achieved that learning, or for one who is not ready for it. We wouldn't expect children of one age or grade level all to wear all the same size clothing. Neither should we give them identical tasks.

2. Learning is incremental. In most instances, the child builds his learning block by block, like a wall. Some learnings act as a foundation for other learnings. It is impossible to achieve a complex learning without first having mastered the simpler component learnings, even though some children may take bigger or faster learning steps than others. For example, in order to do long division, the student must have learned to add, subtract, multiply, and divide, as well as to understand place value.

INTELLECTUAL SKILLS

Having accepted these two premises, we find we can no longer deal out to an entire class, on an assembly-line basis, the books and assignments of one grade level. In individualizing instruction, each objective will be custom-tailored to a particular learner, not homogenized for the whole class and in reality fitting only a few.

Individualizing instruction does not mean that we let certain students "get by" with doing less work. It means we begin where a student is able to perform and move systematically toward better and better academic performance.

Nor does individualized instruction mean that each student must work individually. What it means is that the teacher must thoughtfully and on the basis of the child's learning needs make the decision as to whether for this task he should be learning alone or in a group.

To begin the individualization of intellectual skills, we must first determine what each learner has already achieved in his learning sequence so he may move on to the next appropriate task. To identify a pupil's instructional level in reading, for example, we may listen to him read. If he misses more than two or three words on a page, the book is too hard for him. If he misses no words, the book is too easy—too easy, that is, for us to discover the level of difficulty at which he needs reading instruction. In math, we check to see if he really understands the concepts in addition and subtraction before proceeding to multiplication and division. Thus, by checking what he already knows, we don't waste his time or ours by having him work on something too simple or too advanced for him.

This determination of what each student is ready to learn has two dimensions. One dimension is that which ranges from easy learnings through learnings of increasing difficulty. An example taken from reading would be the learning progression in preprimer, primer, first-grade reader, second-grade, third-grade, and so on. For math this dimension would start with counting, addition, subtraction, multiplication, division, fractions and beyond.

The second dimension is one of increasing complexity in the student's thinking. The simplest level is where the student merely shows that he remembers what he has learned. In further steps, he demonstrates his understanding of that information; applies the information to new situations; uses that information to solve problems or generate ideas by analyzing, then synthesizing, and finally, evaluating.

To individualize instruction, a teacher can work with both of these dimensions, taking a tuck here and letting out a seam there to make the learning task fit the individual child. The task can be made easier—having the child learn addition, or use a first-grade reader. It can be made harder—teaching the child multiplication, or having him read a sixth-grade reader.

Another example of this same type of individualizing takes place when a teacher reaches the subject of Daniel Boone in a class in American history. The subject remains the same, but the teacher demands different levels of thinking from each student. Billy, for example, is required only to be able to answer the question, "Who was Daniel Boone?" He is on the level of simply remembering information. Mary is expected to have some understanding—to answer a query like, "Why did Boone choose that area to explore?" Other students may be given assignments which require them to apply their knowledge (*From this group of statements, select those which could have happened to Daniel Boone*), to analyze (*What factors made Boone's trip dangerous?*), to synthesize (*As if you had been a member of Boone's party, write a story about your feelings and experiences*), and evaluate (*Who do you think had the most difficult trip—Daniel Boone or the moon explorers? Support your position with evidence*).

As you see, individualizing of instruction does not mean that each student will be on a different subject; nor does it mean that individualized instruction is instruction in isolation. Learners can be grouped. It would be a waste of time for a skilled learner to recite the "facts" about Daniel Boone; but he needs that information for analyzing, synthesizing, and/or evaluating. On the other hand, although the less able learner cannot yet perform this more complex thinking, he will benefit from hearing others deal with the information in advanced ways.

TEACHER PRACTICE

To individualize the difficulty of the task—Have each child read aloud a page from his reader. Which children miss more than two or three words on a page? The book is too hard for them; use an easier book for reading instruction. Which children know all the words? For these children, the book is too easy. Find a harder book; or let each select a book of appropriate difficulty— although you must, of course, check the selections.

To individualize the complexity of the thinking—Make up questions at different levels of difficulty for a story interesting to your class. If you chose *Goldilocks and the Three Bears,* for example, your questions might run like this:

1. Remembering information—What are some of the things Goldilocks did in the Bears' house?

2. Understanding—Why did Goldilocks like the Little Bear's things best?

3. Application—If Goldilocks had come into your house, what are some of the things she might have tried to use?

4. Analysis—What parts of this story could not have really happened?

5. Synthesis—How might the story be different if Goldilocks had visited the Three Fishes?

6. Evaluation—Do you think Goldilocks was "good" or "bad"? Why do you think so?

For which of your learners would each of your questions be appropriate? Try the story and questions on your class to check your judgment.

Readings for professional growth

Taxonomy of Educational Objectives, Handbook I: Cognitive Domain, Benjamin S. Bloom, Editor (Longmans, 1956).
Classroom Questions, What Kind? N. M. Sanders (Harper, 1966).

ATTITUDES AND INTERESTS

Individualization of instruction is not limited to the intellectual domain. Individualization can also be accomplished in the development of interests, attitudes, and appreciations.

You must of course first realize that these feelings *can* be taught. A myth exists that we can't teach interests and attitudes, at least not directly and systematically. But much is known about their predictable development.

The first stage of such learning is for the child to *receive* or become aware of the thing beyond himself—to recognize that there is something in which to become interested or about which to form an attitude or appreciation— whether it is an art work, a poem, or another person with rights and feelings. To teach consideration for others is a vain struggle if the student is not aware of anything beyond himself. You will be equally unsuccessful in presenting an "appreciation" lesson if a student has not experienced that which he is supposed to appreciate. Or perhaps a child has been exposed to the experience, but has paid little or no attention. He has not "received," so he cannot appreciate it.

The second step in developing an interest, attitudes, or appreciation is for the child to *respond*. He must do something. He may listen, look, think, feel, enjoy, comment, or in some other way react to that which he has *received*.

Only after he has *received* and *responded* can the student begin to value what he is learning; and, having begun, go on to make it characteristic of himself so he becomes the kind of person who "is interested in," who "feels that way about," or who "appreciates" something.

Now let's translate these ideas into the individualization of instruction. Just as with intellectual skills, children's learning interests and attitudes will differ in their stage of learning, as well as in their degree of possible development.

For example, your objective may be to develop an appreciation of poetry, and you intend to start by reading a selection aloud. To be successful, you must remember that appreciation depends first on "receiving," and select a poem that you judge your group will *listen* to. No matter how excellent a poem is or how valuable the experience would be, students will not develop an appreciation of a poem that "turns them off."

If you individualize, you will accept a wider range of student responses—from simple attending behavior to nonverbal evidence of enjoyment (such as smiles, nods, or body movements), to verbal responses indicating enjoyment or understanding. Individualization can be accomplished by requiring a particular learner only to listen; asking another which he likes better of two poems; giving a third learner a choice and hoping he will request poetry; and giving support and encouragement to a fourth when he begins to write his own poem. Future expectations for each learner will also be individualized. Your aim for the passive listener will be to get him to respond; for the learner who requests poetry, to increase his poetic literacy by teaching him to appreciate different poets and different poetic styles. In such individualized instruction, each of them will thus be given an appropriate learning task.

Similarly, we can individualize the teaching of attitudes such as "respect for the rights of others." We can expect some learners merely to become aware that there are others who are waiting to take a turn. Learners already aware of the need for taking turns can be required to do so. Some children will take turns without our intervention, even if it is only because they know we require it. Still others will take turns because the game goes better. The objective for children is for them to take turns because the other fellow has a right to one. This ideal may not be obtainable for some at this time, but we can take them a step along the way.

TEACHER PRACTICE

To individualize interests—Survey your group to find out what interest each child would like to follow. After considering these interests in the light of accessibility of materials, space, and need for adult guidance, plan a program.

You'll find some students will flit from one activity to another, and are unable to be independently productive; others have the maturity to pursue an interest in depth. To individualize instruction, work carefully with those who need it, and give only occasional guidance to the more independent. The dividends of such a program will be growth in productive independence, expanded fields of interest, and (most important) a growing attitude that learning is zestful and rewarding.

To individualize attitudes—Together with your class, identify some school situations that cause problems. These might include having been a victim of an unfair ruling in a ball game; being teased or hit; finding the assignment too difficult; or any problem related to the attitude you are trying to build. Then ask learners to suggest as many different ways to deal with the problems as they can think of. Don't be surprised if at first students can't think of more than one way; or even if they merely parrot previously heard preaching. One reason such school problems exist is that students have not *received* and *responded* to acceptable alternative patterns of behavior. Proceed by focusing their attention on more than one possible response. When an actual problem occurs, help them identify which response they wish to use, then practice using the response.

Readings

Taxonomy of Educational Objectives, Handbook II: Affective Domain, Krathwohl and Bloom (McKay, 1964).
Developing Attitudes toward Learning, Robert F. Mager (Fearon, 1968).

PSYCHOMOTOR SKILLS

Instruction can also be individualized for the psychomotor skills. These are movement skills through which a child expresses his feelings or demonstrates his knowledge and ability, whether by speaking, writing, jumping, dancing, playing ball, or performing on a musical instrument. Even though student aptitudes vary, each of these skills is learned by building increasingly complex and automatic movement patterns. To individualize instruction in movement skills, the teacher again must determine what the student has already accomplished, and what he is now ready to learn.

To determine the appropriate task, ask these questions:

Has the learner perceived what he is to do—make his letters touch the line, make his voice go up or down, cup his hands to catch the ball? You can waste much time trying to teach a skill when the student has not focused on the critical elements of the task.

Has he a "set" to perform the skill? That is, does he understand what part of his body is involved and does he know what to do with it—put the opposite foot forward, balance with his arms, place his lips correctly? Is he really trying, or simply going through the motions?

Has the student's performance been guided physically (placing his arms for him) or verbally ("Hold your arms this way") so he will get the feel of what is expected of him?

Has he "mechanized" his response—can he perform the sequence of movement without stopping to think what comes next?

Has the skill become an automatic, complex response to the appropriate stimulus—does he automatically track the ball with his eyes, run to where he expects it to land, and position his hands to catch it? In language does he have the movement skills to automatically communicate?

As has been previously pointed out, a teacher who individualizes instruction will have learners working at different stages. This is as true for instruction in psychomotor skills as any other type of skill. In handwriting, for instance, some learners will be working on the correct formation of difficult letters or letter combinations. Others will be writing sentences or paragraphs, automatically using their writing skill to communicate their ideas as they proceed in their learning.

In physical education, a teacher who individualizes will be teaching some students how to use their bodies properly in throwing, catching, running, or balancing. (It is just as unrealistic to put a learner who has not accomplished these basic skills into a complex ball game as it is to expect a first-grade reader to use the encyclopedia.) Students who have mastered the basics will be given the more advanced task of practicing throwing and catching to automate their responses. Still others will be automatically using their skills in a fast ball game, in a complex type of race, or in advanced gymnastics.

Each learner in an individualized program for psychomotor instruction will be using the skills he already possesses to learn more complex patterns. No learner will be trying to work on complex skills without first having learned the simpler component skills; he will never hear, "Just get in the game and you'll learn to play."

TEACHER PRACTICE

Make a list of students for whom you think each of the following learning tasks is appropriate:

Stopping and holding a ball rolled at his feet.
Catching a ball thrown to him between shoulder height and waist height.
Catching a ball thrown high, low, or to one side.
Tracking a ball through the air, running to place his body in the right spot, catching the "fly."

Readings

"The Classifications of Educational Objectives: Psychomotor Domain," Elizabeth Jane Simpson, in *Teacher of Home Economics,* Winter 1966–67.

Developmental Sequence of Perceptual Motor Tasks: Movement Activities for Neurologically Handicapped and Retarded Children and Youth, Bryant J. Cratty (Educational Activities, Inc.).

PROVIDING MANY WAYS OF LEARNING

Each individual finds that some learning behaviors are more productive for him than others. Some children learn more quickly if they read, some need to listen, others find it easiest to learn if they talk about the material.

In planning an individualized program, a teacher should provide different types of activities so a student can participate in the ones that are best for him. History, for example, can be learned by seeing it re-enacted in a movie or a filmstrip, reading about it in a book, writing a story about it, acting it in a dramatization, painting a picture of it, discussing it with another individual or with a group, visiting one of its scenes, viewing it in another dimension through maps or on a time line, or constructing models or dioramas of it.

There are other dimensions of learning behavior which vary with individual students. Some can work productively with a friend; others are distracted. Certain children prefer to work alone and figure it out; others are more comfortable in a group. Boys tend to be active in learning styles, girls more passive. Some students are overwhelmed by a long and complex task—they need shorter assignments which give them frequent feelings of accomplishment. Others prefer a longer learning contract so they can make their own plans and proceed at their own pace.

When instruction is individualized for a certain student, the task to be accomplished is identified first. Next, both teacher and student proceed to seek the behaviors that will help him achieve understanding and accomplish the task.

Note that this does not mean that the student will always find the same type of learning behavior productive. The choice of learning style may vary with the pupil's previous experiences, with his ability, with the task, with the current interest of the student, and even with the style of presentation. A combination of learning behaviors is reinforcing; and, when a choice of learning styles is offered, the student can and should continuously expand his repertoire of learning behaviors that work well for him.

Thus by providing for many ways of learning, the teacher is accomplishing a major objective of the individualizing of instruction, that of helping the student to learn how to learn.

TEACHER PRACTICE

Make a list of learning behaviors which you think would be productive for your students. Be specific. You'll probably find you will have to do some careful thinking to be able to write down precise definitions of the learning behaviors. If you list "concentrate," for example, describe just what the student would have to do to convince you that he is concentrating. If you list "practice," describe what and how the student should practice. Making this list should stimulate you to increase your possibilities for individualizing learning behaviors.

Ask students to tell you what they would do if they really wanted to learn something in a hurry. Give them specific problems such as figuring out how many bottles of soft drink would be needed for a class party, memorizing the lyrics to a new Beatle song, learning enough about Joe Namath to interview him for the school paper, perfecting a trick on the parallel bars for a gymnastic show. Try to get them to reveal some real knowledge about how they themselves work, rather than repeating platitudinous adult admonitions.

Compare your list with the students'. You may find that you'll need to suggest some learning techniques that you know to be productive but that evidently the class does not know. A good example is making sure that pupils after learning something recall it at least once before moving on to new learning.

You may also find that your students have listed behaviors which you have not thought of. If they are productive, incorporate them in your plans.

Start a card file on how your pupils learn. Make a card for each pupil, listing the learning methods that seem to be best for him. Just doing the cards will help you organize your thinking about how each pupil learns best. It may also point out that some use only one or two ways of learning. Plan to have these pupils experiment with other types of learning activities. If a child, for example, seems to learn only by reading and then reporting what he has read, suggest that he broaden his base by reading an article on pottery, then show what he has learned by actually making a small piece rather than by reporting verbally on what was read. As each student moves into new learning methods, add those to the cards.

Set up a tentative plan for individualizing instruction when presenting a unit. Include activities which incorporate many ways of learning. For example, suppose your topic is the settlement of California during the 1850's. Your possibilities for learning might include: making a map showing early Spanish missions and trails; reenacting the discovery of gold at Sutter's Mill; developing a time line of California's historical events; making a report of life in a mining camp from a miner's point of view; preparing an in-depth research paper on those who came to prospect and stayed to farm and ranch.

Include some opportunities for a long-term activity for the one or two persons in your room who learn well when they can concentrate on one topic for a long period. Often day-to-day work is frustrating to the more able student who is anxious to really attack a problem.

ADJUSTING YOUR TEACHING PATTERNS

The third dimension in the individualizing of instruction is for the teacher to individualize his teaching behavior—to decide what he must do to make each student's learning more efficient and more successful. To accomplish this, you must gear your teaching to the needs of the individual student rather than to the demands of the large group.

Some teachers feel that teacher fairness and consistency imply identical treatment of every learner. On the contrary, it's these very qualities that require a teacher to insure that each student receives the assistance and support that are necessary to further his learning. For one student, this may mean a great deal of assistance; for another, it might mean encouraging or even insisting on independent performance.

Many teachers make these modifications in their teaching behavior unconsciously. They joke with one student, are solicitous with another; check every problem with one, spot-check another; praise one, scold another; insist that one work by himself, give continuing help to another. Although the experienced teacher automates these responses, it is important to monitor them constantly to make sure they do not become a rigid teaching pattern rather than genuinely reflecting the needs of particular students. An important factor in this aspect of individualization is the sensitivity of the teacher to varying personality patterns and needs.

This does not mean that teacher behavior can make up for errors in the individualization of the learning task or in the student's learning behavior. If the task is unattainable or the learning behavior inappropriate for a particular learner, failure is likely to occur in spite of any behavior on the part of the teacher. For example, if a student's assignment is to learn to spell words he can't read, writing them fifty times even with teacher encouragement will be a waste of time.

But when the tasks and the learning behaviors have been individualized, the next step is to ask yourself questions such as these for every student:

What can I do to increase his motivation to learn?

Should I praise him or prod him?

Should I give him many short assignments or a few long ones?

Is it better for him to experience continuing success, or does an occasional failure challenge him to greater effort?

How can I increase his speed of learning?

What kind and how much practice helps him most?

What are the reinforcers that strengthen his productive behavior?

How can I make the material meaningful and interesting to him?

How can I encourage him to take more responsibility for his own learning?

What skills or knowledge does he already possess that will help him with this new learning?

How can I make his learning experiences more vivid?

What can I do so that he will remember more surely what he's learned?

How can I add "feeling tone" that will assist his memory?

How can I help him transfer what he has learned into other situations where it is appropriate—transfer his knowledge in spelling into his written work, transfer his good behavior in the classroom to the assembly, transfer his hypothesizing in science into speculation in social studies?

How can I guide him into generalizations rather than isolated bits of knowledge?

You may be asking angrily or despairingly, "How can I possibly know all that about any *one* child, let alone all of them? Where can I find time to ponder each child's specific learning problem in such detail?" You are absolutely right; you can't possibly know all these things. But you will be amazed to find how thinking about these questions in relation to a particular child even at odd moments gives you valuable and productive insights into possible ways to individualize your teaching behavior.

Remember, however, that your purpose is to find out what behavior of yours best helps the child to learn in his own style. Don't fall into the trap of thinking that if you can just find the right technique—the right button or combination of buttons to push—all children will then move in whatever direction you have chosen, like obedient robots. Children know when a teacher is trying to manipulate them and rightfully resent it.

Another idea to watch is the notion that a child will always respond to the same teacher behavior in the same way. His needs and his responses will vary with the task, with the state of his health, with the progress of his maturity, with his mood, with your mood, and even the weather. But this flexibility is just an added dimension to your professional task of adjusting what you do to make it easier for each student to learn.

TEACHER PRACTICE

Make a list of questions for your students which begin, "Which helps you more . . ." "When do you learn more . . ." or "When do you try harder . . ." and complete them with some of your teaching behaviors. For example,

. . . When I give you one long assignment, or several short ones?
. . . When we practice together or you practice by yourself?
. . . When I am firm or when I joke?
. . . When I tell you what to do or let you figure it out yourself?
. . . When I decide which project you should do first or let you make the choice?

Collect the answers from each child. (You may be surprised at some of the replies.) Now proceed to individualize by trying each child's suggestions, afterwards helping him see the results. "You wanted a long assignment, and you do very well when you have one," or "You said you wanted me to joke with you but now you're not settling down to business."

If possible observe several teachers already in an individualized situation, for the specific purpose of noting the ways they adjust their teaching behaviors to the varying needs of the children. Some of these may be deliberate, some unconscious. Make a careful note of the different behaviors and how the child responds. This is even more valuable in a team-teaching situation or when a special teacher takes over your class. Then you can observe someone else with children you know, watching how specific children react to various teaching patterns.

Try different behaviors with your group and note the children with whom they are effective. For example, tell them to be their own teacher for the next twenty minutes and see who sets to work and who takes undue advantage of the freedom. At another time let them know you will not collect their papers, and observe which children stop working or become careless. Offer a reward such as early dismissal for completed learning and see which children try harder or learn faster.

If your school has videotape equipment, request that it be used in your room as you work with children on a particular lesson. Pick one in which you are especially confident and for which you have done some good planning. When you view the videotape later, make a list of the times when you individualized your approach to pupils, another list of times when you tried to reach the entire group. Look for these points:

Observe every person in the class. Was each being reached in some way?

What could you have done to reach the one or two who were not with you? (Perhaps only a nod, or a question worded especially for him?)

View the tape a second time. If you were teaching the same lesson again, what individualized activities would you introduce?

Read these programmed books on learning theory and try the ideas therein with your class: *Motivation Theory for Teachers, Reinforcement Theory for Teachers, Retention Theory for Teachers,* and *Teach More—Faster,* all by Madeline Hunter, published by TIP Publications, Box 514, El Segundo, California 90245. This series of books was written to make available to teachers important psychological knowledge that will result in significantly increased student learning.

YOU CAN INDIVIDUALIZE

SELF-CONTAINED CLASSROOM

To individualize instruction for a self-contained class, begin by throwing out the notion that a student's age or grade determines what he should learn. You will no longer deal out the books of the grade level to everyone. You will overcome your compulsion to "cover the material." Instead, you will accept the responsibility of checking to see what each student already knows so you can plan what new material he is ready to learn. Informal tests and your own observation will show you where to start.

Begin to individualize instruction by checking each child's reading level. Have him read to you so you can see at what level he misses one to three words on a page. Then instruction can begin with groups that are able to use the same book. Slower readers will need daily instruction. More independent readers may not need to meet with you daily, but they will need instruction in certain skills and more practice in independent reading. You'll modify the complexity of the thinking task to suit each of the children reading in the same book. For some, it will be enough to know "what happened"; others in the same group should be able to use their knowledge of "what happened" to do the more complex tasks of comparing, applying, analyzing, synthesizing, evaluating.

The same procedure should be followed in math. Working usually with groups, you will teach new skills, always modifying your expectations for different students. For example, when a group is on multiplication, one learner may be doing the numerical problem, another can be solving word problems, and a third will be creating new word problems to go with the number problems.

Students will increasingly take charge of their own learning, at a rate appropriate for each. Some may work on "learning contracts," pacing themselves and designing their own ways for achieving the prescribed learning. Learning contracts may begin with a diagnostic test that will help teacher and students identify their areas of strength and weakness. Then, assuming differing degrees of responsibility, together they will design instructional procedures, making it possible for those who need to work on certain skills to work alone or in instructional groups.

At other times of day, it may be possible for students to pursue their own interests in other subject areas. However, simply scheduling "free periods" without learning expectations or without accountability is *not* individualized instruction. Other than time allowed for exploration, children should be required to make a commitment for what they intend to do and to present evidence they have done it or a reason why not.

There isn't any special way that individualized instruction should "look." But it must meet certain requirements. Each student must be working on an appropriate task, in the way most productive for him, and with the kind of teacher assistance which meets his needs.

AS A TEAM TEACHER

The staffing design of team teaching makes possible more alternatives in teaching style and competence, more dimensions in grouping, and more professional know-how in diagnosis and prescription.

In team teaching, learners are usually grouped differently for instruction in each subject. When instruction is individualized in a team-teaching setup, the grouping continues. Occasionally the total group will work together, but usually there will be many smaller, flexible groupings. Children may be grouped according to academic ability, but this is only one of the many possibilities. Other bases for grouping are the style of teaching that students need, the interest or the friends they have, the skills they are ready to learn, and the amount of teacher help they require.

Most successful team teachers find that this type of organization provides a richer environment for student learning, and for teacher learning as well.

The nongraded school was created on the basic principle of individualized instruction, whether the staffing pattern is team-teaching or self-contained.

Some schools that call themselves nongraded are really levels systems; that is, all students reading on a fourth-grade level go to this room, all on a fifth-grade level go to that room, and so on. It is an attempt to *organize away* achievement differences, making it possible for one book and one assignment to be used for the entire group. True nongraded instruction is designed to *deal with differences;* in fact, this is the essence of individualized instruction.

In a nongraded school, the learner is diagnosed in terms of the style of teaching behavior that should best propel his learning. He is assigned to that kind of teacher or team. He is also diagnosed as to the kind of group in which he will learn best and assigned to that group. Only then, in an optimum environment of teaching style and peer group, is he diagnosed academically for the purpose of custom-tailoring a program to his needs.

Sometimes the teacher will work with the total class; often he will work with subgroups, and occasionally with only one or two students. If the organizational pattern in the nongraded school is self-contained, a teacher must by necessity leave some students working by themselves when he works with a group. With team teaching, another teacher is available.

When a school is nongraded and instruction is individualized, a student is always working at the academic level appropriate to his present degree of learning. He is using ways of learning and receiving teacher assistance designed to promote his success.

QUESTIONS YOU MIGHT ASK

Should students always be "on their own" when instruction is individualized? Some teachers think that individualizing instruction means turning over to students all responsibility for their own learning. This would be an abdication of professional responsibility. While it is highly desirable for a student to assume an increasing amount of responsibility for his learning, the rate of take-over must be individualized. The learning decisions a student is allowed to make should be commensurate with his ability and experience. The teacher should provide for the growth of each student toward maturity in learning decisions. He will not just hope the student will take over, nor will he expect the same degree of initiative and independence of all students.

Is individualized instruction an all-or-nothing proposition? Completely individualized instruction and assembly-line instruction are at opposite poles, with most instruction falling somewhere between. Many learning activities are individualized in one of the dimensions of task, learning behavior, and teaching behavior, but not in the other two. Sometimes a teacher will individualize his expectations for student performance and his teaching behavior. But if he has the same performance expectations for too heterogeneous a group, he will have to adjust the difficulty of the task in order to individualize it. The behavior of the teacher who wants to individualize must at all times reflect the varying needs of each of his students. The teacher who is an instructional artist will individualize all dimensions: the task, what the learner does to achieve it, and what the teacher does to assist him.

Doesn't individualizing take more time? If you have been arriving in school at the same time as your students and leaving when they do, you'll never be able to maintain that schedule when you individualize your instruction. In the more likely case that you have spent long hours planning and suffering with frustration when students don't learn, then individualizing instruction will save you considerable time.

All good teaching takes planning. When instruction is individualized, however, students work at a level where they can be more independent. They don't have long periods when they can't proceed because they don't understand. Nor do they have free time to get into trouble because the assignment was easy and they finished ahead of the others; so control problems take up less of your teaching time.

Many capable learners can proceed on their own with only occasional stimulation or guidance. This frees you to monitor more closely the learners who would otherwise grind to a halt. Also, as you learn to develop assignments with built-in flexibility the same assignment can be appropriate and stimulating for a greater number of students.

Yes, individualized instruction takes much planning time. But never was your time better spent.

Will my students be ready for the next grade? Since the purpose of individualizing instruction is to increase the amount of student learning, a good program will result in students' being better prepared for their next educational experience than they would have been with the typical instructional routine. Remember that good individualized instruction increases the amount of learning and decreases the time it takes to learn it. The more sturdy a child's educational foundation, the easier it is to build on it.

Doesn't it challenge a child to expose him to more advanced material? If a student does not have the readiness and foundation for his "exposure" to any material, he will not only be unable to learn it, but precious time will be lost that could have been used to give him the learning he needs. Exposing students to fifth-grade reading when they can't read a third-grade book, or exposing them to multiplication when they don't understand addition, is actually detrimental. Imagine the rubble resulting from a bricklayer's putting in the sixth row of bricks when the first five were not securely in place. Just as real is the academic rubble which results from teaching "sixth-grade material" when previous learnings have not been thoroughly achieved.

Don't students feel that different assignments are unfair? Do students feel it's unfair for a teacher to help a student who is having trouble with a problem and not give help to one who has solved it correctly? Of course not! Nor do they feel that assignments are unfair if each has work to do that is right for him.

Occasionally a student will ask, "Why do I have to do this when he only has to do that?" or "How come he gets to do that?" Your response might be, "It's either because I'm unfair, or I like one of you better, or I have a good reason. What do you think that reason might be?" The answer is usually a perceptive one, "Because he has finished his other work," or "Because it's harder for him." If there is a need to explain further, maintain the dignity of both students.

Students usually feel that individualized instruction is infinitely fairer, because everyone has a learning task he can accomplish with appropriate effort. Goldbricking no longer exists; neither are there insurmountable learning tasks.

How do I keep track of student progress? The question of how to keep track of what students are learning is not a new one. It has always plagued conscientious teachers. Individualizing instruction merely brings into focus the fact that the question has seldom been satisfactorily answered.

The answer is not to load yourself down with bookkeeping chores, but to find ways to establish frequent learning checkpoints. Daily correction of work can be done by students who need both the responsibility and immediate feedback. For those who do not have the maturity or integrity to assume this responsibility, you may need to devise a daily monitoring system.

Your records should be simple and easily maintained. They should include this information: What has the student accomplished? Is he floundering, or is the task so easy he does not need to exert learning effort? Is he protected by a check-back system from forgetting something he once knew?

Devices can vary from checklists and anecdotal file cards to teacher-made tests and observations. It is important to have all the information you need, but on the other hand not to waste time collecting useless or obsolete data. Examine your records critically, and keep only those data that are indispensable.

Eventually, the computer will take over this chore. The machine is ready. It is waiting for humans to identify which data are most useful in making educational decisions.

Won't there be some children I just can't reach? Regardless of your teaching procedures, there will be some children who will be very difficult to reach, especially those hard-core cases at low ability or low motivation levels. But with individualized instruction you should have less trouble. Having once accepted the idea that no materials or procedures are inappropriate for any child, you can select those which work best. And a pupil who realizes what you are trying to do is much more likely to be motivated to try harder.

Won't I need lots of materials to individualize? A teacher who follows the ideas outlined in this feature can individualize instruction using whatever materials are available. The more good materials he has, the more alternatives he can make available to learners. No amount of materials, however, can create a good individualized program when the teacher does not have the incentive.

In short, use your materials and supplies to give direction to your individualizing, not as excuses for not doing so. This is not to say good materials are not needed. But demonstrations of good individualized education have a way of stimulating the financial support for material that will make a program even better.

How do I explain individualized instruction to parents? Parents have been individualizing "instruction" ever since their children were born. They know that what is right for Susie can be all wrong for Marty. Although not usually at a conscious level, parents set different learning tasks for each child. Knowing Marty's clumsiness, they don't demand he make his bed as well as Susie, and so on.

Parents also know their children learn in different ways. Susie feels deserted if she does not have the support of a more knowledgeable person in new learning. Marty needs to figure out for himself; he resents assistance, and looks on it as interference.

Parents are reassured by the knowledge that at school their children are not anonymous "desk fillers"—that the individuality and learning style of each child are being taken into account so he will learn more in less time. When you explain your program to parents, don't be surprised if they respond, "Why haven't schools been doing this all along?"

INDIVIDUALIZED INSTRUCTION OR LEARNING?

Roach Van Allen

Every school day millions of children are trying to find and remember answers to millions of questions they did not ask—questions which may or may not be valid for them now or in the future.

What did the clown say to the children?
Why was Bo-Bo tired?
Where did he jump?
How much butter did Greece export in 1948?
When was Mars discovered?

Now as in the past, such questions are asked of large and small groups of children of like or divergent abilities, with one child selected to give an individual response. But today they are also being asked through a voice on a tape recorder, every child giving an individual response by writing his answer or selecting one from a variety of possibilities; they are being asked through

Reprinted from *The Instructor*, 78:33, 86, 92 (November, 1968), by permission of author and publisher.

programmed textbook material which each child pursues at his own speed with no interaction with other children or the teacher; they are being asked of one child at a time through electronic equipment which gives the learner immediate feedback from a remote source; or they may be asked of one child at a time by a teacher during an individual conference on material which the child has read.

All of these methods, labeled as "individualized instructional procedures," have a common design so far as the learner is concerned. He is always in pursuit of answers to questions he did not ask. These routines have become the stock-in-trade of typical classrooms. They have been graced by many labels—individualized instruction; computer-assisted instruction, programmed learning, environment control, and other lofty titles—but too often these labels merely give new status to timeworn procedures and pupil materials.

Such procedures may have moved curriculum content from a teaching format of mass participation with expectancies for uniform rate of learning toward individual pacing with the same educational objectives. They may have moved individualized responses from one child's answering as a representative of many children to *every* child's answering *every* question. As a dubious serendipity, they may have complicated the work of the teacher by expecting him to maintain extensive and accurate records of each child's progress in answering questions he didn't ask.

These procedures for achieving individualized instruction may seem satisfactory to many administrators and teachers; but the changing emphasis has not met the life needs and the learning needs of many of the individual pupils. Life and learning may be better, but they are not good enough until all of the children in our schools experience the satisfactions derived from *individual learning*—from asking valid questions and having available the resources and the guidance to find answers which are valid for each individual asking the questions.

With progress currently being made, we may in the near future be able to determine categories of basic questions which all human beings must ask themselves, and resolve on a continuum which lasts throughout life. This pursuit will be in sharp contrast to the endless hours now spent by professional educators in trying to decide which basic readers should be adopted, which basic science and social studies books have the best questions and answers; and which math series is the most "modern." Instead we may envision programs and select materials which will provide a learning laboratory in which individuals, under the guidance of a team of teachers, can find answers to valid questions.

This will place *individual learning* within the grasp of every child in our schools. Classrooms will cease to be storage bins of facts and will become launching pads for learning. We will cease to view the acts involved in learning as serious problems for any human being with the capacity to ask basic questions.

Some questions persist through life. They have validity for an instructional program promoting individual learning. The child is ever involved in answering such questions as: Who am I? What can I do? What can I observe in my world? How is what I hear related to the print I see? How can I find out what other people have said? What is in my imaginary world? Let us consider what lies behind these questions.

WHO AM I?

No publisher of textbooks can answer this question for the millions of children in our schools. Answers must be pursued in the human environment where children live together and love each other. They must feel confident and secure in asking questions: What is my name? How do other people feel about me? How do I feel about myself? What do I want to be? How can I be of service to others?

Can I help someone by sharing my own feelings through authoring books, painting pictures, composing music, making discoveries, and discussing problems? *Myself, others, society, humanity*—these are words which should spark personal questions to which the individual learning laboratory can contribute.

WHAT CAN I DO?

The school setting should present a positive note for the children who inhabit it daily. Every child should be helped to view himself as already possessing skills and abilities which will grow in the richness of life in the laboratory. A child conceptualizes in this way: I can think about what has happened to me and what I have imagined. I can talk about what I have thought about or I can paint my ideas. The words I say when I talk can be kept if they are written. The same ideas can be enjoyed by people who read what I write. I can help other people understand me if I talk, write, paint, construct, sing, dance, and dramatize. I can choose work which permits me to express myself in ways which are satisfying and rewarding to me. These are the attitudes which grow from "What can I do?"

WHAT CAN I OBSERVE IN MY WORLD?

When children ask this question in school as well as out of school, teachers begin to view the act of teaching as an art of raising levels of sensitivity. Children learn from experience that because of school they can view their world in new ways and have new words to describe their feelings—words of color, size, shape, texture, action, tasting, feeling, smelling, touching. These are the words common to all the literature through which highly sensitive persons have shared something of themselves. They are the words used to say something extraordinary about something ordinary, and something unusual about something usual.

HOW IS WHAT I HEAR RELATED TO THE PRINT I SEE?

Most children, if not all, enter school excited about learning to read. Unfortunately, many of them suffer great disappointment because there is not enough attention given to the abiding question of the relationships between the sounds of language (their own talk) and the printed material in the school and community environment. We can remedy this through activities such as talking, dictating, and listening while observing printed materials. Viewing films, exploring writing, or any other activity which is an honest effort to discover answers to the basic questions must be a continuing resource in the individual learning laboratory.

HOW CAN I FIND OUT WHAT OTHER PEOPLE HAVE SAID ABOUT THINGS WHICH INTEREST ME?

This never ending question holds many of the keys to success and happiness in our society. Because it is such an important issue, especially as it relates to the reading of printed materials, it is often amputated from its natural setting and overtaught. Books authored by children, all kinds of books from our libraries, films, filmstrips, recordings, fine art prints, music compositions, dramatic productions—all such resources must be available and highlighted in the individual learning laboratory if children are to receive valid answers.

WHAT IS IN MY IMAGINARY WORLD?

Imagination is a universal resource. It is free, easy to obtain, and has no strings attached to budgets. It is easily the greatest resource that human beings possess. It is only through the stirrings of children's imagination that progress is made. Facts merely hold the line—imagination extends facts and provides a richness of life.

Is it possible that individualized instruction merely holds the line? Can all of us extend facts and provide a richness of life to ourselves and others? To do so we must change our role as teachers to become dynamic resources in an individual learning laboratory. The answer for each of us is personal—individual!

IMPROVING INDEPENDENT STUDY

Jeannette Veatch

The crux of improving independent study lies in whether or not it *IS* independent. Workbook pages and teacher-made exercises are very much *DE*pendent as they are issued by the teacher. Usually, in the elementary

Reprinted from *Childhood Education*, 43: 284–288 (January, 1967), by permission of author and publisher.

school we refer to independent work as that taking place during the "seat-work" time; i.e., when reading groups are meeting with the teacher.

"Seatwork" centered around such "exercises" will yield little that really educates. The appalling fact is that most teachers, as well as most people who *train* teachers, believe that such paper work is important and educative, a belief not backed up by research data. We read about "well-planned" workbooks. There are no such workbooks; nor can there be, as no author knows what a child in a given class needs at a given time. No planning is good that ignores the children to be involved, so it is nonsense to speak of "well-planned" workbooks. The only hope is that teachers may have a variety of exercises and drill pages to fit a recognized need of a child. This means a dozen different workbooks and hundreds of teacher-made exercises. Even then there is no guarantee that the best-fitting exercise will teach a child whatever that exercise is supposed to teach. We simply do not know *what* workbooks teach, if they teach anything at all. There is little except the opinion of the author of the material to justify their value, even if developed with a modicum of try-outs (but not standardization) with living, breathing children.

To develop improved independent study we need to avoid teacher-assignments of this type. Workbooks are time-killers and should be viewed as such. When and if they should be proven educative, then perhaps will be the time to use them. In the meantime let us discuss learning which can be carried out independently. Children will study independently more often, with greater concentration, and certainly with greater interest when that which they study is of their own choice. Independent study means just that—*independent*. Recognizing a need, the child develops his own means of attacking a recognized problem, seeking the help he needs when he needs it.

Self-recognition of a need is a first step and certainly one of the major laws of learning. When a child *knows* he confuses "b" and "d," he can work on it. When a child realizes he is not sure of certain consonants in the beginnings of words, he can develop a project of cutting out pictures from magazines of objects that start with the needed letter. There are limitless projects in the minds of children.

One point about independent work is that it need not be hurried. When a pupil develops his own project he has the time to work on it during an independent work period without being hounded to finish. When a child is the only one doing a certain thing there is no need on the part of the teacher to rush him through. The child knows when it is time to go out and play or to go home. He can pace his work to the realistic needs of the length of the school day; if he doesn't finish one day, he can plan to stop at such a point so as to finish another. There is a matter of serenity and concentration that must not be ignored. A child works at his own project, and he works on that project at his own pace. While there is no research in independent activities on this matter, there is plenty of self-selection in reading that supports the philosophy of this type of activity.

One interesting master's project [1] showed children, familiar with self-selection practice in reading instruction, to be markedly more independent and resourceful in planning their independent work than were children under a traditional basal reader, workbook program.

CRITERIA FOR IMPROVING INDEPENDENT STUDY

Independent study requires that children make the choice as to what to do. Does the teacher make suggestions? Of course! Does the teacher check on these activities? If he wants to. But those criteria helpful in leading to the improvement of independent study are generally in the tenor of the following:

The activities are child-chosen, self-assigned and largely self-directed, although assistance from the teacher or from friends is possible and helpful.

The activities will require little formal checking, no red-pencil correction, but much teacher approval and knowledge.

The activities may be long-term or short-term without regard to the length of the period devoted to their accomplishment.

The activities must absorb children so that there is little need for the child to interrupt himself or the teacher for any purpose short of emergency.

The activities should use materials that are easily accessible and commonplace. The creative use of ordinary materials should be a hallmark of these activities.

The activities should be done for the pupil's personal satisfaction, producing enthusiasm rather than the feeling of doing a chore.

These activities, however, do not spring full blown out of the thin air. They require a classroom setting full of possibilities for self-determined endeavor. Most useful references [2] describe, in some form, centers of interest that beckon to children.

CENTERS OF INTEREST

With some variation, the centers of interest are set up around the following areas:

BOOK CENTER—where all the books are kept: trade, text and reference.

WRITING CENTER—where writing supplies of all kinds are kept, hopefully a typewriter or two, and including space for blackboard writing or writing on brown paper on the wall.

ART CENTER—where wet media such as clay, finger paint, water paint can be used with clean-up facilities handy; where dry media such as crayons, colored chalk, pretty paper, paste and scissors have a place of their own.

SCIENCE CENTER—where all manner of equipment such as magnets, batteries, terraria, aquaria, collections and exhibits find a spot.

DRAMATIZATION CENTER—where the unit in social studies lends itself to dramatization and exploration or where, for younger children, playing "house" is possible.

MATERIALS CENTER—where blocks and other creative toys and playthings are available for construction and similar activity.

FOLLOW-UP MATERIALS CENTER—where the teacher can assign specific exercises and other work and where children might find material to work upon for their own benefit.

With classrooms set up along these lines, independent work comes into its own. Teachers and pupils plan together so that children work through the problems that face them.

USING THE CENTERS

Given these centers, what can a teacher expect of young children? Which activity comes when? Is there an order to activities? Briefly, order and sequence depend upon the needs of the independent work period itself. Consecutive activities are usually of two types: (1) those that occur during the reading period and (2) those that occur at some other time of the school day. The differences between these two periods lie in the noise level of the activities. In the first, because the teacher needs to be heard by the individuals and groups, a noisy activity cannot be allowed lest there be interference. But when an independent "free" time is set up when no such instruction is required, then pounding, hammering and all manner of noise can occur without causing problems. Planning for either of these two types of work periods should take place when the day is begun in the morning. Teacher-pupil planning comes into its own when there is leeway for pupil-decision.

SEQUENCE OF ACTIVITIES

As far as sequence of independent activities is concerned, the independent work period during the reading time can and should begin with the silent reading of a self-chosen book. Under a program of individualization, self-selection is the motivating force behind reading. Children choose books usable by teachers to improve reading skills. Subsequent follow-up activities can be based on such book choices. A child may prepare his selection to present to his teacher during an individual conference, or he may plan a project that stems from that selection. Beyond those activities that tie directly to reading, there is really no particular need for a prescribed sequence of events. Let the child absorb himself and so be exposed to the excitement of learning independently. The prime test of such an activity is, of course, "What can the activity by itself teach the child?" Upon the answer to this question hangs learning that develops children to their potentials.

NOTES

1. Davida Scharf Goldweber, "A Comparison of the Attitudes of Independence and Resourcefulness of Students Under an Individualized Program and a Traditional Program in the Same School." Unpublished Master's Thesis. Jersey City State College, 1966.
2. The reader is referred to the following:
   Constance Carr (Ed.), *Children Can Work Independently* (Washington, D.C.: ACEI, 1952). *Out of print;* only in bound copies in some libraries.

H. F. Darrow and R. Van Allen, *Independent Activities for Creative Learning* (New York: Bureau of Publications, Teachers College, Columbia University). No. 21 Series. Practical Suggestions for Teaching, 1961.

Jeannette Veatch, *Reading in the Elementary School* (New York: Ronald Press, 1966). Chap. 5.

DO WE GROUP IN AN INDIVIDUALIZED PROGRAM?

Dorris M. Lee

"Hi, Bill! Did you see the notice on the bulletin board? Jim and Kathy are going to discuss Jean Lee Latham's book, *Carry on, Mr. Bowditch*, this morning about 10:00. You wanted to find out about how sailors use sea charts and maps. Let's join the group."

And at 10:05 five boys and three girls join Jim and Kathy in the story-sharing corner of the room. Jim starts by giving the setting and general focus, with an introduction of the main characters and the part they play in the story. Kathy develops the main theme and gives some personal reactions to the author's style and the feeling of reality she has about the characters. Then Jim explains what he has learned about using charts and maps at sea, which is what Bill has joined the group to hear. He begins asking Jim questions about it. Others join in, some with questions, some with comments, and two of them suggest further sources they have found helpful. Kathy then comments on what she has found about Jean Lee Latham's background on this topic and her other biographies. At this point some of the group begins to drift away and back to activities with which they are now more vitally concerned.

Of course there is grouping in an individualized program! The groups are just formed differently, for different purposes, and continue for different lengths of time. But first we must make clear what we consider individualized instruction to be. *Since* a learning situation, to be effective, must be such that each child can bring personal meaning to it, the child must have at least a part in the planning and decision-making. *Since* each learns in his own way and from the framework of his own present understandings, each must have a part in determining his own procedures for learning. Thus individualized instruction of necessity must involve self-directed learning.

Self-directed learning is a far cry from the justly feared do-whatever-you-want variety. Here the learner identifies his own educational needs, decides what he can do to meet them and how he can most effectively carry out his purposes. The teacher may help as little as by raising a question or as much as by extended conferencing. Planning with children helps them learn how

From *Childhood Education*, December, 1968, Vol. 45, No. 4. Reprinted by permission of Dorris M. Lee and the Association for Childhood Education International, 3615 Wisconsin Avenue, N.W., Washington, D.C. Copyright © 1968 by the Association.

to identify needs and procedures in terms of purposes. Individual conferences, in which the teacher can talk with each child about how he can identify needed learnings and how he decides what procedures would meet his purposes, are most useful in developing self-direction.

WHAT IS A GROUP?

In this context, what is a group? It is those children who at that time have common specific concerns, needs, interests or plans. It may be initiated by one or more of the children involved or by the teacher or by the interaction of teacher and children. The group stays together as long as the specific reason for its establishment still exists. Some children may leave and others join as their immediate needs are met or developed.

Groups in which children have a part in deciding their participation or which grow out of self-directed activity have values that do not accrue from teacher-established and maintained groups. Almost by definition, there is involvement and purpose not otherwise possible. This eagerness and single-mindedness develop unique learnings. Self-selection of an individual or group learning activity brings commitment attained in no other way. The child then feels a responsibility to himself or the group.

Mr. Swanson finds that Suzy, Bob, Karen, and Billy have difficulty recognizing base words in derived words. Each one also has become aware that he has not yet learned this, mainly through his or her individual conference with Mr. Swanson. So the group is formed to work together with the teacher in clarifying the problem, each suggesting ways of solving it from his own perceptions and reactions. One child after another gains insight, feels he understands, and leaves the group. With only Bob left, the teacher explores *his* thoughts and perceptions related to base and derived words. He discovers that he has always thought "base" meant "bottom" and never really has been able to bring any meaning to the word in this context. Each time he has thought he understood from the examples, he has become confused by the term. Mr. Swanson clears the meaning and Bob moves another step forward.

PURPOSES FOR GROUPING

Individuals are unique and, while broadly speaking most have common general needs, immediate and specific needs and concerns differ widely. We believe content is primarily for use in developing concepts and understandings about the world of people and things in which the child lives. Further, we believe that a great variety of content may be used to develop needed concepts and understandings. Since children learn most effectively when dealing with material and ideas to which they can bring personal meaning, they will be using a wide variety of content. The number identifying with certain specific content at any one time may vary from one to possibly eight or ten. If the whole group has had a particularly meaningful experience, they may all want to discuss and think together for a while at least. Groups then provide a vehicle whereby those who can relate well to certain content or ideas may work together in a way most meaningful to them.

A sixth-grade class has been having a variety of experiences that have oriented them to South America's problems, weaknesses, strengths and concerns; to its climates and general geography; to the languages of its people. Their familiarity with names of countries has alerted the children to comments relevant to South American situations in newspapers and magazines, on TV and radio, and by parents and friends. One morning Sarah comes in with a clipping relating the concern of American meat packers to the importation of Argentine beef. She asked her mother about it and in the store that afternoon they checked the canned meat shelves in their grocery store. Now she wants to know more about it. Her questions and concerns attract several others and a group of six expresses interest in finding out what it means to cattlemen both in the United States and Argentina. Since the teacher believes that a study in depth of one or two countries provides more real understanding, as well as develops skills in tackling a problem to find answers, she encourages the group to go ahead. She also recognizes that such exploration leads into virtually every aspect of a country's life—economic, political, geographical, historical.

Another purpose for grouping may be to attain needed skills not developed in other ways. When children live in a fluid, exciting learning environment where eager, purposeful activity is ever present, most acquire many such skills as natural, untaught learnings. However, some needed skills may be missed. When this is noted, by teacher or children, those who need the skills will join a group for the purpose of acquiring them, so that they may more easily go on with what they feel they need and want to do.

A fourth grade has been working independently and in small groups to find out the various ways animals are useful to man and how man has affected the animals. They have been doing much reading and discussing and thinking, even copying out of books everything that has any relationship to the study, but some of the children are getting bogged down. Judy and Linda come to Miss Jenkins with the problem. Upon questioning the group, Miss Jenkins learns that ten of them are having trouble with notetaking. Although considerable attention was given to notetaking earlier in the year, this group knows they have not mastered the skill to the point of using it effectively.

Miss Jenkins suggests they and any others who wish meet that afternoon to pinpoint their problems. Twelve come to the meeting; specific problems are shared and ideas exchanged. Miss Jenkins gets them to think about their real purpose in taking notes, what they are going to use them for, how they can decide what to take down. After working for twenty minutes, they agree to try out their new understanding the next day and to meet together again on the following day to share progress, to ask further questions, and to check their skills by reading some of their notes to the group.

Groups form, shift membership and dissolve more or less continuously on the basis of common interest. Sometimes they are instigated by the teacher, but more often in a self-directed classroom they develop spontaneously. Such groups may be for a wide variety of purposes and involve a wide variety of activities. Some of them are:

—to work together in writing a story that may be presented to the class or taped for other groups to listen to and evaluate

—to prepare for the reading of a play of their own or one already written, for presentation to their class or another in the school

—to preview and evaluate a film for use of a larger group or the entire class

—to carry out the various functions necessary to the writing and "publishing" of a class or school newspaper

—to decide on significant and challenging questions to pose to a larger group or class for the purpose of stimulating involved discussion dealing with the understanding of main issues in an area of learning

—to use a listening post with tapes either teacher, child or group made for any of a variety of purposes

—to watch film loops, filmstrips or film and record combinations also for a variety of self-identified purposes

—to solve problems of the moment, as when one or two children say, "We need to discuss this with everybody working on our project" or ". . . with everybody playing baseball at noon" or ". . . with those who want to plan what we need to think about when we write stories for first-graders to read."

HOW TO GIVE THEM THAT PRICELESS GIFT— INDIVIDUAL HELP

Roma Gans

Ask any good teacher what he finds most difficult about teaching and his answer most likely will be: "Finding time to give individual help to a pupil when he most needs it."

Ask youngsters why they consider a certain teacher a "good teacher" and often they will say: "He helps us when we need it."

With so much success, for both the teacher and pupil, depending upon a special boost at a strategic moment, isn't it shocking that teachers rarely include time for individual help in their daily schedules?

The lazy or indifferent teacher may rationalize—"Miss X had no business sending kids to me who can't read any of the books. What can I do with them?" Or he can take the view of the callous teacher who advised a

Reprinted from *Grade Teacher,* 83: 26, 44 (November, 1965), by permission of author and publisher.

neophyte, "Aim at the middle. The smart ones will go ahead on their own, and the dumb ones won't learn no matter what you do."

Such views reveal colossal ignorance of the differences in children and of the main responsibility of teaching.

Conscientious teachers establish these two conditions in their teaching: (1) They encourage youngsters to make known their problems and (2) they organize their time so that individual help can be given regularly. Let's look at each of these conditions.

MORE THAN MERE WORDS

Both at home and at school, a child quickly learns that adults all too frequently are too busy to be bothered with his requests. He may feel that he annoys adults by seeking their help.

A teacher, therefore, shows good judgment by telling children: "I'm here to help you. When you get stuck or don't understand me, ask me."

However, it takes more than just words to assure youngsters that their requests for aid are in line with good classroom behavior. It is the teacher's day-to-day attitude that counts.

WHEN THEY REACH FOR HELP

If a teacher is patient and genial in dealing with a child who is groping for the right word, or one who makes an error, or one who forgets a vital fact, he is putting sincerity in the words "I'm here to help you." This teacher is offering evidence of the type of response a child can expect when he reaches out for help.

Further, a teacher who is ready to admit his own mistakes and weaknesses is both assuring and encouraging to young people struggling with learning problems.

A teacher offers further proof of his helpful intentions by scheduling a special time for individual help—and by discussing his plan with his pupils.

HELP-WANTED SESSIONS

For example, a seventh-grade science teacher with five 50-minute classes each day starts each session with a ten-minute question-answer-help period. If what transpires during this period indicates a need, youngsters are organized into teams for follow-up help or study. Says the teacher: "This helps me as much as it does them because I know when they run into trouble, or when there are important questions that should be discussed. I don't like teaching in the dark—not knowing where my pupils are in their progress. And I don't want them to think I expect them to zip along without meeting clinkers."

Another successful teacher starts each day with "a private enterprise period" in which each of her third-graders work on "what I need most." Some work on spelling, others on arithmetic, and others on reading. During the 25-minute "what I need" period, the teacher works with pupils who ask for special assistance. When two youngsters indicate a similar need, she calls them together to help them. An outstanding result of this operation has been the growth in each child's ability to recognize his own weak spots. Some typical examples: "I skip hard words and then I can't get the sense of the story." "I'm fast, but I make silly mistakes." "I need to practice spelling, so that I'll remember words for good."

"HELP WANTED"

Another teacher puts a "Help Wanted" sign on the blackboard. Children who want help write their names or initials (they are first-graders) in a column under the sign. The teacher sets a period aside at the end of each day to work with those who have signed up.

With a friendly classroom atmosphere and a scheduled time for talking over pupils' problems, the proper trend for good teaching is in operation. The teacher will still face problems: Some youngsters will be slow to seek out help. Others will use help periods as a device to get unnecessary attention. Nevertheless, a planned program of individual help places the teacher in the category of "master teacher."

A PRICELESS REWARD

Many valuable ideas for working with groups and individuals will come from such efforts. They will, for example, make the teacher aware of the appropriateness of his teaching methods and materials. He will find out if the materials he is using are too easy, too difficult, not really helpful, or perhaps as foreign to a child's interests as advanced calculus may be to the teacher.

Through continued close contacts, not only will the children gather increased learning, renewed interest, and more satisfaction, but so also will the teacher. This increased interest and satisfaction in teaching is a priceless reward, indeed.

MEETING CHILDREN WHERE THEY ARE

John J. Goodlad

The University Elementary School of the University of California, Los Angeles, is a nongraded school. Children normally enter before the age of four and move upward through their twelfth year without encountering the grade levels so characteristic of our educational system. They are not promoted from grade to grade; nor do they repeat grades. There are no grades.

This school stands with a small but growing company of schools now abandoning the grade labels—grades one, four, seven, or eleven—in favor of what educators call a continuous progress plan. These nongraded schools are not alike, any more than graded schools are alike. The educators responsible for them are not agreed on what nongrading is or could be. But they all have one feature in common: the grade labels have been removed from a substantial portion of the school. University Elementary School at UCLA is a completely gradeless school.

There is no magic in the removal of grade labels. If this is all that takes place, we have the same old school under a new name and a fraud has been perpetrated. There are fads in education as in everything else. Not to be caught up nowadays in nongrading, team teaching, programmed instruction, or educational television is to be regarded in some educational circles as to be woefully out of touch. Consequently, there are those administrators who have merely removed the labels and then declared a nongraded school to be in existence. Others have replaced three or four grade levels with twelve or more rigidly arbitrary achievement levels. Fortunately, some schools are being redesigned in a much more fundamental way.

Until recently, nongrading was thought of as an organizational device for permitting youngsters to move through a common body of material at somewhat differing rates of speed, according to their individual readiness to proceed. Most thinking and most nongraded schools are geared to this conception. But differentiated progress through what are still essentially graded assignments represents, at best, only significant tampering with a concept of education that has been seriously questioned by educational reformers from Rousseau to Bruno Bettelheim and A. S. Neill.

Nongrading, as used and defined in the balance of this paper, is both a concept and a plan within a larger view of education embracing a few simple but nonetheless compelling principles of child development, learning, school function, and pedagogical practice.

First, children are different, much more different than we have up to now recognized. We have been shamefully remiss in taking these differences into account in our planning and teaching.

Second, in seeking to provide intelligently for these differences, educational diagnosis of and prescription for the individual is essential. Mass techniques and common expectations for all are inimical to these highly sensitive human processes.

Third, there must be alternatives from which to fill the prescriptions. A monolithic school structure providing only pass or fail as the alternatives in regulating pupil progress simply does not square with the range of alternatives necessary to coping imaginatively with human variability.

Fourth, the proper question to ask in starting a child off on his school career is not, "Is this child ready for school?" but, "What is this child ready for?" This is the most pregnant idea and is, indeed, at the heart of nongrading.

Fifth, criterion standards replace normative standards as the measure of pupil progress. Normative standards are sloppy standards based on group performance. They tend to result in unjustified rewards for high but inadequate performance on the part of the able and relentless, punishing failure for the slow and deprived. It has been estimated that 25 per cent of children in school receive 75 per cent of the failing grades based on normative standards. These children ultimately come to regard themselves as failures—not just in school but in life itself. Most of this loss to mankind could have been prevented by asking and carefully answering the question. "What is this child ready for?"

Criterion standards arrange a sequence of difficulty or a meaningful progression in work assignments. Instead of pronouncing the child to be at the fourth-grade level, which tells us very little and most of that misleading, these standards seek to provide a profile of where the child is now functioning with respect to the skills and concepts comprising the sequence of learning. These are really tougher standards, each child pitting himself against the rigor of the material rather than the uncertainties of group competence and variability. Unfortunately, we are still at a relatively primitive stage in the development of these criterion measures but rapid progress is being made in projects designed to change the curricula of America's schools.

Sixth, sound learning is cumulative. That is, the child's progression should not suffer from what psychologists call retroactive and proactive interference. A percentage problem for the child who has no conception of parts and wholes, let alone the number base on which per cent depends, contaminates his present mathematical knowledge and interferes with what follows. Such is the unhappy, cumulative product of several "bare passes" in a graded system.

The graded school was brought into being at a time when we knew little about individual differences in learning. The assumption then, in the middle of the nineteenth century, was that the content of instruction could be divided into roughly equal packages and mastered, a year at a time, by children of the same age. Soon, there came to be graded content, graded textbooks, graded children, graded teachers, and graded expectations for schooling. Graded tests and graded norms came later. The entire graded machinery was efficient in classifying the hordes of children pouring into our schools in increasing numbers throughout the balance of the nineteenth century and into the twentieth.

But the children didn't fit. Some simply could not master the work of a grade in a year; others romped through it. Good teaching raised the level throughout; poor teaching lowered it. A formidable gap between the swift and the slow remained.

Nonpromotion (grade failure) and double promotion (grade skipping) were used—and still are used—to narrow the gap within any one grade.

Neither has proved effective. The nonpromoted child, repeating the grade, rarely is stimulated anew. Studies reveal that nonpromoted children generally do worse than children of like ability and past performance who are promoted to the next grade. In fact, some nonpromoted children fail to equal their own performance of the previous year on the second time around.

The answer, however, is not simply to promote the slow-learning child. Inadequate or faulty comprehension, if not checked, leads to an accumulation and compounding of inadequacy. Promotion and nonpromotion are the ineffective adjustment mechanisms of the graded system. The answer appears to be to transform or replace the system.

The nongraded school is one replacement for the graded system. It is not simply a corrective mechanism. The component parts of grading and nongrading are not interchangeable. The two systems are built on differing assumptions, arouse differing expectations, and demand differing teacher behavior. They require differing language for their description and interpretation but, unfortunately, a language of nongrading has not yet developed. We are forced to think and talk about nongrading using the terms characteristic of grading and, as a consequence, we never quite escape gradedness.

Let us not abandon the graded school out of hand. Let us, instead, create alternatives. There can be no meaningful comparisons of what we now have without alternatives. Let us not create alternatives capriciously, however. Let us instead build alternatives which can be argued vigorously from supporting data.

The facts of individual differences among learners support the nongraded alternative. The usual fourth grade class contains children achieving at second, third, fourth, fifth, and sixth grades in some aspects of their school work —and even occasionally above and below these levels. The average spread in achievement is four years. In a fifth grade class it is five; in a sixth, six years in tested achievement, and so on. These are not fourth or fifth or sixth grades except in name. They are composites of many grades, each graded class overlapping graded classes above and below. In a field such as reading, the picture is even more startling. Children in a fifth grade class commonly range in reading from the second or third to the ninth or tenth.

The commonsense protest here is that, given ideal school conditions, these slow pupils could be pulled up substantially. True, but given equally ideal conditions for the able, they too would move up beyond these performances.

A commonsense solution to managing this vast range of attainments, frequently posed by lay critics of the schools, is to group those of like achievement in a single class. (The term used often but incorrectly for this achievement grouping is ability grouping.) But some additional evidence gives us pause. The variability in attainments within one child sometimes parallels the variability in an entire class. A child, like a class, is not a second, fourth, or sixth grader. Johnny can be in the fifth grade for arithmetic computation, the sixth for arithmetic reasoning, the seventh for spelling, the eighth for word meaning, the ninth for paragraph meaning, and the tenth for language—

and yet be officially registered in the sixth grade. In the same class is Jean, whose scores range from low third to high seventh; Bill, from high second to high fifth; and Pat, from fourth to tenth. (These figures, incidentally, are taken from actual class roles.) Children are downright ornery. They refuse to grow up all of a piece.

Under a plan of grouping for likeness in achievement, Johnny, Jean, Bill, and Pat would join a new group for each subject and rarely would be together in the same groups. Their class groups, to be closely homogeneous (that is, comparable in attainment), would be composed of children from throughout the building, brought together because of their assumed readiness for identical learnings. A monstrous scheduling problem is involved. This can readily be managed through modern computer techniques.

The main problem is not logistics. Three other matters come in for attention: the composition of the class groups brought together in this fashion, the degree of homogeneity actually produced, and the accomplishments of students in such groups.

Strange partners often come together. Is a class made up of pupils ranging from seven to twelve years of age but alike in reading attainment a teachable reading group? Are the same materials for all likely to be appropriate? The answer to both questions, of course, is no. A new and at least equally perplexing problem of dealing with individual differences has been created. This is a caricature, admittedly, but it serves to sharpen the fact that grouping children for likeness in one trait creates groups of vast differences in most other traits.

Still another problem arises from the fact that students grouped for likeness on a trait are not alike on sub-elements of that trait. When two things look alike, this usually means that the viewer is not looking deeply or carefully enough. Children grouped for likeness in reading achievement, for example, usually have comparable test scores representing a combination of paragraph meaning and word recognition. But when one examines these children for six or eight separate factors involved in reading, he discovers that these "homogeneously" grouped youngsters are really very different on each of them. The grouping pattern performs a disservice because it lulls the teachers into proceeding as though the group were one when in reality it is markedly diverse in the components which must be provided for in the productive teaching of reading. Patterns of school organization should reveal, not hide, human variability.

Presumably, students of like ability are brought together to enhance their learning. The evidence is not convincing. Studies in England, Sweden, and the United States show no significant advantages in achievement for homogeneous groups over mixed or heterogeneous groups. The findings in any given study are either inconclusive or, if statistically significant, are offset by another study concluding the exact opposite. Grouping of any kind is productive only when designed to serve a specific purpose and when accompanied by special provisions of an intimate and highly individualized sort.

The potentiality of complex grouping patterns fades and the crucial significance of individualizing instruction looms large. Needed is a system of such flexibility and responsiveness that it is scarcely a system at all. Such a system must reveal individuality, not disguise or obscure it. Once revealed, human variability most assuredly will demand alternatives. The nongraded school is but a part, albeit a significant one, of the total educational system needed for the identification and proper nurturing of precious, individual, human talent.

It will be more helpful now to talk specifically about one nongraded school than to talk in general about the alternatives in content, grouping, pedagogy, and expectations for children available through nongrading. In 1960, UCLA's University Elementary School consisted of seventeen graded rooms: three nursery school, two kindergarten, and two of each subsequent grade through the sixth. Each was largely self-contained; that is, teachers worked alone in providing the daily diet of reading, arithmetic, language arts, social studies, and science but called upon help as desired for art, music, health, and physical education.

Today, five years later, University Elementary School consists of nine nongraded clusters of children and teachers, each cluster ranging in size from as few as twenty-five to as many as seventy-five children. Each child is assigned to one of these clusters and, subsequently, to sub-clusters within these larger ones, on the basis of diagnosis and prescription. Instead of the alternatives being pass or fail, the alternatives are several in number, no one of which is grade repetition or skipping. The clusters were different in number and organization last year; they will be different again next year. The school evolves as the staff clarifies beliefs and subjects them to test.

Most clusters are staffed by teams of full-time and part-time teachers. This team teaching has facilitated the inclusion of part-time personnel, some of them students in the university, in a way that was not possible five years ago. Although the budget is only slightly larger, because of normal salary increases, 50 per cent more people are on the payroll. Not all teachers are in teams. Some maintain about the same pattern of self-sufficiency that existed throughout the school five years ago. Teachers, too, are individuals and deserve alternatives.

Team teaching is not essential to nongrading. There are nongraded schools with self-contained classrooms and team-taught schools with grade levels. But team teaching as a way of clustering children and teachers fits nicely with nongrading as a way of guiding students upward through the school. They are compatible, flexible patterns of school and classroom organization which provide a useful array of alternatives for dealing with pupil variability. Since University Elementary School developed both at about the same time, the two are almost indistinguishably interwoven in practice and, consequently, in this description.

Let no one think that change comes naturally to a laboratory school, especially if its primary function has been demonstration. Such a school is in the public eye. To change what has long been demonstrated and from what have come success and recognition is to suggest that the practices being replaced were never good when, in reality, they may have been first-rate for their time. Further, time for planning change is hard to come by. In a laboratory school, the work load of teaching children, advising future teachers, assisting many university faculty members in the conduct of their research, demonstrating various procedures, and interpreting programs to endless streams of visitors is almost unbelievably demanding. To effect basic changes while keeping the ship afloat is an unsettling experience.

The route from yesterday to today was often a tortuous one. It included changing the function of this laboratory school from demonstration to inquiry, innovation, experimentation, and research in schooling. It began with two aspects of teacher dissatisfaction which were traced to a common source. First, class membership remained rather constant from year to year, as is typical in a graded school. Consequently, children were always the oldest or youngest and rather consistently followers or leaders. They had little opportunity to shift roles and explore new relationships. Second, certain learning ills persisted for some children into the upper elementary years. The problem was less pronounced than in most schools but it was particularly frustrating for these teachers because the school was highly regarded for its instruction, and rightfully so. Teachers did everything possible within the graded organization characteristic of schools generally but often were unable to overcome what appeared to be unfortunate but irrevocable pupil placements. The placement adjustment for inadequate learning appeared to be retention and grade repetition, a solution which these teachers regarded as disagreeable and noncorrective.

They were boxed in by the graded system, a system that they had often stretched to the near-breaking point but had always retained. It is unwise to break away from long-established practice when no reasonably clear alternative is in sight. The search for an acceptable alternative led to better understanding of what was hidden by the graded structure, the fact that the seventeen classrooms were graded in name but not in the attainment of pupils. The graded structure now looked less sacred and inviolable than it had before. Some teachers who had read or otherwise learned about nongrading wanted to abolish the graded system then and there. This decision was not to come for another year.

By collapsing the next three years, we come to the present. The school is now viewed as having three broad levels of function and expectations, each successive level overlapping the previous one both in function and expectations and in the age of children assigned to it.

The early childhood level enrolls children from under four to over six. The primary function is to develop a sturdy, wholesome self-concept. Children are expected to interact productively and satisfyingly with the children, adults, and things of their daily environment. Teachers are there to assist them in working at these relationships. Concern for this wholesome self-concept carries over into the lower elementary level where diagnosis and prescription for needs in this area continue. But now the central function becomes progressive development in the fundamental skills of self-directed learning, especially reading. The age spread is now from about six to eight or nine, but age is not a primary factor in placement. The upper elementary level of function normally embraces children from eight or nine to eleven or twelve years of age. Again, attention to wholesome self-development continues, particularly as it relates to inadequate learning skills demanding special attention. The central goal now, however, is to develop the ability to understand and use man's approaches to studying social and natural phenomena. Hopefully, children will leave the school with a desire to continue learning as well as considerable self-directing proficiency in the process.

These three levels of function are not organizational units of the school, although at one point in the school's recent evolution they were. The nine broad clusters of children are not evenly distributed among them. One cluster, for example, enrolling sixty-five children from age seven to age eleven, obviously cuts across both lower and upper elementary levels, reaching toward the bottom of the former, and well up in the latter. The three-levels concept of function underlying University Elementary School simply emphasizes that the function of elementary education is not unitary throughout but, rather, shifts in emphasis from the early childhood to the early adolescent years.

Each cluster of children, whether large or small, whether team-taught or self-contained, has a wide spread in age. For example, a cluster entirely within the lower elementary level might contain children of age six, seven, and eight. Another conceived to be entirely within this same lower elementary level of function might contain children from seven to nine. One cutting across lower and upper elementary conceptions of function might spread from age seven to twelve.

This system of school organization virtually forces teachers to recognize and provide for individual differences. Several ages together serve as a blinking light reminding teachers that the students are not all alike. A single age group could lull them into forgetting the wide range of differences actually residing in it. With a little care, a mixed age group can be put together so that the overall individual differences are little or no greater than in a single age group. But experience suggests that the revelation of one kind of difference—namely, in age—creates pressure to deal with differences generally.

The learning environment in a cluster of children provides a wide range of activities appropriate to the functions involved. A cluster of forty children from age four through six, for example, shares two rooms that formerly were separate classrooms but that have now been merged by knocking out part of an intervening wall. It is not unusual for them to share other indoor spaces with neighboring clusters and the simultaneous sharing of outdoor spaces is standard practice. The skilled observer would see a certain rhythm to the daily activities. At a given moment, a sub-group is talking about a walk from which the children have just returned; another is busily engaged in a variety of jumping and balancing activities; another is sitting at a table with reading materials; and little clusters of two and three are deeply involved in still other tasks. What one child is doing now, another will be doing an hour from now. The range and variety are in part possible because, in expanding total cluster size, additional personnel also are added.

Each of the tasks mentioned above is believed to be prelude to or part of reading. Each child is working at a point thought to be appropriate for him and, most of the time, selected by him. Progression through such tasks is far from ordered, partly because some of them are parallel rather than sequential and partly because research has not yet defined the most productive sequences. Further, a productive sequence for one child usually only partly overlaps a productive sequence for another. Individual diagnosis and prescription are essential. The child is not incapable of self-diagnosis and prescription, especially if the range of alternatives is broad, visible, and attractive and he is helped to see what these alternatives are designed to accomplish.

Progress through any sequence is only very loosely related to age. The number of years a human being has lived is a poor yardstick for determining what he is ready to learn. Each of the sub-groups above contained fours, fives, and sixes, for whom the task at hand was appropriate. The sub-groups assembled for the next tasks of the day also would contain this age distribution but the children comprising the group would not be entirely the same. Here we see sharply revealed a key difference between grading and nongrading. The graded school is geared rather closely to age and to arbitrary provision of what children of that age (and grade) are to learn. The nongraded school is geared to readiness to learn, which, in turn, is determined from continuing diagnosis.

Another key difference is flexibility in expectations for children. The graded school presents a series of graded expectations. Contrary to much popular opinion, these are not rigorous expectations for all. But they are unfair. As pointed out earlier, they punish the weak and fail to challenge the strong.

University Elementary School provides a broad range of expectations—broad enough to reach from the floor to the ceiling of individual attainment—within each level of function. A child is not expected to reach a set level of reading by the age of six. Nor is he retained in an early childhood cluster of children until he does. But he will have engaged in activities considered basic to reading (many of which, unfortunately, are not seen as such by the layman) as well as in many other kinds of learnings. On moving to join older clusters of children, where these children will now be the youngest rather than the oldest, some will be among the most proficient readers in the new environment, some among the slowest. New groupings for reading will occur to take these individual differences into account. Staff and resources are now geared to make special provision for reading, with a range of expectations far in excess of those normally assumed under the label, "grade."

A child in University Elementary School seldom remains less than a year or more than three years with a cluster of children and teachers, depending on the size of that cluster, the age spread in it, and the diagnosis of that child. In principle, a child is moved whenever placement in another cluster appears to be desirable. In practice, however, every effort is made to keep a child in a cluster of children for at least a year, on the assumption that this continuity contributes to his sense of identity in a world of increasing anonymity. A child in a cluster for three years will have seen children come and go each year, will have had a long-term continuing relationship with some of these children and with several teachers, and will have enjoyed the experience of being at first one of the youngest and then one of the oldest members of the group.

Placement for each subsequent year grows out of a series of meetings taking place in the spring of each year. There are total faculty meetings in which general policies are reiterated and refined. There are single cluster meetings in which teachers who have been closely associated with these children, sometimes for as long as three years, pool data and observations concerning each child. There are cross-cluster conferences in which children likely to be assigned to one of several possible alternative clusters are discussed in relation to the teachers and to the expectations of each cluster. The data come from many sources but particularly from children's present teachers, parents, the school principal, and the children themselves.

At no time is there a squaring of each child's performance with a predetermined set of common expectancies for all four-year-olds or all nine-year-olds. Criteria are derived from the functions of the level of schooling; adequacy from a study of the child's performance over a long period of time. These are decisions for teachers to make, teachers who are close to the data. The principal participates as a member of the team, not as a final arbiter "passing on" each decision.

When the decision is to move a child from his present placement to a new one, the question is, "Which alternative?" In a carefully organized non-graded school, there should be a minimum of three alternatives from which to choose. Each of these alternatives will differ in several strategic ways, the most significant of which are the differences among the teachers. It is the responsibility of the total staff, with the principal's guidance, to determine just how these alternatives will differ: in anticipated learning activities, in the teachers to be in charge, in group size, and in actual group membership. All of these can be and should be manipulated in seeking to set up productive clusters of teachers and children for each subsequent year. Consequently, at University Elementary School, final placements of children are held up until the composition of each tentative cluster has been carefully examined. Frequently, on the basis of this examination, clusters initially proposed are modified through reassigning children.

Teachers find this process to be excruciatingly difficult at first. They must consider much more than the relatively simple alternatives: to promote or not to promote. They need to know a great deal about the children with whom they have been working—parental expectations and their effects, peer group associations, feelings of success and failure, ability to tolerate restrictions or permissiveness, and so on—and about their colleagues. They are uncertain about the criteria to use, largely because, as a total staff or as subgroups of that staff, they have not previously discussed the matter. And, to their surprise and frustration, they usually discover that they possess far too little useful information about the children with whom they have been working. In brief, they are confronted with a new and highly challenging professional task and, understandably, can be somewhat unnerved by it.

Supported and encouraged, however, most teachers learn the behavior required and practice it with growing satisfaction. At University Elementary School, the second round of spring meetings was a marked improvement over the first. Teachers came armed with data and hammered out the criteria in the process of making pupil placements. The third round was strikingly professional. But now a new kind of frustration emerged. The teachers wanted data going beyond their own observations, sensitive test data in all areas of child development—data derived from criterion measures, not normative data derived from graded standards. Such data are conspicuously absent in education. To create a demand for them is to speed their coming. Nongraded schools, of the type conceived here, create this demand.

Needed in a nongraded school is a person knowledgeable in both education and the informative sciences. He might well be the guidance counselor. His job is to set up a system for the collection, organization, storage, and retrieval of data designed to assist teachers in their vital decisions of diagnosis and prescription. He must join the teachers in these processes, learning more about them, bringing data to bear, and refining the information processing system as needed. The necessity for collecting masses of data, for maintaining them over long periods of time, for assembling them in many different ways, and for quick retrieval suggests the potentiality of a computer serving several schools or school systems simultaneously. Computers are now being used experimentally for similar purposes in research projects scattered across the country.

Complex? Yes, at first, simply because these are not familiar modes of thought to most people. It is not easy to escape more than a century of gradedness. The early phases of comprehending nongradedness are something like a first experience with English money. One is forever trying to translate pence, shillings, and pounds into cents, quarters, and dollars (and those half-crowns are maddening!). Or, perhaps better, it is comparable to the way most of us struggle initially and awkwardly with a foreign language. We seek to translate French literally into English rather than to think and to communicate in French. What a revelation it is when the intervening translation disappears and we find ourselves thinking, reading, and speaking French!

Similarly, before the potentialities of this redefined and redesigned school open up we must come to think in nongraded terms. To translate nongrading into graded nomenclature is to stay within the limited possibilities of yester-day's schools. Until fully functioning nongraded models have been carefully developed, meaningful discourse about and comparisons of nongrading and grading will be impossible. But even with models of both standing side by side, experimental comparison will be difficult and, for persons holding differ-ing conceptions of education, probably impossible. For grading and nongrad-ing are fundamentally differing expressions of schooling, based on funda-mentally differing conceptions of what schools are for and of how learners should progress in them. Ask not if this child is ready for school but what this child is ready for.

University Elementary School is still becoming. The promise of the future far outstrips the accomplishments of the past. Three years have elapsed since the faculty committed itself to nongrading and jokingly promised to fine its members for each use of the word, "graded." The school is not yet fully non-graded; it never will be. For, as quickly as one goal is attained, others come into view. As former Chancellor Lawrence Kimpton once said about the University of Chicago over which he presided, "This probably isn't a very good place for the pursuit of happiness, but it's a wonderful place to find happiness in pursuit."

DEVELOPMENTAL ASPECTS OF INDIVIDUALLY PRESCRIBED INSTRUCTION

John Bolvin and Robert Glaser

One of the most pressing needs in education today is the adaptation of instruc-tion to individual characteristics and background. If anything, this need is even more pressing than it was 43 years ago when a publication of the National Society for the Study of Education pointed out: "It has become palpably absurd to expect to achieve uniform results from uniform assign-ments made to a class of widely differing individuals. Throughout the educa-tional world there has therefore awakened a desire to find some way of adapt-ing schools to the differing individuals who attend them" (1).

More than ever, our society is committed to the significance of individual performance as opposed to group categorization. Education dedicated to this end can not only maximize individual competence but also provide every individual with a sense of pride, uniqueness, and a feeling of capability to assist, as a full-fledged member, in the development of society.

The Individually Prescribed Instruction project (IPI) of the Learning

Reprinted from *Audiovisual Instruction,* 13:828–831 (October, 1968), by permis-sion of author and publisher.

Research and Development Center, University of Pittsburgh, represents an investigation into the requirements for and the problems encountered in developing a system for individualizing instruction. The broad goals of IPI are not much different from those expressed by others who have seriously thought about their goals. Perhaps though, as scientists and researchers, we are very concerned about the operational mechanisms by which these goals are attained. To recognize them is one thing; to attempt to approximate them is another. A quotation from Professor Jean Piaget states our goals quite well:

The principal goal of education is to create men who are capable of doing new things, not simply of repeating what other generations have done—men who are creative, inventive, and discoverers. The second goal of education is to form minds which can be critical, can verify, and not accept everything they are offered. The great danger today is of slogans, collective opinions, ready-made trends of thought. We have to be able to resist individually, to criticise, to distinguish between what is proven and what is not. So we need pupils who are active, who learn early to find out by themselves, partly by their own spontaneous activity and partly through materials we set up for them. . . . (2)

We certainly agree with these goals of Professor Piaget, but as educational technologists we are greatly concerned about the conditions and the educational environment which bring about such behaviors in the student (3). Consider creativity and originality and the ability to inquire and question. It is likely that these behaviors are brought about by freedom in the classroom—freedom which preserves the individuality of the student and insures that his behavior is shaped as a function of his own productivity rather than by a group norm and blanket classroom approval. Freedom is also fostered by self-reliance—the kind of self-reliance that comes from being able to do certain things independently of others.

Originality is always a problem for the teacher because, on the one hand, the student must have knowledge and skills to be original with, and, on the other hand, he can be taught too much, with little opportunity to discover. Originality, by definition, cannot be taught since if it were taught it would not be original. What we can do is to teach the student to arrange his knowledge and working environment to maximize the probability that original behavior will occur. This can be taught in the context of school subject learning. It is best taught in terms of an individualized instructional system.

A questioning critical approach to knowledge is probably encouraged by the ability of the individual to challenge opinion. Opinion can best be challenged on the basis of information. Information in our society is exploding, and individuals need to develop the capability for self-learning in order to keep from quickly becoming obsolescent. Individualized instruction offers the possibility for teaching students to recognize that they can learn without undue dependence upon the teacher.

These are the underlying aspirations of individually prescribed instruction.

These are the goals which an operational system for individualized instruction must seek to maximize. These aspects of learning are difficult to measure. However, the most easily measured products of education are not necessarily the most valuable. Nevertheless, attempts must be made to measure what we say we are after, once we are in a position to have analyzed its nature and how it might be fostered.

Different definitions for individualization can be proposed, but incumbent on each definition is the necessity to point to its operational and practical implications. We define individualization as the adaptation of the educational environment to individual differences; put another way, the use of information about individual differences to prescribe appropriate educational environments.

In its present stage of development, the working aims of the IPI project, which are derived from these major goals and the definition of individualization, are: (1) to provide for reliably assessable individual differences among learners, (2) to develop mastery of subject matter as the child moves through the curriculum, (3) to develop self-directed and self-initiated learners through instructional procedures which provide for self-selection and self-evaluation, and (4) to provide opportunities for the child to become actively involved in the learning process. Of these aims, the first two require further elaboration. The individual differences provided for can probably be grouped into broad categories which include:

1. Provision for differences in level of achievement among pupils within a given class. This means that the system is so structured that it is possible to determine what each child now knows in each of the curriculum areas and to determine what he is now ready to study.

2. Provision for differences in rate of learning toward certain goals in the curriculum. In the elementary school, in particular, there is a set of learning goals that is common to nearly all students. In order to provide for individual differences in rate of achieving these goals, it is necessary to restructure the materials, the techniques of instruction, and the learning settings in an attempt to maximize each pupil's rate. For the system to meet this need, it has to adapt to at least the gross learning styles of the students. Hopefully, one of the more important outcomes of the work in individually prescribed instruction will be the identification of the various learning styles among students in the same subject areas and within a particular student for different subject areas.

3. Provision for establishing different learning goals for different students. Even though most of the learning goals in the elementary school are common to most students, there are still those goals that can vary from student to student. This is particularly true at the upper levels of the program. The determination of which goals to establish for which student, at present, is a joint decision of the child and the teacher depending upon the child's past experiences and achievement—his own long-range goals and the structure of the subject matter.

Closely related to the provisions for individual differences is the goal of mastery of subject matter. The assumption is that most children can master their subjects if the instructional environment can adapt to their requirements. In the IPI program, mastery is defined as a specified proficiency level for a given objective, plus a specified retention level over a longer period of time. For instance, when a child is learning to add, he works in this area of arithmetic until he can pass a criterion-referenced test on addition, with an 85 percent score or higher. After he has done this and has spent three months during the summer away from school, his retention is checked; if this retention measure indicates that his proficiency level has dropped below 80 percent in addition, he cycles back through this unit before continuing with other units in mathematics. This concern for mastery means that we have to provide for various amounts and kinds of practice, various amounts of time to achieve mastery, and various instructional techniques.

The developmental requirements to meet these objectives can best be thought of in terms of the following components of an individualized system:

1. The outcomes of learning are specified in terms of observable competence and the conditions under which it is to be exercised. In other words, a fundamental requirement in developing an individualized program is to first describe in terms of measurable products and assessable student performance the outcomes of instructional situations. With all the furor that appears to be going on these days about the vices and virtues of behavioral objectives, it is necessary to say that specifying the outcomes of learning in terms of whatever outcomes we can measure does not at all imply that students need be trained to narrow specifications in a production-line manner. On the contrary, vague specification of desired outcomes leaves little concrete information about what the educational process is to strive to attain. Especially important is the fact that interaction between the specification of outcomes in relation to instructional procedures provides a basis for redefinition of objectives. There is a sustained process of clarifying goals, working toward them, evaluating progress, reexamining the objectives, modifying instructional procedures, and clarifying the objectives in light of evaluated experience. This process should point up the inadequacies and omissions in a curriculum. If creativity, inquiry, complex reasoning, and open-endedness are desirable aspects of human behavior, then this needs to be a recognized and assessable goal. A major failing of education has been that overly general objectives have forced us to settle for what can be easily expressed and measured.

2. Detailed diagnosis is made of the initial state with which a learner comes into a particular instructional situation. Without careful assessment of initial learner characteristics, carrying out the educational procedure is a presumption. It is like prescribing medication for an illness without first describing the symptoms. The diagnosis of initial state should include not only assessment of the learner's knowledge of prerequisite behavior but also the assessment of his aptitudes, his learning style preferences (which we do not know how to measure very well), and his perceptual and motor skill capabilities (e.g., whether the student can visually discriminate letter forms and use a

pencil). This accumulated diagnosis, or long-term history, must be especially relevant to the immediate instructional step that is to be taken. In contrast to the usual kind of test battery used to predict eventual success in school, measures are required to enable us to suggest to the student what choices are available for his next instructional step. Research data have indicated that the predictors of immediate learning success and the predictors of long-range academic achievement are not necessarily the same factors.

3. The immediate instructional step consists of educational alternatives adaptive to the performance profiles determined in the student population. Alternative instructional procedures are selectively assigned to the student or made available to him for his selection. The range of educational opportunities, including instructional materials and procedures, that need to be made available in a particular school is a matter being determined by experience and study.

In many ways, the materials are the key to providing an individualized program that is both workable and economically feasible. In the more conventional teacher-directed programs, it is possible to use textbooks and materials which permit the teacher to explain procedures and operations before the pupils begin their study. However, in an individualized instruction program, the materials have to be developed, in keeping with subject-matter requirements, for some degree of self-study. Without this option available, the amount of teacher help needed would be unmanageable even with a pupil-teacher ratio of 20-1. This does not mean that even when materials for self-study or independent study are available, they are the only instructional technique that should be employed. It does mean, however, that without the availability of self-study materials, group instruction or tutoring is the only technique possible. For this reason, the emphasis to date in the IPI project has been on the development of materials that can be self-instructional.

4. As the student proceeds to learn from the instructional procedures made available to him, his performance is monitored and continuously assessed—at short or long intervals, appropriate to what is being taught. This monitoring serves several purposes. It provides a basis for feedback and reinforcement to the learner and a basis for further adaptation to his requirements. This short-term learning history, together with the long-term history, provides information regarding assignment of the next instructional unit. It also provides information about the effectiveness of the instructional material or procedure itself.

5. Because assessment, instruction, and performance are interlinked—one determining the nature and requirement for the other—what is to be optimized is critical. Is it retention, transfer to other subject matter, magnitude of difference between pre- and post-test scores, motivation to continue learning, the ability to inquire and explore with the subject matter, and/or all of these? If tracking of the instructional process permits the instructional process to become precise enough, then a good job can be done to optimize

some gains and minimize others; and we must take care to assess those ends we are serving and those we are not, although we desire to teach the latter.

6. The recognition of the interrelations among the preceding components leads to the final component of the model: the system has inherent in its design the capability for improving itself. It provides a cumulative bank of knowledge on the basis of which the next time around can be made better than the one that preceded it. One of the real advantages of an individualized instruction program is that this type of system necessitates the collection of large quantities of data just to make it operational. This data that is generated to make the system run can also be of assistance in evaluating the various components of the program such as the objectives, the tests, and the materials. Several examples of the use of data to improve the system are as follows:

Placement tests are administered at the beginning of each academic year to determine general placement of each pupil in each subject-matter area. The information obtained from the placement test shows whether the student gained, lost, or retained the proficiency he showed at the end of the previous school year. Many students who were previously required to meet a high level of mastery showed a lower level of mastery on the placement test and thus were prescribed review work. This pattern has led to an examination of the relationship between the criterion level required for original learning and subsequent retention and review procedures.

A second set of instruments used in the IPI program are the pre-unit tests. These pre-tests measure each of the objectives within a particular unit. Mastery of any of the objectives, as indicated by the pre-test, means that the child can skip these particular objectives and concentrate on those objectives of which he lacks mastery. In addition to providing the student and the teacher with the necessary information about what the child already knows, these instruments also provide the curriculum designer with information relative to sequencing and ordering the objectives within a unit.

Post-tests and curriculum-embedded tests are also used to assist the student and the teacher in making decisions as to when the child is ready to move to the next learning tasks. The curriculum-embedded tests are short check tests embedded within the materials for each objective, while the post-tests are more formal tests given at the end of a unit. In addition to providing information about what the student has learned from a set of lessons, these instruments provide information to the instructional design staff about the curriculum materials, techniques of instruction, and effectiveness of the teacher prescriptions.

Information of the type just mentioned is useful in determining those aspects of the system that need immediate attention and those aspects that can be left alone for the present time. Since individually prescribed instruction is an evolving system, providing information for continuous development and self-correction, one viewing IPI in the 1970's will probably find it very different from what one would see in 1968. Where one now sees the emphasis in testing in assessing achievement measures, in the 1970's one should be able to see instruments measuring other learner characteristics. Where one now sees a rather limited set of materials, one should be able to see a variety of materials designed to meet the individual learning styles of the student. Where one can now see limited kinds of information provided to the teacher, one should be able to see much more information provided quickly and systematically (utilizing computer processing) to assist the teacher in decision making.

REFERENCES

1. Carleton Washburne. "Adapting the Schools to Individual Differences." *Yearbook of the National Society for the Study of Education,* Vol. 24, Part II, 1925. p. x.
2. Quoted by David Elkind. "Giant in the Nursery School—Jean Piaget." *The New York Times Magazine,* May 26, 1968, p. 80.
3. B. F. Skinner. *The Technology of Teaching* (New York: Appleton-Century-Crofts, 1968).

INDIVIDUALIZING INSTRUCTION

Bernice J. Wolfson

Consider these classroom activities:

The teacher reads a story to the class.
The children work at their seats on different workbook pages, story writing, or projects.
Four girls arrange a bulletin-board display.
Two boys share the same book.
Five pupils listen to a tape-recorded story.
Twenty pupils listen to a report about the school store.

Are these manifestations of individualized instruction? Perhaps yes, perhaps no. I observed all these activities in a classroom organized for this kind of instruction, but they could have taken place in a classroom that was not actually responsive to individual needs and interests. Indeed, even a one-to-one relationship does not necessarily meet individual needs, for a teacher can direct an individual conference exactly as she conducts work with the group.

Clearly, individualizing instruction does not mean primarily a tutorial arrangement, though a one-to-one relationship is, of course, included. Nor, I think, does it encompass subgrouping on a permanent or semipermanent basis.

Whether at the elementary or secondary level, groups should be formed on the basis of a common interest, learning problem, or special task and be disbanded as soon as their purpose is accomplished. Some things, such as plan-

Reprinted from *NEA Journal,* 55:31–35 (November, 1966), by permission of author and publisher.

ning for shared activities and offering suggestions for solving a general problem, are more reasonably done in groups (sometimes small, sometimes large) than by individuals.

A crucial concept which separates individualized from group instruction is the rejection of the idea that all learners must move through a predetermined, sequenced curriculum. Merely permitting different rates of speed will not provide for individual differences. Essentially, individualizing instruction requires the teacher to encourage individual interests, allow for individual styles, and respond to individual needs.

Two basic facts support the need to individualize instruction. First, as any classroom teacher knows, students vary tremendously. Not only do they differ in shape, size, energy level, and other physical characteristics but also in rate of development, temperament, motivation, previous experience, and style of learning. Second, the human being is an active, seeking organism that does more than merely react to his environment; he also explores and changes it.

Furthermore, the purposes of education, at least as I see them, support the need to individualize instruction. One of these is the development of individuality. The press for conformity is strong in our culture, and certainly some conformity is essential for living in any society. We are not faced, however, with choosing individuality *or* conformity but rather with the issue of balance and meaning.

Other purposes of the school include promoting an understanding of the world and encouraging each child's self-fulfillment and competency. In order to develop individuality and feelings of competence and to move toward self-actualization, children need to learn how to learn, to think independently, to make choices, to plan, and to evaluate.

The history of education is replete with accounts of efforts by sensitive teachers and administrators to cope with the great range of individual differences. Approaches have included individual projects, tutoring on a one-to-one basis, programed learning, and a variety of organizational plans (for example, cross-grade grouping, continuous progress, nongraded classrooms, and multi-age classes). None of these guarantees individualization of instruction. Organization and materials can only provide the environment and arrangements which free a teacher to meet the educational needs of all the pupils in the class.

What a teacher *is* and *does* remains the crucial variable in the classroom. Inevitably one needs to ask: What is the teacher doing in the classroom? What assumptions does he make about the nature of children and how they learn? What attitudes and expectations does he communicate to the class?

Even those who agree on the need to individualize instruction may have different operational approaches based on conflicting sets of assumptions.

One approach views the teacher as a diagnostician who, with the aid of various tests, subject matter specialists, and consultants, determines what each student should learn. He then prescribes and assigns appropriate tasks and materials. In some cases, the teacher may bypass much of this operation and allow programs, textbooks, and curriculum guides to take over. But, essentially, the teacher is still making the decisions and carrying out the program.

Another approach assumes that real individualization of instruction, in ways that are meaningful to the learner, requires a good deal of self-selection and self-direction by the learner. The teacher in this operation is primarily a consultant to the learner and a manager of the classroom environment. His role is to help students learn to plan and evaluate, to provide stimulating experiences, to make students aware of many alternatives when making decisions, to supply a variety of appropriate materials.

He responds both to the requests of individuals and to his own hypotheses as to what variety of materials and opportunities might be helpful.

Reflection on the two approaches described above should make it clear that nongraded schools may represent the first or the second kind of operation. Most nongraded schools, as they exist today, are in fact graded by reading achievement. Children are grouped for "likenesses" and put through essentially the same curriculum. By contrast, a nongraded class which is multi-age and heterogeneous may be viewed as composed of thirty unique individuals who, from time to time, have common interests and needs.

Programed learning, as developed to date, is mostly related to allowing for different *rates* of learning. It is the manner in which programs are used in the classroom that determines whether or not they facilitate individualization. Self-selected, relatively short units of work would support individualization; long units required of all pupils would not.

Many of the current innovations and restorations (such as programed learning, special grouping, nongraded organization, and team teaching) allow for minor adaptations to individual differences but rest on the old assumption that there exists a graded body of skills and content which is most appropriately learned in a preplanned sequence. This assumption definitely impedes efforts to individualize instruction.

Another impediment is the fact that parents, teachers, administrators, and even children are inclined to define success and failure in terms of graded expectations. A child who is learning and increasing his competency is often labeled as failing because he hasn't succeeded in the arbitrary sequence set up for all learners in a particular grade.

The alternative to trying to patch up a system which rests on values and assumptions contradictory to those which are behind individualized approaches is to reconceptualize both the organization and the content of schooling. Let me say, without going into detail, that I believe the following assumptions are important in working toward the long-term educational goals basic to individualized instruction.

1. For real learning to occur, the learner must see a purpose and meaning in the learning experience.

2. No *best* method exists for all teachers to use in teaching anything to all children.

3. The way a teacher interacts with children affects the amount they learn, their feelings about learning, and their feelings about themselves.

4. There is no best structure in the disciplines nor a best sequence in skill development.

Classroom procedures and organizations which I think are appropriate include:

1. Grouping for diversity (multi-age, nongraded) with opportunities for *temporary* subgroups to pursue special interests and competencies

2. Self-selection in reading and in interest groups from many alternatives (This requires a wide range of human, material, and audio-visual resources.)

3. Opportunities for independent work, alone and in small groups

4. Individual and small-group conferences with the teacher for pupil-teacher planning and evaluation and for teacher assistance as needed.

In the final analysis, the classroom teacher (supported by administrators and parents) must translate his own values and goals into action.

As far as traditional school content is concerned, during the primary years I would emphasize exploratory activities in the various content areas as well as the development of skills in communication, learning, and human relations. In the intermediate years (with overlap into both primary and upper levels), I would provide opportunities for selecting more systematic approaches to developed knowledge alternating with exploratory activities and discussions of personal meanings.

Today's problem of meeting individual needs and providing for individual differences in our mass educational system is extremely difficult to resolve. Although educators may agree on the need to effect changes in this direction, we sorely need to work out some philosophically consistent practices which will develop and support individuality.

Many schools and communities today are seeking to establish an educational climate that fosters individuality. To help them with this important task, the following questions should be useful. Positive answers to a majority of the questions will identify schools and school systems where individuality can thrive.

PHYSICAL FACILITIES

Is the building constructed so that room sizes can be changed easily?

Are the classrooms constructed so as to allow small groups to gather for learning or conferences?

Is provision made in classrooms, library, or elsewhere for pupils to work on individual assignments or to do independent research or study?

Are language laboratories available so that pupils may move at their own rate in different languages?

Do the science laboratories provide opportunity for individual effort and storage space for individual projects?

Does the school have rooms which can be used for individual music or speech instruction, for individual or small-group listening to music, or for viewing motion pictures and slides?

Has space been provided for individualized sports, such as bowling and swimming, and for remedial work in body-building and posture?

Is there a place for relaxation and informal discussion?

Do teachers have access to an instructional center with such physical equipment as duplicators and a photographic darkroom?

ORGANIZATIONAL PATTERN

Do teachers have time at the beginning of the year for preplanning?

Do they have time during the year and at the end to complete records so that what they have learned about individuals will not be lost?

Do teachers' weekly schedules allow for pupil conferences?

Is the schedule flexible enough to allow for class periods to be expanded or contracted?

Does the program make a careful distinction between learning activities which can be carried out in large groups and those which need to take place on a small-group or individual basis?

Are pupil-teacher ratios low enough that a teacher can spend time with each pupil and consider each as an individual?

Do organizational patterns accommodate the continuous-growth concept of learning?

THE TEACHER

Does the teacher have a rich, varied, and creative pattern of experience?

Does he use the clues he finds in the cumulative records and in daily contacts as a basis for individualized assignments and projects?

Does he keep a written record of what he learns about each child? Does he assess its accuracy at intervals?

Is he tolerant of deviations in interests, values, intellectual specialities, creativeness, and competencies? Does he involve his pupils in cooperative planning to bring into the open individual goals, concerns, and aspirations as well as common needs and goals?

Does he provide his pupils with ways to achieve recognition and success?

Does he help his pupils to achieve self-perception, including realistic self-appraisal of strengths and weaknesses? Does he find ways to limit over-selfish ambition?

Does he create a general atmosphere of warmth in the classroom and make each child feel accepted and supported?

Does he inspire the kind of confidence that enables a child to bring into the open his hopes and his problems—personal as well as educational—without fear of recrimination or humiliation?

Does he encourage the free exchange of questions and ideas, the trying out of new experiences?

CURRICULUM

Is the educational program flexible enough to give the teacher considerable latitude in the selection of experiences appropriate for each learner?

Are the learning experiences organized so that pupils of varying abilities and interests can be assured of a reasonable amount of success?

Is the curricular pattern determined only after careful, consistent identification of differences in pupil characteristics, and subject to change when a change in emphasis and direction is indicated?

Is provision made for special programs for groups such as the rapid learners and the gifted, the physically handicapped, the emotionally disturbed, and the mentally retarded?

Do courses of study, syllabi, and resource units contain suggestions for meeting the needs of individual learners, for self-testing devices, for pursuit of special interests and aptitudes, and for wide latitude in exploratory and creative experiences?

Are groupings kept flexible in terms of subjects, interests, and aptitudes?

INSTRUCTIONAL METHODS AND MATERIALS

Do the teaching methods stimulate the student to individual exploration and learning and lead him on to new and widely varied experiences?

Does the way of teaching help learning become a pleasant, exciting experience, leading to the development of a love of learning?

Do pupils feel encouraged to ask questions?

Does the method of teaching provide an active rather than a passive role for the learner?

Is the teaching organized to provide varied ways in which a pupil can be authentically successful? Does it stimulate responses at various levels of ability? Does it stretch the thinking of pupils at all levels?

Can the teaching be adapted to the most suitable method of approach—individualized, small group, or large group—to a given lesson?

Does the method of teaching increase individual responsibility and provide opportunities for each student to organize his own learning?

Does the teacher's way of working foster confidence and make pupils secure enough to try out creative ideas without undue fear?

Are instructional materials selected with an eye to their adaptability for and encouragement of individual study and individual competence?

Is a wide variety of instructional materials available, suitable to divergent individual needs as well as to various levels of ability?

Are instructional materials selected to stimulate individual action—to give learning an active rather than passive character?

STATE AND FEDERAL GOVERNMENT

Do the state and federal governments give financial support to meet local needs?

Do they encourage and reward responsible local action?

Do they provide leadership for maximum individual development?

Do they discourage rigid conformity to standards?

LOCAL COMMUNITY

Are the power structures of the community—the social, political, religious, civic, economic, and fraternal organizations—objective in viewing diversity? Do they tend to accept, even welcome, differences?

Does the community provide a climate of support for ventures with a positive goal regardless of their outcome?

Does the community stimulate intellectual growth and provide a climate for lifetime learning?

BOARD OF EDUCATION

Does the board of education pursue personnel policies that encourage cooperation and diversity within the staff?

Does it help interpret to the community the value of diversity?

Does it encourage careful experimentation with new methods and materials?

Is it sensitive to the varied needs of youngsters and willing to back multiple means of serving them?

Is it receptive to budgets that contain an emphasis on resources for the individual as well as for the group?

Does it encourage provision of an abundance of stimuli for the inquiring minds of both youths and adults?

Does it provide the administration with support for individual staff and pupil development?

Is it receptive to modifying the existing organization and operation of the school when necessary for individualization of the curriculum?

Does the board itself relate to the administrators in a way which encourages comfortable administrator-staff relationships?

Do its policies allow teachers academic freedom to search continually for the truth?

PARENTS

Do parents encourage children to respond to the school's comprehensive and flexible program?

Do they try to understand the school program and give it positive support?

Do they encourage children to try new ideas at home?

Do they accept individuality within the community?

Do they give support to individuality and creativity in their own children and others?

Do they continue their own learning and individual development?

Do they value learning for its own sake?

Do they help their children understand themselves and their relationship to school and community?

INDIVIDUALIZED INSTRUCTION

Alexander Frazier

You must know what you want to hear.—EDWIN ZILZ [1]

When poets repair to the enchanted forest of language it is with the express purpose of getting lost; far gone in bewilderment, they seek crossroads of meaning, unexpected echoes, strange encounters; they fear neither detours, surprises, nor darkness.—PAUL VALERY [2]

For half a century we have been committed to individualized instruction as the answer to the problem of how to teach everybody what everybody needs to know. Yet only now have we been able to put together the elements that will enable us to act on our conviction with the prospect of success.

ELEMENTS OF SUCCESS

Here are some of these elements:

1. *Goals.* We have revived mastery as a goal. No longer is it possible, politically or professionally, to accommodate our behavior to inequities assumed to be beyond our control. Inside as well as around the school, an increasing number of tough-minded persons are demanding that where the road to mastery can be laid down, we must succeed in teaching what there is to be learned.

2. *Nature of the learner.* We now believe that learners start out with much less difference in capacity than we once thought. If at any given point in time learners seem unequal, it means that native capacity has not been properly developed, perhaps that we did not get to some of them early enough, or that we do not yet know how to tap the capacity that is there. At any rate, the idea that capacity is fixed is much in question. Some people are saying, "Don't tell us about their IQ or their home background or anything else. Just tell us what you want them to learn, and leave the rest to us."

3. *Content analysis.* We know better what to teach. Part of our problem has been that we have sometimes tried to teach what is untrue or incomplete

Reprinted with permission of the Association for Supervision and Curriculum Development and Alexander Frazier. Copyright © April, 1968 by the Association for Supervision and Curriculum Development, vol. 25: 617–624.

and therefore has been very hard to learn. The more scientific analysis of the nature of knowledge that has come out of the emphasis on its structure is promising to help us identify what is learnable. The teaching of modern language has been revolutionized by the reexamination of content as well as by the redefinition of the goal as mastery. The teaching of mathematics and of science are being similarly affected. As we learn how to put the pieces together again in our competing analyses of beginning reading, we may anticipate that we will be increasingly successful in teaching the first steps of that most complex and mysterious set of learnings.

4. *Materials.* We have discovered how to prepare materials that are much more studyable. These materials are precise and detailed and geared directly to eliciting the responses needed for learning, much more so than anything we would have been able to imagine in the past as possible, necessary, or perhaps desirable. A recent brochure [3] on 20 programs designed to teach pieces or segments of knowledge describes the reusable booklets as containing "ten short sets of 25–50 frames, each designed to be worked in 15 or 30 minutes." The booklets have been developed in terms of two conditions: "(1) satisfactory terminal behavior (mastery of the subject) and (2) an error rate of less than 10 percent." Topics for which programs are available include "Cells: Their Structure and Function," "Latitude and Longitude," and "Figures of Speech."

5. *Methodology.* We now know how to provide a one-to-one relationship between teacher and pupil. For a long time, we have used as a kind of symbol of individualized instruction the apocryphal image of a student on one end of a log and Mark Hopkins on the other. Now we are faced with the prospect of having a student on one end of the line and, by computer, who knows whom on the other. That part of the problem of individualizing instruction represented by the need for providing a one-to-one correspondence of teacher and learner, however eerie or unearthly or unheavenly their relationship may strike us as likely to be, is resolved.

6. *Evaluation.* We can keep track of independent learning better than before. One of the chief worries in individualizing instruction has been to find out when help was needed and in general to check on progress among 25 to 30 learners working independently. The new care in spelling out specific objectives; the elaboration of study materials, with built-in feedback of some kind to the learner; and now the computer—all have helped or will help to make the flow of evaluative information not only continuous but, in terms of quantity and precision, more than we can handle. In fact, in some situations, clerks are being employed to manage and control the flow so that it will become most useful.

7. *Organization.* We have solved the problem of organizing for individualized instruction. The matter of grouping learners for individualized instruction has been the one element of the problem above all others to which we have been historically most attentive. We have tried anything and everything. Now, however, we have suddenly found ourselves with a choice of alternatives,

partly perhaps because of our inventiveness but also because other elements in the problem have been clarified.

We can organize our pupils in relationship to successive levels of progress through a well-defined sequence of study materials. Or we can organize them in larger units of 100 or so, with an augmented staff and plenty of open space, and leave the internal grouping and scheduling to the teaching staff. Or we can run students through study or learning centers more or less at random, leaving their assignments and supervision to whoever is in charge of their stations. In the latter case, where for a portion of the day the learner is working on his own with programed materials or working under the tutelage of a remote computer, grouping is merely a question of housing.

SOURCE OF DISCOMFORT

How surprised we are, when we view the present situation in this way, to find that we really have triumphed over the problem of how to teach everybody what they need to know. We can truthfully say that when it comes to the education of the whistler, we know what we want to hear. And we can teach just about anybody to whistle "Yankee Doodle" or "Dixie."

Still, we may wonder at what we have paid or seem willing to pay for the prospect of such success. We know, when we think of the realm in which success is to be expected, that in order to succeed we have altered our conception of what education is all about, limited it, reduced it, fundamentalized it.

Thus, we are at this moment uneasy. To some zealots of the new era, it would seem right and proper that the realm of what everybody needs to know should be extended to everything that anybody might ever want to learn. If we can, they seem to be saying, through the use of this process of instruction, succeed with a piece of the program, why not move ahead to all of it?

Yet, while we may be surprised that anybody would conceive of the total curriculum as lending itself to such treatment, most of us are puzzled by and apprehensive about something much more likely to be hard to accept. We believe we can trust to the general good sense to take care of excesses of zeal in the routinization of teaching. But are we ourselves ready to assume responsibility for redesigning our program to provide more adequately for the larger aspects of learning that successful routinization of the facts and skills segment is going to give us?

We have had to spend so much time on this segment in the past that we have not done what we would have liked with the rest of the curriculum. Now the prospect of success in teaching the facts and skills means that we will have the time and space to do more with the rest.

What we are faced with, at the prospect of success in individualizing instruction, is the necessity of redeveloping the curriculum. What is involved in this task? The first thing is to clarify the differences between the lesser and the larger learnings in terms of the elements already defined.

Goals. For the larger learnings, the goal is not mastery. There is no reachable end-point on the way to which highly specific steps or objectives can be spelled out. Continuous growth is the goal.

Nature of the learner. The question of equality of capacity is not central since mastery is not the goal. What is of concern is "an ability, a power . . . the possibility of growth." [4]

Content analysis. With the emphasis on the development of powers or their growth, analysis of what needs to be learned is very different here. It is concerned with the nature of the process through which powers develop.

Materials. The total environment is of greater concern than any piece of material. The concern is for richness and diversity rather than precision.

Methodology. Powers are personal. Their growth comes necessarily from individual use. The concern is to provide many opportunities for their responsible exercise.

Evaluation. Since growth or "carrying power forward" [5] is the goal, evaluation is concerned with the individual rather than the group and is likely to be seen in global rather than concrete terms.

Organization. While room needs to be made to ensure independent functioning, many personal powers require the presence of others in the picture for their proper development. The isolation booth is an inappropriate site for the larger learnings.

Now such a contrast serves to make plain that we are still dealing with individualization of instruction. However, here we talk of the person and of his powers and of their growth. At this point it might be useful if we were to propose two definitions for the individualization of instruction: (*a*) the individualization of instruction *that leads to the achievement of mastery in the lesser learnings;* and (*b*) the individualization of instruction *that leads to the development or growth of power in the larger learnings.* The former aims at success despite individual differences; the latter aims at success in terms of individual differences, perhaps actually seeking to extend them toward a greater range of human variability, at least in all the generally desired directions or arenas of growth.

But the distinction attempted in these definitions may still strike us as abstract and poorly expressed. What we may need in addition is the exemplification of the larger learnings. If we are going to have to redevelop the curriculum to make good use of the newly vacated time and space, what are we going to be trying to do? The growth of which personal powers are we to try to forward? What is the nature of the realm of the larger learnings?

REALM OF THE LARGER LEARNINGS

Perhaps what we are moving into now is the education of the poet as compared to the education of the whistler.

"I believe in individuals." [6] This is the way Anton Chekhov responded to a correspondent inquiring about his politics. "I see salvation in a few people living their own private lives," he continued, "scattered throughout Russia—whether they be intellectuals or muzhiks, the power is in them, though they are few." Elsewhere Chekhov, whom we may take to stand for the poet, defined the realm of personal powers: "My holy of holies is the human body, health, intelligence, talent, inspiration, love, and the most absolute freedom—freedom from violence and lying, whatever forms they may take. This is the program I would follow if I were a great artist." [7]

Let us try to say what such larger learnings are, and, with more attention from us, might be.

PHYSICAL BEING

We may begin with the power of physical being. If we had more time and space in the curriculum to attend to physical growth and development, what might that mean?

For one thing, it would encompass but go far beyond mastery of skills although skills would certainly be there—skills of walking and running, of throwing and catching, of surfing and sailing, of skiing and hiking and dancing. Information would have its place also, of course—about diet and safety, physical structure and function, drugs and diseases.

But in our enlarged program, much more time and space would be provided for free play, for self-chosen games, dancing, swimming, and gymnastics; and for loafing—for refreshment and relaxation. The environment would be designed for physical functioning and physical freedom all day long —and the school would extend its responsibility to outdoor sites for hiking, camping, pack trips; for visits to the mountains but also to the desert and the beach.

The expanded program would focus on more opportunities for physical development, for enjoying the exercise of physical power and for experiencing the world through the body, including not only the natural world (air breathed in deep, the feel of sun and wind and rain) but the world of other persons—through racing, tagging, wrestling, helping up, forming circles, teaming up, pairing off.

We have never had time really to celebrate the physical powers and their growth and development. Now we well may have.

SENSIBILITY

"Experience is never limited, and it is never complete," begins Henry James, in his famous definition of what it means to be fully conscious of one's own existence; "it is an immense sensibility, a kind of huge spider-web of the finest silken threads suspended in the chamber of consciousness, and catching every airborne particle in its tissue." This mechanism of sensibility "takes to itself the faintest hints of life, it converts the very pulses of the air into revelations." Such sensibility is "the power to guess the unseen from the seen, to trace the implication of things, to judge the whole piece by the pattern, the condition of feeling life in general so completely that you are well on your way to knowing any particular corner of it. . . ."[8]

Education of the power or powers of sensibility—of responding fully to experience, of being thoroughly conscious of the world about one in all its manifold meanings—incorporates mastery of certain skills and information, it is true. Being able to identify the structure of the cell or the figures of speech may help. But the development of the powers of consciousness and responsiveness necessarily comes through many encounters with rich, raw experience and the chances one has to respond to these encounters, the demands made upon awareness.

The message of Marshall McLuhan is highly relevant here. We live in an image-bearing environment so rank and dense with multi-layered meanings that we must learn to respond to it all at once. Today the school is often less stimulating than the out-of-school environment, more restricted, blander, relatively impoverished.

What would the school look like to the learner if it were designed to be experienced as were the exhibits of Brussels and of Expo '67?

What kinds of new and specific learnings would be needed if we were to value responsiveness to the broader environment in terms of the visual arts—graphic arts but also sculpture, architecture, landscaping, and town planning? If we were to take films and television seriously? If we wanted to increase awareness and enjoyment of the world of music old and new, eastern as well as western?

If we were to venture deeply into the realms of human awareness outside the arts—the world of feelings and values personally expressed, the verbal and nonverbal clues to feelings and values?

What changes in environment, what additions to specific learnings, the inclusion of what kinds of in- and out-of-school experiences for the exercise and development of sensibility might we have if we were to redesign the curriculum to make use of new time and space for this field of larger learning?

LOVE

How does one learn to love? It is something that can hardly be spelled out, detailed, programmed. Yet the power to emphasize, reach out, relate, identify with, to seek community of some kind in increasingly wider circles is surely among the larger learnings with which we will want to do more as we make good use of our new time and space.

Perhaps love as we are thinking of it begins with simple wonder at and respect for the force of life. Marian Catlin in Wallace Stegner's new novel, *All the Little Live Things,* represents such an aspect of love. Cancer-ridden and pregnant, hoping to live to bear another child, she expresses, through her care that nothing living be uprooted or destroyed, an obsession with life, an obsessive love. Her husband, an ethnologist, mentions that the baby California gray whale gains a ton a month, and the narrator wonders: "What in *hell* is in whale's milk?" Looking back after Marian's death and recalling that metaphor for her agonizing effort to survive with her baby's birth, the narrator supposes her to be saying to him: "You wondered what was in whale's milk. Now you know. Think of the force down there, just telling things to get born, just to be!" [9] The narrator, an old man aroused from what he comes to call a "twilight sleep" of detached retirement, would amend her feeling—but it remains as a symbol of love.

And love extends to and encompasses death as well as birth. In grieving over and reflecting on his mother's death at 80, Sean O'Casey [10] comforts himself by seeing her as having passed into the endless stream.

It wouldn't do to say that each differed from each in some trivial, imperceptible way, blade of grass from blade of grass; leaf of tree from leaf of tree; human face from human face. Who is he who having examined each blade of grass, every leaf of every tree, would say no one of them was like its like? And though human faces might differ, and did, the darkness of hatred, the light of love, the glint of fear, the lightning flash of courage shone the same from every human eye, and the thoughts surrounding them were, in essence, the same in every human heart.

Between the emergence of life and its extinction or translation lies the great range of occasions for valuing and supporting others and expressing love in its many guises. Is this a field in which our power needs to be extended and strengthened? With time enough and space, what more can be done with love in the redeveloped curriculum?

INVENTION

For the poet, the power to shape and reshape his experience is that which he needs most of all to test and extend. What Sartre says of the meaning of history, the poet would say of the meaning of life: ". . . the problem is not to *know* its objective, but to *give* it one." [11]

While there are specific and lesser learnings that need to be there to be called upon, the development of the power to deal creatively with fresh experience, to search it out (to "seek crossroads of meaning, unexpected echoes, strange encounters") and to work with it (fearing "neither detours, surprises, nor darkness") until it yields a union of form and substance—this kind of development depends on openness to new experience and a great freedom of experiencing. When what is to be known is all laid out for the learner, the power of invention gets little enough exercise.

Providing in the new curriculum more time and space for richer experiencing that will stimulate the learner to alter or amend, compose, design, discover, recast, reorder, shape and reshape his world would seem extremely important.

ENDURANCE

Grace Norton, a friend of Henry James, who in his words seemed to "make all the misery of all the world" her own (she "suffered," as they said then), received a letter of consolation from James under the date July 28, 1883:

Sorrow comes in great waves . . . but it rolls over us, and though it may almost smother us it leaves us on the spot, and we know that if it is strong we are stronger, inasmuch as it passes and we remain. It wears us, uses us, but we wear it and use it in return; and it is blind, whereas we after a manner see.[12]

Years later, James wrote to Henry Adams, who had sent him a "melancholy outpouring" of "unmitigated blackness" about their being "lone survivors": "I still find my consciousness interesting—under *cultivation* of the interest." And he suggests that perhaps this survival of interest comes "because I am that queer monster, the artist, an obstinate finality, an inexhaustible sensibility." [13]

Of his reaction to the first-night failure of *The Sea Gull,* Chekhov wrote to a friend: "When I got home I took a dose of castor oil, and had a cold bath, and now I am ready to write another play." [14]

In his account of the San Francisco earthquake, William James,[15] who went into the city from Stanford where he was spending a few months, remarked on the resilience of the victims, of their "healthy animal insensibility and heartiness."

One of the powers, then, that we know we need to include among the larger learnings is the power to endure. In a television interview with Ernest Jones some years ago, Lionel Trilling asked the aging biographer of Freud how he would summarize the lesson of the master. Jones' reply was this: "To look life straight in the face—and endure it." We might find this message a little bleak ourselves, but we would have to concede that physical being, sensibility or consciousness, love, and shaping and reshaping our experience rest as powers on this rock-bottom hardiness, this power simply to be and to continue to be.

An environment arranged or prepared for learning, an environment ordered for simplicity and certainty toward prescribed ends, a failure-free environment—whatever its uses—may be inadequate for developing fully the power to endure. Much of life "out there" beyond the school or around the school, before and after school, is disarranged and unprepared, disordered and complex and uncertain, formless or littered with discarded forms, ambiguous, full of incongruity, lacking in immediate meanings. To learn to live in this world one needs to be in it, with it, so to speak.

Can we set the school scene for adventures into this world, a world that has to be accepted first to be experienced, has to be endured to be shaped, to be loved, to be responded to, to be physically enjoyed? The education of the poet really begins as he is willing to risk his life, so as to speak, in venturing into the enchanted forest. Perhaps we can help him develop the power not merely to endure the darkness, the detours, the surprises but even to welcome them as the crossroads of new meanings.

A SENSE OF URGENCY

What we have tried to do here is first to celebrate the prospect of success in individualizing instruction under what we have chosen to call definition (a): the individualization of instruction that leads to the achievement of mastery in the lesser learnings.

Then we have noted that this prospect means that our curriculum will be open to redevelopment. The teaching of facts and skills will occupy less time and space than in the past.

We have proposed that we use this time and space to individualize instruction under definition (b): the individualization of instruction that leads to the development or growth of power in the larger learnings.

We have tried, overgrandly perhaps and certainly too vaguely, to identify some of these powers—the powers of physical being, of responding, of loving, creating, and enduring.

We have tried to imbue our analysis with a sense of urgency. If we do not see and accept the challenge of curriculum redevelopment on some such terms as these, there may be those less broadly based than ourselves who will move into the freed time and space with something or other, probably more and more of less and less.

NOTES

1. *How to Whistle Songs: An Easy, Enjoyable Guide to Beautiful Whistling.* Los Angeles: The Stanton Press, 1961. p. 19.
2. Jackson Mathews, editor. *The Collected Works of Paul Valery.* Volume 13. *Aesthetics.* Translated by Ralph Manheim. Bollingen Series XLV. New York: Bollingen Foundation. Copyright © 1964. p. 48. By permission of the Bollingen Foundation and Princeton University Press.
3. Coronet Learning Programs. "20 Learning Programs from Coronet." Chicago: Coronet Learning Programs. 4 pp.
4. John Dewey. *Democracy and Education.* New York: The Macmillan Company, 1916. p. 49.
5. *Ibid.,* p. 61.
6. Anton Chekhov. *The Personal Papers of Anton Chekhov.* Introduction by Matthew Josephson. New York: Lear Publishers, Inc., 1948; "Letter to I. I. Orlov, 1899." pp. 194–95.
7. *Ibid.,* "Letter to A. N. Pleshcheyev, October 1889." p. 154.
8. Morton Dauwen Zabel, editor. *The Portable Henry James.* New York: The Viking Press, 1951; "The Art of Fiction," pp. 401–402.
9. Wallace Stegner. *All the Little Live Things.* New York: The Viking Press, 1967. pp. 66, 344.
10. Sean O'Casey. *Inishfallen: Fare Thee Well.* New York: The Macmillan Company, 1949. p. 38.
11. Jean-Paul Sartre. *Situations.* Translated by Venita Eisler. New York: George Braziller, 1965; "Reply to Albert Camus." p. 103.
12. Zabel, *op. cit.,* p. 650.
13. *Ibid.,* p. 675.
14. Chekhov, *op. cit.,* "Letter to A. S. Souvorin, October 22, 1896." p. 173.
15. William James. *Memories and Studies.* New York: Longmans, Green, and Company, 1912; "On the Mental Effects of the Earthquake." p. 226.

Chapter 6

DEVELOPING PROPER PUPIL CONTROL AND DISCIPLINE

INTRODUCTION

The ability to establish and maintain good classroom control is recognized widely as one of the most important factors contributing to successful teaching. Each year many neophytes experience anxiety while attempting to teach in disruptive and near chaotic situations. Research reveals clearly that managing pupil behavior is frequently the major concern and the greatest cause of frustration for both student and beginning teachers. Lack of ability to develop a classroom atmosphere conducive to learning is one of the leading causes for first year teachers leaving the profession.

Unfortunately, the ability to manage pupil behavior is one of the most difficult skills for the prospective teacher to develop prior to entering teaching. Usually little time is given in professional education courses to discussing classroom management. Often students have had little direct contact with children in a classroom situation prior to their student teaching assignment. Consequently, they are totally unprepared for the inevitable "testing" of the teacher that children will do in the first few weeks of the student teacher's experience. Prospective teachers often are misled by overly simplified clichés such as "keep the children busy and you will have few discipline problems." Establishing and maintaining reasonable classroom control is not that easy.

A good percentage of student teachers in the elementary grades attest that they have been poorly prepared to meet the challenge of classroom discipline. Articles in this chapter have been chosen specifically to help guide the elementary student teacher in this challenging area. Student teachers should realize that their cooperating teachers and college supervisors can help them to become better teachers in many ways. However, the student teacher himself must acquire his own methods of establishing and maintaining a classroom atmosphere conducive to learning. Techniques used in accomplishing good classroom control vary from teacher to teacher according to their philosophy, personality, and experience. What works for one teacher may not work for another. Therefore, the student teacher must recognize the importance of classroom discipline, develop a sound philosophy with regard to it, and resolve to deal with it effectively.

278

The potential causes of misbehavior in the classroom are identified in the article by Jerry Wyett. He discusses alternate techniques that may be used to cope with different discipline situations encountered by the classroom teacher.

The presentation by Leslie Chamberlin points out the need to individualize methods in working with discipline problems. The author emphasizes the necessity of understanding individual children within the classroom and the importance of looking at each child's behavior in a different way.

Many classroom teachers are unaware of the "ripple effect" upon the total class when they discipline one child or a small group in the presence of their fellow classmates. William Gnagey illustrates the influence that control techniques have—not on children who are being disciplined—but on the children who are watching and listening.

An increasing number of children in our elementary schools are emotionally disturbed. William Morse discusses potential factors which cause children to be emotionally disturbed and the necessity for these underlying causes to be identified. He offers practical suggestions for working with disturbed children in the classroom.

One of the most frustrating discipline problems confronting classroom teachers is the physically aggressive child. Fritz Redl explains three basic reasons why aggressive behavior develops in the classroom. He emphasizes that the source of the child's aggressiveness must be determined and suggests techniques for handling aggression in the classroom.

Brinson Terry and Alfred Hampton discuss one of the most serious problems facing our profession today, discipline in the inner-city school. These authors illustrate the special problems confronting the disadvantaged child and the frustrations experienced by the teacher in these districts. Both authors attempt to develop a greater understanding of these children and to detail what should be done to meet the discipline problems encountered in the inner-city schools.

HOW DO I HANDLE THE DISCIPLINE PROBLEMS OR WHAT IF THE KIDS DON'T BEHAVE?

Jerry Lane Wyett

During the past several years I have had the opportunity to work with a large number of persons both preparing to become teachers and actively involved in the teaching profession. As a necessary part of this contact with teachers, I have attempted to help them deal with those situations which they perceived as most difficult and essential to their success. I can safely make the generalization that the whole question of discipline and how a teacher

Reprinted from *Peabody Journal of Education,* 46:71–74 (September, 1968), by permission of author and publisher.

manages the problems of classroom control has appeared more frequently as an area of felt concern to these people than any other single area. What if the kids don't behave is the question most frequently posed to me by my students.

I have experienced the same frustration as many of my colleagues in trying to help teachers to view discipline as a function of the dynamics of the whole child as opposed to a series of isolated events. The process is much simplified if the teacher is able to examine the reasons behind the behavior of the child. Discipline should be viewed as a condition which occurs as a result of the way people live together. If a classroom is managed in such a way that the students will be dealt with as individuals, are not exposed to unnecessary pressures, and are achieving some measure of success in satisfying those goals which are identified for them, many of the conditions which typically create discipline problems are eliminated.

It has been my observation that many teachers who are faced with a rather constant barrage of misbehavior become trapped into looking primarily for techniques which will cause the behavior to cease. These teachers are looking for things to do to kids which will cause them to stop misbehaving. Such devices as the dunce cap, writing your name on the board 1,000 times, extra homework, verbal assaults, and sending the misbehaver to the principal's office are sometimes employed in such cases. I seldom talk to a teacher who really believes these techniques to be effective, let alone constructive. In spite of this they are all too often employed. I do not wish to dwell upon this negative approach—it suffices to say a more constructive way exists. Consider with me the following ideas.

Misbehavior in a classroom stems from at least three essential areas:

1. A physical or emotional need which is unsatisfied in the child.
2. A curriculum which places demands on the child which he either cannot or will not meet.
3. A desire on the part of the child to establish limits or test authority.

Each of these problems stems from a different need on the part of the child and therefore requires a somewhat different approach on the part of the teacher. It logically follows that the same techniques are not suitable for each child and/or each situation. Let us consider each of the three areas separately and in some detail:

1. *The Unsatisfied Need or "I have problems too."* Every teacher is at one time or another confronted with a child who is unable to sit still and concentrate on the tasks which are being pursued by the rest of the class. The child may be hyperactive because of some medical reason or because of the conditions under which he lives at home.

Because of this he may need to have a greater opportunity for physical activity. It seems unreasonable to tie this child to his desk (although I once knew a teacher who used this technique). It seems more appropriate to allow the child to get up and move around when he feels it is necessary to do so. At first he may abuse this privilege, but he will soon learn to respect both the privilege and the teacher who cares enough about him to allow it. Some teachers fear that other children will take advantage of them if they extend such privileges to certain children. It has been my experience that quite the opposite is true. Children will respect you more if they come to understand that you care about their special needs and problems. All children are not alike—why then should they be treated as if they are alike? The teacher who cares about children must seek to discover the nature of those problems which cause him to misbehave.

2. *The Curriculum Problem or "I don't see why I have to do this."* Most teachers report that the major portion of their behavior problems come either from those children who are having difficulty doing the work which is assigned to them or from those children for whom the regularly assigned work does not represent a challenge. The remainder of the class, for whom the work is neither too difficult nor too easy, behave reasonably well. The above generalization would seem to indicate that curriculum deficiencies exist in many classrooms. I think most of us would agree that this is true. A tendency exists to aim the curriculum at the so-called "normal range" and let those children who are at either side of this range make whatever adjustments they can. It suffices to say some will adjust and some will not. The "will nots" frequently become behavior problems. While it is not the purpose of this discussion to examine the nature of curriculum in our schools and the pressures which are imposed upon teachers to communicate this curriculum, it seems apparent to most that our curriculum is frequently inadequate. The individual classroom teacher can do much to alleviate this problem by providing additional activities to meet the needs of those for whom the regular curriculum is inadequate. A variety of such activities may be gathered by seeking ideas both from within one's own creative talents and by consulting other teachers regarding activities which they use for curriculum enrichment. It is appropriate to recognize the concept of individual differences, but it is more appropriate to allow sufficient flexibility within a classroom to meet these differences. Teachers who are concerned about children's behavior must realize the fact that aspects of the curriculum are differentially meaningful to individual students and avoid the temptation to teach everyone the same thing at the same time.

3. *The Testing Problem or "You teachers are all alike."* It is a fundamental concern of every child to become adequate as a person. This desire for adequacy may take many directions but is basically concerned with becoming a fully functioning, self sufficient individual. One of the fundamental differences between adults and children is the former's ability to make and execute meaningful and satisfying decisions. In short, adults are free to choose those things which make sense to them and satisfy their needs. Children require more help to do this. We frequently make the mistake of making decisions for children as opposed to helping them make their own decisions.

While it is true that children desire freedom, they likewise seek security. They resist attempts to take away their freedom but at the same time they seek the security of an adult who cares enough for them to provide that much needed security.

The kinds of testing which students frequently engage in are directed toward reaching a condition of equilibrium between their desire for freedom and their need for security which is experienced when reasonable limits are established.

This kind of testing is experienced by a substitute teacher, a new teacher who first meets with a class and any teacher during a period of real or imagined stress. A student may ask for example, "What will you do if I . . . ." He is really asking the teacher to define limits. Because of the pressures we as teachers experience in our day to day operation of the class, we sometimes establish rules and/or limits which are not reasonable for the students. We can expect these limits to be tested. The whole problem of discipline in a Junior High School is best understood in this context. The adolescent is no longer willing to follow the dictates of adults but still needs to test his developing concepts of self against adult standards.

The teacher who consistently experiences these kinds of behavior problems can resolve most of these conflicts by a re-examination of the limits which have been established and a re-evaluation of the level of his own sense of security. A feeling of insecurity in the teacher is readily sensed by the students.

Misbehavior on the part of children is in no small measure a request for help. When someone asks for help he responds positively toward the one who provides the help.

4. *A Final Note or "I feel better now."* The nature of children requires that they be treated as unique human beings and the nature of the teaching process requires that teachers and children work cooperatively toward the realization of their common goals. The teacher who becomes adept at recognizing the motivation behind particular behavior and makes those adjustments which will most effectively direct this behavior in positive directions has made a giant step in the solving of discipline problems. The teacher who makes such adjustments is providing the help which children who misbehave are seeking.

DISCIPLINE AND INDIVIDUAL DIFFERENCES

Leslie J. Chamberlin

Our modern discipline, with its emphasis on self-control and self-direction is one of the most difficult things that a child must master. Any contribution a parent or teacher may make toward the child's development of character, good citizenship and self-control will depend to a great extent upon his skill

Reprinted from *School and Community*, 54:18–19, 24 (September, 1967), by permission of author and publisher.

in managing his children or students in a manner which conforms to a psychology of self-direction. Although a student participates in most school activities as a group member, he may become the center of attention at any moment. The activity that brings the student to the attention of the teacher may be suitable and worthwhile or it may be an outburst of profanity, a temper tantrum or some other unacceptable act. Although lessons are usually planned for groups of students, it is with the individual student that the teacher must ultimately deal. When grades are given, it is an individual who is graded, and when a difficult situation arises, it will be an individual or at best a small group of individuals with whom the teacher must negotiate.

To be a truly successful career teacher, a person must have a thorough understanding of the importance of the individual. He must be prepared to study his class in terms of such general factors as age, environment, race, religion and intelligence. But more importantly, a good teacher will study each individual in his class in terms of that person's past school record, home and family factors, and any other unusual problems that the student may have, such as physical, emotional or mental disturbances. Often, it will be only through a first-hand knowledge of the individual student that the teacher will be able to adequately control certain classroom situations.

Teachers frequently give only lip service to the idea of studying the individual. They deceive themselves into believing that they are "practical disciplinarians" by following a few rule of thumb approaches that can do little more than bring an uneasy peace to a noisy classroom.

Often, much attention is given to the symptoms involved in the disciplinary action with little effort directed at determining the underlying cause or reasons behind the children's misbehavior. When the child misbehaves in the classroom it is frequently a symptom of some maladjustment of his life out of school. Sometimes improper conduct is a warning to the teacher of approaching mental ill-health or delinquency.

Before a teacher can cope with abnormal classroom situations, he must know what is considered normal behavior for a particular group of children. He must also be acquainted with those factors that commonly cause children to deviate from normal behavior.

WHAT IS NORMAL

Different persons look at children's behavior in different ways. A law enforcement officer viewing a youngster is concerned primarily with what the child did and evidence to prove it. A social worker is concerned with the "why" of the behavior. A person directly involved in the misbehavior of a youth will often be concerned with only the harm and hurt that has been caused. Punishment is uppermost in his mind.

Much misunderstanding arises because of the various viewpoints within the community. Teachers need to frequently check their own points of view and reactions to their students' behavior.

The developmental years of life cover four stages; infancy, childhood, pre-adolescence and adolescence. The years from birth through age four are termed infancy. Ages five through nine, the childhood years.

Pre-adolescence is somewhere between nine and thirteen, with boys maturing as much as two years later than girls. Adolescence is that period between puberty and maturity.

Research has verified that individuals show certain characteristic actions, have certain physical development and certain special needs at a particular age.

No two children have exactly the same needs, motivations, or drives at a particular time, and yet all children have basically the same fundamental needs, motivations and drives. Although a teacher may develop a rule of thumb of normal development, he must constantly remind himself that allowances must always be made for individual differences.

In terms of physical development, infancy has the most rapid growth rate of any of the growth periods. The childhood years are a generally slow and steady growth period with some of the portions of the body attaining almost adult size. Pre-adolescence is usually considered a resting period with the possibility of a period of rapid growth in height and weight starting sometime during the five or six year period. Adolescence is usually a period of rapid physical development.

Although children always seem willing to make decisions, this seems to become a more pressing need as the years pass. Beginning at about age nine and increasing through pre-adolescence and adolescence, young people seem to look for more and more opportunities to make decisions for themselves.

Those persons providing direction and supervision for young people of this age category should openly express affection, use a sense of humor, but avoid a nagging or condemnation or talking down to the young person.

Traits such as straining against parental authority, desire for greater freedom, extreme loyalty to peer groups, etc., seem to be characterized during the late teen years. The era that often causes the most trouble might be called the "mating season," that period of time when the youth becomes totally enhanced with the opposite sex. Often everything seems to suffer during this time, including school work, home and family relations, established friendships of the same sex.

Characteristic actions of children vary considerably from developmental stage to developmental stage; and often from year to year. The child who is often careless, noisy and argumentative at eight years of age may be decisive, responsible, reasonable, with a strong sense of what is right and wrong at age nine.

Reactions of a child are controlled to a large extent by his physical development. The child of four may be highly social and talkative where the child of one can be sociable but not talkative.

It can be quite helpful to anticipate a child's reaction to criticism. Below-age-five children are highly sensitive to any type of criticism. At five the child is capable of self-criticism and accepts corrective criticism from adults. The seven-year-old actually becomes quite self-critical. He is anxious to do things correctly and rather cautious in his planning and actions in an effort to avoid criticism.

At age eight, children often become quite sensitive to criticism. Pre-adolescence is a period when children sometimes become over-critical, changeable and uncooperative. The adolescent often seems to return to the habits of younger children, becoming over-sensitive and often unable to accept any criticism.

Adults who have responsibility for developing children need to be acquainted with the characteristic reactions of children in terms of their interests, their ability and willingness to make decisions, ability to assume responsibility, sex interests, etc., if they are to be of real service to the child as he grows, learns and develops.

DEVIATE BEHAVIOR

It is not difficult to recognize misbehavior. It is very difficult to deal with it in terms of the true cause, ignoring the symptoms when necessary.

Too often these days both parents and teachers state that they simply do not know what to do with their child or a particular student. The children are defiant, inconsiderate, even contemptuous of both parents and school officials.

One reason for this situation is that adults often refuse to recognize what the children are saying by their actions. Actions that in the thinking of an adult may be considered misbehavior may really be a demand for attention on the part of the child.

The misbehavior may actually be the child's mistaken way of trying to belong, to be someone who matters. To bring about a lasting improvement in the behavior of a child, it is imperative that the true cause of this behavior be recognized and given consideration.

One of the keystones of good teaching is the teacher's willingness to seek and understand the reasons behind the children's behavior. It is important to make a special effort to understand those children who need it the most; the noisy ones, the sometimes belligerent ones, those children who are most irritating and unlovable.

Of course, it is not only the "difficult" children that teachers must try to understand but they need to also take a close look at the "good" child. These children may be bottling up their real feelings inside of them. Often they need far more help than the outgoing youngster who has been labeled a trouble-maker.

Certainly a thorough understanding of what is considered normal behavior will enable the teacher to make a more valid judgment as to what is abnormal or problem behavior.

A student who is experiencing anxiety over some conflict may often attempt to release this tension through misbehavior. Occasionally, however, some other release is developed, such as a tic, an apparently meaningless habit, such as blinking, lip puckering, twitching or sniffling.

Teachers must learn to recognize other signs of inner-conflict within their students besides misbehavior. A tic or other manifestation of inner-conflict may be caused by anxieties such as fear of displeasing a parent or teacher or failing a test at school.

Releasing the anxiety by way of the tic is a child's way of easing his tension. Children are just as puzzled by their nervous mannerisms as parents and teachers. A child who has a serious nervous mannerism should be examined by a physician.

Some students may need more extended treatment than the teacher can render. Teachers should never go it alone in the business of helping the habitual misbehaving student. Frequently it will be necessary to call upon the help of specialists. The classroom teacher must know how and when to use outside resources in the study-diagnosis-treatment process.

Individual behavior patterns depend upon the factors affecting the individual. Most children do tend toward the norm in behavior, but individuals deviate in a certain area or in general to a certain degree depending upon the severity of the factors affecting their lives. If a teacher studies his class as individuals, he may be able to discover what is causing the deviation. If the teacher is to help, he must be prepared to (1) attempt to understand the situation, (2) compensate where possible for the problem and (3) correct the underlying difficulty rather than depressing the obvious symptoms.

WHAT IS THE RIPPLE EFFECT?

William J. Gnagey

WHAT IS THE RIPPLE EFFECT?

The familiar declaration, "I'll make an example of you!" attests to the fact that parents and teachers have long taken the Ripple Effect for granted. They have realized that by dealing with the deviancy of one student, they were really dealing with the whole class by proxy. It is as though the effects of a control technique spread out from the deviant like concentric wavelets of influence to those classmates who are witnesses to the episode.

Since the Ripple Effect may greatly increase the number of students influenced by a control technique, each deviancy episode takes on new significance. A knowledge of the factors that produce variations in this effect are

Gnagey, William J. *Controlling Classroom Behavior.* What Research Says to the Teacher, No. 32. Washington, D.C.: Association of Classroom Teachers, a department of the National Education Association, 1965. pp. 10–17. N.B.: Copyrighted in 1955; first edition, 1965; and reprinted twice since 1965.

of paramount importance to the teacher who wishes to reduce the amount of deviancy in his classroom.

HOW DO TECHNIQUES INFLUENCE THE RIPPLE EFFECT?

Although we have previously taken space to describe various control techniques, we emphasized those measures that have been effective in influencing a deviant to desist. We now turn to experimental evidence concerning the impact of some of these techniques upon the Ripple Effect.

Let us agree that the major reason for performing a given control technique is to improve the learning situation. Deviancies are stimuli that may evoke responses that compete with those to be learned. It is possible, however, to use some control technique that may stop a deviancy but simultaneously increase the level of behavior disruption for all the witnesses.

The problem then becomes, "What are some characteristics of control techniques that reduce the chances that witnesses will become deviants and that will not produce unnecessary distractions from their studies?"

THREATS EXERT AN INFLUENCE

When Miss Ryan caught Big Jack throwing the eraser, she had at least three choices as to type of control techniques: (a) She could have ignored the incident. (b) She could have issued a simple reprimand such as, "Don't do that again. Please sit down in your seat now." (c) She chose to threaten Jack in a highly agitated manner.

Research studies show that in general, highly emotional threats produce a great deal of distracting behavior-disruption among students who witness the episode. Nail-biting, shifting in seats, chewing pencils, looking around, and so forth are all behaviors that increase after a rough and threatening technique has been used.

What is even more important, these rough, emotional techniques do not lower the number of later deviancies that witnesses perform.

Additional findings indicate that a teacher's use of threatening control techniques causes witnesses to lower their estimation of his helpfulness, likeability, and fairness. His students do, however, tend to rate him higher on his ability to control a class of "tough kids." Treatment of deviancies by rough control techniques also causes the witnesses to raise their estimates of the seriousness of those infractions.

Other things being equal, Miss Ryan's choice of a rough, threatening disciplinary action probably impaired the total learning experience even though she may have succeeded in keeping Big Jack from throwing any more erasers.

CLARITY PRODUCES RESULTS

Verbal commands such as "Hey, cut that out!" have very low clarity. They do not tell who the deviant is, what the deviancy is, or what to do to stop it.

A teacher who reacts to a disturbing noise by commanding, "Jim, stop drumming on your desk and get busy on those arithmetic problems," has performed a control technique of great clarity.

Researchers find that as a teacher increases the clarity of his verbal discipline, witnesses are less likely to become deviants. At the same time, clear control techniques do not increase behavior disruption.

Miss Ryan's declaration, "Jack, if you ever throw another eraser in this room, I will have the principal thrash you," has fairly high clarity. It indicates the deviant and identifies the deviancy in a rather exact way. It does not, however, direct Jack to an alternate, more productive behavior.

FIRMNESS INFLUENCES RIPPLE

A firm control technique may have one or more of several characteristics conveying an "I mean it" quality to the teacher's action. A serious, business-like tone of voice, walking closer to the deviant, or continuing to look at the deviant until he desists: all of these contribute firmness to a teacher's efforts at control. A bland or plaintive suggestion such as "I wish you people would pay attention," has low firmness. It may even verge on helpless entreaty.

Investigators find that increasing firmness of a control technique (as long as it does not become rough and excessively threatening) increases the conformance of both the deviant and witnesses who are oriented toward or interested in the deviancy at the time of the event.

FOCUS AFFECTS CONTROL

"I hear noise in the back of this room. Mrs. Cooper doesn't like noisy children in her room." This is one example of what researchers call an *approval-focused* control technique. It depends for its effect upon the relationship between the teacher and the students.

A *task-focused* technique dealing with the same deviancy might sound like this: "I hear noise in the back of this room. We will never finish learning how to do square root if that din continues."

Findings indicate that task-focused control techniques elicit more desirable student reactions than do approval-focused efforts. Witnesses to task-focused techniques not only raise their estimates of the teacher's skill in handling children, but they gain in interest in the subject matter being taught. These effects are all superior to those noted for approval-focused attempts at control.

When students are convinced that the teacher is an expert in his subject matter, his use of task-focused control techniques causes witnesses to raise their estimates of how much he likes pupils and would be inclined to reward them. It also causes witnesses to rate the deviancy as more serious.

When the teacher combines his expertness with task-centered control techniques, witnesses learn more from the lessons and feel less inclined to misbehave.

If pupils perceive that in addition to being an expert, a teacher likes children, they react to his use of task-focused control techniques by feeling more inclined to discuss personal matters with him.

THERE ARE PRACTICAL IMPLICATIONS

These research results have suggested several ways that a teacher may amplify his influence over a class by using the Ripple Effect.

1. Make use of techniques that are nonthreatening whenever possible.

2. Be sure that control communications are clear: that students know the deviant, the deviancy, and the proper alternative behavior.

3. Increase firmness by changing the tone of voice, moving closer to the deviant, or observing him closely until he complies.

4. Focus control techniques on the learning task at hand instead of contingent teacher approval.

5. As a teacher's subject matter expertness increases, so does his ability to control classroom misbehavior.

HOW DOES THE DEVIANT INFLUENCE THE RIPPLE EFFECT?

As in the previous sections, we shall confine our focus to aspects of the classroom situation. In this section we shall answer the question: "What characteristics of the deviant influence the Ripple Effect?"

THE DEVIANT'S REACTION MAKES A DIFFERENCE

Suppose Big Jack had responded to Miss Ryan's threat in a defiant manner instead of with the meek submission he evidenced. Would there have been any difference in the responses of his classmates?

Researchers would answer "yes" to this question. Witnesses who see a deviant submit to a teacher's control technique rate that teacher as "more capable of handling kids" than when the deviant responds in a defiant manner.

Submissive deviant responses also cause witnesses to rate the teacher as "more expert" than when deviants defy the teacher. It is as though successfully handling a deviancy increases the overall prestige of the teacher.

Classmates who witness submissive responses to control techniques judge those techniques to be fairer than do those who see deviants defy a teacher. The general feelings of the witnesses seem to parallel those acted out by the deviant.

We have agreed that a major reason for controlling deviancy is the maintenance of a good atmosphere for learning. It is interesting to note that research findings indicate that more learning takes place when deviants submit than when they respond defiantly to controls.

We could now infer that Big Jack's quiet acquiescence probably had a number of beneficial effects on Miss Ryan's class.

THE DEVIANT'S PRESTIGE INFLUENCES RIPPLE

If we are to predict accurately the influence of any deviant's response, we must know something about his prestige among the witnesses. Investigators have shown that the reaction of a deviant is far more influential if his classmates hold him in high regard.

If Big Jack is *really* big in social influence in his class, his response to Miss Ryan carries a lot of weight. If Ned Nobody had been handled in the same way, the Ripple Effect of his reaction would have been minimal.

THERE ARE PRACTICAL APPLICATIONS

The following suggestions seem pertinent in making useful applications of the research findings concerning the deviant:

1. The class leaders should be located by sociometric or less formal means.
2. A study should be made of these few high-prestige people.
3. Control techniques should be developed that will cause these leaders to acquiesce.
4. If techniques are successful with a few leaders, more effective control over the entire class will be gained.

HOW DO WITNESSES INFLUENCE RIPPLE?

Thus far we have discussed two facets of the classroom situation that influence deviancy control—the control technique and the deviant. We turn now to some forces residing within the witnesses themselves. In this section we shall try to answer the question: "What witness characteristics influence the Ripple Effect?"

MOTIVATION AFFECTS CONTROL

In predicting the overall effect of Miss Ryan's "Big Jack" episode, we would have to know something about the importance placed by her class on the subject she was teaching at the time.

Research evidence indicates that a deviancy episode is perceived much differently by students who are highly motivated to learn a subject than by their less interested classmates. Highly motivated students rate deviancies as more disturbing and more serious. They see control techniques as more fair and take the teacher's side in conflicts with class deviants.

Students with low motivation to learn a subject see their teacher's control techniques as angry and punitive. They describe these actions in teacher-approval-focused rather than task-focused terms.

Students' motivation also seems to influence their perception of the teacher. When asked to describe their teacher, students who are highly motivated use more task-relevant descriptions. They discuss his competence in explaining material, the quality of his homework assignments, and the like. Low-motivated students emphasize nontask teacher attributes such as fairness and other personal qualities.

Finally, students who are highly motivated to learn pay more attention to the learning task and behave themselves even better after a control technique has been performed.

LIKING THE TEACHER MAY AFFECT RIPPLE

Although it is difficult to separate the influence of a student's affection for a teacher from his motivation to learn, some evidence is available. While motivation influences student reactions toward both the learning task and class deviancy, "liking for the teacher" seems to affect evaluative judgments of the teacher's behavior in a deviancy episode.

THERE ARE PRACTICAL IMPLICATIONS

After examining the research findings concerning the influence of witness characteristics on the Ripple Effect, one might come to the following conclusions:

1. The more interesting a subject can be made, the more effective a teacher's control efforts become. Data from other areas indicate a lower incidence of deviancy in interesting classes. This research, however, associates interest with more efficient control of those deviancies that do occur.

2. If a teacher must choose between being liked and organizing an interesting course of study, the latter should more strongly influence her control of classroom misbehavior.

RIPPLE EFFECTS MAY CHANGE

All of the "ripple effect" studies were based upon students' first encounters with a new teacher. Even in the longer projects, the data were gathered from pupil-teacher interactions during the first week of school. Although it is all conjecture at this time, it seems reasonable to assume that after students become used to the way a teacher operates, control techniques may lose some of their apparent potency.

Firmness of voice, for instance, will probably lose its punch as soon as the students find out that "she doesn't really mean it" or "it's all talk." By the same token, softly spoken desist orders may cause immediate compliance and strong ripple as soon as students find out that "she means what she says" or "you can't get away with anything."

Likewise, the class may soon learn to know the attitudes that their peer leaders hold toward the teacher and may identify with these feelings regardless of any overt response they might make to any specific control effort.

If the specific control technique variables seem to diminish with time, it would be surprising if similar forces did not appear in the total atmosphere. One might be able to show the beneficial effects of a clear *atmosphere* that lacks roughness or threat.

When the rewarding or aversive consequences of certain actions in a given classroom become evident through consistent experience, the characteristics of specific cues may grow less important than the reinforcement and extinction effects cited in the next section.

DISTURBED YOUNGSTERS
IN THE CLASSROOM

William C. Morse

"John can make a shambles of my classroom. The only way I can get any-place talking with him is away from the group. Then he explains very clearly why he does various things. He usually admits that they were dumb things to do, but there is no carryover. He already has a court record.

"And then there are Beth and George. Beth is so quiet and dreamy that she seems here only when I press her with questions and then she drifts away. George is another story. His conversations are non sequiturs. He asks the strangest questions—and always with a worried look. The psychologist has referred him for intensive treatment, but there is a long waiting list. Most of the time I can almost keep on top of the situation, but there are days when I don't seem to be getting anywhere."

An experienced teacher was describing her classroom. Almost any teacher in almost any school could paint a similar picture, and although the per-centage of Johns, Beths, and Georges in the typical classroom is small, it does not take huge numbers of disturbed youngsters to create a critical mass that can confound a teacher and convert a classroom to chaos.

What can a teacher do that will be helpful to the disturbed children in the classroom and at the same time will keep them from disrupting the rest of the class? Source books are not available for teaching attitudes, values, identi-fication, or empathic behavior. Advice ranges from the assured behavior modifiers who direct the teacher to "train" the pupils to the proponents of a leave-them-alone-and-they'll-all-come-home-to-Summerhill philosophy.

These answers are too simple. If the schools are to meet their responsibility toward all children, teachers and schools must change. Teachers need to under-stand what causes the disturbed children in their classes to be that way. They need to develop new teaching skills and to find new ways of using resources. School systems need to look for new ways to use the resources—the time, space, techniques, and personnel—now available and to add new resources.

UNDERSTANDING DISTURBED PUPILS

Some children are disturbed both in their home-community life and in school. Their difficulties are pervasive—with them wherever they go. For example, many a youngster who is rejected and unwanted in his family feels the same way in school.

Reprinted from *Today's Education*, 58:31–37 (April, 1969), by permission of author and publisher.

In other children, disturbance shows up at home or at school but not in both situations. Ralph, for instance, is a skilled leader on the playground and in his neighborhood and gets along reasonably well in his fatherless home. He chafes under the pressure of school routines, however. He is in constant contest with conformity demands and has no interest in school learning. Generally speaking, he is happy-go-lucky and forgets a school disciplinary episode almost before it is over.

Other children who feel supported and do very well in school have difficulties elsewhere. The school is sometimes central in problem behavior and sometimes peripheral, but the aim is to make the school compensatory whenever possible.

The behavior symptoms a child displays are not an automatic revelation of the causes of that behavior. To plan effectively for a disturbed child, the teacher needs not only to see accurately what the youngster does but to understand why he does it. This requires the teacher to do some diagnostic thinking and to gain the ability to see life through the eyes of the pupil.

Let us apply diagnostic thinking first to pupils who are aggressive toward peers, perhaps toward the teacher, and even toward school requirements—pupils who display what is called "acting-out behavior." Children with this broad range of symptoms are the most frequent referrals to special services and special classes. They may provoke fights, break rules, and generally defy the teacher. Older youngsters often turn sullen and hostile. Acting-out children prevent others from working, may react with an outburst if required to conform, and are ready to rebel at a moment's notice.

Since this type of behavior can make conducting classes impossible, no one should be surprised that teachers find it the most vexing difficulty.

When teachers explore beyond the generalized acting-out symptoms, they find some common patterns.

Sometimes aggressiveness results from a lack of adequate socialization. Our culture is producing increasing numbers of children who have never developed social concerns for others, who still function on an impulse basis, doing what they want to do when they feel like it. For one reason or another they lack a suitable prototype for basic identification. Sometimes they take on an omnipotent character—"No one can make me." At best they are narcissistic, bent on following their own desires; at worst they are without the capacity to feel for others. They practice a primitive hedonism.

Sometimes, these children come from indulgent, protective families and become embittered when crossed. When one is asked why he did something, he is likely to say, "I felt like it," until he learns it goes over better to say that he doesn't know why.

Because his delinquent and destructive behavior may stem from a lack of incorporated norms and values, the child with a defect in socialization needs a benign but strong surveillance, so that he is held accountable for misbehavior. He requires clear and specific limits, enforced without anger or harshness. At the same time, he needs models, such as a "big brother," teachers, and older youths, to set an example of proper behavior.

The process of rehabilitation of the unsocialized child is slow and rough, with many periods of regression, because the school is asking the child to give up immediate gratification for long-term goals and to replace self-seeking with consideration for the rights of others. Frequently these youngsters make their first attachment to a single strong teacher and will comply only with his demands. Generalized trust builds slowly. Substantial correction, especially at adolescence, is most difficult. Since the school is the major conformity agent of society, it becomes the natural battleground.

A subgroup among the aggressive children is composed of youngsters who lack social skills but have the capacity to learn them because they have been cared about and loved at home, even though their families have been too disorganized to teach adequate behavior. They are not so much anticonforming as they are untutored in social skills. Role playing and demonstrations by models are useful to show such children the behavior expected of them.

While the reduction of acting-out behavior through teaching basic socialization is difficult, teachers still must try. Learning to value the rights of others is essential for members of a democratic society and recent follow-up studies indicate that neither individual treatment nor institutional custody is a satisfactory approach for such youth.

Another common cause of acting-out behavior is alienation. Estrangement from the educational establishment is occurring more and more frequently. Sometimes, from their very first day, these students find no gratification in the school experience, and their disinterest turns to hostility. The teacher sees these youngsters as problems in motivation. "They just don't seem to care about anything they should be doing."

For the most part, these are not weak children, and they are often well-accepted by peers outside of school. Having found life engaging elsewhere, they can't wait to get at it. One sixth grader had already figured out the number of days until he could quit school. Cars, money, the opposite sex, jobs—these are high demands of the alienated adolescent.

Youngsters like this are usually first admonished, then suspended to "shape them up." Suspension actually works in reverse, since they want out in the first place. If the youngsters are not suspended, too many teachers handle the problem by demanding nothing and letting them do just about as they please.

The better way of resolving the difficulty would be to undertake a thorough examination of the curriculum to see what could be altered. A junior high school pupil, already conducting a profitable business of his own, found nothing in classes with any meaning to him. With visions of establishing himself as an adult, he finally ran away with his girl friend.

Education is turning off an increasing number of able and intellectual youths. Such disenchantment was evidenced first at the college level, but it has already seeped down to the junior high. Many young people feel that school is a meaningless scramble for grades and graduation instead of the authentic education experience they seek. What often needs to be done is to make over the school rather than the pupil, but some teachers still rigidly follow the current curriculum as though it were sacred.

In some children, acting-out behavior in school is reaction to failure. No one wants to fail or even be in a marginal position, and yet thousands get failure messages every school day. The child comes to hate the establishment that makes him a failure, so he strikes back. Some failed first at home, where nothing they did was as good as what a sibling did—where no matter how hard they tried, they failed. The hatred such children feel for adults at home may transfer to their teachers, who may never have been in the least unfair.

The amount of defiling and belittling, to say nothing of direct abuse, that children suffer in our supposedly child-favoring culture comes as a shock to many a protected teacher. If the cause of acting-out behavior is in the home, then acting out in school is merely a displacement, but the acting-out child gets a reputation that is passed along ahead of him and he lives up to it.

School can be too taxing for certain children, grading too severe, and teacher's help too scarce. Although they get along well at home, children with mild learning disabilities or limited academic ability frequently drift into frustration at school. Some of the slow-developing early primary pupils or late-blooming adolescents in junior high are too immature to meet expectations. The solution is for the school to adjust to the pupil by proper pacing. Many of these pupils change surprisingly when a perceptive teacher builds in success.

Still other children who act out are anxious about their lives in general. Often they are hyperactive, driven to release tension through physical activity. They are oversensitive, easily distracted, and given to disruptive behavior. After misbehaving, they feel guilty and promise never to repeat the offense, but in a subsequent period of anxiety they do repeat it, acting out in order to dissipate tension.

Some of this group actually seek punishment because they feel they are bad and should pay the penalty. This feeling of guilt may stem from wrong things they have done or merely thought of doing. For instance, one boy, who was being stimulated by a seductive mother, used to blow up in math class, where concentration was required. He could do the math, but not when he was upset. It took the social worker a long time to help him work this out.

A special category of anxiousness, found with increasing frequency in suburbia, is achievement neurosis. In order to meet overt or covert expectations, pupils who have this affliction feel compelled to be on top. They have lost the satisfaction of learning as its own reward; grades are to prove they are as good as their parents want them to be. These youngsters are frequently tense and driven and overvalue the academic. Their parents are forever inquiring, "How well is John doing?"

Children who are driven in this way need to be made to feel better about themselves. Some of them demand much attention, always seeking resubstantiation by adult approval. If the source of the damaged self-picture is an overdemanding home or neighborhood, it is often difficult to provide enough compensatory success in school to allay it. This is where counselors, psychiatrists, psychologists, school social workers, or referral agencies play their part.

By now it is easy to see why any two acting-out children may not need the same type of help from the teacher. But teachers' concerns are not limited to those who directly disrupt the educational process, for the profession is equally attuned to pupils who have given up. While withdrawn children may not cause the teacher managerial difficulty, they, too, are in need of special assistance.

Many unhappy, depressed youngsters are in school today. Basically, these youngsters have very low self-esteem; they have somehow been taught by life that they are good-for-nothing and important to nobody. Often, internal preoccupation takes over, and they drift into a world of fantasy. They absorb the support sensitive teachers give, but often this is not sufficient to strengthen them to a point where they can sustain themselves.

Sometimes students are confirmed losers. They just know they will fail and usually contrive to make their anticipations come true. Others come to rely on fate rather than on their own efforts. As one youngster put it: "Fifty-fifty, I pass or I flunk. It depends on the breaks." So why put forth any effort?

Another group of the withdrawn children are the lonely ones. The loner drifts by himself at recess or eats alone in the junior high cafeteria or has no one to talk to about his high school lessons. Because he feels that nobody would care, he sees no point in trying to make friends. Many youngsters who are scapegoats in their peer group come from among the lonely ones, especially if they have some physical problem such as overweight, a tic, or odd looks. In these cases, the way the teacher manages the group life in the classroom is just as important as individual attention and counseling.

DEALING WITH DISTURBED PUPILS

No magic, no single cure, no shortcut will solve the problems of disturbed children in the schools. The job demands an extension of the individualization that is the essence of good school practice. This calls for teacher time and specially planned curricular experiences. To provide these, many school systems will add a new resource—the psychological, social-work, or psychiatric consultant. Conflict between specialists and regular classroom teachers used to be commonplace, but teachers have now discovered a new way to use the specialists' help, replacing long discourses on "how Johnny got that way" with discussions of what can be done now, in the classroom.

Frequently, a curriculum expert and the principal should join the teacher and the special consultant in discussions about a disturbed child. Remedial action should be based on study of the deviant youngster's classroom behavior and of his basic personality. Clinical insights provide the backdrop for practical planning.

When the problem is caused not by the school but by the child's home situation, the remedial goal is to have the school provide a supportive environment that will compensate, in part, for what is lacking or negative. Referral services to agencies that can offer individual therapy are vital also. They are not enough, however. Group work agencies, boys' clubs, and big brothers can help the unsocialized child who does not have serious internal conflicts. Such a child is in dire need of basic identification building.

Many disturbed children who can function within normal bounds and utilize the regular classroom much of the time lapse occasionally into disruptive behavior that throws the classroom into chaos. Some schools—secondary as well as elementary—deal with this problem by having a special teacher, trained to work with the disturbed in both academic and behavioral spheres, to whom such a child goes during a crisis. This teacher works with him in a special classroom where he can receive assistance on both individual and small group bases.

While the issue is still current, the crisis teacher and the child discuss the matter, much after the fashion of crisis intervention in community mental health. Close liaison with the regular teacher is, of course, mandatory. Referrals to a school or community service for intensive individual work may be needed, but the crisis teacher is the key person to support the regular classroom teacher and the pupil and to coordinate the entire effort in time of stress. When the pupil has gained control and/or is able to do the task in question, he returns to the regular classroom.

NEEDED CHANGES

The task is to examine the classroom environment and the teacher's role. What changes will improve the helping index?

No one has any idea of making the teacher into a psychotherapist, although many disturbed students form a profound relationship with their teachers. The function of the teacher is to provide pupils with a reasonable human relationship (in itself therapeutic) and the opportunity to grow through academic accomplishment and social learning.

Achievement is therapeutic for a child, especially when he has achieved little or nothing in the past. Having an adult who cares about him and who helps him when he falters instead of getting angry and rejecting him is certainly helpful. Peer acceptance in the classroom has lasting significance for the lonely child.

In this sense, therapeutic intervention has always been a part of school, but some children need much more. Providing that more will require three things:

1. The schools will have to reexamine how the curriculum, methodology, and experiences can be bent to enhance growth and minimize failure.

2. Teachers will have to learn new skills.

3. Teachers will have to become more open about their feelings toward disturbed children, because externalizing attitudes is a necessary step in changing negative feelings.

Since the school operation itself provokes a considerable amount of school difficulty, what is taught and how it is taught will require adjustment. Pupils need short assignments that interest them and that they are capable of doing. Not only the level of difficulty but the rate of learning should be attuned to the child, with provision for remedial teaching of what he has missed.

Individualization for the alienated youngster requires new subject matter that is relevant rather than merely different. Some children with learning disabilities require the use of self-tutoring devices. Iconoclastic curriculums, such as cooperative work programs for older youths, are needed.

Although most behaviorists avoid considering disturbed children in any but symptomatic terms, they offer the teacher two most useful guidelines.

First, they tell teachers to study what the child actually does. Observation of how and to what the pupil responds often shows that much of what the teacher is doing is quite beside his intent. Many disturbed children are adept at controlling teachers by getting them to make inappropriate responses, thus reinforcing just what the teacher wishes to eliminate. If the pupil cares more about having *some* kind of relationship with the teacher than he does about *what* kind of relationship he has, he can get teacher attention by misbehavior. Thus, a teacher encourages repeat performances of an undesirable behavior even as he tells a pupil not to behave that way.

Second, behaviorists emphasize that many pupils do not operate on the basis of high-level gratifications, such as love of learning. Teachers must deal with them on their own motivational level. For example, the attention span and motivation of some who need concrete rewards suddenly improves when the teacher recognizes this need. Free time earned for work done or proper behavior may help get children started who have never had any real success before. They forget their "can't do" to earn free time. Behavior that approximates being acceptable is worth rewarding at first.

Punishment, the major reward many disturbed children receive, is a poor teaching device. Low grades seldom work as a challenge. Emphasis needs to be on accomplishments rather than on failures. Many teachers, wedded to the illusion of homogeneity, have a hard job learning to help these children achieve by accommodating to the special range they present in ability, rate, motivation, and interests. Sometimes the range can be narrowed. In junior and senior high, for example, a student can be assigned in every course to the teacher and the content best suited to him.

When nothing else works, something may be gained by asking a child to do only what interests him. One pupil studied nothing but the Civil War. Another drew pictures. This was no real solution, but the teacher survived and the other students could do their work. Desperate conditions require desperate measures, and it is better to have a student reading about the Civil War than conducting a war with the teacher.

Teachers of classes that include disturbed children need to be particularly skilled in group management. The capacity to establish a work orientation for the class as a whole that will provide psychological insulation is one of the most critical skills in a class that includes disturbed children. Jacob Kounin and his associates have found out that the same teachers are successful in managing both disturbed and normal students.

These teachers focus on the group and its learning activities, actively solicit feedback, concentrate on more than one thing at a time, and select the proper targets for their interventions. The high degree of involvement reduces negative contagion from the disturbed pupils and provides the needed reserve for the teacher to work out the marginal situations that develop.

The first questions a teacher needs to ask are, "How meaningful is the work to these pupils? Can they do it? Do I understand the various roles and relationships in the class well enough to be able to emphasize the things that will maintain stability instead of reacting in a haphazard way to everything that happens?"

The successful teacher knows how to use grouping itself as a tool.

Some classroom groups are particularly stable and constitute a reservoir of peer help for the distraught pupil; other groups have such a thin shell of control that one acting-out pupil means a breakdown. If most members of a class offer support, they can calm down a lot of misbehavior as well as serve as models of proper action.

Pupils whose behavior frightens their own age peers and makes them anxious may not bother slightly older children, so upgrouping a disturbed child may reduce negative group effects.

Sometimes the size of the group is important. Classes with several disturbed pupils should be smaller than others. In fairly large schools, three or four teachers of the same grade or course can arrange to have one small class for those who need it by making the other classes somewhat larger.

When a class needs relief from a pupil's disturbing antics, sending the offender to another class for a visit may be helpful. The teacher needs to make advance provisions for doing this. He also needs to know when to intervene in this way and to find out what the child does that makes his classmates anxious and angry.

Of course, any kind of exclusion must be used with extreme care. It would be ill-advised for a youngster who wanted out in the first place, or one who was so fearful as to be traumatized. Sometimes, however, planned exclusion can produce controls in a youngster.

Teachers need to develop skill in talking productively with children. They spend a great deal of time in verbal interaction with their students and, unfortunately, the typical verbal interplay is largely a waste. Fritz Redl has pioneered with what he calls "life-space interviewing," a technique that is particularly well suited to helping the teacher of disturbed children put an end to the undesirable behavior or at least to take steps in that direction.

The content of life-space interviewing focuses on the ego level and the behavior experience in the "life-space" shared by teacher and student. The technique provides an opportunity for diagnostic exploration, mild probing, and planning for the future on the basis of realistic appraisal. First the teacher asks the pupil for his perception of what happened, and then, step by step, examines what can be done to clarify reality. This leads to specific strategies which can serve to reduce recurrences. Of course, not all students will respond, but this style prevents moralizing on the one hand and passive acceptance on the other. The same principles can be used with groups for classroom problem solving.

Classroom problem solving brings up the concept of crisis intervention. Youngsters are most teachable at a time of conflict, when they are searching for a resolution. Being able to use the crisis at hand and knowing how to talk effectively to children are two skills basic to any classroom management of disturbed pupils. Behind this rests a new concept of acceptance. Psychological acceptance means responding to the student in order to facilitate his adopting more acceptable patterns of behavior. This may mean more strict enforcement of regulations, more listening to his concerns, or doing whatever is relevant to his self-concept and nature.

Three qualities seem to be critical in order for a teacher to develop the right interpersonal relationship with disturbed students: strength to stand testing without giving in or becoming hostile, a belief that the youngster can change (this eliminates the self-fulfilling prophecy of failure that many teachers imply, if only on the unconscious level), and a recognition that the classroom is a good place for helping youngsters. Of course, certain teachers seem to have natural talent with particular types of disturbed children. Definitive teachers, for example, are most successful with insurgent pupils, while a quiet teacher may get closer to frightened youngsters.

Disturbed children require an inordinate amount of teacher time, so there is never enough to go around. Several plans have been used to add teacher power. Frequently, children low in confidence and self-esteem benefit from one-to-one sessions, cause no disruptions during them, and focus on the task. Sometimes, with a mature class, a teacher can borrow a little special time for such students, but in most cases this is just not possible. Often the only feasible learning condition for them is a tutorial, manned by a community volunteer, a teacher aide, or an older student, with the teacher supervising and designing the lesson material.

Other means of stretching the busy teacher's time include the use of a self-tutoring device, task cards setting up individual projects, and prerecorded tapes with lessons and answers. A peer may serve as tutor-listener if proper pairing can be arranged.

Parents are a teacher's resource more often than we have believed. Programs for disturbed students, particularly the alienated ones, are reaching out to include the home. Rather than letting behavior difficulties continue to a point where a student must be excluded, the schools now, at an early stage of a difficulty, schedule conferences in which parents, student, teacher, and a mental health specialist participate. The assumption is that all parties really want to solve the difficulty, and the support of the home may be critical. When parents are hostile to the pupil, the hostility is less likely to provoke unfortunate behavior if the matter can be talked out and plans drawn up to meet the difficulties. While no punches are pulled, the issue is to teach the child what he *must* learn rather than revert to punitive handling.

Help may be needed outside the classroom. Here a "big brother" or "big sister" may be most important in providing not only reasonable recreation but identification as well. Assistance with homework, especially at the junior and senior high levels, may be the only road to survival.

A wise teacher keeps time flexible in planning for the disturbed youngster. Some children may be able to benefit from one hour of school but no longer. Some can make it through the morning but fall apart before the afternoon is under way.

Wise use of space is important. For example, some disturbed students benefit from having offices or study cubicles to reduce distraction. On the other hand, some need to see others and observe what is going on in order to feel less anxious.

The more flexible the concept of space in the teacher's mind, the more he can use this resource to serve the disturbed student. Dividing the room into work centers for various subgroups is one technique. Using the hall not as a punitive place but as a stimulus control may be appropriate. Some older youngsters can do their work better in the library, while others would roam the halls if not under surveillance.

Above all, the teacher and the school need to bear in mind that, for a disturbed child being able to escape temporarily from group pressures is often the key to survival. Each school should have a place and, if possible, a person for a disturbed child to go to at a time of crisis.

Even with the most able consultation and highly skilled teaching it may not be possible to help a child in the regular school setting, and unless he can be helped—not merely contained—in the classroom, he should not be there. The teacher's survival and the other children's welfare, as well as his own, are at stake.

For children who still fail to respond in the regular classroom after everything feasible has been done, the next step is the special class. Such classes provide relief for the whole school system and, generally speaking, they offer the disturbed pupils more individualized planning, with the result that pupil behavior and achievement improve. Some recent research, however, suggests that the improvement tends to disappear when the pupil returns to the mainstream. Indeed, the special class is far from being a panacea. It often helps least the unsocialized youngster, who needs so much, and sometimes it includes very disturbed children, even though the general consensus is that psychotic children need more help than a special class can give.

The special class falls short of the mark for other reasons. Frequently, special class curriculums do not include individual work and family contacts, although classroom work alone is usually not enough. Further, many public school teachers do not have the assistants they need to conduct a special class successfully.

And the special class bears a stigma. Students seldom see the value of being "special" and attitude is a critical part of the impact. Particularly at the secondary level, they resist being set apart. To adolescents, the stigma is so oppressive to their whole quest for a self (and a normal self) that it generates a great deal of friction. The stigma is strengthened because teachers and school administrations are seldom eager to welcome back a "cured" student. Nevertheless, special class provisions, if properly handled and staffed, are part of the sequence of support needed in every school program.

When all is said and done, most disturbed children are, and will continue to be, in the regular classroom, and, like it or not, classrooms and teaching will have to change if the schools are to fulfill their ever-increasing responsibility for the social and emotional development of children.

AGGRESSION IN THE CLASSROOM

Fritz Redl

There's plenty of minor aggression in the classroom that nobody objects to. The real problem is the aggression that prevents good teaching and good classroom life. This aggression comes primarily from three areas.

First, it is an input from the home or from the community. A teen-ager gets hopping mad at his old man, but he doesn't dare let off steam until he gets to school. Now, the teacher didn't produce the aggression, but it's there and he's got to handle it.

Second, is the discharge from within. Some youngster sits there daydreaming, and all of a sudden during a wild fantasy, he thinks of something that upsets him and he conks his neighbors on the head. None of them have done anything to him, and the teacher hasn't either. Something just burst out from within. (If youngsters are seriously disturbed, most of the aggression comes from way within, and neither they nor anyone else knows why.)

Third, the aggression is engendered right there in the classroom. It may be triggered either by what the teacher does that's right but that doesn't

Reprinted from *Today's Education*, 58:30–32 (September, 1969), by permission of author and publisher.

happen to fit the kid, or by God knows what—the kid's reaction to the group or to other kids, or to something that maybe the teacher wouldn't have done if he had stopped to think. But anyway, it's reactive to something in the environment at the moment.

Now, if I were a classroom teacher, I would like to know how much of which of those three packages is exploding before me, because it makes a difference in terms of long-range planning. It also makes some difference in terms of what to do at the moment. Most of the time we are not sure, but different sources of aggression smell different when we are confronted with them. Experienced teachers develop an uncanny skill at sensing "This is something the kid brought with him. I've got to help him recover from it before he acts it out." The outsider, though, wouldn't know.

Some aggression does not affect us directly because certain youngsters may be model pupils in the classroom, but then after school they may go out and rape or murder someone. So a youngster may be full of sick aggression without being a classroom problem.

On the other hand, there may be a great kid sitting over there who's bored stiff. He likes you a lot, but he gets mad at the fact that you bore him stiff. Finally, he's just had it, and he runs out and slams the door. A normal youngster like that whose aggression is classroom-produced is our problem. Too often, an article on aggression in the classroom concentrates on a few examples of youngsters who should have been in a mental hospital for the last 10 years anyway and ignores all the other kids who bother us.

The term *aggression* is so overused now, you've got to watch out for it. Don't ever let anybody trap you into discussing aggression without first asking him: "Listen, brother, which aggression are you talking about? What actually happened?" Because aggression has a wide range—all the way from reacting to boredom to wrestling at the wrong time in the wrong place with another pupil.

Discharge of surplus energy or of displaced needs from the home or neighborhood; loss of control in the face of seductive equipment like a slingshot or a knife or whatnot; personal battles with adults, other kids, the group, or the teacher—all these fall under the heading of aggression.

The way Joe or Jane expresses aggression, while not the end of what we're looking for, certainly should be the starting point. Unless you know what lies behind their behavior, you will have trouble knowing how to handle it. Sometimes you may understand perfectly well how come. So the question then is what do you do to help him, which is a separate matter from knowing what was cooking to begin with.

I want to give special warning here not to make aggression synonymous with violence. The two are not the same, although they are obviously related. There is a theme in violence that we can legitimately call aggression. On the other hand, not all violence comes from aggressive drives. The behavior is aggressive, but the basis may be quite different. Let me give a few illustrations of violence that does not spring from aggression.

Panic coping. A kid may get scared stiff, so scared that he doesn't know what to do anymore. So he does something violent; he tears something apart. The fact that the behavior is violent is important. But this child is not hyperaggressive; he is frightened and desperate.

The need to be heard. A frequent source of violence is the feeling that nobody listens. The child finally concludes that the only way to get someone to listen is to be violent enough. So when other avenues are blocked off, violence is a substitute for verbal and nonverbal communication.

The desire to display guts. If a kid is supposed to be tough, how can he show it? Who is going to believe it? "I'd better not let them know I'm scared. So I've got to find ways to show I'm brave." In order to do this in a peaceful life, he's got to create problems.

Demonstrating loyalty to the group code. This source of violence is not originally meant to be aggression for aggression's sake. ("If the rest of my gang thinks school is no good, I'd better show that I'm with them. So I put a thumbtack in the teacher's chair. I don't hate the teacher; too bad it's her rear that gets stung. But I'm a regular guy and I'm going to prove it.")

Risk taking—to study survival skills. For instance, how can a boy know if he can run fast enough to outrun the cop, unless he swipes something first? Or else picks a rat out of an ash can, swirls it by the tail, throws it in somebody's first-story window, and then hops over the garage roof fast before they can catch him? A kid has to know how good he is in handling a dangerous assignment.

The stink and the dust produced in the decay of group psychology. If a group suddenly gets anxious or panicky or wild or disorganized or elated or mad at each other, you get a lot of behavior that involves violence but that did not start as aggression. Although Joe and Jane may be doing something, they're not doing it as Joe and Jane but as members of a group.

Last on my list of violence that does not start with aggression but is secondary to it is, of course, *an invasion of societal turmoil from the outside.* Someone or something in the community ties a package of emotional TNT to the back of a kid and it blows up in the classroom. The kid responsible wasn't originally aggressive; he carries the whole load of community or neighborhood or subgroup aggression. As his teacher, you're just an innocent bystander. What he does has nothing to do with the way you taught him or whether you bawled him out or flunked him.

In short, there is some relationship between violence and aggression, but not a simple one. For teachers it's very important to begin to sense the difference between Joe's being loaded with personal anger at what you just did and the explosion that results when his TNT package goes off at a given time. They are different problems.

Now let me give a few abbreviated hints of what to do about various kinds of child behavior—hints that are not fancy enough to be written up much in books.

First, you sometimes need to get kids off the hook. The aggressive behavior is beginning but without having really been planned, and if you get pupils off the hook *now,* they don't have to continue. Another way of putting it is that you sometimes need to cut a contagion chain without making a big deal out of it. And in most cases knowing how to do this is very important in dealing with a normally well-behaved child as well as with a wild one.

Take Joe, for example. He's sitting over there shaking imaginary dice, and at the moment you're not too bothered. You catch his eye and he stops, but only momentarily. After a while everybody else gets interested. You want to cut that contagion chain now, because if you wait another five minutes, you'll have a mass problem on your hands.

If you interfere too early, everyone thinks you're a fusspot, a dope, or chicken, and you only aggravate things. If you don't interfere at the right time, you'll have trouble. Getting Joe off the hook at the right moment will stop his behavior without a big scene, and the rest of the group will not be too heavily afflicted. This skill of cutting contagion chains without making too much of a mess is, I think, one of the most important for anybody who deals with groups.

A second important technique for the practical handling of aggression in the classroom is signal interference. Signal interference in time saves nine. Very often teachers underestimate the possibility of stopping minor forms of misbehavior quite casually before the kid gets too carried away by it. They don't take the behavior seriously, because it isn't bothersome enough. So they wait until it does get bothersome enough, and by that time the situation is tense, the kid is already off his noodle, and anything they do now will have an explosive effect.

The big problem is that most teachers lack a good inventory of pre-aggression signals for their pupils. In some youngsters, the signals are easy to spot. Others apparently go aggressive all of a sudden from nowhere. That's because the teacher's radar doesn't pick up their signals. But if the teacher works at it, after a while he begins to get the messages from all around the room. One kid, for example, gets glassy-eyed and sits there quietly in a certain rigid position. If the teacher goes over and taps him on the shoulder, he'll go up like a rocket. Two minutes ago, if the teacher had gone around and said, "Come on, let's start working," that would have been fine.

A good many teachers—particularly those who are new to the classroom—do not know enough about the physiological and gestural signals that indicate the work-up to aggressive behavior. Everybody with experience understands them, but conveying this understanding to the other guy is hard. Apparently we don't think it's important because we don't have any fancy lingo for it, but if I were a beginning teacher, that's the kind of information I would like to have.

If you send me a kid with an unknown aggression work-up potential, I'd like to get to know that kid and figure out what he looks like before he goes off the handle. After that, I can tell at a glance that this is the moment to go over to him.

In observing classrooms and watching teachers with disturbed youngsters, I am constantly amazed at the terrific skill people with experience develop, and they can't ever explain it. What's more, they don't even mention it. They think it isn't worth discussing.

Let me describe one incident I observed:

A kid is sitting stiffly at his desk, obviously determined that he "ain't gonna do *nothing.*" The teacher walks over to him, pats him on the shoulder, and says: "Now, how about it? You don't feel so good, huh?" And he doesn't say anything. What does she do then? She says: "OK, I'll come back in a while. Maybe by then you'll be feeling better." That's all. She doesn't push him. ("Why don't you . . . ? What's the matter with you? What kind of family do you come from, anyway?")

She uses her judgment, and sooner or later he's over the hump. His face clears up; his posture is relaxed. Then she comes over and puts the pencil in his hand and he starts working.

Now, number three: Watch out for the choreography of the dare. In our present society we all have an insatiable, unquenchable thirst for tribal rituals. We still perform tribal dances. Take this scene:

We have what looks like a relatively normal classroom at the moment. Here is Joe back there, who wishes I'd leave him alone. But he knows I'm a nice guy, that I've got to make a living, after all. And I'm pretty harmless, though a little crazy, maybe.

Still, somehow, the noise gets too loud, and I finally say: "Listen, you, you'd better stop that now." Then maybe things get worse, and maybe by this time I'm angry, too. So I say: "All right, now, if you can't be quiet here, why don't you go out and cool off?"

Let's assume I'm relatively lucky in my diagnosis, and the youngster gets up and moves to the door, but on the way he mumbles something under his breath. If I ask him what he said, he probably feels he has to lie—so I make a liar out of him. Or if he is decently honest, I have to send him to the principal.

The foregoing is one way the scene can be played. But it also can be played differently. If Joe is sensitive of his prestige in the group, and I happen to have adults looking over my shoulder, then both of us become involved in a tribal dance. He has to say, "Make me," and I have to say, "All right. I'll make you." So either I try to bounce him or I call the principal or what-not. Then for three weeks, lots of procedures go on—all nonsensical and having nothing to do with the original issue. Joe's become a discipline case, almost.

What I've described here is a personal interaction, a limit-setting process of a very simple nature, really. Most of the time it works like a charm, but in the second instance it became a tribal dance. If I were a principal assigning teachers to study halls or other large groups, I would like to know how vulnerable they are to the tribal dance routine, because in a dare situation the pressure is terrific. If you send me a kid who is tough, I don't mind. But I would like to know how involved this kid is in a tribal dance.

You see, some kids who are plenty tough don't fall for that kind of nonsense. In fact, some of my best delinquents would never be so stupid as that. If I really challenged them, they would think: "All right, so let the guy have his little victory for a change. So what! So I go out. I'm tough enough. Nobody will think I gave in." If, however, the youngster isn't really tough enough, but has to pretend he is, then he has to do the tribal dance in order to impress the others with his plumage, or whatever.

This is a big danger. And many a teacher could avoid many a large discipline problem if he were able to recognize the first drum beats of a tribal dance. Very often we push relatively tough kids who mean well into tribal dances because we are unaware of the position they are in. At other times, we do not interfere when we should because we are too afraid we'll provoke a tribal dance when actually we wouldn't.

So the tribal dance is a whole phenomenon—separate from the usual problem of discipline—that is a rather deep psychological problem.

Number four: Watch out for the subsurface effect. Whatever I do also has a side effect, and it is not always visible right now. If we are aware of what else happens besides the immediate effect of what we do, we won't simply say, "Because I blamed him for being noisy or because I praised him for being quiet, everything is hunky-dory right now."

So it's important to look with one eye to the possible nonvisible side effect. I can do something about it afterwards, but only if I'm on the lookout for it. Like that boy we've been talking about. Let's say he leaves the room and doesn't start the tribal dance. In that case, I'll want to make sure we have a brief get-together afterwards to tell him that I appreciate his doing what I asked and that I'll defend his reputation with the rest of the kids. I'll say that there are no hard feelings; it was just that I couldn't let him get so loud in class. That's all; nothing more.

If you have to live with aggression, at least try not to breed it. We breed it, of course, by exposing even otherwise normal boys and girls to experiences, to space arrangements, to life situations that invariably produce inner frustration.

For instance, if I bore a youngster, I expose him to frustration. Or, if I have to delay giving help that is needed—say, a boy over there is stuck in the middle of a long division problem, and I can't get to him for a while because I have to be over here with the others. Sooner or later he's had it, and he gets mad.

Or I may breed aggression if I intervene with too little sympathy. If a youngster is doing something interesting, something he likes, do I say, "Get going this minute. Do you want to be late again?" when I could just as well say, "Look, I'm sorry to have to break that up, but you know we've got to get out now."

One final point: Don't forget that from time to time, your own aggression will start showing. As you probably are aware, your hostile feelings and how you deal with them make a story no less complex and touchy than the one just presented. That your anger may be righteous and justified is not the only issue. You must ask yourself some questions: How does my anger make me behave in the classroom? Which (if any) of the behaviors it produces in me seem helpful in reducing youngsters' aggressive feelings, and which ones just make matters worse? Figuring this out requires clear thinking and real objectivity, but it is worth the effort. Your professional obligation is to handle your own aggression in such a way that the individual pupil or the class can manage the spillover effect.

INNER-CITY TEACHING:
A PROBLEM OF DISCIPLINE

Brinson Terry

Classroom discipline has taken on awesome and ominous dimensions for the teacher in the ghetto school.

The reasons are multiple and the implications portentous, but invariably they are related to teacher attitude, background and training.

For the average Caucasian, the period of adjustment in the ghetto school is usually stormy and vitriolic. In his initiation, he often concludes that his students are incorrigible, an attitude which is perpetuated by his lack of exposure to Negroes. Or he may undergo a period of cultural shock as a result of conflicting values and ideas emanating from his middle class background.

Another minus is the dearth of knowledge which seems to exist among teachers with regard to the structure of the Negro family. Such ignorance further contributes to the breakdown of communication between black students and white teachers.

In wrestling with discipline problems, too many educators—both black and white—fail to take into account the effect of rioting in the inner city upon the child's attitude toward school. The teacher who perceives this relationship will become less shaken by the "bizarre" antics that may occur in his classroom and more capable of dealing with them.

The subject oriented teacher, confronted with a preponderance of problems in the ghetto school, needs to take a sharp look at his approach. Perhaps he is treating the students like computers by cramming in data which they are not prepared to digest. Conversely the inner city teacher must guard against frustrating the child and stunting potential by assuming that he is inferior or

Reprinted from *Ohio Schools,* 47:13–15, 20 (March, 1969), by permission of Brinson Terry and publisher.

too shallow to grasp concepts that are being taught to suburban children. Finally the teacher must be willing to adopt a creative approach for dealing with the problems presented by black students in the ghetto.

If the teacher in the ghetto school happens to be white, the problem of being a disciplinarian becomes all the more acute. In the majority of cases, the white teacher's training and upbringing have ill prepared him for the black world of the ghetto. Too many of these teachers have grown up in white suburbia where their acquaintance with Negroes has been only casual or spasmodic. A few may have attended high school or college classes with black students, but these associations have come at a point in life when their middle class values are deeply entrenched. His knowledge of the culture and living patterns of ghetto children has largely come from such sources as education journals, lectures in psychology and sociology or TV documentaries dealing with riots and civil rights. If he is lucky, he may have done some student teaching in the inner city for a quarter or perhaps a semester.

This lack of exposure is all too often the crux of the white teacher's problem in dealing with black students. It is at this point that he comes to realize that, contrary to what his parents might have believed about the superiority of the suburbs and the all white school, in reality he has been cheated and miseducated in a kind of incubator that has isolated him from the other half of American society. What a difference attending an elementary school with Negro children or even living next door to them could have made in that crucial first year or two of teaching in the ghetto.

Fortunately, many of these persons are so dedicated to the profession that they somehow manage to weather the storm of the first year. But a great many others either resign, request a transfer to a "good" school (usually the suburban or predominantly white school) or simply go into some other profession. Those who retain their assignments usually make fine teachers and some discover that they are able to relate to their students much better than black teachers.

In short the white teacher, if he is to successfully cope with the problems within the ghetto school, must be willing to reorient his entire frame of reference toward Negro children so that he can maneuver himself into a position where he can accept the student as he is and then assist him to move up the educational ladder. How many rungs the child climbs will not only depend upon his learning capacity, but upon how successfully the teacher can establish rapport.

These factors ultimately play a gigantic role in the teacher's ability to influence his students' conduct. This kind of circuitous interaction between student and teacher is so delicately entwined that a single rash act or mistake in judgment on the part of the teacher could spell disaster. The teacher's role in this case is reminiscent of the mother who is baking a cake, but must tiptoe across the kitchen floor ever so softly so as not to upset the cake as the ingredients react to the heat of the oven. But the end result of her effort is a product in which she can take immense pride. The ghetto child with all of the smears of deprivation, neglect, and despondency must be viewed in this light.

The Caucasian teacher needs to further consider the fact that with all the emphasis on black pride and achievement, black students may react to him negatively simply because he is not one of them, or because they see him as a symbol of the system which has relegated them to an inferior position in our society, or because they have been told that whites who work in the ghetto but who live elsewhere have no real interest in black people, or because he is simply one with whom they cannot identify.

The need for black success symbols is paramount in the lives of many black students. Consequently—wrongly or rightly—the white teacher may be the butt of criticism or accusations which may ultimately cause him to either transfer to another school, or harden his position and create further friction such as in the Ocean Hill Brownville district in Brooklyn. He may, on the other hand, use the situation as a means of bridging the communication gap which exists not only between black students and white teachers, but within our total society.

Many black students have charged white teachers with bias. In general few charges of prejudicial attitudes on the part of teachers have been proven beyond the shadow of doubt. On the other hand it is safe to say that teachers have prejudices just as members of any other profession.

The potential explosiveness of a situation in which overt prejudices are manifested requires that the matter be given immediate attention and steps to eliminate those persons or elements at fault. Otherwise we render our school vulnerable to the attacks of not only the general public but extremist groups as well and we do a tremendous disservice to the youngsters who need our help the most.

While the white teacher faces many problems in the ghetto school because of the hiatus between his world and the child's, educators—both white and black—must also recognize the relationship of classroom behavior to life in the Negro family. It should be understood that the great majority of ghetto children are products of broken homes. Either the mother has never been married or the father has left the family for any number of reasons; in many instances because of his inability to locate gainful employment or because he knows that the fatherless family has an easier chance of getting on the welfare rolls. The structure of American society from the inception of slavery until today seems to have been geared to emasculating the Negro male until he was stripped of every vestige of influence over his community or family. As a result, thousands of Negro youth in America today are still devoid of the essential influence of father identification.

Secondly, Negro family structure has never fully recuperated from the debilitating effects of slavery. When one considers that families were arbitrarily torn apart to satisfy the needs of a repressive economic system, that men were encouraged to be promiscuous simply for the sake of producing more slaves, that legal concepts of marriage and divorce were deliberately distorted by white masters in order to keep slaves ignorant of the vital social influences regulating family life, it is not difficult to understand why the structure of the Negro family 100 years later remains basically unstable. The pattern of broken homes and the old matriarchal head persists.

A major problem in this kind of mother dominated family constellation is that it does not have the kind of stamina in the inner city or Northern ghettos as it did in the simple, rural environment of the South where the folkway of Negro life was relatively uncomplicated and where not only the mother but the grandmother exerted considerable authority over the members of the home. The squalor of the cities with their lack of employment opportunities, and the paucity of services for the poor have further contributed to the breakdown of this system. The sophistication of urban life has almost totally disrupted the simple life of the Negro family as it existed in an agrarian society.

Small wonder that illegitimacy and juvenile delinquency are higher among Negroes than other groups in our society. Small wonder that Negro mothers (many who have been parents since their early teens, but emotionally unprepared for the responsibility) with the staggering burdens of large families and few resources find it difficult to control their adolescents.

Disillusioned over lack of opportunity, bewildered by the pressures of poverty, confused by militant civil rights groups with conflicting goals, deceived by the lure of vice and drugs, and enervated by the absence of strong family ties to render emotional support for a broken spirit, many black students are acting out their frustrations not only in the streets but in the classroom.

No teacher in the ghetto can deal effectively with black students unless he understands these influences. He must understand that "being good" and reacting positively to educational stimuli is no easy task when a child comes from a home where there is a lack of suitable space for study, a dearth of magazines and reference materials to stimulate learning, inadequate funds for the pursuance and appreciation of cultural achievements, and limited exposure to persons who have "made it" in a white man's world. If educators fail to account for these forces as they interact in the life of the ghetto child, they can neither hope to communicate with the child nor handle the discipline problems which he may present.

No one can dispute the fact that rioting in the inner city has had a resounding impact upon black students' attitudes toward school. Looting and burning, black power advocates vying for control of black communities, and almost universal interest in black pride and Afro-American culture among Negroes and the growing wave of counter racism have had a profound effect upon school age children.

The racial tensions in desegregated schools and student rowdyism in predominantly black schools are merely symptomatic of the wide range of civil disturbances within our society. The boiling pot of hate and misunderstanding has simply spilled over into the schools in much the same fashion as the

Vietnam war has transformed the complexion of student life on our college campuses. The teacher must perceive that many students are caught up in the emotionalism of a movement which to them has more relevancy for their lives than the rudiments of the three "R's."

In the heat of their involvement and enthusiasm for what may simply be a fad, black students can create the kind of atmosphere in a classroom on any given day which may render traditional teaching defunct, and the teacher may rue the day he signed his contract. But if he is resourceful and creative, he may be able to channel their enthusiasm for black power, Negro history or African culture into a very meaningful forum for discussion, not only of racial problems but concerns related to learning, individual aspirations or career interests.

In short, what at first may have seemed like a catastrophe could develop into the most meaningful session of the year in terms of establishing a focal point of communication which heretofore did not exist. Utilizing a student's interests as a means of reaching him academically is nothing new. While the concept seems simple enough, the teacher in the ghetto school must remain alert and sensitive to opportunities for employing such a technique. Nor will its application bring instant success. The excitement aroused by civil disturbances could prove to be a blessing in disguise.

With regard to black history and cultural achievements of Negroes, the teacher cannot fail to recognize the almost frenzied interest in this subject by black students. If he is insensitive or lackadaisical to this need, he is inviting negativism and ridicule from his pupils.

Every teacher, regardless of his subject area, needs to do his homework in this area so that he will be in a better position to relate to his black students. Even in a math class, the question could be raised as to whether there have been any black Einsteins or Newtons. The science teacher may point out the achievements of Dr. Christian Bernard with heart transplants, but how important is it to his black students that Dr. Daniel Hale Williams, a Negro, pioneered in the field of heart surgery or that a black man in the person of Dr. Charles Drew was director of the British blood plasma program in the 1940's? In almost any discipline, a careful examination will reveal significant contributions by Negroes.

The teacher who fails to understand or admit the existence of the black students' need for this information or refuses to hear the probing questions of black students with regard to their heritage cannot hope to realize his full potential as an educator of those students.

If educators are to even minimize the discipline problems among Negro youth, they must learn to teach the entire pupil and not simply impart their own sacred subject matter.

Educators must teach life to slum children. Some teachers are so subject and text oriented that they fail to see the pupil as an individual. Rather he is viewed as a kind of computer or machine into which bits of information are fed daily.

Teachers may have to deviate from the text on any given day or even discard the book entirely if it is not getting the job done. One teacher once remarked, "I always have two lesson plans, my own and theirs." This kind of insight will enable *any* teacher to gain a kind of personable relationship with students which will enable him to demonstrate his genuine concern for their welfare and erode much of the suspicion with which many black students regard their teachers. Ultimately he will be able to communicate not only subject matter to them but an intangible something called empathy, compassion—even love. The teacher who deviates from a daily routine or finds it necessary to dismiss a student from her class to see a counselor or participate in some project should not feel that she is failing the child or doing him a disservice. There should be no feeling of guilt or exasperation if he must postpone Chaucer in deference to a discussion on black literature.

Another failure on the part of the teacher of the ghetto child is the proclivity of the teacher to underestimate the child's ability and learning capacity. Some teachers feel that a kind of watered down curriculum will ward off frustrations and permit the child to be successful on his own level. There is some validity to this thinking, but when it is employed indiscriminately, the result is either nonlearning or the wasting of good potential. The ghetto teacher can help the student raise his aspiration level by convincing him that he is capable of achieving as well as any other child regardless of his race or social environment and that he has the same basic capacities as any other human being.

The teacher who discards the idea that ghetto children are inferior in ability can work miracles because he believes that they can. He translates this belief into action by challenging not only their minds but their spirits and their will.

The ghetto child is very adept at spotting phonies. The teacher must be able to communicate non-verbally to the ghetto child that he can rise as high as abilities and aspirations will carry him, even as far as the mayoralty of Cleveland, Ohio or the door steps of the White House if this is the road he wishes to travel.

Finally the ghetto teacher must be willing to be more than a teacher. He must be a counselor and social worker and sometimes a minister. He must be willing to phone or visit the home of that youngster who is acting up in fifth bell science or third period English. In the home he might find the source of the youngster's problem. Contrary to what teachers may think, the average parent welcomes a call or visit, even more so than the suburban parent, for this symbolizes a kind of concern that she sees little of in her society. The conference may reveal serious domestic problems which are adversely affecting Johnny's ability to concentrate on his studies.

None of these suggestions are meant to imply that the teacher must in any manner relinquish his authority as commander-in-chief of his classroom, nor does it suggest that he should become a patsy or milquetoast, catering to the whims of unruly pupils. He must be in a position to deal with violators in a firm but judicious manner, having the assurance that he will be supported by not only the school administration, but by the community at large, black and white, for no learning can flourish in an atmosphere of disorder or rowdyism.

What the article does suggest is that if teachers in the inner city are genuinely concerned about dealing effectively with a plethora of undisciplined students, they must be willing to look beyond traditional approaches such as after school detentions, threatening students with failure and corporal punishment, or sending pupils to the office. These are at best stop gap measures.

Rather teachers must come to grips with the very core of the child's difficulties which are often enmeshed in a complex matrix of social and environmental tensions.

DISCIPLINE AND THE DISADVANTAGED CHILD

Alfred P. Hampton

Parents in disadvantaged homes usually have standards and values which are comparable to those of so-called middle-class families. But economics, lack of privacy and sheer necessity to survive make it virtually impossible for many adults in a severely deprived environment to give more than lip service to such standards.

Abandoning hope for themselves, they cling to the one remaining dream—that their children shall some day be able to live differently.

They say, in effect, "Don't do as I do; do as I say!" They thus impose a dual standard. The inconsistency is quickly sensed by the child, and he resents it. His parents, not realizing that education literally begins at home with the assimilation of adult behavior patterns, see nothing unreasonable in demanding that the child obey. When he rebels, as he does early on, they impose harsher, more unyielding strictures than the middle-class parent is ever likely to invoke.

The small child, of course, has no alternative but to comply. As an accommodation to his environment, he develops a superficial response, a respectful, obedient manner. But his frustration and anger, only temporarily suppressed, lie not far beneath, waiting a chance for release. This is not to say that center-city parents fail to love their children, or that center-city children do not love their parents. As we all know, a child may have conflicting reactions which encompass both love and resentment. As he grows older, the regimen of fiat and fear to which he is subjected at home—for his own good, from his parents' point of view—increases the suppressed resentment and leads in

Reprinted from *New York State Education*, 57:19–21, 50 (April, 1969), by permission of author and publisher.

his teenage years to outright hostility, not only toward his parents but also toward every authority symbol he encounters.

If I took you along with me to visit homes in deprived areas of the city, you might be amazed at how well-behaved the youngsters seem, especially some children who are already beginning to develop problem behavior traits in the classroom. At home, their manners are excellent and they appear to respect their parents.

Comparing their conduct at home with their conduct in school, you might ask: What are we doing wrong in the classroom?

But it should be remembered that aggression is usually manifested first outside the home. For one thing, the young pre-adolescent is still dependent on his home, emotionally and for the necessities of life, such as they are. Moreover, he is vastly more afraid to displease his parent than to displease his teacher, for he has learned that retribution for bad conduct at home is swift and physically painful.

Away from home, the child is likely to become progressively more aggressive toward everyone. Policemen are referred to as "dirty cops," teachers as "old bags," and even his own friends as "fakes."

As his attitude deteriorates, we in the schools become alarmed. We roll up our sleeves, open up our psychology books and invite in the experts in an attempt to find some way to help the hard-to-handle youngster. We have, indeed, made advances in this area and we should continue to seek new techniques and arrangements through which we can better serve these boys and girls.

At the same time, we must view the job to be done as twofold. We must seek to increase our understanding of the center-city milieu and culture, specifically, our understanding of the center-city parent or other adult who stands *in loco parentis* to the disadvantaged child. We must learn to work with these adult figures as well as with the student himself.

Unless we can find some way to educate the parents, and thus to change the center-city home environment significantly, youngsters from disadvantaged areas will continue to bring resentment and conflict into the classroom.

First, let us examine some of the causes why parents or guardians in the center-city milieu are so authoritarian.

To begin with, housing, especially for the Negro, is always a problem. It is not unusual for eight persons to exist in a three-and-a-half room apartment. As many as four or five youngsters, boys and girls, may share one room. In a situation such as this, the belt, ironing cord or the back of the parent's hand is the quickest, most convenient tool for maintaining order. One has only to visit such a home to witness the mother's role as policeman. In her hand is strap or stick. The phonograph is playing, the television blaring, the baby crying.

Constant hubbub and lack of privacy, common to the crowded center-city apartment, tend to immunize children and adults to noise. These children are able to tune on or tune off at will: they hear what they wish to hear. It is not surprising, therefore, that they seem inattentive or appear to be poor listeners when they enter school. Because many of them do not follow directions and have short attention spans as a result of constant noise and distraction at home, they are often erroneously classified as retarded or borderline children.

In some disadvantaged homes, we find parents who are embittered, who are distrustful of the white "establishment." Their goals for their children may be extremely high. If the child lacks the ability to reach these goals, the parents do not accept this fact; they believe he is being discriminated against by white teachers and principals. Their anger spills over onto the child, especially if he brings home a poor report card, for which offense he will generally receive a belting. Such parents also become alarmed and resentful when teachers question the behavior of their children. Again, it is not difficult to see why. At home, Johnny has learned in self defense to be cooperative, almost docile. At school, the lid blows off. He is belligerent, openly defiant of all authority. But the parent simply doesn't believe it.

Another characteristic of the disadvantaged milieu is the home with one parent, a woman. These women love and are deeply concerned about their children. Their own insecurity is often manifested, however, in preoccupation with detail—Did you wash your face? Comb your hair? Brush your teeth? Make your bed, etc.?

Theirs is a heartbreaking task, at best. They must be both mother and father to their offspring, and they must work long hours to provide the bare necessities of life. They have little time and less energy to expend in visiting the school, conferring with the principal or finding out anything about the child's progress. Yet they may be eager to receive a home-school counselor or other school person who will come to see them in their own homes and talk with them as peer rather than patron.

One word of warning, however. It would be a grave error to stereotype all center-city parents. Many parents who have little or no education and whose incomes are marginal still manage to do a very good job of rearing their children. What they lack in the way of middle-class amenities, they make up for in other wholesome family activities. With just a little encouragement, disadvantaged families like this can be drawn into the school orbit, can become active members of the PTA, can develop real pride in and respect for the school system.

We recognize of course that there are, among the disadvantaged as among any economic group, adults who are not interested in their children or who have such severe emotional problems that they are incapable of being good parents. These cases present special problems for the schools, whether the families be economically privileged or deprived.

Now let us consider some characteristics and needs of the disadvantaged child. In a democracy, it is the obligation of the school and of each teacher to accept each youngster, to take him where we find him and lead from that point.

If the disadvantaged child's language is poor, his vocabulary minimal; if he speaks in words and phrases rather than sentences, it is our job to help, not criticize or condemn.

But I cannot overemphasize one point: These children do not need teacher's overt pity or sympathy. In fact, they will be quick to take advantage of it. Like all youngsters, they're glad to find a loophole.

They need limitations, spelled out goals, and a feeling that their teachers believe in them as individuals. Specific instructions geared to the child's ability offer the disadvantaged child a framework of security which he badly needs. He wants to please, and should be able to achieve success by being given tasks which it is possible for him to accomplish, with a little effort.

Building rapport may be the teacher's first job in working with disadvantaged children, for they tend to keep their defenses up until they are sure they can trust you.

The whole question of corporal punishment is involved here. Even though some disadvantaged parents are sometimes strict and use physical force in punishing their children, they nonetheless deeply resent it when any other adult "lays hands" on the child. Especially if that adult is a white stranger, who may be suspect, per se, to the Negro parent.

Just as they admonish their youngsters to "behave" in school, so also do they warn them that they're not to "take anything" from anyone—meaning take no physical abuse from the white establishment.

The teacher's greatest weapon, therefore, is love, understanding and a good healthy dose of adult humility. We aren't God and just integrating a classroom isn't going to solve all our problems.

As educators, we must realize that just mixing children of different races, creeds and abilities isn't going to guarantee good education. We have also to experiment with new ideas, find ways to individualize the program for each child, use cross grouping, large-group, small-group techniques, and any other method we can think of to meet the needs of the children involved. For we know that any child, regardless of his socio-economic background, becomes disruptive if he is insecure, if he is too far behind the class, or if he is so far ahead that he isn't challenged.

Some civil rights spokesmen have accused the schools of trying to impose middle-class standards. I see nothing wrong with trying to inculcate standards and values; in fact, this is one of the school's most important functions. Yet, it is true that we must pause now and then to evaluate those standards. Is it possible for every child to meet them? If not, how can they be revised without lowering our aspirations? Should every child be expected to conform to all rules? Or can some rules profitably be changed or stretched? How can we bring the disadvantaged child into the mainstream?

I certainly do not have all the answers. If I did, I could collect a magician's royalties. However, I do believe that the successful teacher is the pragmatic teacher, the teacher who adapts the ongoing program of education to the raw material, the children. Understanding each child and treating him as a worthwhile individual is the key, as we all know.

Too many rules can be just as foolish as none at all, and rules are made to be broken as well as to be followed. On the other hand, discipline should and must be consistent from day to day. Children want and need the security which derives from reasonable limitations.

Of course, we must always watch our own subconscious biases. This is nothing new. It has always been difficult not to like some children better than others, even in a classroom which is racially and socio-economically homogeneous. The problem is compounded, however, in the integrated classroom because disadvantaged children are acutely sensitive to the attitudes of adults in authority. They will not respond to the teacher who, for whatever reason, fails to treat all pupils with uniform fairness.

Example: Teacher emphasizes at the beginning of the year that she will have no arguments in her class. The children are told that any hitting or name calling is to be reported to the teacher, who will then solve the problem. This arrangement appears to be working very well for several weeks. Some incidents are reported and the teacher does a good job of classroom counseling. But one day a little boy reports that he has been called a racial name. The teacher reminds him that "sticks and stones will break your bones but words will never hurt you." She seems cross because he has reported this name-calling incident. Very shortly, he becomes one of that teacher's most difficult behavior cases.

This boy is convinced that the teacher has been hypocritical from the outset. He is disillusioned. Not only has he no further motivation to seek the teacher's approval, he is now actually motivated to be deliberately "bad," so as to get even.

Why did this teacher fail? Maybe she didn't feel well that particular day. Maybe she honestly thought the incident was too minor to be important. Perhaps she felt insecure about discussing anything which had racial overtones. Or perhaps she had some hidden prejudices. In any event, all of us must aim at the greatest degree of self-understanding if we are to understand our pupils. We may fool ourselves about our own biases, but it's virtually impossible to fool children.

Praise is another valuable tool in the positive-discipline kit. If a child does a job to the best of his ability, even though his work may be poor by more objective standards, reward him with praise. Tell him or write a note on his paper, or give him a gold star, or call his parents and tell them that he has worked very hard. One small success leads to a larger one, and that one leads to another even larger success.

This is not to say that teachers should be all sweetness and light. Legitimate anger has very definite value. Children expect it, in fact, when they know they are being disobedient or careless. If a teacher is justifiably angry, she should let the child know she isn't pleased. Her displeasure may be conveyed in her voice and attitude, or she may write a note on the child's paper indicating her disappointment. The important thing is not to carry over this anger so that it assumes the dimensions of a "grudge." Iron out differences that very day, before the child leaves for the day. And then start tomorrow with a clean page. Never let a child think you have lost confidence in him or that you view him as incorrigible.

Discipline has many facets other than punishment. Too often, we adults put children in a situation where they react negatively in order to save face. I have found, however, that even the toughest child will accept discipline if the approach is skillful and considerate. When a child is causing confusion in a group setting, such as classroom, hall or cafeteria, it's advisable to call him aside and lay the law down privately. Talking quietly with a disruptive pupil and showing him that you are disappointed in his behavior is usually a highly effective method and one which sometimes brings tears to the eyes of an ordinarily obstreperous student. But this same youngster is almost certain to be defiant, talk back and even use foul language if he is corrected in front of his peers. A child with a "reputation" to defend cannot back down in front of an audience.

I have said little about punishment, because I believe it is seldom necessary if discipline is regarded as an art and practiced accordingly. Punishment should be a last resort, after every other technique has been tried. And punishment should always fit the offense. Making a pupil write one thousand times "I will be good" is likely only to make him hate writing. A student could more beneficially be required to remain after school or stay indoors at recess to write a page on how and why he should be a good citizen. This is a logical punishment, which the child will recognize as such, and it is also sound educationally. The student is actually performing an English assignment as well as being put in a position where he must give some thought to his behavior and its implications.

Again, it does little good to correlate the length of an after-school penalty with the seriousness of a pupil's offense. A child can repent just as well in half an hour as in two hours, and he is more likely to do so. Time beyond the first half hour or so is quite likely to be spent in making plans for vengeance on the morrow. Certainly the staying-after-school procedure or any other punishment should be reinforced with an explanation of your point of view, the reasons for the regulations involved and for the punishment.

Discipline, like education, must fit both the situation and the child, and it is difficult to make many specific suggestions. Generally, I believe the guidelines which have worked best in my experience are these: Set limitations for your pupils and be firm when necessary. Be fair. Do not overemphasize small, unimportant things. Try to place youngsters in a position which will enable them to achieve some success. Be generous with your praise. Keep every child as busy as possible. Most important, try to love each child.

One final thought. Effective discipline is not only the key to a good educational experience for each pupil, it is also the key to a happy teaching experience.

Chapter 7

EVALUATING AND
REPORTING PUPIL
PROGRESS

INTRODUCTION

Evaluating pupil learning is one of the most essential responsibilities of the classroom teacher in the elementary school. A comprehensive and continuous program of pupil evaluation is a vital part of any sound educational program. The accurate assessment of each child's potential and his progress toward reaching that potential is all important to the success of the instructional program.

Frequently student teachers do not understand the full significance of classroom evaluation. Such evaluation should, and must, help the teacher determine where instruction is to begin, how and at what rate it should proceed, and to what degree it has been effective.

Possibly the most significant contribution that pupil evaluation can make for student teachers is to give them immediate feedback on the appropriateness of the preparation for and the effectiveness of their individual lessons. Student teachers need this kind of guidance. At the beginning of their assignment they cannot possibly understand such factors as the pupils' interests, abilities, and attention spans; mastery of work and study skills; and rate of learning. Student teachers will discover that good pupil evaluation is not only a prerequisite for but also an integral part of good classroom instruction.

The first four articles in this chapter discuss the measurement and evaluation of educational growth. Paul Allen questions the value of existing programs of evaluation. He stresses that student self-evaluation should be the fundamental purpose of evaluation in the school and challenges teachers to collect the necessary data, make these data available to students, and encourage the students to engage in self-evaluation. Guidelines for assessing the value of an evaluation program are presented by Robert Williams. He criticizes competitive marking systems and enumerates negative effects which often accrue from an overemphasis on school marks. The author presents an alternative program of pupil evaluation which is based on the ability and previous achievement of each pupil. Vergil Ort offers guidelines for planning, constructing, and administering teacher-made tests and presents suggestions for the construction of different types of test questions. Suggestions for organizing test data to enhance interpretation, and the proper use of test results, are made by Robert Walker.

During the school year many decisions must be made regarding each child in a given classroom. The classroom teacher needs accurate information about the children in his room and this data needs to be well organized and readily available. One of the best sources is a cumulative record file. Barbara Musso details what information should be in a cumulative folder and how this information should be used by the classroom teacher.

A necessary component of pupil evaluation is the assessment of the social growth of each child including how well he is accepted by his peers. The classroom teacher should know the social structure of his group and how each child relates to the other members of his class. Melba Huning doubts whether classroom teachers really understand the social structure of their classes and presents information on the use of sociometric questions to determine social relationships within a group.

A natural outgrowth of any program of pupil evaluation should be an attempt on the part of the school to report information concerning pupil progress to each child and his parents. Often, this is one of the most difficult tasks confronting the classroom teacher. Unfortunately, many student teachers miss a scheduled reporting period or at best play only a minor role in the collection, organization, and presentation of data relating to pupil progress.

The latter part of this chapter includes articles that discuss different methods of reporting, strengths and weaknesses of each method, and definite trends in this area. Pounds and Hawkins explain what parents should be told about their child's progress in school. The authors emphasize the school's responsibility to report meaningful and understandable information to each child's parents.

The concluding articles in this chapter discuss the parent-teacher conference. Helen Heffernan attempts to look at the reporting process through the eyes of parents. She concludes that the parent-teacher conference is the best method to be used in answering each parent's questions relating to the progress of his child. Specific goals for the parent-teacher conference are stressed by Barry Herman. He provides guidance for the preparation and execution of the type of conference that would meet these goals. Carol LeFevre discusses the interpersonal relationships involved in the parent-teacher conference. She illustrates the deep personal feelings brought to the conference by both the classroom teacher and the parents and how these feelings affect the quality of communication and understanding achieved during the conference.

THE STUDENT EVALUATION DILEMMA

Paul M. Allen

Evaluation is inevitable. It is also exasperating, frustrating, and extremely humbling.

Reprinted from *Today's Education*, 58:48–50 (February, 1969), by permission of author and publisher.

Nearly every teacher has, at some time, experienced a painful twinge of guilt as he has sneaked into the classroom clutching an examination made in haste the night before. Many teachers have been bewildered by the maze of percentile ranks, stanines, and Z scores they find carefully recorded in students' files. And what teacher, sitting down to make out report cards, has not cried out for an escape from the seasonal task of playing god?

Probably two factors explain why evaluation, which is so completely a part of a teacher's daily life, is frustrating or exasperating. First, the teachers find themselves in the center of an intellectual tug-of-war. And, second, the existing evaluation programs require teachers to play a role that they either don't understand or can't accept.

For the last 15 or 20 years, behavioral scientists and other educational pundits have been choosing sides and bombarding teachers with apparently conflicting truths. Stimulus-response associationists and operant conditioners trade theories and insults with perceptual and field psychologists. The stimulus-response associationists and the operant conditioners claim that behavior can best be explained by a concept of *external causation*. Perceptual and field psychologists, in contrast, espouse a theory of human behavior that might be called *internal causation*. And in between stands the teacher.

In addition, the day-by-day evaluation activities required of the teacher can't help but cause consternation. He is required to sit in judgment on others, even though he realizes that his knowledge about them is fragmentary —probably a close approximation at its best and downright nonsense at its worst. Teachers recognize the potential inaccuracies and frailties of grades and yet they find too many administrators, parents, and students accepting grades as gospel. Testing programs and courses of study require them to do things *to* students, yet they are supposed to teach in such a way that students will become self-realizing, self-actualizing individuals.

Teachers are confronted with a dilemma—a dilemma made up of apparently conflicting theories of human behavior and apparently conflicting demands on a teacher's daily activities. For better understanding, it is necessary to examine this dilemma more completely.

The first of two apparently conflicting explanations of human behavior has been called *the theory of external causation*. To put it oversimply, people who subscribe to this theory believe that human behavior is simply a kind of observable human movement and that environment consists of all of the individual's physical and social surroundings.

The basic premises underlying the concept of external causation are:

1. Man's behavior is initiated by external forces. For example: A student would say, "The *teacher made* me study," or "My *sister made* me angry."

2. Man *reacts* to external forces and consequently his form and function are the results of environmental influences. Man is a passive receiver of stimuli. When he receives a stimulus, he reacts in accordance with the conditioned or innate reflexes it calls into play.

3. The environment is judged good or bad depending on the resultant behavior. The slum environment that produced a medical researcher could be judged "good." The slum environment that produced a criminal would be classified as "bad."

Using this theory as a basis for evaluation, what a man does can be measured against external criteria. Even more important, his behavior can be changed by manipulating his environment, and the success of this manipulation can be judged by measuring the resultant behavior.

Most traditional programs of evaluation stand foursquare in the camp of external causation. The basis of nearly every evaluation plan since 1850 has been a program of testing and measuring. We are told that the test data are important—that with complete knowledge about a student, it is possible to predict how he will behave in every possible situation. As a result, the educators observe, measure, record, and predict. They plan and administer programs of standardized testing. They carefully record in grade books students' scores on teacher-made tests and collect written observations of student behavior in cumulative records. In short, the entire evaluation program is other-person-oriented.

Of course, such information is important. It is necessary in order to discover if valued educational objectives are being reached. This kind of feedback is essential for curriculum development and educational policy making. And finally these data are needed for the record keeping that enables teachers to write letters of recommendation and administrators to send transcripts to future employers and university placement offices. More significantly, these records enable educators to communicate, with some understanding, about students' achievements.

Appearing to be in complete contrast with the concepts just examined is *the theory of internal causation*. People who accept this theory believe that an individual's environment is psychological and consists of what he perceives it to be and not what others describe it to be. Behavior then becomes psychological movement and may or may not be observable.

The basic premises underlying this theory of human behavior are:

1. Man's behavior is initiated internally. For example: A student might say, "The teacher didn't make me study; *I decided* it was a good idea," or "My sister was reading my book and now *I am* angry."

2. Man *interacts* with his environment rather than reacting to it. Behavior is not a matter of a simple stimulus-response; rather it is a state of the total organism. This concept of interaction implies a relationship between an individual and his environment in which he interprets and uses his environment for his chosen purposes.

3. Environment is neither good nor bad. Each person's environment is unique, for it is basically what he perceives it to be. Environment can be a vast dynamic vista of opportunity with which each individual interacts in a unique way.

According to the theory of internal causation, change in man's behavior is self-initiated. Evaluation then would turn toward an inner state of being and the criteria would become personal. An individual's feelings and attitudes would probably be used in the process of making judgments.

Few, if any, existing programs of evaluation are consistent with the theory of internal causation. This theory implies that the primary purpose of evaluation is self-evaluation—for both students and teachers. The process of self-evaluation would provide the feedback to enable the individual to make the changes necessary to keep him on the track toward his chosen goals.

Since change is initiated from within, only the individual can change his behavior. But to change his behavior, he needs the objective data of his own learning. If these data are made available to each individual in a nonthreatening manner, he can compare his action with his intent and his results with his objectives. By this process, he can discover not only the existing gaps in his mastery and understanding but also the personal meaning of his learning.

Self-evaluation has not yet gained acceptance as the most fundamental, the most important outcome of evaluation programs. Even assuming that the importance of this outcome were accepted, the knowledge is not yet available on just how to gather the data that would have pertinence to each individual— or on how to make it available to students and teachers in a nonthreatening manner. The point is not whether self-evaluation should occur, for it is occurring every moment of every day. The point is—what data gathered in what way should be made available? Even more basic—should self-evaluation become the fundamental, structuring purpose of an evaluation program?

Now the dilemma has another dimension. It seems essential that the school system have the information that the traditional evaluation program provides. And for purposes of self-evaluation, a new program of evaluation based on the theory of internal causation must be developed. Can two apparently conflicting goals in education be accomplished? *If it is necessary to make a choice, which program should be chosen?*

A parallel to this question arose in the field of modern physics. Since Newton's time, scientists had believed it possible to observe and track a particle, whether grains of dust or a planet, to determine its speed, and to predict its position for any moment of time. This is the doctrine of causality— the certainty that cause produces effect. If the laws and relationships among observable phenomena should be discovered, the state of the universe would be known, for an observable cause will produce a predictable effect.

Surprisingly, such certainties collapsed in observations of the world of the atom. If an electron started out on its rounds at a certain speed, it would be impossible to predict its time of arrival at a given point. The reason is that it is not possible to observe the electron without disturbing it. The observer's beam of light will actually change the electron's course and speed.

Niels Bohr, world-famous Danish physicist, has said that any observation regarding the behavior of the atom will be accompanied by a change in the state of the atom. Interaction with unpredictable results takes place between the observer and the phenomenon observed. Yet without disturbance, there can be no measurement and no knowledge. Heisenberg called this *the theory of uncertainty.*

The implications of all this for the dilemma in human behavior are apparent. The proponents of operant conditioning have presented ample evidence in support of external causation. The perceptual psychologists and the field psychologists are proposing and competently defending the theory of internal causation.

The manner in which the physicists resolved their dilemma is a milestone in man's intellectual development. Niels Bohr did not see helplessness in the quandaries. Instead, he proposed *the concept of complementarity,* a new way of looking at the problems. This concept recognizes the existence of two explanations rather than one. Both theories are valid and useful for a better understanding, but they are mutually exclusive if applied simultaneously. The knowledge of the position of the particle is considered complementary to the knowledge of its velocity, but the two cannot be computed simultaneously.

In our own camp, human behavior can be explained by both external causation and internal causation. The two theories together complement each other and offer us a more complete view and understanding of human behavior, education, and evaluation. So, like a house of cards, our dilemma has collapsed. *We don't need to make a choice.* Instead we need to learn how to build an evaluation program that will utilize as completely as possible the potential of both theories.

If we listen to teachers for 10 minutes, we will hear more complaints about evaluation than any other aspect of education. When teachers discover themselves spending hours gathering data for the purpose of marking and grading and additional hours recording these data, frustration results. When they are placed in the role of sitting in judgment on others, they feel deeply their inadequacies and their misgivings about playing such a role. And still both teachers and students cry out for the objective feedback essential for making the profoundly important, personal decisions in teaching and learning. But because evaluation programs do not produce these data, guesses, biases, and the opinions of the uninvolved and the uninformed too often form the basis for decisions.

Teachers are now becoming aware of what is missing—*the data for self-evaluation.* By knowing what is missing and by recognizing that what seems to be conflicting is not necessarily so, perhaps teachers can channel the energy now expended on frustration and exasperation into a search—a challenge. The challenge then is to devise the ways to gather the data of self-evaluation, discover how these data are to be used, and find a way of doing something about them at the classroom level.

And one more challenge. The data justified by the concept of external causation are also needed. Find a way to combine the two. Fortunately, it is possible to have both.

ON SCHOOL MARKS

Robert L. Williams

What is the most appropriate way for teachers to evaluate pupils' academic achievement? This question is one of the genuinely important issues in education. Despite many vociferous arguments to the contrary, competitive evaluation policies have persisted in most school systems. Typically, pupils of varying abilities and sociological backgrounds compete for academic marks.

Children of low ability perceive early in their academic experiences that they have little chance for success. However hard they try, they simply cannot compete with brighter pupils. Consequently, school becomes a succession of experiences in failure.

Several school systems, having an uneasy conscience about competitive evaluation, have tried to work out policies that provide positive appraisal for all pupils, including slow learners. Yet most of these systems have retained certain components of competitive appraisal.

Ability grouping is one such attempt. With this arrangement, the pupil is evaluated according to his ability level. On the surface it might seem that homogenous grouping would be effective, but in actuality it is often a miserable failure. After reviewing relevant studies, Johnson concluded that retarded children in regular classes achieve at a significantly higher level than retarded children in special classes (1). According to Johnson, placement in special classes does not enhance the school achievement of retarded children. Other researchers have found that placement in special classes is also ineffective in enhancing personal adjustment (2, 3). Slow learning groups often have a stigma that seriously undermines achievement and adjustment. One must admit, too, that a child is graded by the very act of being placed in an ability group. Assignment to a low group may give a pupil a more humiliating and lasting sense of failure than low marks in the regular classroom setting.

Some educators have explored the efficacy of a dual grading policy. With this arrangement, each pupil gets two school marks. One mark is based on achievement in relationship to individual ability; the second mark is based on competitive standing (4, 5). In the main, educators seem unwilling to eliminate competitive appraisal and the practice of assigning marks.

ASSESSING AN EVALUATION POLICY

Three considerations are of paramount importance in assessing the efficacy of an evaluation policy. They are the effect of the grading system on the

Reprinted from *Elementary School Journal*, 69:1–5 (October, 1968), by permission of Robert L. Williams and The University of Chicago Press. Copyright 1968 by The University of Chicago.

pupil's self-respect, on his achievement, and on his attitude toward school-work.

Specialists on theory about the self-concept believe that the perpetual negative feedback that low ability pupils characteristically receive produces pernicious feelings of self-abasement (6, 7). Research indicates that indices of self-esteem in a competitive milieu correspond closely to assigned school marks and standardized measures of ability and achievement (8, 9, 10, 11).

Proponents of competitive school marking often contend that while pupils of lower ability may suffer emotionally in a competitive milieu, the total result of competitive appraisal is higher academic achievement. Negative evaluation is said to motivate pupils by causing them to work harder to raise their standing.

This argument is based on the erroneous assumption that all pupils have the capacity to work at the same level. Pupils of low ability, however hard they try, cannot compete successfully with much brighter pupils. Therefore, increased efforts to compete only confirm and intensify the pupil's sense of failure and inadequacy. Feelings of inadequacy produced by competitive appraisal typically lead to diminished academic achievement (12, 13, 14). Consequently, competitive evaluation may cause the slow learner to perform far below his potential (15). In a competitive milieu the only way a slow learner can maintain a modicum of self-respect is not to try at all. He can at least tell himself and others that he could do better if he chose to expend the effort. Furthermore, since the child of high ability can with very little effort compete successfully, he may produce far less in a competitive milieu than his capacity would permit.

A competitive atmosphere often creates the impression that school marks are all important. If a pupil does not get acceptable marks, he is likely to feel that all is lost. Conversely, if a pupil gets high marks, he automatically assumes that the academic venture has been successful. Strom has reasoned that if grades become the primary goal of learning, the individual, once outside the educational setting, is likely to make little effort to continue learning (16).

In a competitive situation, defeating others may be construed as far more important than learning itself. In one extensive survey of adults enrolled in organized classes, an overwhelming majority of the students wanted grades as well as examinations (17). Students who preferred grades generally thought that a grade indicates "who is better or worse than someone else." The attitude of attaining success at the expense of others is not the kind of orientation needed to deal effectively with the excruciating social and inter-national problems of our time. A co-operative, not a competitive, spirit is necessary to resolve the human conflicts of the day. Also, by emphasizing the glory of successful competition, we often discourage the bright pupil from developing his lesser capacities.

Competitive marking may be a major cause of behavioral problems in academic settings. Briggs contends that cheating, extreme anxiety, and student irresponsibility typically accrue from an overemphasis on school marks (18). Many pupils feel that if acceptable marks are the only means of maintaining the approval of teachers, parents, and, in some instances, peers, then appropriate marks must be attained at all cost. The cost sometimes includes cheating. Counselors in academic settings recognize that many emotional problems pupils have may result primarily from the pressure of marks. Furthermore, if the teacher's appraisal is all that matters, pupils refrain from pursuing projects and ideas that run counter to the teacher's bias. Consequently, pupils become increasingly dependent on the teacher for direction in the learning process (19).

What effect does competitive evaluation have on the pupil's attitude toward school? Apathy and outright antipathy toward school are among the more serious problems in public education. Research in learning has demonstrated that if Stimulus A, a neutral stimulus, is frequently paired with Stimulus B, an aversive stimulus, Stimulus A also acquires aversive qualities. If academic experiences are repeatedly paired with derogatory feedback on the competence and the achievement of a particular child, such experiences soon acquire highly aversive connotations for that child. The present author, studying pupils in competitive settings, has found a highly significant relationship between attitude toward school and grade point average. Undoubtedly, schools that have stringent competitive marking policies produce in many pupils irrepairable despair concerning education (20).

A FEASIBLE ALTERNATIVE

To deplore the evils of competitive marking is not enough. One major reason why school systems have continued to use competitive evaluation may be the lack of a feasible alternative. It is the author's belief that the most equitable, efficacious policy for enhancing self-esteem, achievement, and affinity for school is to appraise a pupil's work primarily on the basis of his ability and previous achievement. As long as a pupil is trying to surpass his previous performance, he has ample opportunities for experiences in success. This individualized evaluation should not be couched in the form of school marks. To be of optimal value, appraisal ought to be frequent and specific. A mark of C in a content area after six weeks of work provides little information that would facilitate subsequent learning (21). A more productive approach would be to provide frequent feedback—daily or weekly—that would indicate the areas of a subject in which the child is making suitable improvement and the areas that need special attention. One major virtue of automated instructional devices is that they provide specific and frequent feedback for pupils.

What would be the repercussions of eliminating competitive marking in the public schools and using instead individualized, specific, and frequent appraisal of pupils' achievement? School systems that have tried to use the individualized appraisals described have encountered considerable resistance from teachers, pupils, and parents (22, 23, 24). Most of us have been conditioned to think that school marks are indispensable and consequently feel shortchanged if no marks are given. Resistance to change, however, is hardly an adequate index of the soundness of existing policies.

Another reservation often voiced with respect to individualized evaluation is the difficulty of assessing a pupil's preparation for a certain academic level without some type of competitive appraisal of his previous work. For example, how do we know that a high-school graduate is prepared for college work if we have no index of his high-school rank? If employers, colleges, or parents demand information about a student's competitive rank, scores on standardized ability, aptitude, and achievement tests would provide more complete and objective evaluations than assigned marks (25). Certainly, specific assessment of a pupil's strengths and weaknesses in a content area tells more about his readiness for subsequent work in that area than one global mark in a course. In an individualized evaluation the question of preparation would not be "Can the student pass the course?" but "Does the student have the knowledge that would enable him to profit from the course?"

Proponents of competitive marking often declare that anything less would create in the thinking of the child of low ability unrealistic expectations of success in adult life. These advocates of competitive marking contend that the adult world is highly competitive. In contrast, the individualized approach tells the child that what matters most is not his competitive standing, but the use he makes of his capacity. Whatever the nature of the adult world, would several years of bitter frustration in a competitive academic setting adequately prepare one to deal with the demands of adult life? The individualized approach does not purport to convey to the child the idea that he is as bright as someone else or that he can expect to be the president of a large corporation some day. The individualized approach simply sets forth the proposition that the primary test of human success is the use of one's capacities and opportunities, be they great or small. Individualized appraisal does not camouflage a child's limitations, but rather allows him to accept his limitations without losing self-respect. The individual most adequately prepared to deal with the realities of an adult world is the one who has used his intellectual potentialities appropriately. A completely individualized appraisal would be far more effective in producing this kind of person than a highly competitive atmosphere.

REFERENCES

1. M. Johnson. "Solving the Mess in Marks," *Education Digest, 27* (February, 1962), 12–14.
2. H. Goldstein, J. W. Moss, and L. J. Jordan. "The Efficacy of Special Class Training on the Development of Mentally Retarded Children." U.S. Department of Health, Education and Welfare; Office of Education; Cooperative Research Project No. 619. Urbana: Institute for Research on Exceptional Children, University of Illinois, 1965.
3. J. H. Meyerowitz. "Self-Derogations in Young Retardates and Special Class Placement," *Child Development, 33* (June, 1962), 443–51.

4. M. Alpren. "Fair Grading System," *Clearing House, 35* (October, 1960), 113–14.
5. E. D. Doak. "Grading: A Deterrent to Learning," *Clearing House, 37* (December, 1962), 245–48.
6. A. W. Combs and D. Snygg. *Individual Behavior: A Perceptual Approach to Behavior.* New York: Harper and Brothers, 1959.
7. E. C. Kelly and M. I. Rasey. *Education and the Nature of Man.* New York: Harper and Brothers, 1952.
8. S. Coopersmith. "A Method for Determining Types of Self-Esteem," *Journal of Abnormal and Social Psychology, 59* (July, 1959), 87–94.
9. P. H. Stevens. "An Investigation of the Relationship between Certain Aspects of Self-Concept Behavior and Students' Academic Achievement," *Dissertation Abstracts, 16* (1956), 2531–32.
10. R. L. Williams and S. Cole. "Self-Concept and School Adjustment," *Personnel and Guidance Journal, 46* (January, 1968), 478–81.
11. R. L. Williams. "Personality, Ability, and Achievement Correlates of Scholastic Attitudes," *Journal of Educational Research, 63* (May 1970), 401–403.
12. E. D. Alexander. "The Marking System and Poor Achievement," *Teachers College Journal, 36* (December, 1964), 110–13.
13. E. Drews. "Evaluation of Achievement," *Instructor, 75* (April, 1966), 20.
14. A. M. Walsh. *Self-Concepts of Bright Boys with Learning Difficulties.* New York: Bureau of Publications, Teachers College, Columbia University, 1964.
15. L. E. Peterman. "Let's Junk Our Grading System," *Michigan Education Journal, 35* (February, 1958), 223.
16. R. D. Strom. "Academic Achievement and Mental Health," *Journal of Secondary Education, 39* (December, 1964), 348–55.
17. E. E. McMahon. "Report Cards for Adults?" *Adult Leadership, 13* (December, 1964), 169–70.
18. F. M. Briggs. "Grades: Tool or Tyrant? A Commentary on High-School Grades," *High School Journal, 47* (April, 1964), 280–84.
19. R. N. Bostrom. "Grades as Reinforcing Contingencies and Attitude Change," *Journal of Educational Psychology, 52* (April, 1961), 112–15.
20. L. F. Malpass. "Some Relationships between Students' Perception of School and Achievement," *Journal of Educational Psychology, 44* (December, 1953), 475–82.
21. R. H. Muessig. "How Do I Grade Thee? Let Me Count the Ways," *Clearing House, 36* (March, 1962), 414–16.
22. G. Bloom. "There Should Be No F's—Students Should Be Judged on the Basis of Whether or Not They Are Achieving Their Potential," *Business Education World, 46* (March, 1966), 13–14.
23. J. W. Halliwell. "The Relationship of Certain Factors to Marking Practices in Individual Reporting Programs," *Journal of Educational Research, 54* (October, 1960), 76–78.
24. I. F. Johnson. "Injustice of Grades," *School and Community, 54* (October, 1967), 24–25.
25. W. A. Yauch. "School Marks and Their Reporting," *NEA Journal, 50* (May, 1961), 50.

TEACHER-MADE TESTS

Vergil K. Ort

Since millions of tests are given yearly for purposes which are veritably legion, a growing concern has developed among the populace regarding aspects of

Reprinted from *The Clearing House,* 41:396–399 (March, 1967), by permission of author and publisher.

tests and testing. It would seem that when most products come under the tester's scrutiny, the nation either nods its acquiescence or chooses to disregard the research with an indifferent shrug. But when the tester's focus is placed on the education of the young and/or on the child's own unique ability to be educated, then passivity and indifference no longer characterize the prevailing public posture. Rather, such focus often stimulates the voice of public opinion to make itself clearly manifest. For example, there are those today who think that certain tests delve too deeply into the private lives of individuals, others think that intelligence tests are not sound indicators of personal potential, and some feel that testers (by whatever name) are often rather non-percipient probers. Hence, it is not uncommon to hear, *"My* child knows all the right answers, but the teacher always asks the wrong questions!"

The crux of the problem does not seem to reside in any one test or even in the number of tests involved, but rather the focus addresses itself to the tester's ability to construct or select valid tests, to give tests competently and discriminately, to interpret tests with sensitivity and sagaciousness, and to apply the knowledge which tests yield with a discreet beneficence that acknowledges pupil growth and development as its major goal. With this approach as a guide, consider, then, some basic competencies needed in developing and refining teacher-made tests.

The process of making, giving, and interpreting tests is a task and responsibility assumed by nearly every classroom teacher. While some teachers have received in their college courses pre-service instruction concerning the making, giving, and interpreting of test results, others have not. Frequently, in the construction of test questions, teachers simply emulate the testing structures and testing techniques they experienced during their own school years. Thus, many tests reflect and perpetuate testing which may range from that which might be termed effective to that which might be classified as being inferior. Too often, however, tests are in need of much improvement.

When asked the question, "Why do you give tests?" the most common answer elicited from teachers is that they need a basis for giving a grade, and testing serves as one way to determine that grade. Perhaps another reason would be to provide a kind of classroom motivation. One teacher observed, "My students just won't study if I don't give them tests."

It is true that in most of our present school systems teachers are required to give some sort of an evaluative symbol at periodic intervals, and tests are often used for this purpose. A more professional reason for giving tests is that tests can serve effectively to improve instruction. Primarily, testing helps the teacher to discover which particular aspects of a discrete body of knowledge a student does or does not know. From this information a basis for new learning situations may be identified.

Secondly, through diagnostic teaching a teacher may discover certain of a student's deficiencies, and, guided by this knowledge, an intelligent approach to corrective or remedial help may begin. Thirdly, testing may be used as a pedagogical yardstick to determine how well the teacher himself has presented learning situations which should have contributed to the meaningful and fruit-ful development of pupils. Hence, the teacher may use testing results to improve his own teaching effectiveness. Fourthly, since students are usually as eager as the teacher to have tangible evidence of their progress, testing—at least to varying degrees—satisfies this need. Each student will be just as interested as his teacher in learning how he ranked among his classroom peers. Here, then, are four plausible reasons for giving tests.

Why bother with teacher-made tests to accomplish the above-mentioned ends? There are hundreds of standardized tests available for this purpose, and most of these tests are well organized and skillfully presented. On the other hand, some of the reasons why the teacher can not and should not use standardized tests exclusively are here presented. First, commercial tests do not always meet the distinctive needs of local situations. Secondly, they are expensive to purchase. And, thirdly, standardized tests rarely give students an opportunity to synthesize their understandings or to express themselves uniquely. Although it may appear that the intent here is to decry standardized tests, this is not the case. Rather, the purpose is to point out the necessity for the teacher to know how to construct the best possible tests in order to meet the objectives of the particular group of pupils within a given classroom situation.

Volumes are available on the subject of the construction of teacher-made tests, but the purpose of this article is to present in a rather terse manner some basic suggestions which may be helpful to the teacher in constructing tests.

The construction of teacher-made tests is not an easy task, and, if a valid test is to be designed, the process is one which cannot be performed during a recess period, a noon hour, or in an evening while propped comfortably before a stimulating television program. Test items, ideas, or questions must be gathered by the teacher as an outgrowth of each day's classroom prepara-tion, presentation, and exploration. These discrete items should then be placed *individually* on index cards, filed, and kept ready for that time when a test is to be prepared.

Just as in building a house the contractor needs a blueprint, so in making a test the teacher needs an evaluative blueprint, a plan based upon the objec-tives which the test is to serve. Before preparing a test, the teacher needs to make a survey of the material which the test is to cover and to decide upon the importance of the various possible parts. An example of weights and balances in structuring a test might be this: one-eighth of the question is to be based on terminology, one-fourth on facts, one-eighth on sequential data, and one-half on the application of principles. This, of course, is a purely hypothetical example, and the balance desired for a particular test will depend upon the objectives, the subject, the students, and the teacher. The amount of time spent on the various aspects of the unit of work will also help to determine where the emphasis should be placed in planning the test.

The teacher may ask himself, "Should I structure objective or subjective questions?" The answer is quite clear if the findings of research are considered. The objective type of question is the best type to use in the large portion of cases, but this does not exclude the essay-type question which is so often associated with the subjective-type test. The important thing to remember is that each type of question serves a specific purpose, and it is the teacher's problem to determine that purpose. A broom is not used to clean a plush carpet when a vacuum cleaner would perform the task more effectively. So, too, discrimination must be carefully exercised when selecting the tools to elicit best answers.

Essay questions can be used to best advantage when the teacher wants to measure complex learning, and when his purpose is to encourage students to study and learn material in large and interrelated units, rather than in small segments isolated from the whole. Tests in the social studies and in English definitely call for well-planned essay questions.

On the other hand, questions which can be answered by who, what, when, or where should not be included in this category. Essay questions are best characterized by such words as, "explain," "exemplify," "differentiate," "evaluate," "contrast," "compare," etc. The subjectivity of essay questions can be lessened by constructing model answers which have been assigned weighted values for scoring purposes. Objectivity can be further enhanced by scoring at one reading all the answers written by a class on any *one* test question. Further, each paper which is being scored should not reveal the owner's identity, for anonymity enhances objectivity. Subjectivity may be further reduced by having, whenever possible, a second teacher evaluate the papers using model answers as an evaluative guide.

The objective-type questions usually fall into five categories: multiple-choice, matching, rank-order, completion, and true-false. Of these types, the multiple-choice question is, in most respects, the most versatile. If the teacher knows his subject well, has a clear picture of what understanding or application is to be tested, and is willing to take the time to develop effective test items, these questions are capable of measuring skill, understanding, knowledge, and application. The teacher should keep in mind the following factors: each item should have a central problem; if the best answer is called for, each option must be stated with grammatical correctness; the plausible answers should all be about the same length, and they should be arranged in a vertical column.

The matching-type question is a variation of the multiple-choice question. Here the problems are placed in a left-hand column, and the answers, which are greater in number than are the problems, are arranged in a right-hand column. This type of question can be used in testing such factual knowledge as dates, names, and places. The answers should be relatively short, of about equal length, and arranged in chronological or alphabetical order. The number of problems in each group should be homogeneous and limited in number.

The rank-order type question may be used to advantage in the social studies or perhaps in the sciences when some need is present for ranking various elements or happenings in a chronological or logical manner. Care must be taken in selecting items which can be listed in some order of importance, for if this is not done, a problem will be created in scoring. Unless there is a positive listing or several possible alternatives for which credit may be given, these items should be avoided.

Completion items requiring very short answers are more nearly like essay questions, but since they are of the short-answer variety they are classified as being an objective type of question. They can be used to advantage when factual data (such as are sometimes desired in science and mathematics) are to be tested. Elements of caution to be observed by the teacher in constructing this type of question are these: use completion items which can be answered with a unique word, phrase, symbol, or number; avoid using completion items having too many missing words; if computational problems are included, specify the units desired.

True-false items are the least desirable of all the objective-types of questions. Although these items can be used in almost any subject area, the number of true or false questions used in a test should be held to a stringent minimum, and care must be followed in constructing items which are 100 per cent true or 100 per cent false.

When constructing tests, teachers should consider the following general suggestions which are applicable to all kinds of questions: (1) avoid using statements taken directly from the book; (2) avoid writing negative items; (3) avoid the use of *always* and *never* which are taboo words in constructing questions; (4) write down and file ideas for questions as they occur to you; (5) give a second person an opportunity to read and criticize the test items, and, if this is not possible, put the test aside for a cooling-off period and then reread; (6) keep the reading level of the test approximately one grade below the reading level of the class for which the test is intended unless, of course, the test is designed to measure vocabulary; (7) include specific directions with every part of the test and provide examples if the class has never experienced the types of questions which have been prepared; and (8) construct the format of the test so that a key can be made for ease of scoring. (Overlay keys are excellent and will save much time in scoring.)

With the increasing number of students and the greater demands which are being placed upon every teacher's time, it would be advantageous for schools to purchase scoring machines so that tests could be constructed by teachers for a standard answer-sheet form similar to the type used with many standardized tests. This latter suggestion would also permit students to receive their scores on the day following a test, and, more importantly, it would delineate a student's weaknesses as determined by the test. This, in turn, implies that still another learning experience could be had with the test while the interest level of all students is still at a high level.

Teacher-made tests are still among the most useful educational instruments which contribute to the improvement of classroom learning, and, if used with professional integrity, skill, and discretion, they should contribute vitally to student-teacher dialogues—dialogues which focus on the student's own behavioral change and growth through learning. If, however, this is not representative of the actual aim and nature of the classroom testing program, then the value of tests can and should be seriously questioned and their use considered a waste of time, money, effort, and emotional involvement.

HOW TO UNDERSTAND AND USE TEST RESULTS

Robert N. Walker

Filed and forgotten. This, all too often, is the criticism leveled at test scores—which teachers perspire so diligently to secure and find so difficult to understand . . . and use.

But this needn't be so. There are simple, uncomplicated strategies you can use to make test scores meaningful and helpful in understanding how—and what—your students are learning. All you need is 10 good fingers, the ability to count to 35 or 40 . . . and a real desire to extract from standardized test scores the valuable clues they give for planning instruction.

I want to make two points in this article. First, I want to describe a means of organizing test scores so that they make more sense than the alphabetically arranged class record sheet or roster report usually do. Second, I will suggest how this method of organization can lead you to insights into pupil learning behavior and can be used in your instructional planning.

ORGANIZING THE SCORES

First of all, let's arrange your pupils' individual test results so that you can really understand them. This can be done by simply arranging each test in a pile in descending order of scores—highest on top, lowest on the bottom. You can use the scored test booklets themselves for making these piles or the scored answer sheets. If only a class record sheet is available, transfer each pupil's name and his scores to a 3 x 5 card, listing only such scores as percentile ranks, grade-equivalents, stanines, IQ's, etc.—not simple "number right" scores. Sometimes pupils' names and scores are reported on gummed labels which can be affixed to cards. You may want to request such labels when they are not regularly available. They are great work savers.

If two or more sets of scores, such as mental ability and reading achievement, are being studied it is preferable to put them on separate sets of cards. You can use the word recognition score on the reading test for arranging that stack.

Having arranged the scores into stacks, count down the number of tests representing *one fourth* of the class—eight booklets, say, in a class of 32. Set this group aside. Now continue counting down the pile until you have counted out a number of tests equal to *half* the class—or 16 *more* booklets for the class of 32. Set this group aside also. Each set of tests is now divided into three groups—one representing the upper fourth of the class, one the middle half, and one the lower fourth. The tests are now organized and the process of *interpretation*—that is, determining what the scores mean—can begin.

WHAT TO LOOK FOR

There are four points of reference to look for in interpreting your test scores. First, look for *likenesses* and for *differences*. Ask yourself to what extent the scores of individuals or groups on a test are like the scores of other individuals and groups on the same test. If the scores are different, how great are the differences? Second, look for *consistencies* and *inconsistencies*. Is the performance of an individual or group comparable and consistent from one test to another, or is it erratic? Is there consistency or inconsistency between pupils' performances on tests and other behavior—classroom behavior or recitations, for instance—which you have observed elsewhere?

Keeping these questions in mind, turn to your pile of answer sheets and begin making some educational deductions. Look, for example, at two IQ tests—the highest and the lowest in class. Are they widely different or rather close? How does the range of your class compare with others in the building? In the school system? Is your class rather typical—suggesting that the system's routine curricular materials and methods can be used? Or is it so different as to call for special attention? Look at the top two or three and bottom two or three ability papers. Are these pupils pretty much in the normal range or are they so different as to suggest need for special instruction, even special class placement? Repeat this procedure with all other test scores you may have available—reading, achievement and so forth.

Now find the paper in the middle of your group of test booklets or cards (remember, there are 16 of these—count down eight to the middle). The score on this will roughly represent the class average and can be used as an index of the performance of the class as a whole. Is it high, *very* high? Perhaps low or *very* low? How does it compare with other classes in the building? In the city? Does it suggest a need for modified instruction for the *entire* class?

Take a look at the 16 center-group booklets as a whole. These pupils are the "solid middle" of your class. Are the abilities and skills they indicate pretty much in line with what you would expect? Will the students who made these scores progress more or less satisfactorily on their own while you give extra attention to the top and bottom groups in the class? Perhaps the *bottom* group in your class is more like typical pupils and the center and top groups are bright and capable and need to be taught as such. Or perhaps the reverse is true—only your *top* group fits the "typical" picture.

Study the top, center and bottom group scores of your class individually in the same way you have studied the performance of your *entire* class. They will give you further clues about the ability-achievement patterns within your class. Note also how different your top-fourth group is from the bottom fourth, or how similar they are. Again, wide differences suggest one kind of educational planning while similarities suggest another.

HELP IN GROUPING

Next, spread all the booklets out in a row, maintaining the low-to-high order of scores from left to right. Look for natural clusterings of pupils with similar ability scores and about equivalent reading achievement levels. These clusters may represent a basis on which small, homogeneous groups can be organized for instruction. Sometimes this kind of grouping is most effective when based on ability scores—when you introduce new subjects, topics or activities, for example. In continuing instruction in skills or subject sequences started earlier, however, it may be better to group by achievement level.

Grouping may not be indicated if your test scores run rather smoothly from lowest to highest. You may have to work more on an individualized basis with such a class or join with another teacher in organizing instructional groups of similar abilities from both classes. In this case, since natural clusters haven't presented themselves, compose your groups more or less arbitrarily, using given scores for cut-off points.

Do your scores tell you anything about boy-girl differences in your class? We know that the sexes tend to respond differently to classroom programs yet we rarely look at this phenomenon as a guide to planning. Examine your scores again. Do either boys or girls cluster disproportionately into the higher or lower ability groups? Where are the boys found in reading achievement as contrasted to girls? Does one sex tend to average higher in ability than the other? These observations may indicate a need for planning instruction that will be more appropriate, interesting, challenging, or meaningful to one sex or the other.

By now you should have a good idea of the basic strategy for test score analysis—stack, count, study, look for *similarities* and *differences*. The examples given are only indications of the kinds of information you can look for and find. You can go further. You can analyze the likeness-difference patterns of your class in relation to age, just as you did for sex. And you can extend your comparisons to other achievement and aptitude scores, if you have them.

CONSISTENCIES AND INCONSISTENCIES

Test scores that are consistent among themselves and with non-test information tell you that what you are observing is almost surely the way things really are. When inconsistencies among test scores or between scores and non-test information appear, however, you can be equally sure that something's wrong somewhere. Such signs should *never* be ignored. At the very least they call for a second look at the "inconsistent" pupil—even if only to reassure yourself that it's the test score that's out of line.

How do you go about looking for consistencies and inconsistencies? Largely, by comparing each pupil's scores on one test with those on another and by comparing his test scores with all available non-test information. Start by comparing ability scores with reading comprehension scores. Do the pupils who score high in one also score high on the other? Or do you find some pupils who stand one or two from the top on one score and near the bottom in another?

Now consider discrepancies between individual *ability* scores and *classroom* achievement and review these in the light of your personal estimate of each pupil's abilities. When you find inconsistencies, try to resolve them—that is, look for the cause of the discrepancy. Continually ask yourself, "What accounts for this inconsistency?" When you find the answer, chances are excellent that you will also have found a clue for remedial action.

Now make a three-way comparison among ability, reading comprehension and word meaning scores—or any other aptitude or achievement scores you may have available. You can make consistency-inconsistency comparisons according to rank in class as established by your grades or your pile of score booklets, on the basis of percentile rank, stanine, or whatever. Compare each pupil's rank or score on the ability test with his score on comprehension tests. Check ability against word recognition, word recognition against comprehension. Are there a disproportionate number of discrepancies in one such comparison or another? If so, one aspect of your instructional program isn't getting through. On the other hand, can you find a comparison in which achievement is consistently *better* than ability would predict? Here you must be doing something very right! Find out what it is and use it in other subjects or skills.

Bear in mind that *sometimes* discrepancies appear because a test score is simply "off." It just doesn't reflect a particular pupil's ability or achievement accurately. In a class of 32, for example, two or three pupils are almost *certain* to have scores so erroneous as to be unuseable. You can detect them because all other evidence about the child will be of marked and consistent contrast to the score. By all means don't accept test evidence uncritically. But don't be too quick to second-guess the test either. Look at *all* the evidence; then make the appropriate decision.

Equally important: Remember that very small differences between scores should not be considered as inconsistencies. Discrepancies of two, three, or five points are not generally worth concern. It's the larger ones you need to look into—and the larger they are, the more likely it is that they reflect the true situation.

A LOOK BACKWARD

Still another source of consistency-inconsistency evidence is the comparison of current test results with those of a previous test. This kind of comparison is not recommended if there are more than two years between tests. However, highly worthwhile inferences can be drawn from comparing end-of-year scores with those from, say, the previous September or October, or the previous spring.

The comparison strategy remains the same—stack the previous tests and the present tests into piles and look for patterns. Do individual pupils show consistent growth from test to test? In ability? In achievement? In some skills but not others?

Is there more consistency between the pretests or the post-tests? Do you find highly erratic growth patterns, maybe even losses? Can you associate discrepancy patterns in achievement scores with any of the ability, age, socio-economic, sex or racial characteristics of your group? Such identifications should suggest that remedial steps are in order.

To sum up, inconsistent test performance patterns identify pupils who, more than their classmates, need some special attention from you. You can uncover these inconsistencies with the stacking and counting method of test analysis described above. The strategy will give you a far better understanding of your children's academic and mental growth patterns and problems. And your test scores won't be "filed and forgotten" again.

THE IMPORTANCE OF CUMULATIVE RECORDS

Barbara Musso

There are numerous ways to study pupils and to gather material about them. A list of means might well include the following: (1) autobiographical information, (2) health records, (3) standardized test results, (4) school grades, (5) anecdotal records, (6) teacher notes, (7) notation of parent conferences.

All of this vital information tells a story and provides data for understanding a pupil's potential and his progress as well as the strong and weak points of his physical, mental, social, and emotional behavior and capabilities. Thus the cumulative record becomes a center of information for teacher study. The study of cumulative records becomes a *must* for teachers.

ITEMS FOR THE CUMULATIVE RECORD

The following paragraphs discuss items in the cumulative record.

1. *Autobiographical information.* The pupil's autobiography should include information about early childhood, number of siblings, youngster's interests, parental educational and occupational background. From such information teachers and counselors may often gain insight in working with the pupil and his parents.

Most teachers bring to classrooms a life experience very different from that of the families whose children they teach. Appropriate perception of reasonable objectives and expectations needs to be understood. The teacher must become aware of the child's whole life, including all of his life which contributes to his success or failure in school. With this understanding the teacher can work more effectively with the problems of children.

2. *Health history.* All health records should include professional medical data. The teacher, school nurse, physician, and dentist need this information to evaluate properly the pupil's physical development and progress.

3. *Standardized test results.* The teacher and school guidance counselor need standardized test information as one instrument for evaluation of mental progress. The name of the test, form grade level of the test, date administered, norms used and effective conditions upon the person or group should be recorded by the person administering the test, while the person evaluating the results must know the advantages of giving such examination and how the resulting information should be most effectively used.

Only recently has it become publicized that standardized tests do not give a true picture of the culturally deprived youngster. Other approaches are new tests with different vocabularies which must be devised for these children of limited backgrounds. Examination of administered tests reveals not only important factors regarding the test but also how a pupil actually responded.

4. *Individual tests.* Among the types of tests that may be administered are the individual tests administered by an examiner who observes and records the examinee's response as he responds to oral questions and performs manual tasks. Examples are Stanford-Binet, the Wechsler Intelligence Scales, Thematic Apperception Test and the Rorschach Ink Blot Test.

5. *Group tests.* A group test given to a number of pupils at one time may be classified in the way the test was designed to be used.

(a) Tests of mental abilities, intelligence or scholastic aptitudes are basically measures of intelligence. These tests measure reasoning and vocabulary. The results are produced either in compiled or separate scores of verbal and non-verbal response. Educational and vocational guidance may be given as a result of this testing.

(b) Achievement tests are in battery form of broad subject area or diagnostic form. These are designed to determine the achievement in such skills as reading, mathematics, and subject areas as science, social studies, etc., as well as in thinking critically. Academic strengths and weaknesses may be observed.

(c) Aptitude tests estimate future success of a person in further education and occupations. Interest inventories are a test to record preferences and make choices. These tests are useful in vocational guidance.

(d) Personality inventories measure personal adjustment. They are believed helpful if used by adequately trained personnel in conjunction with other knowledge about the subject.

6. *Teacher-made tests.* Tests are often constructed by the teacher, usually for his own use to evaluate classroom teaching and learning. These teacher-made tests might be classified according to subjective and objective types. The subjective requires the examiner to use great care in evaluating the written or oral responses of the pupils. On the other hand, objective exams require little judgment, for a key scores the true-false, multiple choice, or matching responses. Teachers' tests are, as a rule, kept in the cumulative file only when some unusual quality of a pupil's work is to be kept on record.

7. *School grades.* School marks provide an on-going accumulation of strengths and weaknesses. These grades show significant personal attributes and learnings that standardized tests of one or a few days' taking cannot dispel. Many questions should come to mind when one looks at grades—questions concerning the teacher and the teacher's standards, the school and its facilities, the pupil and the total knowledge of him.

8. *Anecdotal records.* These should include teacher-written, dated, short descriptions of behavior patterns—good or poor. These reveal personality traits of character, attitudes and interests.

9. *Teacher notes.* These should consist of records of participation in cocurricular, extracurricular, or work activities. Talent and positions of leadership should also be noted. Work experiences should be recorded. This record helps the teacher and counselor in planning educational courses and offering vocational guidance.

10. *Notation of parent conferences.* These notes of parental conferences are a reminder of information the school has given the home, of plans made together for the pupil's welfare, and of the hopes and expectations of the parents.

GUIDE SHEET

The following guide sheet is one devised by the writer to encourage the teacher's thinking and response in using the cumulative record. Cumulative file material, if properly kept, can reveal a great deal.

In this day of crowded classes, teacher turnover, curriculum revisions, and new programs such as "Head Start" and "Job Corps" as well as many other work and study programs, it becomes essential that schools earnestly and conscientiously keep these records. Teachers need to understand cumulative records—their merits, their weaknesses, their proper purposes, their intelligent use, and their real strength as an educational resource.

GUIDE SHEET FOR CUMULATIVE RECORD EXAMINATION

Please answer the following questions which are pertinent to the cumulative folder which you are examining.

1. What kinds of information have you learned about this student from viewing this folder?
2. What knowledge or impressions have you gained about his family?
3. How do you evaluate the student's present status as to the following areas of development? (Make notes for each area)
   A. Physical development
   B. Mental growth
   C. Personal growth and development
   D. Emotional development
   E. Personal-social growth
4. What types of tests have been given to the student?
5. What guidance does the student need in respect to the following factors? (Make notes for each factor)
   A. Teacher notes
   B. Health records
   C. Psychological evaluation
   D. Grades
   E. Vocational area
6. What efforts have the following persons made to help the student?
   A. Teachers
   B. Administrators
   C. Other
7. In view of your responses in this guide sheet, what can you do in your programing to help this student and others like him?
8. What benefits do you gain by examining students' folders, such as this? (Make a brief statement)

HOW WELL DO YOU KNOW YOUR CLASS?

Melba A. Huning

Each year as teachers come back to the classroom, they try to evaluate the group that they have. Physical characteristics are obvious, but what about the inner feelings of the children? Does the teacher know how John feels about Mary or Tom or Peter? Of course, the teacher can learn much by careful observation, but she can't always learn enough.

Each child is an entity in himself. His growth patterns, background, attitudes and the way he gets along with others, make up his individuality. The teacher should make the most of each child's characteristics. She should provide personal security in the classroom and help each child develop to the utmost. The teacher should know the social structure of her group and how each child relates to the others.

By analyzing the classroom social structure, she can learn a great deal about her group which will aid in making her teaching more effective. Casual observations should be enhanced with objective data. By using a combination of tools, techniques and ideas, a better environment for learning can be made in the classroom.

SOCIOMETRIC QUESTIONS

One of the tools a teacher can use to learn about the structure and relations of her group is the sociometric question.

Sociometric questions can be used to show the social interaction of the group. The questions are simple to draw up, take a short time to administer, and the only cost is for paper!

Through sociometric questions, imbalances in the social atmosphere of the class can be found. The teacher can see whom children like and don't like, what children might be natural leaders, what subgroups or cliques there are, how cohesive the group is and what children are completely left out. By knowing all of these important factors, the teacher can rearrange activities to improve the group effectiveness.

The individual teacher constructs the sociometric questions. When making up the questions, she should keep in mind that they will identify only the present situation and should be used with other pupil information. The questions should be meaningful to the students, based on some common interest. The children should see that the questions will be of benefit to them, and they should understand that responses will be kept strictly confidential.

A person who has good rapport with the children should give the questions to the group, and the classroom teacher would be the logical person to do this. She should adapt her questions to the abilities, nature and maturity of her group, and should not administer them until after the children have had plenty of time to get acquainted. It would be best to change criteria and use this device at intervals throughout the year.

TYPES OF QUESTIONS

The children are instructed to choose individuals for association in some activity or situation. The number of choices can be limited. The questions can vary according to the use that is to be made of the results. General or specific questions can be used, and to find out what children are not liked, negative questions must also be used.

Some examples of sociometric questions that could be used by classroom teachers are:

What classmates would you like to have sit on either side of you?
Whom do you prefer not to sit by?
What person would you like to have help you with your homework?
What person would you rather not have help you with your homework?
Whom would you like most to have as your project partner?
Whom would you like least to have as your project partner?
What classmate would you choose first to attend a school party with you?
What classmate would you choose last to attend a school party with you?
What person would you like to have work with you on a report?
What person would you rather not work with on a report?
What three people would you like to work with on a mural?
Whom do you prefer not to work with on a mural?

Resistance to the efforts of the teacher to look into the inner feelings of the children will be overcome if the questions are explained in a friendly, understanding manner.

The teacher must be proficient in using any technique in order for it to be effective. Certain terms must be mastered in order to have complete comprehension of the sociometric data collected.

The *star* is a person who receives a large number of positive votes from his classmates.

The *isolate* receives no choices either for or against him. He is a physical member of the group, not a social one.

The *reject* attracts attention which is not acceptable and receives negative choices from the group. The rejects and isolates cannot be distingiushed without using a negative question.

The *neglectee* is disregarded or overlooked by the majority of the group and receives relatively few choices.

When one child chooses another and the choice is returned, it is called a *mutual choice.*

A *clique* is a small group of children who choose each other.

With a large group, the teacher may find several children in each individual category, and several mutual choices and cliques may be found.

TABULATION

In tabulating the data collected, the purpose of the test should be clearly in mind. Some tabulation forms are simple and others more complex to make. One type of tabulation lists the names of the children and shows the choices that they received (See Fig. 1). Another type shows who made the choices

Figure 1
SOCIOMETRIC TABULATION

Name	Choices received	Totals 1's	Totals 2's	Totals 0's
John	1,2,0	1	1	1
Mary	0,0,0,0,0	0	0	5
Sally	1,2	1	1	0
Cathy		0	0	0
Sam	1,1,2,2	2	2	0
Mike	1,1,2,2	2	2	0

1 = First choice
2 = Second choice
0 = Rejection

The teacher can easily see that Mike and Sam are the stars of the group. Mary is rejected and Cathy is an isolate.

Figure 2*
SOCIOMETRIC TABULATION

	Name	Chooses	Chosen by	Rejects	Rejected by
1	John	**5,6**	5,6	2	2
2	Mary	3,5		1	1,3,4,5,6
3	Sally	6,5	2,4	2	
4	Cathy	6,3		2	
5	Sam	**1,6**	1,2,3,6	2	
6	Mike	**5,1**	1,3,4,5	2	

Each child could make two choices and one rejection. Mike and Sam are the stars of the group. Mary is rejected and Cathy is an isolate. Mutual choices are indicated by bold face type.

*Adapted from *The Role of the Teacher in Guidance* by Edgar Grant Johnston and others, Prentice-Hall, Inc. Englewood Cliffs, New Jersey.

Figure 3*
SOCIOGRAM
Data from Figure 2
Only choices are shown

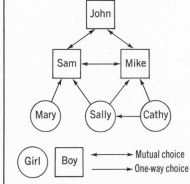

*Adapted from *Practical Guidance Methods for Counselors, Teachers, and Administrators* by Robert H. Knapp, McGraw Hill Book Company, Inc. New York, N.Y.

Figure 4
INDIVIDUAL SOCIOMETRIC PATTERN FOR MIKE
Data from Figure 2

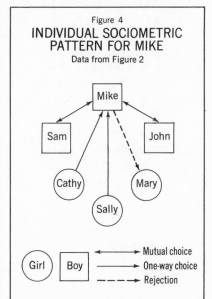

(See Fig. 2). Tabulations can be found to show examples of choices, rejections, how the class rates an individual and mutual choices. The teacher should use her imagination in devising a tabulation form to fit her particular purposes.

The sociogram is a chart or graph which pictures the interpersonal choices of the children from the tabulated data (See Fig. 3). Sociograms are more complicated to make but they clearly show the social structure of the group. Individual sociometric patterns can also be made (See Fig. 4).

By carefully studying the sociogram, the teacher can see clearly the lines of communication in her group.

The sociogram only shows the structure of the group; it does not explain why the choices were made. It shows desires for social contact, leadership potential, cleavages between groups of boys and girls and identifies those who are not involved to any extent with the group.

THE RESULTS

Each child wants the approval of his peers and the teacher should do everything possible to make a good learning climate. The data can be used as a basis for organizing activities within the class, organizing clubs, arranging seating or for organizing home rooms or committees.

Isolates and rejects can be integrated into the group through skills, interests, hobbies or common problems. The group will not give overnight approval to the child, so the teacher will have to know many things about the pupil in order to help him integrate effectively.

When children work with whom they like, they will have personal security and the working situation will improve. Children can help each other through understanding and patience. More creative work should come about, and fewer tensions within the class should be noticed. The flow of communication should improve, and natural discipline should develop from children wanting to please others in the group.

Learning can be affected by the pupil's position in the group, so the teacher should try to develop an emotional climate which will stimulate the class to better learning.

IN CONCLUSION

Social adjustment is important in modern education. Sociometric techniques are an objective approach to reveal the structure of the pupil society. The teacher must be able to communicate with those she teaches, and she cannot be indifferent to the class structure. From sociometric data collected, she will have a better picture of her students. Group life should be such as to bring about better learning, more motivation, greater maturity, personal security, improvement in working together and high morale in the group. Individuals should stimulate each other instead of competing with one another, and they should contribute to a greater total achievement. Each child should add something to the group. His peers give him security by recognizing his merit.

It is necessary for the teacher to accept preferences from sociometric data and utilize them, to get complete cooperation and understanding from her group.

The possibilities for using sociometry in the classroom are dependent on the ingenuity of the teacher. With better integration of pupils and groups, a richer life with enhancing experiences will develop and a more effective school program will be had.

HOW MUCH SHOULD YOU TELL PARENTS?

Haskin R. Pounds and Michael L. Hawkins

Collecting information is now big business, with machine data processing and computer techniques making data input and print-out a matter of seconds. But for years schools have been in the business of collecting data about their students, although in a somewhat less sophisticated manner. School principals, counselors, and teachers have long been concerned with the ethics of data collection, and even more with the ethics of output. Who should know that John's intelligence quotient is 98, or that Susan has a percentile score of 80 on the Stanford Achievement Battery?

In the past, parents have been judged too emotional, too unlettered, too unsophisticated, to share in the special knowledge the school possesses about individual students. Undoubtedly, confidential information in the hands of those who do not need to know can do considerable harm. Everyone agrees that some information should be kept confidential, but there is disagreement as to what information should be so classified.

Test results are the most notable example. Are test results to be seen and used only by professionals—and never discussed with parents—or should test scores be common knowledge, both in and out of school? A desirable operating position lies somewhere between these two extremes.

The decision really revolves around the question of whether parents are to be considered as partners in the educational process, and therefore made privy to the school's special knowledge. While there is no absolute answer, some guidelines can help teachers and administrators handle the problem.

1. Parents are concerned with the education of their child. They have a right to be made aware of the information that the school has collected about him. Recent legislative actions and court decisions in several states have

Reprinted from *Instructor* 78:55,77 (August, 1968), by permission of author and publisher.

emphasized the legal right of parents to such information. (See References 1 and 2.) Upon parents rests the final responsibility for the upbringing of a child. This responsibility requires that they have access to information bearing on educational and vocational decisions to be made for and by the student. Although parents delegate part of their responsibility for education to the school, they do not abdicate it.

2. *Parents possess all levels of understanding, thus making it necessary for the school to examine its obligation for interpreting student information to them.* Uninterpreted test scores may help some parents understand the student's status, but with other parents they could definitely harm the student and the school. The school therefore has an obligation to present information in a meaningful manner, so that the parent is not left to make judgments without adequate knowledge of what was being measured by the test.

Teachers and principals must be certain that they are giving *understandable* knowledge to parents. If a total picture of the student's ability and aptitude is being presented it should include, where possible, measures of intelligence, aptitude, achievement, and teacher-made test results, as well as reports of observable work habits and attitudes.

Before the school can transmit understandable information to parents, the staff itself must have an understanding of these scores and test procedures. Teachers need to know what the test score means and how much confidence can be placed in it. Teachers need more than a nodding acquaintance with the evidence indicating the validity and reliability of a particular test. They need to know the probable error in prediction based on the test. The counselor should have the necessary training to be able to provide such information to the staff. Further, most test manuals contain this type of information as well as information concerning interpretation of test scores. (See References 1 and 3.)

3. *Teachers and principals must be able to transmit information to parents in meaningful terms.* Parents have greatly varying backgrounds, so careful terminology should be used, to convey true meanings to them. Various devices are helpful to increase parental understanding. Expectancy charts, graphic displays showing percentiles, student profiles—all convey an added dimension to the parent. The counselor can also assist teachers in constructing such devices.

Probably the most publicized misunderstandings are those connected with intelligence tests. There is a great danger that parents, students, teachers, and principals may look upon an intelligence test score as a fixed characteristic of the person tested, rather than a useful piece of information for further thinking and planning. Because of the misunderstandings resulting from the interpretation of intelligence test scores, it may be advisable for grade placement scores or some other sort of standard score to be used instead. Lyman (Reference 4) recommends that where possible schools use a percentile score, as probably the most informative method of reporting and the most easily explained. The explanation should include specific information on the group with whom the student is being compared, and emphasize that the percentile score refers to the percentage of students whose performance the pupil has equaled or surpassed, not to the percentage of questions answered correctly.

SUMMARY

In this age of instant recall of voluminous amounts of information, the school has a dual responsibility—to give information about a student and safeguard him too. Test scores or other confidential information should rarely if ever be made public. The schools do have the obligation of dispensing information to the student, with the parent many times as intermediary agent. The person presenting and interpreting information must consider every parent's deep emotional involvement with the well-being of his child as well as the parent's ability to understand.

Further, staff members must put themselves in the strongest possible position to interpret test information by understanding the test administered. They should have the answers to questions such as "What is being tested?" "How is it tested?" and "What does it mean?" They must arm themselves with evidence that the instrument used has validity and reliability. They must then select the language and methodology for interpretation to insure·that the terminology used will have meaning for parents.

Parents have a right to any information the school has about their child. But to provide for the best interests and welfare of the student, the school has a responsibility to make certain that his parents are provided with information in a form that is both understandable and usable.

REFERENCES

1. Georgia Sachs Adams: *Measurement and Evaluation in Education, Psychology, and Guidance*. Holt, Rinehart and Winston; 1964.
2. Dugald S. Arbuckle: *Pupil Personnel Services in American Schools*. Allyn and Bacon; 1962.
3. Robert L. Ebel: "How to Explain Standardized Test Scores to Your Parents," *School Management*, March 1961.
4. Howard B. Lyman: *Test Scores and What They Mean*. Prentice-Hall, Inc.; 1963.

QUESTIONS PARENTS ASK

Helen Heffernan

Report Cards or Parent-Teacher Conferences?

A parent asks:

Last summer our family moved to another state. Recently our son who is in the third grade brought home a letter from his teacher asking us to come

Reprinted from *Grade Teacher* 81:22, 105–107 (May, 1964), by permission of author and publisher.

to an individual parent-teacher conference to discuss Gregory's progress in school. At home, we have always had report cards and have rewarded the children for good marks. We think this makes them "toe the mark." Are these parent-teacher conferences better than the old-type report card?

May I answer your question by telling you a story?

Yesterday Timmy Thomas brought home his report card. He gave it to his mother with a half-bewildered yet expectant expression that characterizes many children at report-card time. Timmy knew from past experience that his report card brought forth responses from his parents that were often difficult to understand. He was either praised, scolded or punished because of the marks his teacher put on the card. He knew that for several days his parents would discuss him and his shortcomings to his painful embarrassment. Home ceased to be a comfortable place for Timmy. He felt unwanted and unloved because somehow he had not lived up to parental expectancy.

Mrs. Thomas took the card with her usual puzzled expression. Timmy had an *S* in reading and an *S* in oral expression but he had an *I* in spelling and a *U* in arithmetic. Mrs. Thomas knew that *S* meant satisfactory but she asked herself: "Satisfactory for what? Does that mean he reads as well as others in his class? Or, considering Timmy as the boisterous, active little boy he is, does it mean satisfactory for him? The *I* means improving. Well, I should hope so," she commented to herself. "That is what he is going to school for, isn't it?"

That should be good enough for a nine-year-old but she knew that *I* was poorer than *S* and she should not be pleased. She would have to talk to Timmy about that *U* in arithmetic. Why should Timmy be unsatisfactory in anything? Was it his fault? Should she blame him for not understanding arithmetic, or should she blame herself? She recalled her own childhood struggles with mathematics. Poor Timmy, he must have inherited her weakness. Mrs. Thomas was developing a feeling of guilt that made her less able to cope with the problem objectively.

Then Mrs. Thomas turned the card over to the section marked citizenship. In *Working with Others,* the teacher considered Timmy satisfactory. *Dependability* was followed by another *I*. Mrs. Thomas stopped to think of the many times Timmy had taken good care of his baby sister, of how competently he handled family shopping chores. Wasn't that dependability? Just what did the teacher have in mind? The term *Work Habits* rated a *U*. "That's strange," thought Mrs. Thomas. "Timmy helped his father wash the car on Saturdays, and often did a commendable job washing the dishes. To be sure, he was childishly messy about his work but he always worked with a friendly, cooperative spirit."

These marks were really meaningless to Mrs. Thomas. She did not know the basis on which the teacher had arrived at these judgments. The symbols on the report card shed no light on her questions about Timmy's progress in school.

Mrs. Thomas looked at Timmy. He read her bewilderment and said, "Jim got four *U's* and three *I's*. I did better than that. Mary got all *S's* but I don't think the teacher is fair. She likes Mary better than me and Jim. She gave me *U's* just because I didn't finish my arithmetic paper on time. Besides, I don't like arithmetic, or that teacher, or Mary either." And Timmy rushed outside just ahead of an unmanly torrent of tears.

Mrs. Thomas put the card on the table and stopped for a moment, lost in thought. "Is this good for Timmy? Should he be comparing himself favorably or unfavorably with Jim and Mary? They are his neighbors and should be our friends. Is this report card making Timmy dislike his teacher and his school? Timmy has always been so cooperative. Can it possibly be right for the school to put this emphasis on competition?"

Incidents similar to this one occur in the homes of several million children in our country many times a year. Certain parents greet the report card with nonchalance but to others it is a matter of serious concern. For certain children, severe punishment and rejection follow poor marks; others add money to their piggy banks as a reward for good marks. Report cards are as traditional as candles on the birthday cake and as inevitable as taxes.

But rational parents and teachers approach any problem related to children with one question: "Is what we are doing or what we propose to do in the best interests of the children?"

What are the best interests of children? What do they need to help them grow up?

They need assurance that they belong, that they are wanted in their homes, their schools and their neighborhoods. They need friends with whom they can work and play. They need lessons they can understand and learn. They need guidance that is just and kindly and that will help them to learn self-direction and to accept responsibility for their acts. They need opportunity to explore the stimulating aspects of their environment.

What purpose does the report card serve in meeting these needs? What do parents and teachers think is its usefulness? Many of them would say that the report card informs parents as to the progress of children in school. What is the evidence on this point? Research indicates that teachers' marks vary even when applied to the same piece of work. One study showed that a geometry paper was graded from excellent to poor by different teachers. Certain teachers included neatness in their evaluation, others considered the method of doing the problem important, while others judged solely on the basis of the correct answer.

Do teachers want report cards? Many teachers and those who understand children best do not want them. They realize their invalidity and their detrimental effect on children and on the all-important parent-child relationship. But ineffective teachers cling to them. They like the power of the weapon they wield. They can reward or punish children who do or do not accept their standards of behavior or accomplishment. It makes such teachers feel important to be able to control the lives of others in this manner. A teacher can shift responsibility from herself to the child by the mark she gives. "You earned the poor mark," she says in effect; not, "I have been unsuccessful in teaching you."

By holding the threat of a poor mark over a child, certain teachers believe they are able to get children to swallow unpalatable doses of subject matter for which the child sees no need. The effectiveness of this coercive weapon is an illusion because it creates tension which is often an insurmountable barrier to learning.

For certain teachers, report cards are a defense against change in their methods of working with children, and change is a painful process. It is easier to point to the child and say, "You are not working," than to find new ways to encourage him to learn those things that will be useful to him. It is easier to blame the parents because the child does not "work well with others" than to find out why he does not and then do something to help him make a better social adjustment.

Will parents and teachers forever cling to this educational evil? Will they always place the blame upon the children? Will many parents continue to feel guilty and thus destroy the rapport which should exist between the home and school? How long will we continue this competitive race for marks among children of unequal ability? Most schools have not been able to break away from tradition.

Some schools, stimulated by intelligent parents have broken with tradition entirely. In these schools, parents visit the classrooms and teachers help them to understand the work in progress. The parents have regularly scheduled conferences with the teachers in which the progress of the child is discussed. Samples of the child's work, the results of standardized tests, written descriptions of the child's behavior provide the scientific and objective data for these conferences.

Most individual conferences result in far better understanding of the child's progress. In the classroom in which Gregory is enrolled, a mature teacher will meet his mother when she and—hopefully—his father come for the conference. They will find her a friendly person who knows how to make other people feel comfortable. She may ask a question so the parents can get any worries they have about Gregory off their minds. She listens attentively for cues which will help her understand Gregory better. She will attempt to keep the conference focused on Gregory. She will emphasize a particular strength on which home and school may build. She may discuss some remediable weakness on which mother, father and teacher could work together.

Gregory's parents will leave the conference with some positive and mutually acceptable courses of action. They will feel "in" and not "out" of their son's education. They will recognize that education is a joint enterprise in which parents and teacher play supportive roles in the drama of Gregory becoming the finest human being he is capable of becoming.

THE PARENT-TEACHER CONFERENCE

Barry E. Herman

A parent-teacher conference can be a most important part in the education of each child. Even though the child may not be present, a conference expresses the need for both the parent and the teacher to examine their roles in helping the child succeed.

The teacher, whether a beginner or veteran, regards a parent-teacher conference with mixed feelings. However, he will feel more secure, if the purpose of the conference has been clearly defined so that both teacher and parent understand why a conference has been called.

MANY PURPOSES FOR CONFERENCE

A teacher may request a parent-teacher conference to become better acquainted with the parent, to learn about the child's background and interests, to obtain information about social problems at home, or to discuss the child's academic achievement, his personality, his behavior, or his relations with his peers. The parent, on the other hand, has an opportunity to learn about the child's progress in school, how to help the child at home, and to become better acquainted with the teacher and the total school program.

Preparation before the conference is imperative. The parent should be contacted by letter, bulletin, or telephone. In most schools, parent-teacher conferences are scheduled during the year. Sometimes, children are dismissed early so that conferences can be held in the afternoon. A personal conference should be set up by appointment. Personal conferences should not be held when school is in session unless the parent is unable to come at another time. If such a conference has been set up, arrangements should be made with the principal for someone to cover your class.

When the teacher seeks a conference, give the parent ample notice, with an alternate date and time and a clear understanding of what will take place. If the conference is held in the teacher's classroom, it will give the parent a chance to see what a modern classroom is like and to see the teacher in the classroom environment. Sometimes, it may be a good idea to hold the conference in the library, in an empty office, or in some other place other than your own classroom. Your classroom on the particular day of the conference may have a negative emotional reaction for you. A change of scenery may be the right ingredient to set a positive tone when the conference begins.

A HOME VISIT

If a parent is not able to come to school for a conference, a home visit is in order. If you are nervous about making a home visit, talk to the school nurse or social worker. They regard home visits as common routine and can probably give you pointers about the family to be visited. Because many parents have fears or an awe of the school, you achieve good public relations by going to the child's home. Furthermore, meeting parents on their own home territory contributes to better rapport. You can also receive a good picture of the home situation which might modify your attitudes toward the child.

PREPARE FOR A CONFERENCE

Become acquainted with the background of the child before the conference. Make a thorough review of his cumulative record. Keep an anecdotal account of his attitude and behavior in school and take samples of his work to show the parent. A folder on each child with samples of work should be kept by the teacher. I always include the child's first paper in September and samples of work done in the different subjects as the year progressed. I filed both good and bad papers, which eliminated embarrassment for a teacher when she goes to the child's desk for samples of work to show the parent and the desk is mysteriously clean with all class papers gone. In June, on the last day of school, I always presented each child with his folder. The children enjoyed looking over their papers and comparing their first paper with work done throughout the year. Besides having samples of the child's work, you should be familiar with all school policies and regulations.

The success of a parent-teacher conference usually depends on the teacher, who probably initiated the conference. A few basic techniques will help. Greet parents warmly and try to create a mood of friendly interest. Having coffee or tea handy often helps create the right mood. Parents will feel more at ease if you exert no pressure, but talk about the child without criticizing or condemning the home, and give encouragement to the parents about their child. Always allow enough time for the parents to talk and share their feelings about the child and the particular problem. Try to make the parents feel that your job is to help their child and that it is an important task. Convince parents that their child is very important to you as a teacher and that you need their cooperation. I usually initiate discussion by saying, "I am having a little problem with John, and I need your help," or "What can we do to help Mary with her problem?" No matter what their education level, parents know when a teacher is sincere. All the parents I have talked with are more than willing to help, if they are convinced that I am genuinely interested in the welfare of their child.

Do not take notes, but make mental reminders of what is discussed. A parent may not feel comfortable or speak freely when you are busy jotting down what is being said. Speak "straight English" during the conference. Avoid educational jargon, which confuses parents more than it impresses them. Most important, choose your words and expressions carefully so as not to offend the parents. In his book, *School Public Relations,* Leslie W. Kindred offers lists of expressions which have negative and positive effects. He stresses the use of positive expressions when meeting with parents. He cites:

NEGATIVE EXPRESSIONS	POSITIVE EXPRESSIONS
Lazy	Can do more when he tries
Unclean	Poor habits
Stubborn	Extremely self-confident
Trouble maker	Disturbs class
Sloppy	Could do neater work
Selfish	Seldom shares with others
Below average	Working at his own level
Uncooperative	Should learn to work with others
Show-off	Tries to get attention

PLAN FOR FOLLOWUP

At the end of a conference a brief review should be made by the teacher so that both parent and teacher understand what has transpired. Also, some provision for followup should be discussed. This may be another conference, a weekly letter or phone call to the parent by the teacher, or the parent contacting the teacher. The parent should be kept informed of the child's progress or else the conference is just a waste of time. After a problem clears up, contact between teacher and parent can be very infrequent.

A good practice for a teacher is to contact a parent to let him know that his child is doing well and is progressing nicely. Often teachers will contact a parent only if there is a problem. Parents like to hear nice things about their children also. Promoted to my room was a youngster who had been a problem to his teacher the year before. Deep inside I dreaded getting the youngster after hearing what his last year's teacher had experienced. However, the youngster and I became good friends immediately and he was a wonderful addition to my class. He did his work, made no trouble, was popular with his peers, and, in fact, was one of my top students. After three months of school, I called his mother to give her a glowing report about her son. She was so thrilled that she thanked me again and again for the glad tidings. She told me confidentially that she expected a different kind of report and that my call was the first favorable comment she had received about her son. This call changed an uncooperative parent into a sincere friend of the school and one whom I knew I could turn to if a problem ever developed with her son. However, no problem ever developed and the boy, now in high school, continues to call and visit me.

A parent-teacher conference can and should be a valuable method of clearing up any school-home misunderstanding and cementing a better relationship between parent and teacher. The conference should always end with a feeling of cooperation and the assurance that the door will be open for possible future meetings.

Receiving an SOS from a parent of a child I had taught the year before, I went to the home and met with the mother and boy. I gave my advice to a terrible problem the mother was having with her son. One week later, I received a friendly letter from the mother, thanking me for taking time with her son.

Every teacher over the years has received such letters from grateful parents. These letters are worth saving and, when you have had an exceptionally rough and trying day, they should be taken out and read again and again. A little note or kind letter makes every dedicated teacher of children yearn for the next day. A parent-teacher conference can be the means to start parent-teacher friendships and to let the world know that here is a teacher *who really cares* about children.

FACE TO FACE IN THE PARENT-TEACHER CONFERENCE

Carol LeFevre

The day set aside for conferences with parents is a special day. The teacher puts on her prettiest suit and her best smile and awaits the first parents with a mixture of trepidation and elation.

If the teacher is young and inexperienced, she may be wondering how she has measured up in the eyes of the parents. Are they aware of all the mistakes she has made in the classroom? What joy if they reassure her that she is a good teacher.

If the teacher is older, or more experienced, she may be wondering how she can get the parents to see Johnny more as she does.

If the teacher is sensitive to others, her chief concern may be how to listen and observe and respond so that she may enter into and understand the world of the parent, and through empathy create a more fruitful relationship between parent, teacher, and child.

The parent, like the teacher, may come to the conference with something less than an objective interest in the child's progress. As one father said, half humorously, "I resent parent conferences. I resent the teacher, and I resent

Reprinted from *Elementary School Journal* 68:1–8 (October, 1967), by permission of Carol LeFevre and The University of Chicago Press. Copyright 1967 by The University of Chicago.

my kid. I even resent my wife's placid attitude toward these affairs. The instant she and I walk through the door and I see the teacher smiling frostily at us, my blood curdles and I regret that schools were ever invented" (1).

To many parents the teacher remains a formidable figure, one who still, long after the parents' own school days are over, has power to "pass" or "fail." Now the power is exercised through her judgment of the child, not the parent. Yet the identification between parent and child is so close in the minds of parents and teacher that the difference is negligible. The judgment may be a mere nuance, or it may be expressed quite openly, but it is there in every conference (2).

The avowed purpose of the parent-teacher conference is open, face-to-face communication between parents and teacher so that each may function more adequately in promoting the child's development. The teacher can teach more effectively if she is aware of the special interests, abilities, anxieties, problems, and circumstances of each child. More than this, she can know the child much better if she knows his parents, the most important people in the child's life. The parents, in their turn, can co-operate with the school's efforts if they know and have confidence in their child's teacher, and can exchange information and discuss mutual problems with her. But somehow those trained and impartial professionals, the teachers, are usually considered as the experts especially qualified to give advice, rather than as equal partners in a common undertaking. Rarely is the parent credited with knowing as reliably as the teacher what is good for the child.

Many feelings lie beneath the objective, professional discussion of the child's progress in school. Implicit in the talk about Jane's progress in arithmetic or Johnny's reading level are hidden questions parent and teacher are asking each other. How am I doing? Am I all right? Is my child as successful as I need him to be? Am I a good parent? What kind of person are you? How do you make me feel? What are you doing to my child? Can we trust and respect each other enough to work together as partners in the child's best interests?

THE ROOTS OF APPRAISALS

Each arrives at his judgment of the other person's trustworthiness and capability through his own inner feelings about himself and about his relationship to the other person. If the parents feel fairly confident in themselves and satisfied with their child, it is relatively easy for them to find the teacher an attractive, competent, reassuring person. If the teacher feels she is a good teacher, she can meet parents more warmly and openly. Where class, racial, or cultural distance must be overcome, or strong feelings of inadequacy or hostility, the problem of trust and relationship becomes more delicate and more difficult.

Every parent comes to a conference with a knowledge of weakness and inadequacy as well as strength and sufficiency. Every teacher is aware of failures and feelings of hostility toward children as well as skillful teaching and loving kindness. The balance of forces may lean strongly one way or the other, but no one is free of weakness, and no one is all kindness. Each is vulnerable, and each seeks reassurance, consciously or otherwise.

A BLOWER OF BUBBLES

Parent and teacher may especially seek approval, or fear criticism, from each other because each often finds it hard to see or measure the results of his efforts with children. The teacher has been described as a blower of bubbles (3). When the school day or school year is over, and the bubble has burst, it is difficult to know whether much of permanent value has occurred in the child. For the parent, deeply involved emotionally with his children, there is even less objective measurement of success or failure. Thus the personal approval or criticism that each gives the other may assume considerable importance as a source of needed feedback. This is particularly true of the parents of young children, and of relatively new teachers.

How do parents and teacher cope with feelings of uncertainty and need for reassurance in the conference situation? One method that almost everyone uses is apology. If we admit our weakness, even exaggerate it, surely the other person will reassure us. If he does not respond positively to our apology, our worst fears are confirmed. If he does reassure us, we cannot really trust him, for we had to ask for his affirmation.

DEFENSES

We can attack the other person, blame him for any weakness in the child, punish him, often quite unconsciously, for the problems and failures we have endured. We project the badness outside ourselves onto the other person, keeping the goodness and successes for ourselves. We are left with our frustration, which cannot be projected, and with our certainty that the other person will reciprocate by feeling the same hostility toward us, making us more vulnerable than ever (4).

We may adopt an attitude of indifference and superiority. If we convince ourselves that the other person is unworthy of being listened to, we do not need to hear. Professionalism may be a mask to hide behind, or a way of belittling or attempting to impress another with our supposed wisdom and authority. Such defense mechanisms are particularly tempting when there is a considerable difference in culture or status between the teacher and the parents.

Talking itself may be a form of defense used by either parent or teacher. As long as we are talking, we cannot hear. If we are talking, the other cannot question, contradict, or criticize us. But we should not be surprised if we reach the end of the conference and find that no communication has taken place.

To a person who has strong narcissistic needs, the conference may be an opportunity to elicit praise and admiration. Any effort to discuss a child's needs will run counter to the adult's need to see himself as a perfect parent or teacher.

To another person, the conference is an opportunity to dominate. The teacher or parent is seen as someone to be manipulated to carry out one's own aims and policies, not as an equal with whom to work co-operatively for the child's best interest (5).

PRAISE

The solution would seem to be that we should be nice to each other, if we can manage it. If I am a teacher, I will protect myself by praising the child and reassuring the parent. If I am a parent, I will disarm the teacher by telling her how good she has been for my child. Then surely we can both feel good, both like the child better, both be confirmed in our adequacy.

But even this rose has its thorns. However much we may want to believe the nice things the other person says, we know within ourselves that this is only part of the picture. A person who admits only of good qualities in the child and in us leaves us with the feeling that he has not dared enough or cared enough to see us as we actually are. Or perhaps he feels that our bad qualities are so bad as to be unspeakable. More likely he is simply being polite or acting out a professional role, rather than being a genuine person whom we can trust.

If our need is so great that we accept an exaggerated picture of our goodness—and often in most of us the need is that great—then we must live a degree of falseness even to ourselves. With falseness there is always the fear of being found out, discovered as we really are, doubly disapproved because hypocrisy has been added to our original faults.

If these are some of the pitfalls parents and teachers encounter in their efforts to work together, then a modicum of common sense and sensitivity and a smattering of knowledge of defenses should lead to more productive and more amiable parent-teacher conferences. But there is another dimension that is more difficult to fathom or deal with.

SHADOWS OF THE PAST

Neither parent nor teacher comes to the conference with open eyes and objective judgment. Neither sees the other as he really is, but only as he seems to him. We come to other people not only with our own strengths, needs, and vulnerabilities, but also with a host of feelings about all the people we have known. Often we are totally unaware that we have transferred an attitude toward some person from the past to a person we have just met. Something about a parent—a mannerism, a tone of voice, a detail of appearance—unconsciously reminds us of an uncle who often embarrassed us as a child. Without knowing why, we, now adult, may be as tongue-tied and as awkward in a conference with this father as we were at the age of six when our uncle joked about us at the family dinner table.

IMAGES FROM CHILDHOOD

For the teacher, especially the young teacher, the children's parents are her own parents. She feels something of the same ambivalance toward Dick's mother and father that she felt toward her own parents, whose love was present but not perfect, whose approval was sought but not always gained, who could scold as well as hug. The teacher has a special need for the parents' acceptance, and a special fear that they cannot fully accept her, or would not if they knew what she really is and feels.

To the parents, the teacher is the composite of the teachers they had in childhood: Miss Newell, of the awesome reputation; Mr. Wilds, who ridiculed a book report; Miss Jennings, the spellbinding storyteller. Parents, like the teacher, come to the conference with a special need for reassurance. They seek confirmation from this powerful, judgmental figure of childhood who gave and withheld praise and blame, love and punishment. The schoolroom may look very different from the austere one remembered from childhood. But squeezing into a small desk, smelling the chalkdust of ancient memory may be enough to evoke once more the feeling of being a vulnerable child before that important authority, the teacher (6).

Attitudes toward authority may range from hostility to submissiveness, from awe to cynicism. Each of us has had experiences with many different people who had some kind of authority over us. Each of us has a mixture of feelings that may be called forth by any person in a position of authority.

The teacher may have ambivalent feelings about being a person in authority. She may enjoy the power and the prestige her role gives her with children and parents. But bearing the criticism and the hostility this role brings forth from some people may be difficult. Then, too, the weight that others attach to what she says may make her uncomfortable. Many teachers find satisfaction in working with children partly because they are more at ease with children than with adults. Such teachers may be especially sensitive to both the hostility and the excessive respect given them by some parents (7).

RIVALS

A parent and a teacher may see each other as rivals for the child's affections. Each may be a little jealous of the child's interest in the other. A teacher may take an unholy delight in being told that the child hates to miss a day of school. The parent may be quite annoyed that the child has quoted the teacher to refute some statement the parent made. Rivalry for the child's affection and respect may stem from an identification with the child that leads to undue possessiveness.

This rivalry may be linked to feelings of competition. If we are ambitious, it may be important to us to prove that we teachers are better with Mary than her parents are. It is difficult to be better. It is tempting and easier to point out the other's weakness, and the teacher is in an excellent position to do so.

When we compete, we are likely to look for the flaws in others and emphasize the good points in ourselves, fearing to see either realistically. Such attitudes interfere with our ability to work constructively and harmoniously with parents.

THE CHILD THE TEACHER SEES

As teachers we carry into conferences our distorted perceptions of the children we teach as well as our personal reactions to parents. Every teacher soon becomes aware of the difference between the way she feels toward a particular child and the way another teacher feels toward him. A pretty girl may be "beautiful but dumb" to one teacher. Envious of her sister's attractiveness, choosing the path of academic accomplishment as a means of competing with her rival for her father's love, it seems unfair to this teacher that any girl should be beautiful as well as successful in school. Quite unaware, she may sabotage such a child's efforts to learn and emphasize her academic shortcomings. Another teacher may have been her father's favorite, lovely in his eyes. She identifies with the pretty girl, sees her own younger self in the child. This teacher gives the child special help and attention and speaks warmly of her accomplishments in the parent conference. Each teacher has acted differently toward the child, and each selects different qualities and incidents to report to the parents. Each feels that she is being professionally impartial, but the weight of approval and disapproval of the child varies sharply in the conferences of the two teachers. Neither sees the child as she actually is.

What about sex in the parent-teacher conference? Of course there is no sex in the parent-teacher conference. But it may be exciting to a woman teacher to find that she can charm a critical father into approving her, or make another parent defensive by unconsciously well-chosen comments about his daughter. Even harder to recognize or admit is the elation of triumphing over a mother, or of seducing praise from her.

FACING OUR FEELINGS

What are we to do about these feelings, which permeate every conference whether we recognize it or not? Limiting ourselves to the good things is not the answer. Neither is being "honest" about the problems. Somehow we need to try to understand these subterranean feelings better. We have to bring as many of them as we can out where we can examine them. Only then are we free to decide what to do about them and to begin to subordinate them to our conscious goals.

Teachers can help one another by comparing reactions to children and parents. Considering different points of view may help us become aware of some of the selective perception each of us brings to each person we meet. When we find ourselves excited or depressed after seeing particular parents, we would do well to examine ourselves carefully and to compare notes with other teachers who know these parents. If a child in our classes particularly appeals to us, or causes us difficulty, again we might well seek out others who know the child and can help us correct or enlarge our vision of him. The reason for our deeper involvement with a particular child or adult may be carefully hidden from our conscious awareness, but a deliberate effort to know ourselves, even when it hurts, and to be open-minded to others' views of people, may help us to a less biased view.

Parents and teachers can remind themselves that each tends to view the other through the lens of childhood feelings toward important authority figures. Each needs to make a special effort to see the other as a contemporary, individual fellow human being.

THE ART OF LISTENING

We need to discipline ourselves to listen more and talk less if we hope to become more aware of others as unique human beings here and now. As teachers we can seek to be more receptive to what a parent is saying to us, in his words, in his manner, in his tone of voice. Listening is an active art, not a passive state. With practice we can develop an empathy that will help us to enter, in some small measure, into the parent's world, to begin to see and understand his attitudes and feelings, his joys and problems, his hopes and fears for his child. Only as we can do this can we hope to say anything that will be helpful to a parent and his child in the circumstances of his life (8).

Teachers are not, and should not be expected to be, family counselors. Their purpose and profession is teaching children, and the purpose of the parent-teacher conference is to further the child's education. But some of the very qualities that make good teachers may at times make for poor parent-teacher conferences. One strength of an able, confident teacher may be her firm convictions about what others should know and do, and how they should do it. But such an attitude expressed toward parents is likely to arouse resentment: "Who does she think she is, telling us what to do?" A poor parent-teacher conference can seriously interfere with the relationship between the teacher and the child. A teacher who responds inappropriately to what a parent is saying may stir up a defensiveness and even a hostility that will be communicated, intentionally or not, to the child. There are times when a teacher may make definite, concrete suggestions to a parent who may accept them and find them helpful. The teacher needs to be sensitive enough to this parent at this moment to judge when a suggestion may be helpful, even if it is not accepted, and to recognize when a suggestion will be harmful because it will be seen as threatening, or as lacking in perceptiveness of the parents' situation. The spirit prompting the suggestion, the feeling tone underlying it, are often far more important than the words themselves (9).

WHEN DOES INFORMATION HELP?

It is not enough for the school to decide that certain kinds of information must be given to parents and that certain things must be expected of them.

If the purpose of education is to be fulfilled, we have to ask several questions: What will this information mean to this particular parent at this time? Will it help him to help his child grow? Or will it only reinforce his fears, which are already undermining the child's sense of adequacy?

As teachers we shall make many mistakes. But we can try our best to distinguish between what we want to say out of our own needs and what we might say that would have meaning and would be helpful to parent and child. We can only begin to understand another person as we are "with" him. We have to have a basic respect for his particular personhood, however different it may be from ours. Only as we have such respect for another individual can there be communication instead of "talking at." If we genuinely respect another person, we see our role as accepting him as he is and perhaps helping him see new possibilities from where he is, not as telling him what we think he should do from where we are.

REFERENCES

1. Charles H. Wilson. "Ordeal by Conference," *NEA Journal, 54* (November, 1965), 17.
2. Virgil Murk. "Parent Conferences Supplement Teaching," *Illinois Education, 53* (March, 1965), 302–4.
3. Philip W. Jackson. "The Way Teaching Is," *University of Chicago Magazine, 58* (February, 1966), 15–19.
4. Benjamin D. Wright and Shirley A. Tuska. *From Dream to Life in the Psychology of Becoming a Teacher: Student and First Year Teachers' Attitudes toward Self and Others.* Cooperative Research Project No. 1503 for the Cooperative Research Program of the Office of Education, U.S. Department of Health, Education, and Welfare. 1966.
5. Fritz Redl and William W. Wattenberg. *Mental Hygiene in Teaching,* pp. 360–84. New York: Harcourt, Brace and Company, 1951.
6. Benjamin D. Wright. "Why Do We Keep Bad Images of Teachers?" *Elementary School Journal, 66* (November, 1965), 66–67.
7. Barbara W. Merrill. "Under the Surface of Parent-Teacher Relationships," *The Instructor, 75* (November, 1965), 35.
8. Charles A. Nicholson, Jr. "Parent-Teacher Conferences—a Positive Approach," *Ohio Schools, 43* (December, 1965), 32.
9. Donald G. Cawelti. "Creative Evaluation through Parent Conferences," *Elementary School Journal, 66* (March, 1966), 293–97.